Denton Jacques Snider

**System of Shakespeare's Dramas**

Vol. II

Denton Jacques Snider

**System of Shakespeare's Dramas**
*Vol. II*

ISBN/EAN: 9783337034023

Printed in Europe, USA, Canada, Australia, Japan

Cover: Foto ©Thomas Meinert / pixelio.de

More available books at **www.hansebooks.com**

# SYSTEM

OF

# SHAKESPEARE'S DRAMAS.

By DENTON J. SNIDER.

IN TWO VOLUMES.

## VOL. II.

ST. LOUIS:
G. I. JONES AND COMPANY.
1877.

*St. Louis: Press of G. I. Jones and Company.*

# CONTENTS.

# COMEDY, OR MEDIATED DRAMA.

## THE IDEAL CLASS.

That class of comedies in which the mediation takes place wholly through the Real World has been already considered. There is a conflict in society portrayed, but it is healed through the ordinary instrumentalities which man employs for this purpose. Institutions are made to correct their own wrong. But now we are to treat of a class of comedies in which the mediation is relegated to a new realm — distant, wholly different in character, essentially ideal. The logic is that the Real World of institutions, since it is in conflict with itself, and productive of wrong to the individual, must be entirely abandoned, and a human abode be sought in which conflict cannot exist, and, hence, in which institutions are not found at all, or only in their simplest state. This may, in a general way, be called the Ideal World, as it is an abstraction from the real life of society.

It will be noticed that such a dramatic idea is more profound and more consistent than that which lies at the basis of the previous class of comedies. When institutional life becomes utterly self-contradictory, and it cannot mediate itself, it must be left behind, and a non-institutional life has to take its place. Moreover, the fact is deeply consonant with human experience; men do flee from society when its collisions become too strong for endurance, and betake themselves to a simpler social condition — sometimes even to the woods; but more frequently they remain in society, and construct, with the aid of the imagination, some purely ideal state, in which they may dwell free from all conflict. Indeed, pretty much everybody gets to building imaginary republics in times when the external political world has become utterly corrupt and hopeless.

Still, such an ideal realm is an irrational abstraction, a transitory figment of the brain. It offers, however, a glorious field for poetic creation and embellishment — that beautiful sphere of pure fiction in which a poet is at home. But it is essentially comic — comic in the highest degree — for through it the individual is led forward in the pursuit of an end wholly absurd and self-annulling. For, when he has realized his Ideal World, at that moment it is annihilated, since it must be real then, and no longer ideal. This is the essence of the comic character — his purpose is null in itself, and breaks to pieces in its very accomplishment.

Hence the Ideal World must vanish, and the true poet will not fail to portray both the manner and cause of its disappearance. The distinction is worthy of notice; it is only the sentimental half-poet that remains wholly wrapped up in his idyllic scenery. Though there be a flight from society to a pastoral or rural life, there must be likewise a return to society, and the poet should be able to comprehend it, and to portray it in its true nature. Let him not flee to the country and stay there, in his poetry; the complete circuit of experience must also be reflected in the artistic product. Hence there is a deep necessity for restoration to society, which alone is the rational abode of man, and the true work of Art will not fail to embody the same thought in a faithful picture of human spirit.

The return to civilized life, therefore, is certain to take place ; the individual must again produce those very institutions which he has abandoned, or perish ; society will spring up of itself even in this Ideal World. Hence the latter disintegrates within ; it rapidly develops internal conflicts which destroy it — which compel it into some form of social organization. But the twofold result of its existence must not be forgotten — on the one hand, it has brought back the individual to institutional life, and healed the wounds of his spirit ; on the other hand, it has harmonized the conflicts of society by removing the wrong which caused the flight, for this new society which has resulted from the Ideal World is free from the original injustice towards the individual. Thus the mediation on both sides is complete, and is effected through this Ideal World.

It will be manifest that a dramatic form of this kind involves three essential movements. First is the Real World of conflict ; man falls out with institutions which have become the means of oppression and wrong ; usually both Family and State are involved in struggle ; hence comes the flight to an opposite condition of existence. Secondly, this is the Ideal World, whose prime function is the mediation of the conflict ; the guilty must be brought to repent, the injured must be restored, and, above everything else, society must free itself of wrong and contradiction. Then the Ideal World passes away, for the evil to which it owed its origin is cured, and there remains nothing but the return of all the conflicting elements to harmony and to society. This last is the third movement.

The plays of the ideal class of comedies differ much from one another in the coloring, which may be sportive or serious, with all the intermediate hues. Some verge toward a tragic depth of earnestness, others tend toward the light gayety and capricious humor of Pure Comedy. But they cannot here be classified by this characteristic; there is a deeper principle which distinguishes them, and by which they are to be arranged, namely, the presence of an Ideal World. But, if the reader so chooses, he can easily place them in groups of Tragi-Comedies and Pure Comedies, as was done in the previous class, and is usually done by writers. Such a distinction, however, is now not the essential one.

The forms of this Ideal World in Shakespeare are various. Already, in *Love's Labor's Lost*, there was an attempt to realize a realm of study — an Academe — but it was not successful. Now we are to consider the different kinds of ideal life which appear in this class of dramas, and thereby divide them into groups. It may be the Church, in its *Monastic Life*, to which the individual flees in order to get rid of the struggles of the world. This is a religious realm, organized, and existent alongside of the secular realm, for the very purpose of mediating the conflicts of the latter. Such is the principle of the First Group of this class. Of the Second Group, however, the principle is *Idyllic Life*, which belongs to the country — to the woods; it is the most primitive social order, to which man goes back in seeking refuge from the complex, feverish organism of civilized society, for from this it is far removed, both in Time and in Space. It has, nevertheless, a tinge of reality; it may be — indeed, it has been — though it belongs to a period which has long since vanished for the civilized community. But the Third Group sweeps away the last faint shade of the Real World, and has as its mediating principle a romantic realm of supernatural shapes — the *Pure Ideal World*; that is, the individual absolutely creates out of his own imagination a mystic land, with its own peculiar forms, among which he seeks abode and reconciliation.

There is but one play in this Group — forming a kind of transition out of the real comedies, which have gone before, into the more purely ideal comedies, which are to follow. The contrast is between the secular and religious spheres, though religion has always in it a strong ideal element, and, hence, its mediation may be classified as ideal in the present case. Monasticism had its chief function during the Middle Ages in being a refuge for the weak and oppressed — those who sought a new life outside of the violence and fierce tumult of secular society. The cloister, therefore, is just the ideal world placed amid civil institutions, and embodied in a special organization, with the design of reconciling the collisions of the real world. Still, monasticism, like all kinds of ideal life, is transitory, as opposed to the rational existence of man in society — but all these matters will be best illustrated by examining the play itself.

# MEASURE FOR MEASURE.

This play belongs to the class of special or mediated dramas, in accordance with the distinction made in the preceding essays. The collision has a tragic depth and earnestness; the fundamental tone of the whole work is serious, and even dark, notwithstanding the comic nature of certain portions. The conflict, however, is mediated, and the persons are saved from a tragic fate by the intervention of the World of Mercy. This form of mediation is the main thing to be noticed, and constitutes the distinguishing characteristic of the play. Hereafter we shall see pastoral communities and ideal realms of various kinds introduced for the purpose of healing the disrupted elements of society. Now it is religion, as an organized system, which is brought in with its principles, and which seeks to determine the affairs and harmonize the conflicts of the Family and the State. Another peculiarity of the present drama is that the religious world is not transferred to a territory entirely removed from the political world, but both exist together in this country of Vienna. The ideal realm is, hence, the Church in one of its manifestations, namely, monastic life. The treatment will be, accordingly, somewhat distinct from that of the other mediated dramas which are to follow.

There are three general movements of the entire action. The first is short, but must be considered as a part coördinate with the other two. It shows the disruption which

is taking place in the whole social fabric of the country.
The ruler, who is the embodiment of mercy, is unable to
administer the law on account of excessive leniency
towards crime; he leaves the State and betakes himself to
the religious realm — enters a monastery. The woman,
who is the representative of chastity, is preparing to abandon society and the Family; she also is eager to lead the
religious life of the cloister. That is, Mercy and Chastity
have taken flight from the secular world. The second
movement portrays the conflict in this secular world
between formal justice and incontinence; the religious
sphere, as a distinct, organized system, undertakes *from
without* to mediate the difficulty, and fails. The third movement indicates the true solution — the diremption between
the secular and religious elements is overcome, and both are
united into a principle higher than either taken separately;
mercy becomes a constituent of the State, and chastity a
constituent of the Family; formal justice — or, rather,
injustice — ceases, as well as the illicit relation of the
sexes, in the two grand ethical institutions of man. The
merciful monk returns and becomes the just ruler, while
the chaste woman is made his wife. It is thus a double
restoration from a double disruption.

I. 1. In the first movement the first thread has its central figure in the person of the Duke. Mercy is his predominating trait, but mercy in its one-sided manifestation.
Through the pardon of offenses and their tacit permission
he has suffered the law to become of no validity, and,
indeed, to fall into utter contempt. The result is universal crime and disregard of all authority. He is aware
of the evils, but cannot bring himself to execute those
enactments which he has permitted to be violated. He

must, therefore, abandon the helm of government to others and flee. The office of ruler, who is to administer justice, is too severe for his merciful nature, and, moreover, he has a preference for a retired, contemplative life. Accordingly, the very first scene of the play represents him as transferring his authority to his deputy.

He recognizes his mistake to be excessive leniency; to restore respect for law, and to secure society, there is need of a sharp, decisive remedy. He, therefore, selects as his substitute a man of quite the opposite character, a man who will enforce the law rigidly to the letter. Angelo is taken, whose temperament is cold and inflexible, and whose knowledge of the statutes is most ample. But his chief characteristic is the strictest adherence to formal justice. He is, therefore, the person best fitted by nature to enforce the old enactments which have fallen into desuetude, and, in general, to restore the reign of law which seemed to have taken its departure from society. Angelo, too, seems to be as rigid with himself as with others; he has reduced to submission the fierce appetites and passions of the body; he is ready to subsume himself under his own principles. Such are the grounds for his selection by the Duke. We may now expect the sway of justice in all its severity, for it is the world in which Angelo moves — is the fundamental consciousness from which spring all his convictions and actions.

It would seem, however, that the Duke, notwithstanding his laudation of Angelo, has still a lingering suspicion of his deputy's weakness, or at least believes that mercy cannot be entirely banished from the administration of the law. One ugly fact in Angelo's history is known to him, as will hereafter appear, namely, the treatment of

Mariana. Hence the Duke will not leave Vienna, though he gives out that he has gone to Poland; but he must remain in the country to watch an experiment whose success he does not regard as absolutely certain, if he be true to his sense of duty and his benevolent character. He cannot deliver his people over entirely to formal justice, if he have any faith at all in his own principle of mercy. His stay is, therefore, necessitated by the situation.

The Duke has also thrown up another bulwark against the extreme tendencies of Angelo's disposition. Escalus has been appointed to the second position in the State, with large authority, and he possesses also great influence on account of his character and his age. In this man the element of mercy again becomes the predominant trait. He will try to tame the legal ferocity of his associate, and in his own judicial capacity he will decide with moderation — indeed, with leniency. The Duke, to a certain extent, reappears in him — not as supreme now, but as subordinate; for it is the principle of both of them which has broken down the administration of the State, and, hence, must not again be made paramount. Such seems to be the reason of this double authority, and such the true relation between Angelo and Escalus. Mercy and justice thus form the contrast of their characters.

But whither will the Duke go when he quits the State, with its laws and institutions? He can only follow the bent of his nature and enter the pure realm of mercy, if there be such in existence. He will find it in the organization of the Christian Church. When, therefore, he abandons secular life, he can betake himself only to a religious life. Accordingly, he enters a monastery — assumes the habit of a holy friar, whose life is devoted to works of benevolence and mercy. His special duty is now that of an adviser, confessor, mediator; he is to soothe the individual in affliction, and harmonize the struggles incident to weak humanity. He is not of the world, but descends into it as a power from without — as a messenger from Heaven — in order to reconcile its difficulties and to banish its doubts. Religion means mediation, and the priest must mediate, not only between God and man, but also between man and man. Therefore the Duke, as friar, henceforth becomes the chief mediator of the play.

But we must not fail to notice the other determinations which flow from his situation. He will have to be in disguise, for he remains in his own city; in his ordinary garb could not help being generally known to the citizens. He is thus compelled to act a species of falsehood from the start. Moreover, his influence is external—comes from a sphere beyond — for he no longer possesses any authority to realize his views and intentions. He is, hence, forced to resort to trickery and deception in order to accomplish his ends. Thus a taint is thrown upon his character and calling which no plea of good results can wholly remove. But his shrewd devices totally fail of their purpose. The lesson seems to be that this separation of the secular and religious worlds has a tendency to pervert both from their true nature, for both thus become immoral, though in different manners; they must be united and reconciled in the institutions of man.

Let us now attempt to state, in abstract terms, the movement of which the Duke is the center. Mercy finds itself unable to stem the lawlessness of the time; it is too kind-hearted, and rests too much in the emotions. It

permits offenders to go free and violence to remain
unpunished; it, therefore, saps the foundation of law and
institutions, which must always rest upon the responsibility of man for his deed.   The whole realized world of
right seems to be crumbling to ruin; such is the result of
mercy in its one-sidedness.   It, therefore, takes its flight
from the State, after resigning all authority into the hands
of justice — justice in its extreme severity — which now,
in its turn, undertakes to control society.   The course of
the play will show that justice, too, breaks down; it
destroys what it ought to protect, and violates its own
principle; it becomes, in fact, just the opposite of itself,
namely, the direst wrong.   Such is the outcome of justice in its one-sidedness.   Mercy, therefore, must return
to the world — but not in order to destroy, or even to
displace, justice, for thus the old conflict would be
renewed; but both must be reconciled and united in one
principle.   Each one, taken by itself, is inadequate and
one-sided; only their unity is true justice or true mercy.

   2.  We are now ready to take up the second thread of
the first movement.   The Duke alone cannot completely
represent the dissatisfaction with the present condition of
society;  he must have his counterpart in the other sex,
whose principle is chastity, and whose institution is the
Family.   Isabella is the embodiment of this element of
female virtue; but we observe that she, too, is about to
abandon the world for a religious life.   The motives to
this step on her part are not fully stated, but are sufficiently implied.   The licentiousness of the time must
make society distasteful to her pure nature; she will,
therefore, leave it, and seek a life of perpetual chastity in
the nunnery.   But even there the rules are not strict

enough for her, as she says when she is seeking admission. The intensity of her principle is thus made manifest. Religion is, hence, the ideal realm to which she flees in order to avoid the conflicts of life, and to preserve intact her deepest conviction. She will also perform important mediations hereafter in the play.

To express this thought abstractly, chastity sees itself assailed and disregarded in the world; it can find a solution of the difficulty only by an entire annihilation of the sexual relation — that is, mankind will be pure when it is destroyed. Chastity, therefore, betakes itself to a realm of its own, and leaves behind merely incontinence, which is also destructive of man. Both sides are thus negative, inadequate. The true solution of the problem is that chastity and the sexual relation must be reconciled and united in the Family, which then controls both elements, and becomes a religious institution in the truest sense. The Duke and Isabella, in their devotion to one virtue, or to one phase of a virtue, have abjured the domestic relation; the Poet, in order to bring about a positive solution, has to make the monk a husband and the nun a wife.

Let us now sum up our results, and mark the necessary transition to the next movement. There has taken place a spiritual breach, which produces two worlds — the religious and secular. The religious world has two principles — mercy and chastity — which principles have been taken away from the secular world. In the latter, therefore, remain abstract justice on the one hand — for mercy has departed, and the illicit sexual relation on the other hand — for chastity has fled from society to the cloister. Such is the logical result of the flight of the Duke and Isabella to their monastic life. In the secular world, therefore, two principles are now found which can produce only the most bitter conflict — formal law undertakes to root out licentiousness.

II. 1. The second movement exhibits this conflict, which is the main theme, and constitutes the greatest portion, of the play. Its elements have already been indicated, and may be divided into three threads. The first thread comprises the religious element — the Duke and Isabella, and some other minor characters, who, by their functions, are the mediators of the conflicts which are about to rise. They will be considered in their relation to those upon whom they work.

2. The second thread is made up of the instruments of justice, from the deputy down to the pettiest officer. The characters in this class are contrasted on the principles of mercy and justice. The difference between Angelo and Escalus in this respect was before noted. In the humane Provost of the prison, mercy becomes again the predominant trait, while in the brutal executioner, Abhorson, justice shows its most revolting feature. The constable, Elbow, in a low sphere, is a stickler for legality, like Angelo in a high sphere; both, too, are guilty of a violation of the law which they execute.

The law must now be enforced in all its severity. The particular form of its violation which will be taken by the Poet can easily be inferred from the flight of Isabella, the representative of virgin purity. One of the primal institutions of man is the Family, whose true existence depends, not only upon the mutual fidelity of husband and wife, but also upon the chastity of man and woman. Hence legislation has always sought to erect barriers against the passions of the human race, in order to protect this institution. But in spite of every effort the evil has not been extirpated, and in all civilized societies there is a despised and outlawed class which has been called the negative Family. So it is, so it has been, and will probably continue to be; the fact alone is sufficient for our present purpose.

The law against incontinence was the one that was first taken by Angelo, and of whose enforcement there was, of course, the greatest need. An old enactment which had long lain dormant, and which prescribed death as the punishment for the offense, is suddenly raked from its obscurity and executed with rigor. Here was formal justice, undoubtedly. Angelo was technically correct — the law had never been repealed — yet his conduct under the circumstances was palpably unjust. But the character of the deputy is to adhere simply to this formal side, to the neglect of all others.

3. The third thread is now to be unfolded. The whole world of incontinence, in all its phases, must come up for portraiture, since it is the object against which the law directs its shaft. Angelo proposes to sweep it out of existence; hence it must appear, in order to be swept out of existence. Such is the reason for the introduction of this element; to be exhaustive, the theme had to be treated. But it has brought the play into great discredit. The question has been asked whether such a subject is suitable for artistic treatment. If Art excludes the Ugly and Repulsive — in general, the Negative — then there can be but one answer. But a critical canon of this sort would exclude from Art every great poem of modern times. Such a subject cannot, upon any general principle, be stricken from the list of artistic themes; the most that

can be said is that the Poet was unnecessarily coarse and revolting in his portraiture. But, to any one who takes delight in depth of thought and completeness of treatment, this drama must furnish a great and permanent satisfaction.

(*a.*) The incontinent world, which the critic has also to consider, is divided into two very distinct groups of people, between whom the Poet makes the greatest difference — quite the difference between guilt and innocence. Yet both are liable to the law, and must suffer punishment. The first group is composed of the most degraded members of the negative Family above mentioned — those who have lost both chastity and fidelity to the individual, these two virtues being an object of purchase and sale. Here we remark that loathsome sore of modern society popularly known as "social evil." As before stated, it assails the existence of the Family, since the latter depends upon the absolute and unreserved devotion of one man and one woman to each other. "Social evil," therefore, destroys the primitive natural basis of the Family.

The Poet has laid much stress, and gone into great detail, upon this not very attractive element of his play. All its essential phases are portrayed — the persons, their talk, their consciousness. The woman is there, the "unfortunate female;" also the besotted *habitués;* still again the more fashionable customers — soldiers, apparently — Lucio, and two other "gentlemen." Upon them the law falls with a heavy hand; they are dragged before court, and dismissed with an admonition by the good Escalus. For a second offense they are again brought in, and all sent to prison, which is now full of this class of people, so that the clown compares it with Mistress Overdone's own house.

Lucio, one of these persons, seems to be not very consistently drawn in his various acts and relations. His connection with Isabella is surprising, since they cannot have much in common. He is, perhaps, the meanest character to be found in Shakespeare. The only purpose of his life is lust; he is utterly devoid of any ethical principle — hence is absolutely hollow. Decency, truth, fidelity, are meaningless to him except as they may subserve his passion. He jeers at and betrays the clown, his own tool; he villifies the Duke; he informs on the woman who has taken care of his own illegitimate offspring. Thus he is faithless, lying, slanderous, as well as lecherous. Shakespeare has elsewhere portrayed villainy in colossal proportions, yet with some powerful motive, but meanness he has concentrated in Lucio. The reader will be ready to excuse any further details upon this part of the drama, though the Poet evidently considered it of great importance.

(*b.*) It is the second group, however, of this incontinent world which gives rise to the leading incidents of the play. Its persons differ from the persons of the first group in the fact that both parties — men and women — have fidelity, but have lost chastity — that is, they are true to one another, though they have violated the commandment. It is the class which are often said to love "not wisely, but too well." Such are Claudio and Juliet. It will be noticed that these possess the essential basis of the Family, namely, fidelity to the individual; but their fault, equally with the former case, comes under a violation of law which inflicts the penalty of death upon the man.

2

Claudio is willing to have the marital right performed; his intention is to be true to his betrothed; but nothing can help him against the stern deputy. Such is the conflict; Claudio is, in spirit, the husband of Juliet, but has failed to comply with the form, which, however, he is ready to do at once. Shall he now suffer the same punishment as one who transgresses in full — one who is both unchaste and faithless?

In order to rescue him from death, the mediations of the poem are introduced. Claudio's sister, Isabella, who is just about to become a nun, is hastily called upon to intercede with the deputy for the life of her brother. She at once strikes the heart of the subject; she pleads the cause of mercy against the rigor of the law; she alludes to the redemption of all mankind through the Savior against the strict demands of justice. Her thought is similar to that of Portia, in *Merchant of Venice*, on a similar occasion. Finally, she bids him think whether he is not guilty of the same offense, and so condemns himself in his own sentence. In the second interview the deputy says that he will save the life of her brother on condition that she yield up her honor to him, to which proposition she gives an indignant refusal.

Let us consider, for a moment, the logical bearing of these two scenes. Virgin innocence comes to plead for incontinence. Isabella feels the conflict within herself in making such a plea, but, on the other hand, the life of a brother is at stake. She tries to soften the offense in every way — she who has placed chastity the highest in her vow. This is what seduces the deputy, with all his severity of character. Virtue pleading for its own overthrow can alone touch his rigor. Accordingly, he replies

in substance, with logical precision: If incontinence be
so trivial an offense, yield to me. Thus Angelo falls —
becomes the violator of his own deepest principle, namely,
legality. The man who adheres to form alone must always
exhibit the same weakness. If he had loved chastity as
much as he did the law, he could never have fallen. Just
the opposite is the case with Isabella. Though inconsistent in her request, she spurns his proposal; for her,
chastity is the highest principle. Isabella, therefore, can
no longer plead for her brother on such grounds, and
Angelo can no longer assert his own innocence. Angelo
has lost his integrity, but Isabella has not obtained her
request; Claudio's safety must be brought about by some
new means.

But another conflict and more anguish await Isabella.
She goes to her brother and tells him of her rejection of
the base proposition of the deputy, expecting his admiration and approval. Great is her disappointment. But
how could she expect that her brother, who cared so little
for chastity, would be willing to sacrifice his life for her
purity? He asks her to submit, but she, true to her
principle, again indignantly refuses, and breaks out into
a curse upon her incontinent brother. Thus Isabella
passes triumphantly through her double ordeal against
deputy and brother.

This plan has now failed to save Claudio; another mediator must be brought to his rescue. This is the Duke,
disguised as a friar. He designs to overreach Angelo in
his lustful proposal. A young lady once betrothed to,
but now abandoned by, the deputy is substituted for Isabella. This is the essential turning-point of the drama,
and it must be carefully noted. The disguised Duke, in

order to save Claudio from death, brings about the very same offense for which Claudio was condemned. It is the demand of mercy to rescue the unfortunate man, for law has inflicted an unjust punishment—has become wrong. To get rid of the injustice of law, the offense is repeated; law thus condemns—indeed, logically destroys—itself, since it forces the very crime which it seeks to punish, in order to thwart its own injustice. Also, the highest officer of the law is made guilty of the same crime which he unrelentingly punishes. Thus the inherent contradiction of law is shown in the plainest manner.

The injustice of the statute is amply motived by the Poet. It is, in the first place, an old enactment which has long lain unexecuted and unknown; in the second place, the punishment is wholly disproportionate to the offense. But the main point of its wrong is that Claudio is still true to the spirit of the law, whose whole object was the protection of the Family; for he was faithful to the one person, and ready to fulfill the ceremony. He is caught in the letter of the enactment, which, no doubt, he had violated. To avoid the monstrous injustice of the penalty, the law is trampled underfoot.

But even by this last scheme Claudio is not rescued; Angelo violates his promise to release him. It is perfectly natural that the deputy should act thus. He has violated his own deepest principle—why should he now be restrained merely by his promise? In fact, it is just the strength of that principle of abstract justice within him which drives him to disregard his word and to give orders for Claudio's death. The deputy had previously broken loose from his principle; now his fall is accomplished in act. He can hardly be called a villain, though he is narrow, bigoted, and even cruel. His conduct springs directly from his conviction, which is adherence to the form rather than regard for the spirit of justice. He loves the law more than the essential object of the law; hence he falls into contradiction just at this point. His abandonment of his betrothed was from a formal ground — she did not live up to her contract in furnishing dower. Finally, he exhibits the same trait in the last words which he utters in the play, when he says, in substance: "Execute me according to law." He thus shows what is his ultimate principle, as well his own readiness to have it applied to himself.

The result of the disruption between the secular and religious worlds is now manifest — the one has become criminal, the other helpless. Justice has turned out utterly contradictory of itself, and mercy has sought in vain to mediate the wrong. The nun, whose vow is eternal chastity, has been compelled to plead for incontinence, and even then has failed. The monk, who left society for religious works, has been forced to resort to trickery and deception in order to accomplish his humane end; and he, too, has not succeeded. The purposes and principles of all are shattered and broken, and death is still hanging over Claudio. It is clear that external mediation cannot rescue him, nor, indeed, can it save society. There remains one alternative — the return of the Duke to power, to the secular world.

III. This is the theme of the third movement, which is now to be considered. We shall, therefore, behold the restoration of mercy to the State, which cannot dispense with it. The abstract form of justice grinds the world to death. That form, however, is necessary to society; the

purpose here is not to underrate it; only, it is not absolute—it has limits. The question always is to ascertain
these limits. Also, mercy without justice is equally impotent—means social disorder and violence. The play
starts from an anarchy produced by undue leniency. The
Duke must come back from his religious life; the result
is true justice, of which mercy is a constituent.

The Duke is now to judge the world before him in
accordance with his two principles. The first class of
offenders are left in prison to atone for their guilt; the
Duke does not discharge them, for they are truly amen-
able to justice. Their punishment was mild in the first
place, compared to the penalties of the law. The gentle
Provost and the good Escalus receive his approbation
for the happy blending of mercy and justice in their
actions. Barnardine, the prisoner from youth and the
victim of the forms of law, is brought in and pardoned.
This character does not fit well into any particular thread
of the play; still, he is a striking illustration of its general
theme. Each person gets his dues, yet none perish—
not even Angelo, who repents of his deed, and must be
forgiven; he has, too, a wife, whose claim cannot be
forgotten. The Duke has learned to be just as well as
merciful.

Four pairs are brought up before us, representing various phases of marriage. Lowest of all is the union of
Lucio, who is compelled to wed one of his kind as a punishment. Man and woman are in this case both unchaste
and faithless, yet the child born to them necessitates the
Family. The second pair is Claudio and Juliet, who love
and are willing to comply with the inherent result of their
conduct; they have been faithful to one another, but

unchaste. The third pair, Angelo and Mariana, represent the same phase in general; the woman here has at least love and fidelity. In all these cases the Duke makes marriage the solution of the difficulty, instead of destroying the offender. The object of the law could have been only the security of the Family; yet that object would certainly not be obtained by killing the husband. Thus the Duke by his decision reaches the great purpose of the law, and at the same time shows mercy in its true sense and limitation. But the fourth pair, the Duke and Isabella, have the indispensable condition of the true union, for they alone possess chastity before marriage. This element has been dwelt upon by the Poet, in other dramas, with great force and beauty. Isabella intended to take the vow of perpetual chastity; that is the best reason why she should enter the Family. It is Mistress Overdone and her class who ought to take such a vow. The Duke also has entered monastic life, but his virtue cannot be spared from a society in which there is none to throw away. He and Isabella are thus modeled after a similar pattern, and go through with quite the same experience. Both of them, independently of each other, fled from the prevailing corruption; they sought to annihilate the sexual relation entirely, since it is productive of so much evil. But they discover their own chastity and fidelity, which form the true ethical basis of marriage; thus they belong together, and are united at the end of the play. Conventual life is inadequate, and passes away; the disruption between the secular and religious worlds is healed; their reconciliation and union are found in the institutions of man, in which religion becomes the most potent principle, but loses its forms, its organization, and even its name.

The historical groundwork of this drama lies deep in the development of European nations. The same separation is witnessed; the various monastic orders—and, indeed, the Church—have stood outside of the life of society, yet have tried to control it by manifold instrumentalities—very often in the manner of the Duke—by intrigue and cunning. A time of general violence like the Middle Ages may receive much benefit from such a system. But monasticism gives only a negative solution to the problem of sin; it makes the world holy by destroying it. Man is, hence, not likely to remain contented with the solution. The Reformation struck at celibacy and attempted to sanctify the Family, so that it became, not merely a tolerated evil, but a positive religious institution. Luther the monk, like the Duke, took a wife. The Poet has presented both sides of the subject in their truest aspects; he manifests no bigoted or partisan prejudice in his treatment; there is portrayed the pure conflict between two principles, but it can be seen that he has given the solution of his own age and nation to the question of monasticism.

We now pass to a group of plays whose essential principle may be called idyllic. There is the conflict which drives the individual from society; he, therefore, seeks a place in which society exists only in its simplest form, in order to free himself from the struggle and wrong in which he is involved along with social institutions. The idyllic life belongs to the country — to the woods and mountains — whose actual inhabitants are a primitive people, living in the simplicity of Nature. But those who flee thither have to be cured inwardly and brought back — they cannot remain permanently in such a natural condition; so this idyllic world acts as a restorative for both society and the individual when they are spiritually sick with strife and contradiction. Each gets rid of the other for a time; the result is a happy reconciliation. There are four plays of Shakespeare which may be placed in this group; in each of them some form of idyllic life is the mediating principle.

*Two Gentlemen of Verona.* — Here the reconciliation is accomplished through the World of Outlaws, who have been driven to the woods, and to whose realm the conflicting members of society flee. The conception of this kind of mediation is here in an incipient and imperfect stage.

*As You Like It.* — This play exhibits pastoral life in its full glory; the shepherds constitute here the idyllic realm, to which there is a flight from the institutional world, and in which all social wounds are healed — when there takes place the restoration.

The two plays just mentioned have a predominating comic tinge, while the two which follow have a tragic seriousness in most parts.

*Winter's Tale.* — Here we see again the World of Shepherds introduced as the essential element of mediation. Thus Shakespeare repeats himself, but covers up the repetition by an entire change in the tone and character of the drama. Repentance, as the inner principle of reconciliation, is more strongly emphasized here than in any other play.

*Cymbeline.* — In style, in coloring, and in characterization to a certain extent, this work resembles *Winter's Tale.* The structure is also very similar; the idyllic realm is changed, doubtless with design, from a Shepherd World to a Hunter World.

This is, doubtless, one of the youthful plays of Shakespeare. Its theme is the passion of youth; fullness and warmth characterize its descriptions, and, at the same time, there is a feeling of resignation to the power of love which amounts to weakness. The coloring is peculiar and uniform throughout; there is felt the lassitude of the stricken shepherd; there is seen the complete absorption of the individual in the fancy and emotions. The mood of the Poet is diffused through the entire work, giving it the fragrance as well as the languor of early Spring — the season which in so many ways represents youth. The tone often resembles that of the pastoral romances of Spain and Italy; it is the feeling of the lorn lover, who has lost himself and wanders round in a dreamy quest like a shadow. Such is the artistic hue which colors this drama, and gives its distinctive characteristic; it is the true poetic element, which no analysis can reach, and which can only be felt. For the poetry, therefore, the reader must go to the poem; criticism may unfold the thought which is the controlling principle in every work of art, though it cannot be expected to take the place of that work.

In the present drama the thought is not so profound, the organic structure is not so perfect, the characterization is not so rich, as they are seen in later works; but the germs of many of the most beautiful parts of Shakespeare are to be found here. The reader is continually reminded of scenes, incidents, and motives which occur in other plays. But the peculiar and striking fact is that the Poet now gives the outlines of his most notable literary form, namely, the Mediated Drama, together with the introduction of the idyllic realm to harmonize the conflicts of life. Here it is, though in an incipient stage ; the outlaws in the forest form a world of their own, which becomes the great instrumentality for doing justice to the wronged, for inflicting retribution upon the guilty, and for restoring to society its banished members.

We may now pass to consider the organization of the drama. There are three movements, though they are not marked with such precision as in some other plays, nor have they quite the same order and signification. The first movement exhibits the two chief male characters as devoted friends on the one hand, and as devoted lovers on the other. The emotional unity which cements one individual to another, and makes both, as it were, a single person, is here shown in its two most important phases. Friendship and love, therefore, constitute the theme — the former existing, in its highest and truest manifestation, only between people of the same sex, the latter only between people of different sexes. The second movement shows the disruption of this unity in both directions ; through the faithlessness of one person the friends are separated and the lovers torn asunder. Here occur the struggles and conflicts which give to the drama its serious tone, and remove it from the realm of Pure Comedy. The third movement portrays the return out of this state of disruption, the restoration of friendship and love, and the harmonious solution of all the conflicts. The instrumentality is the world of outlaws.

I. 1. The two friends are first introduced, who, how-

ever, at once separate — the one, Valentine, is eager to
set out on his travels; the other, Proteus, remains at home
because he is inthralled by love. Valentine derides the
condition of his friend, who is so utterly absorbed by his
passion, and then departs. The thread of which Proteus
is the center may now be followed to its conclusion, in the
first movement. Julia is the name of the loved one;
through her shrewd waiting-woman she has received a
letter from Proteus containing a declaration of his affection. After a pretended resistance and various strange
caprices she yields to the influence of the winged god —
the sufficient reason being because she is loved, and must
requite the affection unless there is some good ground for
not doing so. Nor is any motive given for the love of
Proteus, except that he loves. Man and woman belong
together, and will come together unless there is some
excellent reason for their remaining asunder; the burden
of proof lies on the side of separation — not of union,
which can always be taken for granted. Nature, with a
whip of scorpions, drives the human being as an isolated
individual into his rational existence in the Family. Love,
with its unrest, is just the manifestation of insufficiency;
the single person is not adequate to the truest and happiest life. Proteus and Julia thus, in a rapid whirl, love,
declare, pledge.

But now comes the painful separation. The father of
Proteus is not yet satisfied with his son's education; he is
determined to send him abroad to see the world and to
gain its experience. Proteus, while reading a missive
from the fair Julia, is surprised by the old man; the boy
fibs stoutly, but thereby falls into his own trap. Off he
must; the parent will not be trifled with. There ensues

the parting scene between the lovers, with the oaths of eternal fidelity — soon to be broken — and the customary accompaniment of tears and sighs. Such is the external separation. The destination of Proteus is the court of Milan, where he will meet his old friend, Valentine.

2. We shall now go back and pick up Valentine's thread, and see what he has been doing. We beheld him setting out upon his travels with many a jibe and derisive taunt against love and its thralls; but retribution has come, and the mighty traveler has been stopped in his journey, at Milan, by the eyes of Silvia, the Duke's beautiful daughter. But the most gratifying news comes through his knowing servant, Speed — his affection is reciprocated. Indeed, the young lady herself writes a note, which conveys the same information in a somewhat circuitous, yet quite intelligible, manner. But, alackaday! the course of true love never did run smooth — at least in a comedy; the much-employed, time-honored obstacle rears its front — papa is opposed. Also, the old wealthy suitor, that goblin of youthful lovers and favorite of parents, puts in his appearance, and is, of course, supported by the father. Thurio is his name. The conflict is inevitable; it opens with a few flashing sky-rockets of wit between the combatants, but it is clear that heavy artillery will be brought in before the war is over. The principles which collide are the right of choice on the part of the daughter against the will of the parent. The outcome of the struggle is indicated in the mere statement — the daughter must triumph, her right must be maintained, even at the expense of disobeying and deceiving her father. If he demands conditions which render the Family impossible, the Family must set him aside; such, at least, is Shakespeare's solution.

Just at this most interesting point of the struggle Proteus arrives at court, and by his conduct changes the whole attitude of affairs. Instead of the ordinary two-sided combat, it becomes an intricate triple fight, with abundance of stratagem and treachery. This part will be developed in the next movement. We have had brought before us the double relation of friendship and love ; there has also been an external separation in each. Still, the internal bond has not been destroyed by absence ; fidelity to both principles remains as yet in the hearts of all.

A word may be said here upon the two clowns and their function in the play. It will be noticed that both Valentine and Proteus are each provided with such an attendant. The main duty of the clown is to give a comic reflection of the actions of his master. The latter is in earnest, employs elevated language, moves in high life, and the Poet usually puts his words in a metrical form ; while the former belongs to low life, deals in coarse jests, and speaks the rude slang of the hour. It is the same content viewed from the poetic and from the prosaic stand-point— from refined sensibility and from gross sensuality. Nor is the most serious, and even affecting, theme to be treated without presenting its ludicrous side. Thus there is always a double reflection of the action, which makes the work complete. The clowns seem to be partly imitating, and to be partly mocking, the manner and circumstances of their superiors ; the effect is that of a burlesque. Their prototype is to be found in Spanish and Italian comedy, from which Shakespeare in his earlier plays was in the habit of freely borrowing. Hereafter he will elevate these somewhat stiff and conventional figures into living beings; instead of a clownish and monotonous imitation, he will pour into them a varied and independent comic character, which is connected with the main theme through itself, and not through another person of the play.

Between Launce and Speed a close examination will find a few, but not very important, differences. The perplexing fact is that each is so different from.himself at different times. Launce, for instance, is in one place a stupid fool, while in another place he manifests the keenest intelligence. The same discrepancy may be noticed particularly in the case of Valentine. In fact, the characterization in this drama is by no means fine and consistent always; it betrays the youthful, uncertain hand. Still, the outlines are all here; the interest is to trace the development of these rude features into the most beautiful and ideal forms.

II. 1. The second movement, which portrays the conflict and dissolution of the ties just mentioned, is next in the order of explanation. Proteus has come to the court of Milan; is immediately admitted into the Duke's confidence upon the recommendation of his friend, who also receives him with affection and joy. But he, faithless to his Julia, at once falls in love with Silvia, the chosen one of his friend. This sudden change rests in his susceptible disposition; it requires the presence of the fair object to keep up his fidelity. He is unable to subordinate emotion to reason; in his soliloquies he states the true principle of his action — love is above duty. The result is, he commits a deed of triple treachery — he is faithless to friendship, to love, to hospitality. He is truly the victim of passion, the thrall of love, which drags him from one object to another in hopeless bonds. Such is emotion without the

permanent, rational element; it drives man into a violation
of all honor and virtue.

The conflict of Valentine with the will of the parent, the
Duke, has been already noted. To bring his purpose to a
triumphant conclusion he proposes an elopement, the time
and manner of which he confides to Proteus, who goes at
once and tells it to the father. The Duke, by a very ingen-
ious scheme of dissimulation, succeeds in making Valentine
reveal his plan, and then upon the spot pronounces his
banishment. Thus results another separation of lovers.
Throughout this scene the reader is continually reminded of
*Romeo and Juliet*, both by the incidents and the coloring.
Proteus now must continue his treachery; he has to be
false to Thurio and the Duke. But his suit is unsuccessful; Silvia, whose character is fidelity to love, reproaches
him for his faithlessness to his betrothed, and thrusts
home with logical keenness the nature of his deed — you
have been untrue to her, you will be untrue to me.

The clowns perform their function as before — they give
a distorted, but comic, reflection of the main action. The
romantic love of the high-bred suitors is caricatured in the
affair concerning the milk-maid, whose homely qualities
have the force of real life. Launce foreshadows the faithlessness and villainy of his master. He, too, has a subordinate, namely, his dog; this relation is a humorous
image of his own relation to those above himself. Launce
makes long speeches, and has more to say than Speed,
who seems to be the more prying and the less clownish
character. Lucetta, the serving-woman of Julia, ought perhaps to be placed in the same general category with Speed
and Launce, though she surpasses both in refinement.

2. The second thread of this movement is the actions

and adventures of the two women, Julia and Silvia. The Poet has not made the separation here implied by these threads except in a few scenes, but, for the convenience of the analysis, some such division may be permitted. Both these characters have the fundamental type which is seen in all of Shakespeare's women — devotion to the Family. Those whom he wishes to portray as good are endowed with this one highest purpose, to which all their other qualities are subservient. They are depicted with various degrees of intellectual ability, and with various degrees of power of will; but they are all women, and ultimately unite in the single trait of supreme womanhood. Julia, here so modest and gentle in her nature, assumes the garments of a page in order to go to Proteus; her devotion supplies the courage to accomplish such a bold act, though its audacity in no sense taints her innate modesty. She discovers the faithlessness of her lover; the premonition of her waiting-maid has turned out true. With her own eyes she beholds Proteus wooing Silvia; indeed, she, in her disguised habit, carries to the latter a missive of love and her own token of betrothal from the perfidious gallant. What will she now do? Not revenge, nor even jealousy, fires her bosom — she remains true to her principle; her feeling with Proteus is so intimate that she even pities his unrequited love for Silvia. His case is also her own; her affection blends with his suffering and partakes of it, though her success depends just upon his want of success. Love has here reached quite the point of self-contradiction; it hugs the object which destroys the end of its being. Essentially the same character and essentially the same incidents will be repeated by the Poet in at least four of his later plays.

Silvia has also the characteristic trait of devotion, and manifests it in its full intensity. Her struggle is different from that of Julia — it lies with the will of her father. She has also to withstand the importunate suits of Thurio and Proteus, but this does not cost her much trouble. She has been separated from her lover by the violent mandate of her parent, but the separation is only external; both are still one in emotion, though asunder in space. Julia's case is more difficult, for the separation is internal, since Proteus has proven faithless. Silvia thus has only to get rid of the intervening distance in order to reach her purpose, which requirement she at once proceeds to carry out; for the true existence of the Family is her highest end; her courage and daring will rise to the emergency; she will even defy an otherwise valid ethical principle, namely, parental authority. Now follows her flight: she finds a certain Sir Eglamour, who lends both sympathy and aid. But whither will she go? She must follow Valentine, and, hence, it is necessary for us to go back and look after him.

At this point we observe one of Shakespeare's most peculiar and effective dramatic means. It is the transition to a primitive or idyllic state in order to cure the wrongs of society. The latter falls into strife and injustice; it becomes destructive of institutions which lie at its own foundation; man can no longer find his abode in it, but must leave it in order to get rid of its oppression. Valentine and Silvia desire to form a family, placing it upon its true and only possible basis; the parent, who is also the ruler of the State, interferes to disrupt the union. The Family must flee unless it cease to exist, since its very essence is assailed by the supreme authority of the country. It must find a spot where there is no such authority; hence it betakes itself to the woods — to an idyllic life, in which it is free from the conflicts of society. The lovers thus have gone to a forest, whose sole inhabitants are outlaws — that is, those who have renounced the civil authority of the land.

III. The third movement, which now follows, will portray this World of Outlaws, and that which it brings about through its influence. Already in the first scene of the Fourth Act is a description of its nature and origin. The outlaws tell what they have done — it is some offense against the laws of the country which they have committed and which compelled them to flee from society; yet the Poet has shaded lightly their deeds, for, though they were guilty, they were not mean in their crimes. The allusion to Robin Hood, the English ideal of chivalric brigandage, gives the true tinge to their character. The superior breeding and learning of Valentine, who happens to pass through their abode, conquers at once their esteem; he consents to become their chieftain on the honorable condition that they "do no outrages on silly women and poor passengers." But they have never done this, and strongly asseverate that they " detest such vile practices." Robin Hood is clearly the model of these Knights of the Forest. They have violated and deserted the institutions of men, but they still seek to preserve personal honor.

1. Silvia also flies in order to avoid the conflict with the mandates of society. She must, therefore, go where she will find no oppressive social order standing in the way of her purpose; there she will find Valentine, who has been forced to depart for the same realm. Union is now possible, since all restriction is removed; the Family

can be built up from the foundation. But this new world has thus become antagonistic both to the authority of the parent and to the authority of the ruler; it has also defrauded the two unrequited lovers of their prey. The result is that, when the flight of Silvia becomes known, the Duke, Thurio, and Proteus — the latter attended now by the faithful Julia — follow at once the runaway to the forest. Society thus attempts to assert itself against this other world which has sprung up at its side ; its representatives try to restore by force what it has lost. It will be seen in the end how they succeed.

Silvia is at first captured by some of the outlaws, but is retaken by Proteus, who seizes the opportunity to press his suit anew. She rejects his advances with her old reproaches of his infidelity to Julia ; then he dares to es- say violence. At this moment Valentine, who has heard the whole conversation in his hiding-place, comes forward ; he has discovered the treachery — his supposed friend has been the cause of all his misfortunes. But now follows the sudden change. Proteus repents of his conduct and expresses the deepest contrition. Surprise awaits us again. Valentine just as suddenly forgives him, which alacrity may be tolerated on account of the previous friendship ; but when Valentine offers to surrender to him the devoted Silvia — to subordinate true love to treach- erous friendship — both feeling and reason protest to Heaven. It is almost impossible to think that Shakespeare is the author of the passage. But Julia is here to settle the difficulty. She now throws off her disguise ; her pres- ence restores the affection of her inconstant lover ; the two pairs are thus free from both the internal and the external conflict; friendship and love have passed through their struggle into complete harmony and reconciliation. Such is the result of the love-collision.

2. Now comes the final act — the restoration to parent and to society. The Duke and Thurio are brought in by the outlaws; Thurio cowardly resigns his claim to the hand of Silvia in the presence of Valentine; the latter has the true element of union, namely, requited love, whose right can now in this realm be enforced. The father then relents and is reconciled; this obstacle is thus swept away. Finally, the Duke, as ruler, pardons the bandits at the intercession of Valentine, and they all go back to the place whence they had fled. Thus the World of Outlaws is dissolved, and no longer stands in hostility to legal authority; the internal disruption of society is also healed, and the conflict in the Family has received its solution. This is the return to the world of institutions; the reconciliation with Family and State is complete; and the personal relations of friendship and love, which were so disturbed, are restored to their pristine energy.

The elaboration here presented is, no doubt, fuller than the mere text of this play warrants. But, for the sake of the light which is thrown upon a whole series of the Poet's works, and for the sake of illustrating his most peculiar and original dramatic form, the present play is worthy of the most careful study and analysis. It is, however, only a germ, which has not yet unfolded, but which shows the future flower in all its details. A comparison with his later procedure in the ideal class of mediated dramas will demonstrate the immense advance in depth and completeness of treatment, but will also prove that every essential element is to be found embryonically in *Two Gentlemen of Verona*. Hereafter he will free his idyllic realm from its

present taint of illegality and crime, for now he almost
seems through its use to excuse the wicked deed; he will
also portray it with far greater fullness and beauty, and
give to it a more definite place in the action. Hereafter,
too, he will assign supreme validity to repentance, which
is now so lightly and so unsatisfactorily dismissed. The
restoration also will be more strongly emphasized, and,
indeed, will be of itself elevated to an entire movement of
a play. Finally, the divisions of the action will be
changed to their true logical order: The Disruption, the
Mediation through an idyllic world, the Restoration. It
will be seen that this play belongs to the class of special
or mediated dramas, whose form and instrumentalities it
has throughout; it cannot be called either a comedy or a
tragedy.

Such is unquestionably the species to which *Two Gentlemen of Verona* belongs, but its other relations to the
works of the Poet are worthy of notice. Julia, with her
disguise and her situation, is reproduced in *Twelfth Night*
in the person of Viola, though the latter is in every way
more complete. In fact, no comparison can better show
the difference between the youthful possibility and the
mature realization of a great artist than a comparison of
these two characters. A less distinct adumbration of the
traits will be found in Portia, Imogen, Helena, and others.
Then, again, the reflections of Valentine in the forest
recalls vividly the soliloquy of the gentle Duke in *As You
Like It*. But the resemblance to *Romeo and Juliet* is the
most intimate of all. The two stories of the dramas
often seem to run together; there is the same collision
with the parent and with the rejected suitor; there are
often noticed the same incidents and the same instrumen-

talities, even down to the ladder of ropes; there is the same style of imagery, language, and versification; we observe a like extravagance of the emotions, particularly of love; there are the same general outlines of characterization. But the quality which links these two dramas together most closely is the tone which runs through each, the indescribable coloring which leaves all its hues in the feelings and fancy, so that the mind is strongly impressed with the conclusion that both plays must have been written in the same mood and about the same time.

# AS YOU LIKE IT.

In this drama we see placed in striking contrast the actual and the idyllic world. The former contains society, state, business, and their manifold interests and complications; the latter is the simple pastoral existence, without care, struggle, or occupation—almost without want. The former is the world of Reason, and exhibits man in his rational development, and for this very cause has within it the deepest and most terrific contradictions. The loftier the summit the greater the fall; the more highly organized a society the mightier are the collisions slumbering or struggling in its bosom. But an idyllic existence is almost without contradiction, and, hence, it happens that men sometimes flee from a more concrete social life, in order to get rid of its difficulties, and betake themselves to a simple state of the shepherd.

More commonly, however, they remain in society, but construct, with the aid of imagination, a world of their own, suited exactly to their notion of things, whither they can flee out of the rugged and disagreeable reality surrounding them. Such a realm may be called the ideal, as distinguished from the idyllic, though both have the same fundamental principle, since they are abstractions from actual existence. An imaginary world of this kind has always been a favorite theme with a certain class of minds, particularly with the poets and theologians. But in some social conditions, especially in periods of revolution and disintegration, it is the resort to which all intelligence flees, and the construction of ideal societies becomes a phase of national consciousness. Such a state is generally thrown back into the distant past, long antecedent to history, when man was absolutely innocent, and even the lower animals shared in his condition—that is, the negative side of man and nature is wholly eliminated—thought away. Of this character was the Paradise of the ancient Hebrews and the Golden Age of the ancient Greeks. It will be noticed that there is a great advantage in placing this world in the past, since we are thus continually receding from it, while, according to the well-known law of distance, it is increasing in enchantment to the spectator. But more hardy spirits have dared to project this world into the future, where it is in danger of being overtaken. Still, the Millennium has thus far always kept a thousand years ahead, and it is likely to do so for an indefinite time to come.

But, now, this consciousness—so general, so deeply grounded in human nature—the Poet proposes to make the subject of a comedy. That it is capable of a comic treatment is manifest when we reflect that the very realization of the ideal world must be its annihilation, for then it is real and no longer ideal. Thus the pursuit of such an end, as absolute and final, is contradictory and null in itself, since it must terminate in just the opposite of that which is sought. Now, Comedy exhibits the individual pursuing ends which are nugatory, and, therefore, destroy themselves in their realization. That the Poet had this consciousness in mind is clear from his allusions to Robin Hood, the English ideal hero of the forest; and still more plainly does the same fact appear when he speaks of

"those who fleet the time carelessly as they did in the
golden world," an obvious reference to the Greek ideal
realm. To this latter he likens the Forest of Arden, a
comparison by which he lets us know what he meant by
that forest.

But it is through beholding the organization of the
drama that the purpose of the Poet will be most clearly
revealed. There are three movements, which, however,
are merely the essential phases of one and the same general process. The first movement depicts the Real World
of Wrong, in which institutions have fallen into conflict,
and in which the individual is assailed in his personal
rights. Here there are two threads, of which the central
figures are, respectively, a man and a woman — Orlando
and Rosalind. Both are the victims of wrong in this
unsettled society; both have to flee from domestic and
political oppression; they also become enamored of one
another — the common bond of misfortune easily changes
to the common bond of love. The second movement
portrays the Idyllic Realm to which the individual has fled
in order to get rid of the institutional world and its injustice; it is the simple pastoral and sylvan life before
society. Here also there are essentially two threads; the
first is the banished Duke and lords, who have been driven
off by the existing wrongs of the civilized State and have
gone to the woods, there to dwell in the primitive peace
of nature; the second thread is made up of three groups,
which must be considered together — that of Orlando and
his servant, and his brother; that of Rosalind and Celia,
and the clown; and, finally, that of the native shepherds.
The third movement is the restoration of the Real World
of Right — the idyllic realm dissolves of its own inherent

necessity, and there is a complete return of the banished
members to society, which is healed of its wrong by the
departure and repentance of the usurping Duke.

I. 1. We shall now glance at the incidents of the play,
and trace the first movement through its various parts.
The first thread of it brings before us at once the Real
World of Wrong. Orlando has been deprived of his share
in the paternal estate by his brother Oliver, and, what is
much worse, his education has been utterly neglected, in
violation of the will of his father. Here is shown the
wrong in the Family; but this is not all. The rightful
Duke has been expelled from his government by his
brother, and thus we see that the wrong extends into the
State. The play does not unfold, but rather presupposes,
these two great acts of injustice, and, hence, society is
portrayed as in condition of strife and contradiction. But
Orlando has developed his physical nature, though his
intellect may have been neglected; he exhibits his prowess
first against his brother, and then at court he overcomes
the Duke's wrestler. A curious result of this adventure
is the love which springs up between himself and Rosalind,
which, however, has received the most ample and beautiful motive from the Poet. Nowhere has he more successfully shown the budding, blooming, and ripening of the
tender passion.

But soon this world of injustice comes into full activity
and manifests its inherent character. The Duke, as the
violator of all individual right, must naturally become
jealous of all individuals; hence he has banished a number of lords who seemed dangerous to his power. And so
this process must continue as long as anybody is left in
the country, since the existence of one man must be a

continual source of fear to such a tyrant. Hence Orlando, as the son of an old enemy, excites his suspicion, and has to leave the court with precipitation. The innocent youth has simply thrown the Duke's wrestler in a fair match; but this, together with his name, is sufficient to cause his speedy flight.

But the wrongs of Orlando do not end with his departure from court. He returns to his brother's estate only to find his life conspired against there, and his condition more hopeless than ever. Accompanied by his trusty servant, Adam, a second time he betakes himself to flight. It is impossible to mistake the meaning of these scenes. The Poet has here portrayed society in contradiction with its fundamental object; it has driven off those whom, by every tie of blood and of right, it was bound to protect; both State and Family have become the instruments of the direst injustice; on all sides we behold the *world of wrong.*

2. Such is the first thread of this movement; the second thread has as its central figure, Rosalind, daughter of the former Duke, who has been driven off by his brother, the present usurper. She is not disposed to be merry under the circumstances; her cousin, Celia, tries to enliven her spirits; Touchstone, the devoted clown, also seeks to drive away the heavy hours with pleasantry. Then Orlando appears for the wrestling match. The modest, sad-visaged youth seems unequal to his enterprise, and at once excites the warm sympathy of Rosalind, who feels her own sorrowful lot in his sorrowful words and looks. But, when she finds that he is the son of an old friend of her banished father, her sympathy rapidly ripens into love.

Rosalind now meets with the same treatment from the

suspicious Duke that Orlando has received. She is driven out of his dominions in the most wanton manner, but is accompanied by the daughter of the usurper — a just retribution upon his own family for the wrong done his brother's. The two young ladies now disguise themselves for their journey. Rosalind assumes the garb of a man, which she retains through all her adventures in the idyllic land. Here we have the chief instrumentality of comic situation — Disguise — which furnishes the intrigue of the play, though this is by no means its sole, or even its leading, element.

Both Orlando and Rosalind have, therefore, to flee; each is the victim of wrong in the Family and in the State. Moreover, we see in the background the general condition of society. There is no rightful authority; the true Duke has been expelled by an usurper; many lords have been compelled to leave their country. Such is the first movement. We are now prepared to make the transition to the second movement, in which will be portrayed the Idyllic World — the sphere of mediation.

II. But whither must these people go? Society has banished them, has wronged them, and, hence, their object is to find a place where the injustice of society does not exist, where there is no civil order. Such is the Forest of Arden, into which we are ushered in the beginning of the Second Act. Its nature has already been sufficiently indicated by the Poet when he compared it with the Golden Age. Its logical character is determined by the fact that it is the negation of all social organization — that simple primitive state before society.

1. Moreover, we find already here the banished Duke and lords, those for whom the social contradictions were too

strong, and, hence, have betaken themselves to a less
complex existence. The Duke rejoices in the new situation; he makes a glowing contrast between their present
life and that which they have abandoned. Here is no
flattery, no ambition, no crime; he can find quite all the
advantages of society in the trees, the stones, and the
brooks. Nature, were she only looked into, can furnish
all the content of reason. Nothing can surpass the fresh-
ness and the idyllic beauty with which he describes their
life in the forest; the aroma of the country is in every
line. Then comes Amiens, the lyrist of the company,
who embodies these sentiments in the most ethereal song.
The poetic representation of their abode is thus complete.

But hold! a disagreeable contrast arises. The Duke
feels that even in this new life he has not wholly avoided
the old difficulty, for there still remains the struggle with
the animal world — the burghers of the wood — for physical maintenance. Nay, there is one of these lords who
cannot find here any solution of the trouble — who declares
that injustice is as rife in the Forest of Arden as in society.
Witness the slaughter of the innocent beasts of the field,
and that same usurpation of their domains by the banished
Duke and lords of which they themselves were the victims in society. This is Jaques, whose negative character can find repose nowhere; he even sees in Nature herself only discord and evil; the deer is as bad as man — it
leaves its wounded neighbor to perish, while it passes
haughtily on. Thus is our Idyllic World, from which we
had thought to shut out all negation, disturbed by its reappearance, like a ghost among children. Indeed, man can
hardly get rid of the negative in this way; though he flee
to the woods, he will find it there. In fact, his very

existence depends upon destruction — upon swallowing a certain amount of vegetable and animal existence. Hence, in order to get rid of the negative, he must first get rid of life. Such is the logical result of abandoning State and society with the design of seeking a solution of their contradictions, namely, suicide — a result which men seldom insist upon practically realizing, though it is not unknown in the history of the human species that this result has been carried out to the bitter end.

2. These persons the play presupposes to have already gone to the Idyllic Realm, but now behold the new arrivals. First, Rosalind and Celia, in their disguise, appear at its entrance. Their difficulties, weariness, and hunger are specially noticed; they find the transition from the Real to the Ideal — from the luxury of the court and conveniences of society to the meager life of the shepherd — by no means easy. Though they are in an Ideal World, the Real makes itself very unpleasantly felt. But the nature of the place is soon made manifest. Two beings, called Corin and Silvius, suddenly rise upon their view, natives of the land, whose appearance shows them to be shepherds. Moreover, their language assumes a poetical form, and has for its theme the wail of unrequited love. Also, their names sound quite familiar — are, in fact, some old familiar names of pastoral poetry. With one of them Rosalind enters into conversation, and the result is that the new-comers buy a shepherd's hut, and are firmly planted in the idyllic land. Strange to say, Orlando and his old, devoted servant, Adam, have arrived in another part of the same territory, a proceeding which seems at first somewhat arbitrary on the part of the Poet. Yet, whither else had they to go? They have fled society, and,

hence, must proceed to a place where social order is unknown, which place has been identified as the Forest of Arden. We also find that they have the same difficulty, on entering this realm, which was experienced by the last party; Orlando even thinks of violence in order to obtain food, but he is soon changed by the gentle manner of the Duke, who, of course, could not do harm to any human being. With the end of the Second Act we find everybody fairly established in the new country.

The next question which arises is: What are they to do here? What is to be the content of their lives? We are not long left in ignorance, for soon we find Orlando wholly occupied with love, carving the name of his fair one upon the bark of trees, making love-ditties and hanging them upon the bushes — in fine, consumed with the most intense passion. Nor is Rosalind much better off, though she preserves her disguise in his presence. Touchstone — the clown — too, becomes infected with the prevailing frenzy, and the native shepherd Silvius, who is also heart-stricken, is again introduced, together with the disdainful shepherdess, Phebe, who, in her turn, falls in love with the disguised Rosalind. The result of the Third Act is that we have three pairs of lovers, native and foreign, to whom one pair is added in the following Acts. Thus our Ideal Realm is, for the new-comers, transformed into a sort of love-land, where the young people seem wholly occupied with their passion, though the old-comers are not so affected.

That such a state of existence should take this form is in the natural order of things. Let us analyze this remarkable transition. Man without society is without content to his life. Here society exists not, business is

impossible, ambition in the State is cut off, the physical
wants are reduced to the smallest compass and are satisfied with the smallest amount of exertion. Without occupation, without incentive — in general, without content
to his life — man is reduced to the *natural individual.*
Thus left alone to himself, his finitude begins to show
itself in every direction; for man, single, is one-sided —
a half — as is manifest by reflecting a moment on the
sexual diremption. He is thus the half, yet would be the
whole, and his entire nature drives him to overcome the
contradiction; for, in truth, he is not himself; his existence is in and through another, namely, one of the opposite sex. Such is the feeling of love, for it is here not
conscious, not in reflection, but the impulse of the natural
individual to cancel his own finitude. Now, we have just
seen that this natural individuality was quite the sum of
pastoral life, and, hence, its chief content is love. Thus
the Poet is true to the character of this realm, when he
makes those who dwell in it totally occupied with the tender passion.

But there is another consequence of this life, which the
Poet has not neglected. We see here the origin and the
purport of the idyl. Pastoral poetry, in its native simplicity, is mainly amatory, and allows but little reflection —
which belongs to a more cultivated period. Moreover, it
is here that poetry begins, as the simplest expression of
the primitive human passion. The Imagination gains
absolute control and paints the loved one in the fairest
colors; the stricken shepherd sees in the bush, in the
flower, in the clouds, her fleeting form; all nature is
turned into the image of her shape — love is his whole
being. When man thus transmutes his existence into

forms of the Imagination and gives them expression, the result is poetry. It does not seem a forced interpretation when it is said that Shakespeare meant to indicate the nature and the presence of the poetic element by the introduction of the native shepherds, Corin, Silvius, and Phebe. Their language falls at once into verse, their theme is some collision of love, and their names are taken from the pastoral poets. Moreover, Shakespeare has introduced perhaps the most common theme of this species of poetry — the neglected lover and the disdainful shepherdess; in fact, it occurs twice — Phebe disdains Silvius, and is herself disdained by Ganymede. Certainly the greatest charm of pastoral poetry is this simple idyllic love, springing from nature direct, with the faintest shadow of social forms and conventionalities. Description of rural scenery and of pastoral manners is quite subordinate to the amatory element; but, when reflection enters, or allusions to a more complex social organization are brought in, the pastoral loses its native relish, without attaining the higher forms of poetry. This play is not, therefore, a pastoral drama in the sense of *Aminta* or *The Faithful Shepherdess*, both of which do not get beyond the shepherd's life, while here the pastoral element is merely a transitory phase of both poetic and social development. Such is the second movement of the play.

III. 1. But what is the outcome of the drama? The complication, which rests wholly in the disguise of Rosalind, is solved by her appearance in woman's clothes, and the four pairs are united in the presence of the Duke. Hymen is thus the magician who reconciles these collisions of love-land, and the result of the pastoral world

is Marriage — the Family, which again results directly in
society. So, viewed on this side, the Ideal World cancels
itself — passes over into a system of social order. The
four pairs, who quite represent the various classes of
people, make already a little State.

2. But the banished Duke and lords cannot thus return
out of their idyllic existence, for it is supposed that they
are too old for passion, or have previously entered the
family relation. It is the State which has driven them
off, and through the State they must be brought back.
So the Poet introduces a new — and, of course, the
true — motive for their return. The world of wrong, of
which the usurping Duke is the representative, must continue its assaults upon the individual, since it is based
upon the destruction of personal right. The result must
be that soon a majority — or, if injustice be carried to
its extreme logical end, all — of the people will be driven off
to the Forest of Arden, where the rightful Duke resides.
In such case the Idyllic Realm is at once converted into
the same State from which they have fled, lacking only the
soil and the usurping Duke. But the return must be complete — must be to the old territory. Hence the usurper
is made to repent when he sees that he is deserted, and
the old ruler and his attendant lords are restored *peace-
fully* — an important point, for it would ill comport with
their peaceful character, and their simple, unoffending
life in the woods, to come back by violence. Thus the
reconciliation is complete; harmony is restored; the world
of wrong dissolves of its own accord, the world of right
returns with the rightful Duke. The diremption with
which the play begins is now healed over, the Ideal World
being the means whereby the regeneration takes place.

It will be noticed, however, that there is one of the company who does not return. Jaques is the completely negative character, who believes in society as little as in anything else. Even the Forest of Arden called forth in him only sneers; it was as bad as the court and possessed the same unjust features; hence it had no mediation for him. He finds a fool in the forest, whose nonsensical moralizing calls forth in him the wildest delight; he thinks the fool is the only wise man, and he himself wants to turn fool to reform the world. Here we have a sample of not a few of our modern reformers, who, of all people, are themselves most in need of reform. He snarls at all reality, apparently for no other reason than that it is; the moment anything becomes actual it becomes bad; mere existence is sufficient for condemnation. It does not surprise us, therefore, when it is hinted that this reformer has himself waded through the depths of sensuality, and traveled over the whole world in search of something positive, which, of course, he cannot find. He is, hence, wholly negative; man and even nature are to him worthless. He does not return, therefore, with the rest, but goes to the new convert, the Duke's brother, who has now "left the world" in his turn, but whose career in the world was also negative. Jaques is one of those psychological characterizations of Shakespeare which are true to the most rigid logic, yet are so completely vitalized that we never feel the abstraction. Such is the third movement of the play.

To sum up, this drama gives a poetic statement and solution of the problem of the Real and Ideal. First comes the struggle of the individual with the actual world, whereby he is trampled into the dust, his rights taken

away, his life endangered.  It becomes the Real World of
Wrong, and ~~destroys that which it was~~ called into existence
to ~~protect,~~ and thus has the contradiction within itself
which must bring about its destruction.  Secondly, the individual, therefore, must flee; ~~abandon State and~~ society,
which oppress and try to destroy him, and go — whither?
Not to another State, for the thought in its universality is
that the State as such assails him; hence he must find
some spot quite out of its reach.  The simple primitive life
must, therefore, be sought; hence he betakes himself to
the woods — the Forest of Arden — where only a few
.  scattered shepherds eke out a scanty existence.  Thus
the individual is established in his Ideal Realm, far away
from institutions, from the conventional usages and struggles of society, in ~~simple unity with nature and~~ the beasts
~~of the~~ field.  But, in the third place, this mode of life is
found to be of very short duration — is, hence, not a true
and permanent condition of the human race.  There
arises simultaneously a twofold movement for its dissolution.  On the one hand, the members of this ideal land
are still natural individuals — hence must love, and, what
is more, must marry; thus the Family appears, which
again in good time brings forth the State, and the Ideal
Realm vanishes into thin air.  On the other hand, the Real
World of Wrong continues its warfare with the individual
until it drives all away into the Forest of Arden; for its
principle is the destruction of the individual, who has, of
course, to flee.  The ideal land thereby is converted into
the old State minus the tyrant, since the citizens of the one
have become inhabitants of the other.  So, by a double
process, this realm cancels itself and passes into the higher
form of civil and social organization.  The Poet, there-

fore, indicates that such an idyllic life is an irrationa
abstraction; that man's rational existence is in the State
and in society, whose collisions he must endure, bitter
though they be. The absurd notion that a pastoral,
dreamy existence is the highest finds here no toleration
—is, in fact, reduced to a comedy, which shows it dissolving in its own absurdity.

Such is the lesson for life; but the Poet's work cuts
deeper, since it includes the literary and artistic products
of the same consciousness. All those ideal commonwealths of which literature is full may here obtain their
final judgment. But particularly the nature, extent, and
limits of pastoral poetry — the art-form of such a life — are
brought out with a hey-dey of laughter. For this species
of poetry also must end with the entrance into society; it
belongs only to the simple shepherd on his native hills; it is
the first and least concrete — and, hence, least interesting —
of all poetry, being without the presupposition of society.
The course of the drama, therefore, is the contradiction
in the world of reality which results in the wrongs done to
the individual; the mediation is through the Ideal World,
whereby a reconciliation is brought about and the individual is restored to the world of reality. The three steps
may be generalized as the Diremption, the Mediation, and
the Return. They exhibit a totality of society, with its
corresponding Art and a hint of its Literature.

Some have considered this play to be a mere caprice — a
wild and irregular sport of fancy. But, if we have succeeded in our interpretation, we have shown it to be an
inherent and necessary development out of one fundamental thought. Again, it has been taken for a pastoral
drama. But its very aim, its comic germ, is to show the

limits of pastoral poetry—in fact, of idyllic life generally
—and, consequently, of the poetic form which springs
from such a life.　Still more frequently it is held to be an
ordinary comedy of situation, of intrigue and love, as if
the incidents connected with the disguise of Rosalind
were alone to be considered.　It has, undoubtedly, a pastoral element—it has also intrigue; but both are subordinate—are only means to bring forth the grand result.
It is thus a comedy within a comedy, or, rather, two comedies within a comedy.　The pursuit of an idyllic life
calls forth the pastoral, the love gives the basis of the
intrigue.　But the third and highest comic element is to be
found in the return to society; in the fact that these people
of the Ideal Realm are, in reality, doing just the opposite of what they think they are doing—they are trying to
accomplish ends which are in themselves contradictory
and null.　In general, this play may be called the comedy
of the Imagination as against the Reason, or of the abstract
Ideal as against the Actual, wherein the Imagination in
pursuing an object is at the same time destroying it.　Its
content thus reaches deep into the history of the world.
All visionary commonwealths—Plato's Republic, More's
Utopia, Harrington's Oceana, Arcadias, Icarias, Atlan-
tises, etc.; also, many of the so-called ideal lives, par-
adisaical societies—in fine, the whole consciousness
upon which such bodiless creations of fancy repose—
constitute the theme of this drama, and are exhibited in
their finitude.

# WINTER'S TALE.

This play is characterized by its frequent and direct defiance of the senses. Time and Space, which constitute the basis of the great world of sensation, seem to be entirely given over to the capricious play of the Poet's imagination. Even the so-called truths of the Understanding are laughed at in wanton mockery. History, Chronology, and also Geography are violated with an audacity which has often called forth the sneers and the ire of pedantic erudition. Christianity consults the Delphic oracle, Pagan customs are mingled with those of the English people, ancient Greece is one of the modern European system of states, Bohemia is made a country bordering on the sea. Indeed, the Understanding becomes utterly confused by the disregard of its facts and its laws, and can make nothing out of the play. It is plain to be seen that there is an utter neglect — or, rather, an intentional defiance — of all external probability. In fact, Probability, as a canon of Shakespearian criticism, is wholly meaningless and inapplicable; there is scarcely a play in which it is not violated. The time has come when it ought to be eschewed altogether. The Poet seems to have proceeded thus on purpose. In other dramas, as in *Tempest*, he has gone to work indirectly by portraying an ideal world removed from the common consciousness; but in *Winter's Tale* he takes pains to give the lie direct to all sensuous and immediate elements. But, notwithstand-

ing these contradictions — or, indeed, by means of these
contradictions — the deep purport of the play stands out
in bold relief ; we are compelled to seek beneath the surface to find its meaning.  Our senses are confused with
the design of forcing us to turn to its creative thought for
the solution of its difficulties.  In this realm — that of
thought — the drama is all harmony ; and here we must
seek for its unity, since the sensuous unities of time and
place, and the abstract laws of the Understanding, are
everywhere ignored.  To develop the formative thought of
the work will be the object of the present essay.

There are three grand movements or divisions of the
drama.  The first portrays the guilt of the King of
Sicilia, and ends in his repentance ; it is the world of
strife, contradiction, and wrong, which necessarily causes
a separation, a flight from its iniquities.  The second
movement shows the new world called into existence by
the tyrannical conduct of the monarch, which is Bohemia,
the simple pastoral realm that is free from the tragic conflicts of Sicilia.  But it, too, will ultimately develop a
collision within itself, which will bring about its own dissolution.  The third movement is the penitent world, in
which the King, having repented of his deeds, sees those
who were dispersed brought back, and those who were lost
restored to himself.  The logical thought of the action,
therefore, is that guilt produces the second or pastoral
world, and repentance the third or the restoration.  If
we take general terms to express these different elements,
we may name them the Diremption, the Mediation, and
the Return.  All the special or mediated dramas of Shakespeare, as distinguished from his tragedies and pure comedies, have three movements of a similar character.  For

the guilt of man can be atoned for only by repentance; and Art, the representation of man, must employ the same instrumentality.

I. The single thread of the first movement is Leontes, about whom the incidents and characters will be grouped. The starting-point of the action is the friendship between the two kings, Leontes and Polixenes. The first scene shows also the good feeling existing among their subordinates. Polixenes, King of Bohemia, has been paying a long visit to the friend of his youth, King Leontes of Sicilia. Nine months have passed delightfully away, and the royal visitor is about to return to his own country. The harmony between the two kings and their courts is thus indicated; now comes the rupture. The wife of Leontes, Queen Hermione, at the request of the King, urges Polixenes with great ardor to prolong his stay, and, to enforce her appeal, she seems to have given a caress and indulged in some familiarities. Her husband, Leontes, is fired with jealousy at her behavior; from friendship for his guest he changes to deadly enmity, from affection for his wife he turns to the deepest hatred. Jealousy is based upon the complete unity of marriage, and when the unity is disturbed by infidelity that passion is manifested, and should be manifested, in all its intensity. But a suspicious nature may imagine a wrong, or draw conclusions from totally insufficient grounds. Such a nature Leontes undoubtedly possesses.

The Queen's regard for Polixenes proceeds chiefly from the fact that he is her husband's dearest friend — she loves him only through her husband. This is manifest, not only from her conversation with him, but also from her defense in the Third Act; and the very warmth of her conduct toward Polixenes results from the desire of pleasing her husband in the entertainment of the companion of his youth. This consideration, however, does not enter the mind of Leontes; he views her external behavior only in its worst light; the spirit of it he does not — indeed, cannot by his nature — comprehend. Perhaps her conduct might be called indiscreet under certain circumstances, but the present case is certainly one in which she ought to abandon all coldness and formality. The King in his soliloquies has stated the principle of his action. He has a vague feeling — an affect — that his wife is false to him; and because he imagines it, therefore it must be true. That is, he entirely yields to his first impulse, and justifies his first fancy. Her former character and life weigh as nothing. He is now fully possessed of his purpose to destroy both his friend and his wife, which he as king can carry out in all its destructive consequences.

What are these consequences? They will involve in their sweep the destruction of the entire Ethical World, from the merely individual relations of man up to the highest and holiest institutions of civilization. In his mad passion and stubborness he assails everything which is considered right and sacred. Let us try to seize these various elements in their gradation. First, he wantonly tramples underfoot the deepest and most honorable personal relations — those of true friendship and honest service; he casts away Polixenes his friend, and Camillo his counselor. Having firmly determined upon his course, he seeks to make Camillo the instrument of murder. The honest servant is shocked, and will not believe the charge of infidelity against the Queen; he has independence of

character, though a subordinate, and will not surrender his
conviction in obedience to a master. Still, he seems to
assent in order to save Polixenes and the Queen; he lays
his plan evidently while talking with the King Leontes.
Here we have the fundamental traits of Camillo — devotion to the highest ends, combined with a secret and decep-
tive cunning in attaining them. He is the chief mediator
for both Kings; he has often "cleansed the bosom" and
soothed the excited mind of Leontes, like a priest at the
confessional, and the latter now foolishly expects his aid
in a scheme of infamy. Hereafter he will stand in the
same relation to Polixenes. He unites the loftiest purpose to politic shrewdness; his deception must be justified
by the end. The other personal relation which is assailed
by the jealous King is his friendship for Polixenes. The
life of the latter is to be destroyed under the hospitable roof,
but the plan is thwarted by the intervention of the mediator, Camillo, who warns him in time and provides means
for his flight. But Camillo, too, has to leave Sicilia; he
is given the same relative position in the court of Polixenes as in that of Leontes, and so transfers his allegiance
to another king and country.

Now, let us consider for a moment what is involved
in this act of the Sicilian monarch. He has logically
destroyed friendship by his jealousy; no man can consistently be **a** friend to him. He has, furthermore, driven
away honest counsel; for has he not made it impossible
by his conduct to Camillo? No friends, no honest servants, can live with him. They have fled; but whither
do they go? They are not lost, but they have a world of
their own which receives them. It must be in many
respects the opposite of that realm which they have left.

The Poet will portray it hereafter; indeed, he must do so to complete his work. We shall watch, then, for the place where Camillo and Polixenes are next found, being assured that it must have some entirely new characteristics.

Leontes has thus destroyed, under the influence of his ferocious passion, the sphere of personal relation in the true friend and in the devoted servant. But he has at the same time assailed something far more important — the Family. He has unjustly and wantonly struck it in the most tender point, namely, in the chastity and fidelity of the wife. The consequences are shown in all their rigor. The wife is a mother; her offspring must be stained with the suspicion of illegitimacy; her high-spirited boy, Mamillius, perishes from the wound of his name. She is also about to become a mother — her highest maternal hope is turned into dishonor; her innocent child is bastardized. Thus little is left of the Family. But what is the fate of poor Hermione herself? Every wrong and every indignity which the wife can suffer is heaped upon her by the jealous tyrant. At first Leontes tells his suspicion only to Camillo; but, after the flight of Polixenes, he considers all his imaginings to be confirmed, and now he accuses his wife of infidelity in the presence of the whole court. Thus he tries to blast her honor before the world. But several of the courtiers, and particularly Antigonus, are ready to assert her innocence in the most emphatic manner, and it is evident that public opinion is strongly against the King. But, to confirm his suspicion by religious sanction, he sends to the oracle at Delphi — not so much for his own information as "to give rest to the minds of others." The Queen is thrown into prison, where to her mental anguish is added the physical suffering and anxiety of a premature delivery of her child. Still, though spirited and asserting her innocence, she is patient and wifely under the atrocious inflictions of her husband.

But Leontes is now to have his deed held up before his eyes; he is to be told in the plainest terms of the nature of his conduct. No courtier was bold enough to tell him this; the most any one of them said was to declare the innocence of the Queen. But to proclaim openly the guilt of the King was reserved for a woman — one who could best know her sufferings and feel her wrongs. The Queen, with her gentle, loving character, could not assume such a part. Hence Paulina appears — certainly a strong-worded, perhaps a strong-minded, woman. Her deepest principle of action is devotion for the Queen. She is married, but her love for her husband was evidently not so strong, for she seems to treat him pretty rudely. Her husband is Antigonus, who was the boldest of the courtiers in the defense of Hermione; yet he has submitted to his wife, who must, therefore, be still bolder than he. This Paulina brings to the King his infant, and holds up before him his actions in language lacking in neither strength nor precision. The King cannot get any of his attendants — and, least of all, her husband, Antigonus — to put her out of his presence. But Leontes is not touched with compassion, though he has "no rest nor day nor night;" he ascribes it to the wrong cause — to danger from the weak and imprisoned Queen. Paulina leaves the infant with the King, who, after deceiving Antigonus into a pledge to perform any command that he might enjoin, orders the unfortunate man to expose the child in some remote and desert place.

Hence Antigonus falls into guilt and perishes. His promise was not binding, and, indeed, he does not seem at first to have purposed the exposure of the child. But a dream appears to him — he thought that the ghost of Hermione commanded him to do the deed; in fact, he loses his former belief in the innocence of the Queen, and now deems that the child belongs to Polixenes. Finally, religious superstition adds its mighty power; he considers it to be the will of Apollo that the babe should be exposed. Excited by his imagination, against his own deepest conviction he leaves the infant in a desolate spot, where it is picked up by some shepherds; but he receives retribution for his deed in his own destruction. The babe is thus removed from the court and civilized society; it has been cast into an opposite world — among the rude, but honest, natives of the wilds — where, however, it obtains nourishment and protection, which it did not find in the civilized court of Sicilia. This is the second separation — the second departure to the new realm — that of Camillo and Polixenes being the first. We shall also watch with interest for the reappearance of the little outcast.

Leontes has now committed a new and graver offense against the Family; he has, as far as his will is concerned, destroyed his own offspring. His jealousy has driven him to the point of first branding with infamy and then exposing the child of his loins. Now, the graet purpose of the Family is to protect and rear the tender and helpless scions of the race. That end is here annihilated by the King; he has on this side, too, destroyed the Family, as before he destroyed its unity, by assailing the character of his wife. The child is thus sent out of the realm; it must be taken elsewhere that it may be preserved, for here there is no longer any family to guard its infancy. The one to which it belonged has perished; it must find the Family in another place — it must pass to some land in which domestic ties are possible.

But the final wrong is about to be inflicted upon the poor wife, Hermione. She has to undergo the ordeal of a public prosecution; the indictment charges her with adultery, and with the intention of murdering her husband — just what she is not guilty of. But the crowning trial of her life manifests only the more clearly the crowning trait of her character. Her defense has one key-note through all its variations — wifeliness. She always has been, and always will be, true to the Family — true to her function of wife and mother. As to Polixenes, her love toward him was such as Leontes himself commanded —

> " Which not to have done I think had been in me
> Both disobedience and ingratitude
> To you and toward your friend."

" It was for your sake that I loved your friend." She is ready to die because the Family, the object of her existence, is destroyed; her husband's favor, the crown and comfort of her life, is lost; her children are taken from her; her reputation is publicly blackened with the basest accusations. Not life, but honor, she pleads for, since this descends to her children. It is the most heroic assertion of the Family, in spite of the most terrible wrongs that can be perpetrated upon a human being. She is the glory of her sex; nothing can shake her devotion to the deepest principle of womanhood. The Poet has given to her a will of Titanic strength, yet she is gentle as a dove. Her husband inflicts upon her the sum total of injustice,

5

he pours upon her innocent head all the vials of iniquity, yet she does not cease to love that husband, and in the end forgives him. To bring to the highest possible pitch her heroism, these wrongs fall upon her in the most delicate condition of woman — in the very throes of maternity. Still, she is unshaken in her devotion; in comparison with her endurance the old Greek heroines dwindle to pygmies. Hermione is the absolute wife; her character is the apotheosis of wifehood.

The King is inexorable; his jealousy is not yet satiated; the Queen is condemned to death. She receives her sentence, not from an impartial tribunal, but from the lips of the King himself. Though he has repeatedly promised a just and open trial, according to the English sense of right, it is the mockery, not only of the essence, but also of the forms, of justice. Herein the King commits a new offense against the ethical order of the world — he destroys the end of the State. For its great object is to secure justice to man, but in the present case the purpose is perverted by the ruler to the grossest injustice. Thus the State can no longer exist in Sicilia; it must logically perish with the annihilation of its end.

But one more institution remains to be destroyed. The messengers return from the Delphic oracle with the response of the god totally adverse to the acts and purposes of Leontes. It simply reflects the existing ethical sentiment of the community, as it ought. What will Leontes now do? He blasphemes, he asserts the falsehood of the oracle, he denies religion. The highest principle of his people he tramples underfoot; the most complete expression of their conviction he ignores — indeed, gives to it the lie direct. Further he cannot go in his

destructive tendencies — he has assailed the highest. Now
follows speedy retribution; the death of his son is announced to him, whereat Hermione is borne out apparently
dead. It ought to be noticed that these incidents, which
seem to be a consequence of blaspheming the oracle, are
motived clearly and adequately in other passages. Thus
the boy, Mamillius, has been observed to be pining away on
account of the supposed dishonor of his mother; the
apparent death of Hermione, and the circumstances
attending it, are unfolded in a later part of the drama.
And the oracle itself tells only what everybody knew
already — what the Poet had amply motived before. It
simply gives in a religious form the universal conviction
of the time. Why, then, does the Poet employ the oracle?
Because he wishes to portray the negative conduct of
Leontes in its completeness and final culmination. He
is made to deny religion — or, the profoundest principle of
his nation and his age.

Let us now turn back and mark the gradation of guilt
through which Leontes has passed. This is the single
thread in the first movement. He has destroyed the realm
of personal relation in Polixenes and Camillo; he has
destroyed the Family in all its elements by the dishonor
and legal murder of his wife and by the loss of his children, which loss is but the direct result of his deed; he
has logically annihilated the State by perverting its end
to the most wanton injustice; and, finally, the religious
principle of his people he has trampled underfoot. To
sum up his conduct, he has destroyed the entire Ethical
World, as far as his act goes. This World interfered, as
it ought always to interfere, in order to prevent wrong
and shield the innocent; the result is, he has ruthlessly

destroyed it—that is, Sicilia can no longer be the abode of man. For it is just these ethical relations and institutions which society stands on; without them it falls to pieces. The monarch who is to administer, uphold, and vivify them has become their destroyer.

Though the King, as the head of the civil tribunal, may condemn Hermione, she has been acquitted by the highest tribunal—Universal Reason—or, at least, the ethical feeling of the nation, which is represented in the oracle. The god has declared the innocence of the Queen; the entire basis of the King's jealousy is thus swept away. All his acts have had the one motive—the infidelity of his wife. But even the highest of all tribunals does not at once change the mind of the King. It is only when retribution is upon him that he begins to see the consequences of his action. His son, Mamillius, is torn away by death, the cause of which was the unjust accusation of his mother. Leontes now comprehends that his deed is returning upon him; that the destruction of the Family means the destruction of his child and heir; that all his other iniquities will bring forth the same fruits. He realizes that the annihilation of all will include his own annihilation. It comes like a flash upon his mind. Hitherto he has not felt the evil consequences of his wrongs; but the moment they are brought home to his own person he changes, and with him the course of the play must also change.

He is now ready to make his wicked deeds undone — in other words, his soul is ready for Repentance. He recounts his bad actions and seeks forgiveness; first of all, he reconciles himself with Apollo — with the highest ethical principle. He confesses in deep contrition his wrongs

against his Queen, against Camillo and Polixenes. To all
he will make the most ample restitution in his power. But,
in order that he may still more profoundly realize the enor-
mity of his offense, and in order that his pride and stub-
bornness may be humbled to the dust, Paulina, whom he
had formerly driven away in anger and disdain, now comes
to preach her previous sermon with increased vigor, severity, and length — a courageous, strong-worded woman,
who is a little too free with her tongue over a penitent
wrong-doer. A lord has to restrain her; but Leontes
even asks for her castigation — a good sign that it is no
longer needed. The King declares:

> —"Once a day I'll visit
> The chapel where they lie; and tears shed there
> Shall be my recreation; so long as nature
> Will bear up with this exercise, so long
> I daily vow to use it."

Here we see stated and enforced the great mediatorial
principle of the race, namely, Repentance. Man has the
power of making his wicked deed undone; he can reverse
the wheels of life and can become fully reconciled with
himself and the world. Spirit is able to heal its own
wounds — is able to master its own negative elements;
for its characteristic is to be universal, and, hence, it is
sovereign over all forms of finitude. The doctrine is not
merely a religious one, but also a philosophical one, and
must be recognized and practiced by every rational being
of whatever creed. But Repentance is to be complete;
it involves confession of the wrong, deep contrition, and
full restoration of every advantage derived from guilt.
Then the deed is undone; the crime is wiped out; the
penitent individual returns to his previous condition of

innocence and repose — becomes reconciled with himself
and with the world.  Such is the general purport of Repentance in the dramas of Shakespeare, which, however, is
more prominent in this play than in any other.  It sounds
like a Christian sermon, though its dress is Pagan.  Its
thought belongs to the modern world, though its external
form is mainly cast in a Grecian mould.  Leontes repents —
repents fully, deeply.  This repentance involves the restoration of the world which he has lost through his guilt; it
will be given back to him in the third division of the
action.  Thus the work becomes a special or mediated
drama, whose principle is mediation through repentance;
for how is the guilty man to be saved, even in a play,
except by a penitent heart?  The King, however, has to
unmake his disposition — has to reconstruct his entire
character — since it is tainted through and through with
jealousy.  The process of elimination will be as slow as
that of growth; day by day the vicious element must be
plucked out, till finally the regeneration is complete.

But guilt has done its work — the diremption has taken
place, the ethical world has been destroyed; Sicilia, the
civilized realm of institutions, now disappears.  The
King enters upon his penitential life, which will be prolonged, but whose exact period is determined by the
external requirements of the play.  The exposed infant
must have time sufficient to grow up to be a young
woman.  We have, accordingly, to leave the court of
Leontes, and cast our look upon the new realm which has
already arisen.

II.  We are now ready to consider the second general
movement of the play — the pastoral realm of Bohemia.
Though it has a king whose act will again call forth a

collision similar to one of those in Sicilia, yet its chief
tone and character are derived from the life of the
shepherds, and the entire action is laid in their rustic
abodes. This is the land where all have arrived who
were cast off by Leontes. The logical connection of it
with the preceding movement has been already noticed;
it is the product of the tyrannical guilt of the King of
Sicilia. These persons can no longer exist in that country; they fly, or are brought, to a place where it is possible
for them to live. Such a place must be quite the opposite
of Sicilia. The latter is portrayed as a wealthy and civilized State, which, however, is in internal struggle on
account of the character of its ruler. Bohemia, therefore,
is wholly different; it is a poor, mountainous, uncivilized
region, inhabited by shepherds. But it is free from the
strife and calamity of Sicilia; its people are simple and
humble, yet at the same time they are joyous and humane.
We shall here have a continual round of jollity, in contrast to the tragic severity and gloom of the first part,
because the country is not harassed with the deep social
contradictions of Sicilia. Pastoral life in its full hilarity
and freedom from anxiety will be unrolled before our
eyes—a primitive condition of man, almost before evil
enters and introduces strife, will be depicted.

But such a society is transitory; it must rise to civilization. It develops contradictions within itself by which it
is destroyed. Its destiny is to return to Sicilia, which has
passed through such difficulties and has harmonized them.
There alone it can find peace and reconciliation; hence
the entire pastoral world will return to the contrite King
Leontes. Bohemia is thus the means whereby those whom
Leontes has driven away are restored to him, and where-

by the leading diremption of the play is healed. Its function is, therefore, mediation, since it is the external instrumentality of the return, which, however, has its necessary
logical ground in the repentance of the King.

1. The threads of this pastoral world are three. The
first thread shows the life and occupation of the shepherds, with their sports and merry customs. They give
color to this entire part; it is essentially their world.
Their kindness and humanity are shown in the rearing of
Perdita, and in their sympathy for the fate of Antigonus.
Their rustic love, with its petty jealousy and rude direct-
ness, their songs and dances, their manners generally,
are portrayed with a broad, comic license; everywhere is
seen an honest, hearty merriment; simplicity, honesty,
and even stupidity, are the marked traits of these people.
It is the idyllic land of primitive innocence. But even
here there is contradiction; in the lowest group of this
world is found a negative character — Autolycus. The
simplest form of existence would seem not to be without
conflict.

Autolycus is, however, not wholly a product of shepherd life, but apparently of the court also, having been
formerly a servant of Prince Florizel. He is, moreover,
negative only to the honesty of the pastoral character,
while he participates in its free joyousness and sportive
nature. He is one of Shakespeare's higher efforts in
comic delineation, ranking under the same genus as Sir
Toby Belch and Sir John Falstaff. He is a rogue not so
much from malice as from pleasure; he takes delight in
thievery for its own sake rather than for its gains. He is
aware of his misdeeds, and laughs at them; his life is
folly, to be sure — but, then, he wants to enjoy his own

folly. His cunning is the source of a continuous chuckling to himself; the property won is of far less account. He is comic to himself and plays a comic part for his own special amusement. He, therefore, belongs to the class of consciously comic characters, who make fun and enact folly chiefly for themselves. He celebrates his vagabond life and thievish disposition in verse; it is a theme for Art with him. Such a person stands in contrast with the simple, honest shepherds; but, still, he is of them, and harmoniously blends with their world. He furnishes the intrigue and disguise of this little realm, and is, hence, the source of its comic situations. Under many deceitful forms he appears to the shepherds, picking pockets, peddling worthless trifles, extorting money by threats and lying—a cunning rogue on a small scale, whose function it is to make a ripple in the tranquil life around him. He will assist in breaking up the pastoral world and transferring it to Sicilia, where he will repent.

2. The second thread is the love of Florizel, son of Polixenes, and of Perdita, the supposed daughter of an old shepherd who is the chief figure here. but she is in reality the daughter of Leontes. The exposed infant has grown up and belongs to this world, for Sicilia has cast her off. She has inherited the chief trait in the character of her mother—devotion to Family. But she is her mother as a young maiden; the relation, therefore, in which she appears will not be that of wife, but of lover. With the quiet strength and deep ethical feeling of Hermione, she combines all the warmth and simplicity of youthful love. In her modesty she thinks herself unworthy of Florizel, and has a presentiment of the collision which will interfere with their union. She dis-

tributes flowers to the company — the most beautiful
emblem of virgin purity; they are also her language.
Only the natural bloom she will have; no flower artificially
streaked will be allowed to remain in her garden; no
deception, no artifice, is her meaning, and such is also her
character. The abstract reasoning of Polixenes on nature
she does not understand, though she assents; she is herself the simple flower, unconscious of its own beauty.

Florizel, who had accidentally met her when he was
engaged in the chase, has the same intensity and devotion;
the King's son descends to a rural maiden. He acknowledges love to be the highest and strongest principle; it
has even subdued the gods. His conduct is in accord
with his declaration; he is ready to sacrifice all to his
affection. This pair must be logically connected with the
first part. In Sicilia the Family has been destroyed by
the act of the King, who has condemned to death Hermione, his wife, though the deepest principle of her
nature was domestic fidelity and devotion. Here, now, the
Family in general, and that of Leontes in particular, must
be built up anew through the child of Hermione and the
heiress of her character. Hence it is necessary that in
this pastoral realm, as the mediatorial world, there should
be a restoration of the Family destroyed by Leontes.
This thread has a highly poetical coloring, as distinguished
from the vulgar, prosaic style of the rude shepherds.
Still, the love is idyllic; Perdita is a shepherdess, and is
thus the connecting link between the two main groups.

3. The third thread shows the doings of Polixenes and
Camillo. Both were driven off by the wrong of Leontes;
both have evidently found in Bohemia what they did not
obtain in Sicilia. Polixenes, it is true, was king of this

country before he visited the court of Leontes; he, therefore, only returned to his own kingdom. It is, therefore,
slightly different from the purely pastoral realm, such as
we see in *As You Like It*, for it has a monarch, though its
institutions and its court do not appear. Camillo has
made himself indispensable to the ruler; again we behold in him the faithful minister — having been compelled to flee for his honest service, he has found it possible here. But he longs to return, and lay his bones in
his native land; he has, moreover, heard of the repentance
of Leontes, and the deep desire of the latter for reconciliation and forgiveness. It is manifest that the strongest
wish of Camillo's heart is to be restored to his country,
especially since that which separated him from it has been
wholly removed. He is the great manager — he will find
some means of accomplishing his end. It must be observed
that he expressly declares that the repentance of the King
of Sicilia is what motives his return.

Both Camillo and Polixenes have heard of the strange
love of Prince Florizel, who has of late quite abandoned
the court, and is seldom absent from the house of a lowly
shepherd, the fame of whose daughter has also reached
their ears. The father is naturally anxious; his plan is
laid: Camillo and himself, disguised in a strange garb,
are to go to the house of the shepherd and take observa-
tions. Here we have the comic disguise so often used by
Shakespeare in various forms; it is the element of intrigue
which he commonly employs in the more refined and
courtly part of the dialogue. Camillo and Polixenes carry
out their scheme; they converse with the maiden and are
charmed with her pretty ways; they talk with the old shepherd, who tells them concerning the love of the pair.

Finally, Florizel himself is examined by the disguised
father, and declares in the most absolute manner his passion for the fair shepherdess; he protests that all, even
the greatest empire of the world, would be naught without
her love. Now comes the conflict; the father asks his
son: "Does your father know of your choice?" The
Prince says: "No; nor shall not." At this point the
knot is untied — the parent throws off his disguise; in his
kingly wrath he condemns the old shepherd and the
maiden; he threatens to bar his son from succession to
the throne if he does not at once return to court. Thus
the pastoral world is destroyed by the harsh judgment of
the monarch; the aged shepherd laments his wretched
fate; Perdita weeps, and tells Florizel to follow the command of his father. But the Prince has before emphatically stated his principle — everything, even the kingly
dignity, is subordinate to love. He, therefore, determines
at once to flee with Perdita — but whither? Now comes
Camillo, who is himself anxious to return to his native
country, and he at once suggests Sicilia. The whole
matter is easily arranged; a little deception, indeed, is
practiced upon Leontes, but a mediator cannot be a severe
moralist, and Camillo is no exception to the rule. Scruples
must be passed over, to some extent, in all reconciliation
and mediation; rigid obstinacy, even to principle, is not
going to produce harmony.

The lovers hasten to a ship conveniently at hand and
take passage for Sicilia. In that country the Family is
now possible, since Leontes has repented of his wrong
against it, while Polixenes, in his turn, has here assailed
its existence. Camillo will follow them in company with
Polixenes, who is seeking to bring back his son. Even

the two shepherds, together with the rogue Autolycus —
who, true to his negative character, has brought about
this departure — are carried away in the ship to Sicilia.
Thus the pastoral world is quite depopulated, and now disappears; the same contradiction, essentially, has overwhelmed Bohemia which formerly destroyed Sicilia.
Bohemia, however, has now performed its function — that
of mediating a restoration to Sicilia of all those who had
been driven away; it is the external instrumentality of the
Return. But the internal movement is that, as it was
called into existence by the guilt of Leontes, so it must
necessarily cease with his repentance. Pastoral life is at
best a transitional stage of society; it must pass into a
higher principle.

This second movement has quite all the elements of a
Shakespearian comedy. It has the low group of characters speaking in prose, and it has the genteel group speaking in verse. It has also a double comic disguise — that
of Autolycus on the one hand, and that of Polixenes on
the other. As the first part is weighed down with a tragic
severity, so the second part moves with a frolicsome light-
ness. This change has been generally condemned or
misunderstood; it has been said that it divided the play
into two disconnected and irreconcilable portions. But
a true insight will reveal the intimate logical relation of
the two parts — that the second movement is directly
derived from the first. Besides, Shakespeare has certainly as great transitions in other dramas. In *Midsummer Night's Dream* we at once pass from the real
world into the fairy realm, and in *As You Like It* there is
a sudden leap into a comic pastoral existence very similar
to that of the present play. The same is the case with

the entire ideal class of mediated dramas. The only
means of solving these difficulties is to have recourse to
the logical movement of the thought which creates the
work.

III. The third and last movement is now prepared for,
whose theme will be the Return, which, as before stated,
was involved in the repentance of Leontes. We are at
once transported back to Sicilia, and there we find the
same personages whom we left sixteen years before. The
King is still full of deep contrition for his former conduct;
the character of the court seems entirely changed — it is
like a house of mourning; on all sides we behold the
world of penitence and sorrow. One of the courtiers
thinks that the wrongs done by Leontes have been sufficiently atoned for, and is urging him to take a wife for
reasons of State. Paulina opposes, and extorts a promise
from the King never to marry without her consent. Here
begins the little intrigue of this part, which will be solved
by the reappearance of Hermione. The King's devotion
to his wife, supposed by him to be dead, as well as the
fullness and sincerity of his repentance, are seen in every
act and word. The widower's conflict between duty to
the living and affection for the dead has arisen; the latter
is shown to be the more powerful. We are thus forced to
conclude that Leontes has made his wicked deeds undone
to the extent of his power, and has completely remoulded
his character.

While they are all still conversing, news is brought of a
strange arrival, and shortly afterwards the son of Polixenes with Perdita appear before the King. Here again the
penitential sorrow of Leontes breaks forth; he is full of
confession for the wrong done by him to the Prince's

father and to his own children. But upon this fair scene a thunderbolt suddenly falls; a messenger rushes in, announcing that the pair are runaways, and that Polixenes has arrived in pursuit of them. That is, the conflict of the pastoral world is transferred to Sicilia, where alone it can be reconciled. The lovers beseech the King to intercede for them and to maintain the right of the Family, which of course he must now do, since he has repented of his own sins against the Family. Leontes has thus changed from being the cause of conflict and guilt to being their mediator, a trait which is the necessary consequence of his repentance. He is the more ready to act on account of a strange instinctive affection for the maiden, who has recalled to his mind the image of Hermione.

The scene of recognition and forgiveness follows, which, however, is not brought upon the stage, but is narrated by eye-witnesses, in order that the reappearance of the Queen may form the climax of the drama. Before the King come Polixenes and Camillo, with whom there is at once reconciliation. The friend and the honest servant are restored, from whom he parted company in the First Act. But also Perdita is discovered by the most certain evidence to be his lost daughter, who is thus restored to him, together with a son-in-law in place of the deceased son, Mamillius. But, to complete the influence of this realm, Autolycus, the rogue of the pastoral world, sees and confesses the mistake of his former life — repents and asks the intercession of the two shepherds, who have been rewarded for their humanity and honesty, and are now in high favor with the rulers. Thus even the negative character of the humble class is transformed in this atmosphere of repentance, and both the collisions of the pastoral world are here harmonized.

But the final and supreme restoration is yet to be accomplished. The entire company, at the earnest request of Perdita, who longs to behold her mother, go to see the statue of Hermione in possession of Paulina, the fame of which has been artfully noised abroad. The theatrical effects and beautiful motives of this scene need not be given in detail; the statue moves, descends, and embraces Leontes — it is his living wife, Hermione. Her existence has been prolonged only in hope of the return of her daughter, though her son was dead and her husband alienated. That hope is now fulfilled in Perdita, who kneels and receives her mother's blessing. Thus the original diremption between husband and wife, which caused the play, has been overcome — the action is ended. If we turn back to the first movement, we find that every principle there violated has been made good — Personal Relation, the Family, the State, and also Religion, which has been satisfied by Repentance. Two persons, however, do not return — Prince Mamillius — whose loss is, partly at least, compensated by the gain of a son-in-law — and Antigonus, the husband of Paulina. But she, too, obtains her reward in a new husband, one whom we may suppose to be more congenial to her nature than Antigonus. Camillo, at the request of the King, is united to her; the male and the female mediatorial characters of the play belong together.

If we now bring before the mind the various elements of the drama, we observe that there is first portrayed the civilized State in which a diremption takes place, being produced by the guilt of its King. This guilt causes a flight to a primitive condition — to a pastoral world — which, in its turn, develops contradictions which bring about its dissolution. But the monarch repents of his guilt which called forth the diremption; he undoes his

deed without and reconstructs his character within.
Hence there results a third part, whose theme is the restoration of the separated members, and the resulting unity
and harmony of the two previous contradictory spheres.
Guilt produces the division, repentance produces the
reconciliation. Repentance is, therefore, the pivotal principle of the entire drama, and helps give to it the stern,
somewhat ascetic, coloring which is its special characteristic.

6

# CYMBELINE.

The relation in which this play stands to *Winter's Tale* is very intimate, and it is evident that both were constructed after one pattern. There is the same disregard of external probability, the same mingling of Pagan and Christian customs, the same defiance of the facts of History and Chronology. The main pathos in each play belongs to female characters, and is the same, namely, devotion of the wife to the Family under the most trying circumstances. Yet the surroundings and incidents are quite different: Hermione is mother as well as wife, while Imogen is the young bride. The difficulties of the former come from the husband alone; the difficulties of the latter come at first from her parents, and then from her husband. The structure of the two works is also similar: Both are special or mediated dramas, in which a tragic collision finds mediation; the earnest theme is brought to a happy conclusion, and, hence, they cannot be classed under Tragedy or Comedy. There is also introduced an idyllic realm, in distinction from the court and civilized society, which is the chief instrumentality in restoring the injured and overcoming the wrong of the State. Repentance, too, is made the spiritual ground of the reconciliation of the offenders, though it has not so complete and prominent a development in *Cymbeline* as in *Winter's Tale*. The resemblance in thought and structure is, therefore, very decided; still, the setting of each play, the incidents and characters, are altogether different.

The entire action, accordingly, will be divided into three parts or movements. The first movement portrays the world of conflict and disruption, which has its center at the court of Cymbeline. Family and State are in a condition of strife and wrong; the union of Posthumus and Imogen, representing the Family, has to endure a double collision — from within and from without ; Britain, representing the State, is involved in a war with a foreign power. This movement, therefore, exhibits struggle and contradiction on all sides ; because of such a condition of things there will necessarily result a flight from the world of institutions to a primitive life. Hence we pass to the second movement, which is the Idyllic Realm — the land of peace and harmony, inhabited by hunters, and far removed from the conflicts of the time. But this narrow existence will disintegrate from within, and will be swallowed up in the conflict from without. The third movement, therefore, is the Restoration, involving the repentance of those who are guilty, the return of those who have been wrongfully banished — in general, the harmony of all collisions of Family and State.

I. 1. The presupposition of the action is the love and marriage of Posthumus and Imogen. It is in the highest degree a rational union ; the characters of husband and wife seem just fitted for one another. Moral worth, strong emotion, intellectual gifts, are all present. Posthumus has been instructed in every kind of knowledge ; he is also endowed with the fairest exterior and noblest manners. But that which he lacks is a long line of noble ancestry, though his father and brothers had rendered the most important services to their country — in fact, his entire family had perished, directly or indirectly, in its defense, and he had been left an orphan. This untitled origin, then, is the sole ground of objection to him; the play emphasizes the conflict between birth and intelligence. Imogen, the daughter of the king, has chosen him in preference to the degraded and half-witted nobleman, Cloten, against the will of her father and against the plans of her step-mother. Her choice, however, meets with the secret, but unanimous, approval of the courtiers. Now, to break this union so true and so deep, the most powerful instrumentalities are brought forward in the course of the play. But particularly the wife, Imogen, is subjected to the sorest trials, and passes through them in triumph — nothing can undermine her devotion. Here we see the inherent necessity for the restoration and final union of the pair, since the Family reposing on so deep and rational a basis cannot be destroyed without violence both to thought and to our most sacred emotions.

(*a.*) Against the marriage of Posthumus and Imogen there is a double assault, giving what may be named the external and internal collisions. These two phases manifest all the possible forms of conflict with the Family. The first phase will exhibit the external collision, in which there is an attempt to destroy the union of the married pair by force — by violent separation. Three persons of consequence are engaged in the undertaking — Cymbeline, the Queen, and Cloten. Cymbeline, the father of Imogen and King of the land, has fallen completely under the influence of his Queen, who is his second wife. At her instigation he has forbidden the marriage of his daughter with Posthumus, and is ready to force the pair asunder. It is a phase of the Poet's frequent theme — the collision between the will of the parent and the choice of the child.

The Queen, however, is the lever of the whole action, and her great object is to place her son upon the throne. She is the perfection of cunning and ambition. The easiest way of attaining her end is to marry her son, Cloten, to Imogen, the heiress of the throne; but, if this plan does not succeed, she is ready for the secret poisoning of all obnoxious individuals. In the use of deadly drugs she has already had some experience, and she declares that the King himself will be put out of the way if necessary. Still, Imogen understands her dissimulation, and with the greatest firmness resists all attempts to break the marriage. The Queen is, therefore, the villain of the play, and assails the subsisting ethical relations.

Cloten, her son, is the type of the brutalized nobleman, indulging in every species of degrading amusement. He is the designed contrast to Posthumus in all respects; a rational union with him is impossible — at least to a woman of the character of Imogen. Braggart, overbearing, a low gamester, he yet possesses a brute courage; intellectually he is a fool. Still, he aspires to the hand of Imogen, and presses his suit with great pertinacity, being supported by both King and Queen. The result is, however, that he is rejected with firmness, even with insult. These are the three persons who assail the marriage; in the very beginning of the play Posthumus has to flee, being banished by the King; Imogen, the wife, is left alone to withstand the anger of her father, the machinations of her step-mother, and the rude courtship of Cloten. This she does in the most heroic manner, aided and comforted by a servant, Pisanio, who is the leading mediatorial character of the drama. His character is devotion to the pair — fidelity under the most trying difficulties. Forced by the stress of circumstances, he will be faithless to everybody else in order to be faithful to his master and mistress.

(*b.*) With the departure of Posthumus the separation is accomplished; external force has thus disrupted the members of the Family. Still, they are one in emotion, though far apart in space. Now comes the internal collision — the bond of emotion which unites husband and wife is to be assailed. This assault, if successful, must destroy the foundation of marriage, which is based upon the fidelity of each party. Let either man or wife be brought to believe that the other is untrue, the emotional unity upon which the Family reposes is destroyed. The character whose function it is to undermine their reciprocal love is Iachimo. He is incited to his act by the wager of Posthumus, who thus shows both his confidence and his folly. The scene in Philario's house at Rome, where the bet is made, is not without offensive features, but its necessity is manifest — it motives this assault upon the internal unity of the Family. The nationality of Iachimo is repeatedly emphasized; he is the crafty Italian who utterly disregards all ethical principles. First, he comes to Britain and assails the chastity of Imogen. He begins with casting suspicion upon the fidelity of Posthumus at Rome. The latter is jolly, laughs at lovers' sighs, ridicules devotion, attacks the character of woman, and, to complete his transgressions, is untrue to his marriage vow. Imogen wavers for a moment in her confidence. Iachimo thinks it is the favorable moment; he urges her to take revenge upon her husband by being untrue also, and offers himself as the means. Imogen at once detects his purpose, and is on the point of having him seized, when he succeeds in gaining her confidence a second time by an artful apology, as well as by extravagant laudation of Posthumus. The assault upon Imogen has, therefore, failed; her confidence in her husband is unimpaired; the wily Italian has not succeeded in destroying the union in her bosom.

Next comes the assault upon Posthumus. Let us see how he stands the trial. Iachimo returns to Rome; the trick of concealment in the chest has furnished him with certain kinds of evidence, which he employs to the best advantage. No doubt the chain of suspicious circumstances was very strong; it convinces the impartial Philario, but it ought not to have convinced a husband who was very partial towards his wife, and who firmly rested on the belief in her fidelity. But Posthumus hastily yields the wager, and concludes that his wife has lost her chastity — a conclusion of which he afterwards bitterly repents. Posthumus, in his anguish, turns against all womankind, and reproaches them with infidelity; he does not even spare his own mother, and thus casts the suspicion of illegitimacy upon himself. This is, however, only carrying misogyny to its necessary conclusion — a universal slander of woman returns to the calumniator.

Thus Iachimo succeeds with the husband, though he failed with the wife; as regards Posthumus, the confidence upon which the Family reposes is destroyed. He is even ready to murder his wife, and gives instructions to that effect to Pisanio. But the latter again is false in order to be true; he disregards the wicked command of his master, and is faithful to the ethical relation of the pair. Imogen now leaves the court of her father and directs her journey to Milford Haven, where she hopes to see her husband. On the way Pisanio tells her the dreadful secret—her husband has lost confidence in her fidelity. The fact is now revealed to her that their union is destroyed in the bosom of Posthumus. She, too, momentarily turns against the fidelity of men; her passionate utterance is: "Men's vows are women's traitors." She also begs Pisanio to execute his commission; death is preferable to the loss of union. But Pisanio has not lost confidence in the integrity of his master; and he, the skillful mediator, proposes still to save the Family, though its members despair. He tells her that she must disguise herself and take service with the Roman Lucius till she finds out the truth concerning her husband. Imogen accedes; for it is her deepest principle to maintain the union—to be true to the Family through all adversity.

Thus we behold the bond of union between Posthumus and Imogen in almost complete disruption—suspended, as it were, by a single thread. First, external violence separated husband and wife—Posthumus has to leave the court, and Imogen remains behind. Then comes the internal attack, which aims at undermining their emotional unity. With Imogen it fails, but succeeds with Posthumus; and, finally, the wife becomes aware of the alienation of the husband. Such are what were before called the external and internal collisions of the Family. Only Imogen remains faithful to the union, though assailed from without and from within. The beauty of her character lies in this devotion to the highest principle of her sex. Against parent, against the most powerful enemies, and, finally, against the very husband who rejects her, does she assert her unconquerable fidelity to the Family, and in the end saves it from destruction.

2. The second thread of this movement is the conflict between the two States, though it is much less prominent than the first thread.   Britain has ceased to pay tribute to Rome; an embassador is sent to demand it; the refusal of Britain causes war to be declared.   It is national independence against foreign subjugation.   The King announces the right of revolt, and asserts the duty of maintaining the ancient laws of the land.   But the chief instigator and active supporter of the rebellion is the Queen; without her strong will the weak King could not have been brought to undertake such an enterprise.   It must be said that her conduct in this case is not only defensible, but noble; she appears as the champion of nationality against the greatest power in the world.   Even Cloten is arrayed on the same side — not from any merit in him, perhaps, but through the influence of his mother. Her motive was doubtless selfish; she wanted to possess absolute authority for herself and for her son as successor to the crown.   Still, it is in itself a noble ambition to desire to rule over a free country.

Here occurs the great jar to our ethical feeling which has always been felt in this play, notwithstanding its power and beauty.   The wicked Queen, who, on the one hand, assails the Family in its loftiest and purest manifestations, on the other hand vindicates the State, the highest ethical institution of man.   What, therefore, is to be her fate? She ought not to live — she ought not to die; she is a contradiction which runs through the entire play and blasts its effect.   Nor can she be called a tragic character, which goes down in the conflict of institutions, for her support of the State in no way necessitates her hostility to the Family. To the class of villains she rather belongs — those whose nature it is to defy all ethical principles. We feel the discord, the double pathos of her character, from this time forward. The Poet undoubtedly seeks to condemn her as the enemy of the true marital relation; but, then, on the other side, she stands the main supporter of national independence. When it is added that the drama ends with undoing the whole work of the Queen — that not only the sundered pair are restored to one another, but also Britain returns to the Roman allegiance, and thus nationality is destroyed — we can see how deep is the violence done to the feelings of an audience — especially of a British audience. This play has never been popular, compared with most of Shakespeare's pieces, and never can be, for the reasons just given. There is no other work belonging to the Poet which shows so great a discord in his Ethical World.

II. 1. Such is the portraiture of the first movement — the realm of conflict — from which we pass to the second movement, or the Idyllic Land. The Poet has here introduced a new variety of inhabitants, namely, the hunters, corresponding to the shepherds of *Winter's Tale* and *As You Like It*. But the transition is not so decided; this world is not marked off so plainly here as in other plays. It is mingled with foreign elements. The Poet breaks off describing it, in the middle, and passes to the court of Cymbeline, and he also introduces into it the Roman thread. The outlines of the Hunter World are, therefore, by no means so distinct and separate in the play as might be expected from other works. Still, it consti-

tutes an essential element of the action; it performs also
the function of mediation; its character, too, is thoroughly
idyllic, and it causes the present play to be ranked with
the ideal class of mediated dramas.

(*a.*) The Hunter World is the contrast to the court,
and it logically springs from the latter, which has become
intolerable as the abode of man; in fact, the Poet has
made it the direct product of the King's injustice. Many
years before the time of the present action, Cymbeline
wrongfully condemned Belarius, a nobleman who had done
great services to the State; he flies from society and calls
into existence this Hunter World. But he also steals and
takes along two children, sons of the King. These three
persons now compose this world. The boys are grown up
to manhood; are ignorant, however, of their royal origin.
The country is mountainous, their house is a cave, their
clothing is made of skins, their food is derived from the
chase. The old man, Belarius, whom they take to be their
father, is full of the praises of their wild life, and utters
much detraction of the court; he has even a natural
religion — the worship of the sun. But the young men
are anxious to go forth and know more of life; the very
dissuasion of Belarius has excited their intense desire of
experience. So at the beginning we notice the seeds of
dissolution in the Hunter World.

It is manifest, therefore, that this realm is both the
contrast and product of the court of Cymbeline. Belarius,
driven away by injustice, has created a world of his own —
or, rather, has returned to a primitive, natural life, as
opposed to a concrete, social existence. Such ideal
realms are the natural fruit of a disordered society. Suspicion, intrigue, flattery, wrong, are triumphant at
court; but among the hunters are found simplicity, hon-

esty, true bravery, united with a manly independence. It is a condition of peace; of calm, idyllic repose; a still life, to which the individual, harassed by social collisions, gladly takes refuge — in imagination if not in reality.

(*b.*) Imogen, fleeing from the court, comes to its opposite — this idyllic land — and is most kindly received by its inhabitants. The inner, spontaneous feeling of kinship which springs up between her and her brothers, though wholly unknown to one another, is one of the most beautiful situations of the play; in fact, they unwittingly declare their very relationship. But the transition from a civilized state to such rough life is a hard one; poor Imogen falls ill, and takes some of the Queen's drug, whose effect, however, is merely to produce a long sleep. But the innocent hunters think that she is dead, and we have her burial ceremonies portrayed. It is the primitive view of death; a cheerful religion of nature breathes through their utterances; their love is manifested by the floral decorations supplied immediately from the soil. This is apparently only the second time that they have seen death; their supposed mother, Euriphile, had died before among them. Their chief rite is the song, whose theme is that death frees man from all the finite struggles of existence. The conflicts both of Nature and Spirit are then settled. The internal necessity of this burial scene is not apparent, inasmuch as the death of Imogen is only fictitious. But it gives fullness and beauty to the portrait of idyllic life. It shows, too, how the hate of the real world pursued Imogen to her humble place of refuge, and the striking contrast in the treatment of her by the hunters and by the parents.

The second arrival from the court in this idyllic land is

that of Cloten. The pursuit of Imogen has led him hither. His design is to inflict upon the poor fugitive the most brutal outrage, and drag her back to her angry parents. The wretch meets the elder of the brothers, begins to treat him as if he were one of the servile courtiers, and addresses him in a most insulting manner. The work is short — Cloten's head is cut off in a trice. It was only the court and civilized society which could protect such a monster. In this realm of nature birth conveys no privilege, unless supplemented by other endowments. But observe the contrast between these two adversaries: Cloten, the probable successor of the throne hitherto, is slain by the true heir, one who possesses, not only the royal blood, but the royal character. The Poet has taken pains to portray Guiderius, the elder of the two boys, as animated with the worthy spirit of his high lineage. The aristocracy of birth is shown on its good and bad side in these two personages — in the degraded nobleman, Cloten, and in the generous and high-spirited Guiderius, whose humble life has not extinguished the spark of his royal origin.

Such is the fate of Cloten in this idyllic world. He is laid by the hunters alongside of Imogen. She wakes and sees the headless trunk with her husband's clothes on; She thinks that it is Posthumus, and that he is dead. Pisanio is accused by her of treachery; the last one who was faithful seems to have turned false. It is the culmination of her trials; the object of her life is gone; the unity of marriage appears now impossible. She has endured the external and the internal disruption, and still did not despair; here is the final stroke. In a swoon she falls upon the corpse.

2. The second thread also is introduced into this Hunter Land, namely, the collision between the Roman and

British states. It necessarily swallows up the idyllic realm, which has always a tendency to return to society. The battle-ground is in the neighborhood of the hunters' territory — that is, the latter cannot be wholly withdrawn from the conflict of the nation. Lucius, the Roman general, finds Imogen lying upon the supposed body of her lover; she revives, and makes the best of her situation by entering his service as a page. The means of return is thus provided for her; suicide she cannot commit, on account of her moral nature.

But the Hunter World dissolves now within itself. The germ of its dissolution was noticed before; the two young men are dissatisfied with their narrow sphere of action when they have discovered that there is another world beyond, of which they know nothing. They hear the noise of the conflict round about them. The old man, Belarius, with the bitter remembrance of his wrong, wishes to go higher up the mountain, out of the way; he desires still to preserve his idyllic realm. But the youths cannot be restrained; their thirst for activity is so great that they have come to prefer death to their present condition. They descend, therefore, into the plain to participate in the struggle of nationality, and the old warrior, Belarius, cannot stay behind. Thus the Hunter realm vanishes, being disrupted from within and disturbed from without. The civilized State must show itself stronger than such a narrow, abstract existence. These hunters, therefore, will also return; the Roman war is the means. They must on the one hand be restored to the State, and the State on the other hand must make it possible for them to live under its protection — must free itself from wrong and contradiction.

III. 1. Next comes the third movement — the Restoration — which will bring all the separated and colliding elements of Britain into harmony. The external means for accomplishing this purpose has already been stated to be the war with Rome. Connected with it, in one way or another, are all the characters for whom reconciliation is prepared. The battle takes place; the Romans are at first victorious, but are afterwards beaten back and defeated by the three hunters, aided by Posthumus. Thus the idyllic land has been the instrumentality of saving the King; his own courtiers and soldiers have degenerated into cowards. The indignant speech of Posthumus to a British lord shows to what pass the courage of the nation had come under the rule of Cymbeline; the fresh, independent spirit of the mountains rescues the country. The Roman commander is taken prisoner, together with Imogen; all the persons to be restored are collected in the tent of the British King.

2. The battle, being only an external instrumentality, is of minor importance; hence the Poet does not dwell upon it, but has it pass before our eyes rapidly in the form of pantomime. The point, however, which is of the highest significance is the internal ground for the return and salvation of the different characters. They who have done wrong can be saved only through Repentance; they must as far as possible make their deed undone. There are at least three persons who manifest contrition for their conduct — Posthumus, Iachimo, and the King. But the worst character of the play, the Queen, will not, or cannot, repent; at least her repentance is of that kind which does not purchase reconcilation, for she

—" Repented
The evils she hatched were not effected; so,
Despairing, died."

Her violation of the ethical world has taken such deep possession of her nature that it could not be cast off — renunciation of ambition and crime means death.

The chief of the repentants is Posthumus. He supposes that his order to kill Imogen has been fulfilled by Pisanio; he is full of the deepest tribulation for his hasty action. Though he is not yet aware of the innocence of Imogen, he nevertheless repents of his command; for thus she has not had the opportunity to repent. He courts death; he would gladly offer up his own life as an atonement for his deed. Repentance can go no further. When the individual is ready to sacrifice his existence, what more can he give? Posthumus seeks death from both Romans and Britons; but his wish is not fulfilled — he still lives. It is evident that he has made his deed undone as far as lies in his power; the sorrow within and the action without indicate the deepest repentance. In two lengthy speeches he is introduced as giving expression to his contrite feelings. Reconciliation must be prepared for such a soul — it is a necessary logical consequence.

Here the Poet might stop, for he has amply motived the reunion of Posthumus with Imogen, which will hereafter take place. But he has chosen to go further, and to give a detailed representation of the above-mentioned reconciliation in another form — to present a literal image of the repentant soul harmonizing itself with the rational principle of the Universe. Posthumus falls asleep and dreams; his dream is of forgiveness. He sees his father, mother, and brothers interceding for him with Jupiter — greatest of the gods — who grants their prayer. The restoration to Imogen is promised, and also release from affliction. It is but a dream, yet it shows his state of mind, and intimates his internal absolution. He wakes

# CYMBELINE.

again; doubt and sorrow assail him; again he sighs for death. But the reality soon comes to confirm the vision; he is reconciled with his father-in-law, Cymbeline, and restored to his wife, Imogen.

This passage, including the dream of Posthumus and his conversation with the jailers, has often been condemned for its manifold defects, and sometimes declared not to be the work of the Poet. That its literary merit falls below the average literary merit of Shakespearian composition is hardly to be denied; that it is not strictly necessary to the development of the action is also true, since the repentance already manifested by Posthumus logically involves restoration. The example of the Poet may also be cited, for, though he has often employed Repentance in other dramas, he has nowhere introduced such an intercession of divinity to secure its results. Still, even if it is not absolutely requisite for the action, the plea may be made in its favor that it gives an imaginative completeness to the mediation. Deity is introduced in person, manifesting grace for repentance. It is thus the most profound Christian doctrine in a heathen dress, and this dress is taken, instead of the real Christian dress, for the purpose of avoiding the charge of blasphemy. To bring God upon the stage, pardoning the repentant sinner, would be a pretty hazardous undertaking. Such a liberty may be taken with an old, worn-out Greek divinity, though even this procedure is not strictly that of the drama, which should exhibit man as determined from within, and not from without. But the introduction of the tablet, with its prophetic inscription and its interpretation, is not only useless, but also ridiculous. The authorship of the entire passage, however, cannot well be taken away from Shakespeare, in the absence of positive testimony, though one may wish it were not his. It is also jointed too closely into the rest of the Act to pass for an external interpolation.

The second of these repentants is Iachimo, who has been guilty of defaming a pure woman, and destroying the internal bond of union of the Family. He also has come with the Roman army; his first declaration is sorrow for his wrong. The main ground of his change seems to lie in the fact that he has lost his former valor; the guilty soul paralyzes the strong arm; he is vanquished by one who seems to him to be a mere peasant. Before the King and the entire company he confesses his deed, and, finally, asks for death at the hands of Posthumus, whom he has so deeply wronged. Thus his repentance has carried him to the point of a necessary reconciliation; he has offered for it the highest possible price, namely, his own life. At this price it cannot be withheld — for how could his punishment obtain more? The character of Iachimo, as well as that of Posthumus, is not tragic; their complete repentance, going so far as to make a voluntary sacrifice of their own existence for their wrongs, forestalls the tragic end, since the latter, at most, could exhibit their lives taken for their guilt. Repentance is the mind's sacrifice; it is the individual sitting in judgment upon his own act, and condemning himself, even to death. Such a decision, however, should not destroy the rigid and upright judge who makes it. But a system of external justice can by no means be regulated by this purely internal element.

The King also repents of his conduct toward Imogen, and is reconciled with Belarius. Thus his two great acts of wrong are undone; the two deeds which disrupted his family—one of them causing the loss of his sons, the other the loss of his daughter—are recalled. The result is, sons and daughters are restored to him, and his family is once more united. But not only the Family, but also the State, is restored from its internal diremption. The Hunter World is reconciled with it, and no longer separates from it—creating a distinct realm. Even in the external conflict Britain is successful against the Romans; but the King voluntarily surrenders his victory, and again becomes the vassal of Rome. The object is, no doubt, to undo entirely the work of the wicked Queen, who was the chief instigator of the revolt, even to the extent of throwing away national independence. I have already said that to make this detestable woman the heroine of her country's freedom was a jar to our ethical feeling; but to reject that freedom because it was achieved by a wicked person seems to grate even more harshly upon the sentiment of nationality. The management of the part of the Queen must be declared to be unfortunate—it is, indeed, the chief defect of the drama.

The critics have not been very satisfactory in their views of this play. To determine its true nature has evidently given them great difficulty, and, as a consequence, they have employed to designate it certain high-sounding phrases, which, however, add very little to our knowledge. It has been called a dramatic novel, mainly on account of the supposed loose connection and the unwieldy number of its incidents and characters; it has also been called a dramatic Epos, chiefly because of the introduction of Jupiter in the last Act. The idyllic element, too, has been declared to be foreign to the action and unusual in the Drama. In general, this play is considered peculiar in its kind among the works of Shakespeare. But the Poet has elsewhere frequently employed epical elements, and to say that *Cymbeline* is the most loosely connected and the most varied of all his plays is a hazardous statement. If the preceding analysis has been successful, it has shown that the drama before us has the same unity, the same fundamental thought, and the same essential structure as the other mediated dramas of the ideal class. Let the reader make the comparison, and he will find fundamentally the same general movement in all of them, and will have revealed to himself one of the deepest principles of Shakespearian Art.

This group of plays still has the underlying form of the whole class of mediated dramas to which it belongs. There is a breach in the Real World ; then comes the transition out of it into an Ideal Realm of Mediation ; last is the return to the Real World.  But the religious and idyllic phases of the two previous groups had still a tinge of actual life ; now, however, this last tinge is swept away, and there remains a purely Ideal or Romantic World of Mediation, with its own inhabitants of a peculiar nature. These are not shepherds, not monks, not even human beings ; but they belong to a supernatural realm, and flit amid an ideal scenery.  That is, they are types which the Imagination no longer takes from real life, but creates purely out of itself, and for its own purposes of reconciling the conflicts which have to find here a solution.

But there is something more now than a return to institutional relations — there is also a return of the mind upon itself in order to view and portray its own operations.  The Ideal Realm becomes the pure realm of poetry, and, therefore, reflects itself in its own crystal fountain. The Imagination still unfolds a dramatic action, but at the same time unfolds itself in that process.  Thus both the artist and his work are shown in one movement ; both sides are united, and there is reached a totality of representation.  Two plays belong here.

*Midsummer Night's Dream* has, as its ideal realm, the lighter Fairy World, which mediates merely a conflict of love,

and pertains, therefore, only to the Family.    *Tempest*
has, as its ideal realm, the far profounder Spirit World,
which mediates conflicts, both of Family and State, as
well as the most universal spiritual struggle of man — that
between sensuality and rationality.    The former play is
purely comic in its treatment; the latter is serious in
tone for the most part, and from this point of view would
have to be ranked as a tragi-comedy.    Also, in *Midsum-*
*mer Night's Dream* the self-reflection of the Poet's process is a burlesque, and, too, a thread distinct from the
other threads; in *Tempest* it is serious and interwoven
with every thread, which thus mirrors itself in its very creation.    In the former the transitions from and to the
Real World would occur within the play; in the latter, they
occur outside of the action — before and after the play.
*Tempest* alone, therefore, lies wholly in the Ideal World,
and, hence, is the supreme work in the ideal class of
mediated dramas.

# MIDSUMMER NIGHT'S DREAM.

*Midsummer Night's Dream* is, perhaps, the most popular of Shakespeare's comedies. Its weird, ethereal scenery captivates the purely poetical nature; its striking sensuous effects impress the most ordinary mind; while its faint rainbow-like outlines of the profoundest truths entice the thinker with an irresistible charm to explore the hidden meaning of the Poet. There is no work of our author that is so universal — that appeals so strongly to high and low, to old and young, to man and woman. Its shadowy forms appear, disappear, and reappear in the wildest sport, and the critic may sometimes doubt his ability to track them through all their mazy hues. Nor can it be denied that there is a capricious play of fancy over and around the underlying elements of the drama. Still, like all of Shakespeare's pieces, it is based on thought, and must look to the same for its justification. Our attempt, therefore, will be to seize and fix these fleeting, iridescent shapes in the abstract forms of thought. To be sure, the poetry of the play is thus destroyed — but criticism is not poetry, but prose. For, if criticism were poetry, it had better keep silent in the presence of this piece, and not vainly attempt to imitate that which is inimitable, or say over again that which the Poet has already so adequately said. The only justification of the critic, therefore, is that he expresses the content of this drama in a new form — the form of thought — for his reader, instead of the imaginative form, which the dramatist has chosen, and, in fact, must choose.

We are well aware that not a few people will regard any attempt to make out a consistent unity in this play as wanton and absurd refinement. Moreover, the great interpreters of Shakespeare will be pointed to, who call it a caprice — a dream without necessary connection in thought of its various parts. That is, the work is a chaos. But every person who reads this play with admiration must grant that there is a profound harmony pervading it throughout; that he feels all its essential parts to be in perfect unison with one another; that the effect of the whole is not that of a discordant and ill-assorted poem. Thus, however, the notion of caprice, or of a dream, must be abandoned as the fundamental idea of the work. Both these elements undoubtedly are present; there is a capricious ingredient in certain parts, and also the Fairy World is likened to the dream-world; but they are only subordinate members in the organization of the whole. If, then, it must be granted that there is a deep, underlying harmony throughout the entire piece, it must further be granted that the attempt to ascertain and state the law of such harmony is not only reasonable, but necessary.

The procedure of this essay will be twofold. First, it will attempt to state the phases or movements of the entire action, and their transition into one another; second, it will seek to trace the various threads which run through each movement of the play. The former divides the total action of the drama into a certain number of parts; the latter unites the characters together into groups. This will give a complete view of the structure of the work, which must be the foundation for all future conclusions.

But, after such preparatory labor of method, the chief part of the critic's work remains to be done. All the above-mentioned stages must be explained for thought; the transitions must be shown to be logically necessary; the different characters, if important, but particularly the different groups of characters, must be elucidated in their unity — in their fundamental idea. In other words, the language of imagination, which is that of the poet, must be translated into the language of thought, which is that of the critic.

Following the principles above laid down, we are now ready for the statement of the various phases or movements, which, however, must finally be grasped together into the one complete movement of the play. These are three: First, the Real World, which is embraced in the First Act, and which is called real because its mediations and its collisions are those of common experience, and are based upon the self-conscious Reason of man; second, the Fairy World, the Ideal Realm, which terminates in the course of the Fourth Act, so named because its mediations and collisions are brought about through the agency of supernatural beings — the creatures of the Imagination; third, the Representation in Art, which, together with the return from Fairy-land to the world of reality, takes up the rest of the drama, except the final scene. In this last part, then, the first two parts mirror themselves — the action reflects itself, the play plays itself playing; it is its own spectator, including its audience and itself in one and the same movement. Thus there is reached a totality of Representation which represents, not only something else besides itself, but represents itself in the act of Representation. The very limits of Dramatic Art are touched

here; it can go no further. In this reflection of the play
by itself is to be found the thought which binds together
its multifarious, and seemingly irreconcilable, elements.

The reader will notice that there is very little portraiture
of character in the play. The sketches of persons are
true, but light and superficial; there is no profound and
intricate psychological painting, such as is to be found in
other of Shakespeare's works. This is, therefore, in no
sense a character-drama, and the criticism which proceeds
from such a point of view would assuredly fall short of
the true conception of the whole. No doubt there is some
characterization; there must be in a drama, but it is not
the principal element. The chief interest is centered in
the groups, in the transitions, in the different phases
which are above called worlds, as the Real World, the
Fairy World, and their Representation. We shall, therefore, indulge very sparingly in character-analysis, believ-
ing it to be quite out of place here. Our object will be to
unfold and connect these various movements and threads
logically, and unite them into one central thought. For
the work of the Poet moves in images — in individual
forms which are apparently independent; but thought
must unify all these distinct elements, and thus must free
itself from the pictures of the imagination by exhibiting
the underlying ground of their order and connection.

I. 1. We shall, therefore, begin with the Real World,
and carefully separate the various threads of which it is
composed. The first of these threads is the part of
Theseus and Hippolyta, whose love hovers over the whole
drama — the beautiful arch which spans the entire action.
In them there is no diremption, no collision; the unity is
perfect from the start, and remains undisturbed to the end.

They are thus the type of that harmony in which all the
difficulties of the lovers must terminate, and in which all
the complications of the play must be solved. But the
essential function of Theseus is that he is the head of the
State. He, therefore, represents the highest rational institutions of man — he is both judge and ruler; through him
the Real World is seen to be controlled by an organized
system of law and justice — such is the atmosphere which
surrounds him everywhere. Hence he stands above the
rest and commands them, but does not himself become
involved in their collisions. At first he sides with Egeus
and asserts absolute submission to parental authority, but
in the end he alters his mind and commands the daughter
to be united to her chosen lover. The grounds for this
change of judgment are carefully elaborated by the Poet,
and, indeed, the movement from strife to harmony lies
just between the two decisions of Theseus.

2. Next comes the second thread — Egeus and the
group of lovers. Here, now, the negative element, discord, is introduced, and the contrast to the preceding pair
is manifest. Egeus comes before the Duke Theseus with
his refractory daughter, who insists upon marrying the
one whom she loves, without regarding the selection of
her father. Thus it is the old collision, involving the right
of choice on the part of the child against the will of the
parent. It is a theme which Shakespeare has often hand-
led, and for which he seems to have a particular delight.
But this is not the only difficulty which arises. There
begins also a complicated love-collision, by which is meant
the struggle which takes place when individuals of either
sex find out that their love is unrequited by its object.
Here two such cases are portrayed — Helena loves and is

repelled by Demetrius, Demetrius loves and is repelled by
Hermia — the reciprocal love being between Lysander and
Hermia, which, however, has to endure the conflict with
the will of the parent. Yet even this sole harmony will
hereafter be destroyed for a time in Fairy-land. Such
are the collisions from which the action starts, and which
must be solved by the play.

The law at Athens demands the most implicit submission to parental authority, under the severest penalties,
and the Duke will abate none of its rigors. The harsh-
ness of Egeus, the father, and the decision of Theseus,
the ruler, force the lovers to flee from their home and
their city — from Family and State. But whither are
they to go? It is just at this point that we must seek for
the basis of their transition to a new order of things.
We hope the reader will observe carefully the nature and
necessity of this transition, for here lies the distinctive
work of the critic. It must be borne in mind that the
lovers do not run away from the world of organized
wrong ; on the contrary, it is the authority of the parent and
of the law — certainly a valid authority — from which they
are fleeing. Hence they abandon the world of institutions, in which alone man can enjoy a free and rational
existence, and they go to the opposite, for it is just these
institutions and the law which have become insupportable
to them. They cannot enter another State, for it is the
State as such with which they have fallen out, and, hence,
the same collision must arise. Thus the nature of their
place of refuge must be determined by what they reject.
The next place we find them is in a new and strange
world, called by the Poet a "Wood near Athens."

The similarity at this point to the idyllic group of

mediated dramas, and particularly to *As You Like It*, becomes apparent. In the latter play there was also a flight from society and an entrance into a wood — the Forest of Arden. But mark the distinction; it was a flight from the World of Wrong — society was without justice — while in the drama before us it is the flight from the supremacy of law and just authority — in general, from the World of Right. Hence, in *As You Like It*, those who flee must begin to build up society from its foundation; they must commence with the primitive pastoral existence, which develops into society. Such was the course of that drama. But here there can be no such movement, for society in its just and rightful form is already present, and the flight is from it.

On their entrance into the wood the lovers must, therefore, leave behind them the realized world of Reason, the State, the Family, and the other institutions of society. Now, the object of all these institutions is to secure freedom to man and to shield him from external accident. By them he is protected against incursions of enemies from abroad, against injustice at home, against every species of rude violence; through civil institutions brute force is shut out, as it were, by mountain-bulwarks. Man is only in this way secure of his freedom and can enjoy his existence as a self-determined being. For in the State all action is determined ultimately through Reason, in the form of laws and institutions — in other words, is determined through man himself; thus it is his true abode, in which he sees everywhere the work of his own Intelligence, whose mediations are, therefore, perfectly clear to his mind, and not the work of some dark, extraneous power. It is Theseus who represents such a world in the drama before us.

The lovers, therefore, enter a place where all these mediations of Intelligence no longer exist, but they are brought into direct contact with the mediations of Nature, which determine them from without. Such a place is, hence, represented by the Poet as a wood dark and wild, a pure product of Nature, inhabited by a race of beings foreign to man and unknown in the world of Reason. The lovers are, therefore, at once exposed to all sorts of · external influences. They have now no State above them whose action is their own highest rational principle — hence clear to their minds; but the world which is here at work is beyond them, outside of their Intelligence — the world of Nature, of Accident, of Externality. Now, it was seen to be the great function of the State to subordinate these elements hostile to freedom, and to protect man against them; but, when the former is wiped out, or has been abandoned, the latter must have full sway. Therefore the one fundamental property of the "Wood near Athens" must be that it exhibits a world of unfreedom — of external determination.

But how is such a world to be represented by the Poet? Here, too, there need be no doubt, for an adequate statement of this phase of consciousness has frequently been given in the course of human history. In certain stages of culture man's profoundest convictions repose upon a system of external determination; it is his deepest belief that he is the sport and the victim of extraneous powers, and, consequently, he must elaborate a corresponding expression of his faith. While he has not yet freed himself from the trammels of Nature by means of institutions and thought, what else can he do but portray himself as he really is? Such is the character of all Mythologies. The activities of Nature, and of man in relation

to the same, are conceived to take place by the instrumentality of supernatural agents; the most common phe-
nomena have behind them the demon, angel, fairy, god,
as producing cause. Man is not seized in his freedom,
nor is Nature subjected to Law, but all mediations are performed by a power superior to both. Mythology is,
therefore, the adequate expression of this world of external determination.

The mythopœic epoch of nations, hence, will furnish
the Poet numerous examples for his purpose. Which of
the many Mythologies will he then take? Evidently the
one which has been elaborated by the nation which he is
addressing. It is known as an historical fact that the
belief in fairies was common, at the time of the writing
of the play, throughout England. To this consciousness
already existent the Poet appeals, and at the same time
portrays it to itself.

But there are two more characteristics which follow
from this one fundamental principle. In the first place,
the Fairy World is not the product of Reason, which is
here the State, and has been left behind, but of the
Imagination, which objectifies the processes of Nature
and Spirit in the form of images and external activities.
It projects some personality behind every kind of mediation. Hence, when it takes complete possession of the
mind, all occurrences are transferred to the realm of the
Supernatural. But the content of the Imagination is,
nevertheless, the genuine expression of the consciousness
of a nation —its statement and solution of the profoundest
problems of existence. But, in the second place, this is
also the world of poetry, since everything is transfused
into images and external influences; the prose of real life,

with its means and ends, its wants and utilities, is banished
— man seems to live in a perpetual dream. The abstract
Understanding, with its categories of cause and effect,
laws of Nature, etc., has no validity here ; all is pictured
— abstract terms are quite unknown. Whole nations, like
the ancient Hindoos, seem to have lived in this dreamy,
sensuous state. The Fairy World is a phase of this consciousness, and, hence, the ethereal poetical existences
which flit through it are not merely the capricious products
of the Poet's fancy, but strictly necessary.

These are the essential qualities with which the Poet has
endowed his "Wood near Athens." It is a world of
external determination ; it has a Mythology, which is the
product of Imagination, and thus resembles dream-land,
where all rushes in without cause ; it is poetic, as contra-
distinguished from the prosaic life in society.

3. Such is the second thread of the drama — the love-
collision and that which springs from it, namely, the
poetic Fairy-land. The third thread is the learning and
representation of the theatrical piece by the clowns.
This is motived on the first page of the play, in an external manner, by Theseus calling upon his Master of Revels
to stir up the Athenian youth to merriments — to produce
something for the entertainment of the court — that is, a
demand for Art has arisen. For man's highest want is,
after all, to know himself; he desires to behold his own
countenance, as it were, in a mirror, which Art holds up
before him. Moreover, there is an official attached to the
court, and generally to all courts, whose duty it is to pro-
vide for the above-mentioned want.

The theme will, therefore, be that which gives a picture
of the court — of its chief thought and business at this

time, which is love. The content of the drama of *Pyramus and Thisbe* is thus a love-collision. Now, to exhibit such a work adequately demands the highest skill, both in actor and poet. They must be gifted by nature with true artistic conception; they must polish nature by culture; Art must be their life and living; they must be professional. Such at least is the general rule; dilettante-ism beyond the private circle is intolerable, and never was it more happily ridiculed than just in these clowns. Shakespeare has, therefore, chosen not to give a poetic, ideal picture in this part, but a prosaic one; and necessarily so, for what would the second picture otherwise have been but a repetition of the first? In fact, this play of the clowns is the contrast to his own true play; he has exhibited thus in the one and the same totality the negative — that is, humorous — side of his own work.

The idea of the third thread now before us may, therefore, be given in the statement — Prose is trying to be Poetry. The result is a burlesque of the legitimate kind, for it is not Poetry, or any other high and holy thing, which is wantonly caricatured, but the prosaic conception of Poetry. The contradiction is real—inherent; the Prosaic attempts to be what it is not, and can never be — the Poetic; its efforts to put on such ethereal robes are simply ludicrous. But we have also the True alongside of the Burlesque; genuine Poetry is to be found just here in the same piece. Thus the Poet does not leave us with a negative result; after his wit has ceased to sparkle there is not left merely a handful of ashes, but the positive side is present also.

In this connection another distinction must be noticed which the Poet has carefully elaborated. It is not the cultivated, refined, prosaic Understanding which is here represented; that will be shown hereafter, and has quite a different manifestation. But it is the dull, uneducated, prosaic consciousness of low life, of mechanical employments, with a feeling for only the most gross sensuous effects, without even cultivated taste, not to speak of artistic conception. The lowest form of prosaic life thus proposes to undertake to represent the very highest form of the highest art, namely, Dramatic Poetry; hence the clowns, too, must go to the poetic Fairy-land — the mystic wood of the Imagination.

II. These are the three threads which the Poet has unfolded in the First Act. They embrace the Real World, from which the play suddenly leaps into the Ideal Realm. The logic of this transition has been already given — the lovers flee from civil society, with its manifold mediations, whose object is to secure freedom and enter a Wood whose characteristic was defined to be external determination. That is, man acts there through influences from without, and not through the mediations of his own Intelligence — through institutions. The reader will note, therefore, that Theseus and his world here disappear, and their place is taken by the fairies; the former cannot consist with the latter. Moreover, when Theseus reappears the sway of these supernatural beings at once vanishes. If we now examine the nature and attributes of the fairies as here represented, it will be easy to discern their common characteristic. They work upon man — deceive him, lead him about by appearances, victimize his senses; in general, manifest external determination. But it must not be forgotten that they exhibit only man himself; they are simply a portraiture of his own unfree stage of consciousness — of his own delusions. Such must be their interpretation — they are symbols of some phase of human Spirit.

1. Let us now consider the organization of this Fairy World, for it is a regular hierarchy. First comes the common fairy, with a description of her functions. She is the servant — she dews the orbs upon the green, spots the cowslips, hangs dew-drops in the flower's ear — that is, she performs the operations usually ascribed to Nature, which is thus mediated in its activity by the fairies. Next are told the doings of Puck, a servant of a higher order, having also a sphere of independent activity, in which he is the embodiment of mischief, and causes what are usually called accidents. He seems to stand in a nearer relation to man than the other fairies, and has a certain external power over him. Also, the repulsive element of Nature is not forgotten; it stands in open hostility to these beings of beauty — snakes, newts, worms, spiders. Negative Nature, as it may be called for the occasion, is warned off, once for all, from the sleeping fairy queen; only Philomel, with her melody, may approach. The Beautiful cannot abide the Ugly. But the central principle of the fairy organization, and its chief figures, are the pair Oberon and Titania, to whom all the rest are subordinate.

The main fact here to be observed is that the highest fairies are king and queen; hence are not only sexed, but coupled, or, if the term is applicable to these beings, are married. Such is not the case with the other fairies. This hint will furnish the key to what follows, for the sexual diremption is the deepest contradiction of Nature, and the sexual unity is the profoundest harmony of Nature. The pair, therefore, are monarchs, and are placed on the

apex of the physical world, whose highest effort is self-
production.   At present, however, their unity has been
disturbed; the two sexes are in opposition; Titania and
Oberon have quarreled.   What is the result?   All Nature
is out of joint — in strife with itself; the seasons do not
come in their regular order — winter is in summer and
summer in winter; the waters have taken possession of the
land and destroyed the labors of man — all of which evils
are produced by the quarrel of the royal pair.   The cause
is explicitly stated by the Poet in the speech of Titania:

> "And this same progeny of evil comes
> From our debate — from our dissension;
> We are their parents and original."

For, when the central and controlling principle of Nature
is thus deranged and in contradiction with itself, the
effects must be transmitted to all the subordinate parts.
Such is the poetical conception of the hierarchy governing Nature.

But the cause of the unhappy separation of the fairy
couple has not been forgotten — it is represented to be
jealousy.   This passion is based upon the absolute unity
of man and wife; it asserts that each individual shall find
his or her complete existence in the other.   If a third
person is taken by either, the tie is destroyed.   Jealousy,
therefore, rests upon the monogamic nature of marriage,
and will, and ought to, be manifested in all its intensity
when that relation is disturbed.   The king and queen of
Fairy-land reproach one another with their gallantries —
quarrel and separate. LConfusion and strife must now
reign in the kingdom of Nature. ] Leaving out of account
the mutual charges of infidelity, as equally false or equally

true, the fault of the separation would seem to lie with
Titania. However this may be, Oberon resolves to assert the husband's right to be head of the family, and is
determined to subordinate his refractory wife. His aim
is unity and peace — not only in his own domestic relations, but in the entire realm, of which he is the supreme
ruler.

Thus the action sets in towards the reconciliation of
the conflict in Fairy-land. Accordingly, he prepares the
means for his purpose. It is by dropping the juice of a
certain flower upon the eye-lids of Titania when she is
asleep, in order to make her fall in love with some ugly
monster, the opposite of her nature. The retributive
character of this punishment is obvious — if you cannot
live in peace with me, one of your own kind, then try the
contrary, a horrid brute. Titania, therefore, becomes
infatuated with Bottom, the ass. It is the Poetic under
the yoke of Prose — the natural result of her separation
from her husband, since she has abandoned for the time
the beautiful world of the fairies, and its monarch. In
this service she undergoes the deepest indignity; in vain
she lavishes her choicest love; her ideal perfections are
soiled and unappreciated by the gross clown. The cause
of the quarrel being at last removed by the submission of
the wife, Oberon takes pity on her like a dutiful husband,
releases her from her thralldom, and restores her to his
bosom.

Thus the conflict which harassed Fairy-land has been
harmonized, and peace reigns. But mark! now occurs
one of those transitions upon which so much stress was
laid in the first part of this essay. Night flies away; the
darkness of the Wood is driven off by the light of the

day; the Fairy World disappears with its own reconciliation; the Real World dawns. But this is not all. Theseus, the monarch, is on hand, ready to judge; Egeus is here, with his former collision; all transpires in the clear sunlight of consciousness; external mediation has ceased. Is it not evident that we have returned to the realm of institutions which we left some time ago?

2. Having thus brought the first thread to its termination, we are now ready to take up the second thread — the lovers. They arrive from Athens, and enter the Wood in the height of the strife between Oberon and Titania. They also bring along collisions among themselves, for two of them have an unreciprocated love. Fairy-land, therefore, is a picture of the condition of the lovers, for both have collisions, and indeed similar collisions, namely, those of the Family. Hermia has left her father; Titania has left her husband; and also the conflicts of the rejected suitors may be reckoned under this head. Here is the point where the relation between the real and ideal worlds may be seen — the one reflects the other. The internal state of the lovers is thus pictured in the world of the Imagination, which was before said to be this Fairy-land — the poetic abode of such forms.

It was also shown that the flight from society must be a flight to a world of external determination; here it now is in full operation. The lovers are wholly influenced by powers outside of themselves; the chief means, for example, is a flower wounded by Cupid's bolt. But these external forms, like the Fairy World itself, are poetic — are symbolical of the inner spirit of man — and, hence, must be interpreted. The common and most natural view is that this flower represents the effects of what the Poet calls

"Fancy," a combination of caprice and love, which chooses and changes with wanton whim the objects of affection. The part of the lovers in the "Wood near Athens" may thus be interpreted to be a play of fanciful, capricious love.

On account of the externality of the means, a mistake is possible — the mediation is not in the heart and emotions. Puck anoints the wrong person. The effect is quite the same as that of a comedy of intrigue in which there is some form of disguise. This mistake, therefore, produces all the results of that very common dramatic instrumentality, Mistaken Identity. In fact, Shakespeare has in several places indicated that the influence of Mistaken Identity is like that of a dream, since it places man in such new and strange relations that he seems to himself to have been carried into an unknown world. The mistake destroys the only remaining reciprocal tie; the collisions are now completed; each individual hates his lover and loves his hater. There ensues a love-chase through the woods, which furnishes sport for all Fairyland, till the parties, weary with fatigue, lay down on the ground and go to sleep. The solution of the collision is also external, and is brought about by command of Oberon, the central power, whose highest object has been all along the unity of the Family in his own case; and, hence, to be true to his character, he must manifest the same trait to the lovers who have wandered into his realm. The separation cannot, therefore, continue; for, as before stated, the highest point and goal of Nature is the unity of the two sexes, whereby the two individuals are made into a mysterious one. Such has been the aim of Oberon — or, if you please, the aim of Nature — from the

beginning.   To take another phase of the same interpretation, the lovers have run the course of caprice, and are
now ready to experience the permanent affection upon
which the Family reposes.

The lovers awake, and, their difficulty being harmonized,
Fairy-land disappears like a dream.   Not that they have
actually dreamed; on the contrary, the contrast is very
distinctly drawn—they sleep, but do not dream, in this
realm.   In their waking state they compare their night's
experience to a dream, on account of the external mediation.   The fact is to be noticed, for critics have generally
tried to explain the whole work from this single element.
The lovers thus find themselves again in the world of
institutions—before Theseus the ruler and Egeus the
parent.   But, now, the two pairs are in perfect harmony—
their love is reciprocal; hence the rational basis of union
is present in both couples.   Theseus, therefore, reverses
his former sentence; he decides in favor of the right of
choice on the part of the daughter against the will of the
parent—a solution which Shakespeare uniformly gives in
all similar collisions.   Nor can Theseus consistently do
otherwise; for what is he himself doing but celebrating
his own union with Hippolyta?   The return of the lovers
from the Ideal to the Real World is thus accomplished.

3.  The third thread must now be resumed—the clowns
in Fairy-land.   Why are they, too, here?   The question
forces itself upon the mind, for this would seem to be a
place most uncongenial to them.   And so it is; the poetic
world is certainly not their natural abode.   But in the
present instance they have left their prosaic occupation;
they are transcending their own sphere, and are trying to
represent a play—a work of Art—which lies far out of

their comprehension. The attempt, however, brings them into the Fairy-land of Poetry, which is soon found full of strange beings, and they are compelled by terror to leave it with precipitation. A man cannot make, nor indeed act, a drama without entering the mystic Wood—the world of the Imagination. To be sure, the clowns themselves, for going there, can give only a common-place reason—"lest our devices be known;" since, if the plot should be revealed, then there would be no "surprise." But the principal thing to be noticed is how they reduce everything to the dead level of Prose. Their solicitude for the audience is touching; it must be perpetually reminded that these characters are not real, but that they are merely assumed—that I am not Pyramus, but Bottom, the weaver; that I am not a lion—be not afraid!—but Snug, the joiner. The clowns, therefore, have not the primary notion of the drama; they do not comprehend that it is a representation and not a reality. The imaginative form must be at once destroyed, and the illusion of Art is always extinguished by their prosaic explanations. This trait is common to all these "mechanicals," and lies deep in their nature; it forms the essence of their comic characterization. They are, verily, mechanical; they reduce all poetic form to Prose. Thus their end is a nullity; they are simply destroying the object which they are seeking to produce—are annihilating their own end—which principle is the essence of Comedy.

Another trait must not be forgotten—how realistic they are! how true to nature and probability! No sham moonshine for them; they must have the queen of night herself present in her own person, if possible; no pretended wall, or, if it must be represented by a man, let him be plastered. All is to be real, natural, probable. Thus, however, the thought is lost, for the attempt is, not to portray Spirit, but to reproduce the meaningless forms of Nature in their fidelity. One might almost think that the Poet was satirizing the modern generation of critics, so true does he hit their canons. But Nature has to illustrate and portray only Mind in an artistic work; when it ceases to have this significance it is worthless.

Their flight from the land of the Imagination cannot be long delayed. Bottom, the hero of the clowns, appears to them suddenly with an ass's head on, the appropriateness of which might be shown in various ways, but it will be manifest. Such does Bottom turn out to be in the realm of Art, and is thus represented even to his own comrades. Terror-stricken at his image, which is without question their own fate if they remain, they flee in all speed in order to avoid being "translated" also. Such is the lamentable outcome of the rude Prosaic in its efforts to reproduce the Poetic. How much of this satire was intended for his own age by the Poet cannot now be told. But since it was his special calling — the Drama — which is here the theme, we may suppose that it had some foothold in the circumstances of his time.

One other phase of this realm remains to be mentioned. We have just seen with what effect the prosaic clowns woo Poetry; what, now, if Poetry should become the lover and servant of Prose? Such is the scene when Titania falls in love with Bottom — the queen of Fairy-land with an ass. The contrast in all its ludicrousness is here portrayed — the two elements are brought face to face. The motive for her strange conduct has already been stated to lie in her separation from Oberon. The Ethereal is thus subjected to the Gross and Sensual; Imagination and her handmaids, separated from beings of their own spiritual nature, must obey the behests of Prose — nay, be swallowed in its voracious appetite. Her rapt poetic utterances are reduced to groveling common-places; her ambrosial food seems to excite no desire; her sweet caresses are turned into grossness; she has at last to tie up her sweetheart's tongue. When she returns to her first love, how she hates the brute. The result, therefore, of the clowns' visit to Fairy-land — the realm of Art — is that they have produced and also beheld a picture, but a picture of their own asininity, and that they have been rudely driven off from the mystic Wood by its inhabitants. Thus they also have returned to the Real World.

We have now traced to their conclusion the three threads of the second grand movement of the drama — the Fairy World. Again we are ushered into the presence of the old society from which we parted at the end of the First Act. The difficulty upon which a separation from it was based has disappeared — the collision which created the Ideal Realm has been harmonized; hence the ground of its existence has been taken away. Theseus, who represents the State, no longer gives absolute validity to the will of the parent; and, since it was his adverse decree which caused the flight, there must now follow the return to, and the reconciliation with, the Real World. Here the work of the Poet might be made to end — here it does end in the two previous groups of ideal dramas, for they conclude with the general restoration. But in the play before us he has chosen to make a higher synthesis; he wishes not only to portray an action to the spectators, but also to make the action portray itself.

III. Hence we must now pass to the third movement
of the work, which has not yet been developed — the
Representation. The court has demanded Art in which
to see itself, or at least by which to amuse itself. The
two actions which have hitherto run alongside of each
other are now to be brought up before Theseus and his
company, who henceforth assume the part of audience
and critics. The poem, therefore, after beholding and
reflecting itself, is to criticise itself. But these criticisms
will only illustrate the points of view of the different
speakers.

1. The first thread of this movement is the story of the
lovers, which has been told to the company, as we see by
the words of Hippolyta at the beginning of the Fifth Act:

> "'Tis strange, my Theseus, that these lovers speak of."

Shakespeare, however, could not well repeat the same
story in the same play, and, hence, it is here omitted.
The main point dwelt upon by the Poet is the criticism of
Theseus. How will he treat the Poetic as it was shown
in the strange tale of Fairy-land? His conception is
purely prosaic; hence in him Prose again appears, but it
is now altogether different from the groveling, sensuous
form which was manifested in the "rude mechanicals."
Here we see education, refinement, abstract culture.
Theseus, therefore, represents in this connection the
Prose of the cultivated Understanding, whose skepticism
assails all poetic conception and tears its forms to pieces.
He derides the "antic fables;" he scoffs at "the lunatic,
the lover, and the poet," placing them in the same category; the Imagination itself is made the subject of his
sneers — it is full of "tricks," and is placed in striking

contrast with "cool reason." The poet's function is to "give to airy nothing a local habitation and a name"— that is, the Poet's work is without any actual or rational content. Old Theseus was a downright *Philister*, as the Germans would say. It is the prosaic Understanding attempting to criticise Poetry, whose essence is totally outside of its horizon. Theseus will not acknowledge that under this fabulous form may be found the profoundest meaning; it is not his form, and, hence, worthless.

The reader will, perhaps, be surprised at this interpretation of the famous speech of Theseus, since the passages above mentioned, which are taken from it, have been quoted by critics of high authority as the most adequate definitions of Poetry and of the Imagination that have ever been given. The fact is, however, that Theseus intends to ridicule both; and his language, on a careful examination, will be found to be that of skeptical derision. Look, too, at the answer of his wife, and see how she understand him.

This wife, Hippolyta, is of quite a different character; she, with all the appreciation inherent in the female nature, is inclined to gently dissent from the negative judgments of her husband. She mildly suggests that there may be some content in these wild, poetic forms of Fairy-land; that the story of the night—

> "More witnesseth than fancy's images,
> And grows to something of great constancy;
> But, howsoever, strange and admirable."

With this quiet remark she ceases; she does not pursue the discussion further, for she is a woman, and possesses, perhaps, the immediate feeling and appreciation of Poetry,

rather than the ability to give the grounds of her judgment.
Such is the contrast: Theseus has at his side the opposite
form of consciousness — the husband and wife exhibit
opposite phases of critical opinion. It may be added
that the Poet does not represent, and cannot represent,
the highest critical comprehension of his work, for that
involves the statement of the entire content in an abstract
form, while he must necessarily employ for the same content a poetical form.

2. But the second thread — the play of the clowns —
now comes up for representation. It must also be subjected to the criticism of the audience, mainly composed
of these two mental principles — Theseus and Hippolyta.
The Duke wants to be amused; he rejects the old plays;
he must see something new; he, therefore, chooses *Pyramus and Thisbe*, both on account of its novelty and its
absurd title, though against the strong protests of his
Art critic. The clowns appear and go through with their
play. We again observe in them the same elements which
were before characterized — the destruction of all artistic
form; the introduction of nature in its immediateness
simply for its own sake, and not as the bearer of any
spiritual meaning; rant, which lays equal emphasis on
what is important and unimportant, without any relief;
ignorance of all technical requirements of acting, with a
strong infusion of general stupidity and self-importance.
Indeed, it may be said that the separation of the lovers
in *Pyramus and Thisbe* rests, not upon a moral obstacle,
but a natural object; the basis of the collision in the play
is a wall. It exhibits the realistic style reduced to absurdity. The critical judgment of the audience serves to
bring out more strongly the contradictions of the piece,

beneath whose sneers it perishes, Theseus pronouncing upon it final sentence. It will be observed that the clowns have fared hard in their artistic efforts. After a very uncomplimentary picture of Bottom — and, in fact, of themselves — they are frightened out of Fairy-land, and thus excluded from the world of Poetry; and now their work is torn piecemeal by the critical Understanding. Neither Gods nor Men, Poetry nor Prose, can endure mediocrity in Art, much less stupidity. It will also not escape the attention of the reader that the Poet has portrayed in the drama before us the two essential phases of the prosaic Understanding in its attempts to attain the beautiful realm of Poetry. Theseus and the clowns have thus a common element.

The three pairs of lovers retire to rest in perfect happiness and peace, and the Poet again allows the Fairy World to flit for a moment across the stage, as if to give one more hint of its meaning. This world is now, too, in harmony; Oberon and Titania, the ideal couple, besides the three real ones, enter with their train and sing an *epithalamium*, whose content is the prosperity and concord of the Family. Thus Fairy-land has done its last duty — it has reflected the peaceful solution of the struggle, whereas previously it had imaged the strife.

At this point the drama must end; its three movements, with their various threads, have been wrought out to their natural conclusion. The reader will probably consider some of the above explanations to be far-fetched, and it must be confessed that the faintest hint of the Poet has often been expanded in full. Such, however, is the duty of criticism; it gives what Poetry cannot, and Poetry gives what it cannot. Besides, in the present drama one often feels that Shakespeare did not always adequately realize his conception; he wrestles with his idea, and sometimes does not succeed in embodying it with clearness and completeness. Especially the third part — the Representation — caused him great difficulty, and is the least perfect of the three parts. The thought of making the play reflect itself in the course of its own action never lost hold of him during the whole period of his dramatic career. The poem has other inequalities of execution, and bears numerous traces of the youthfulness of the author. But the conception is one of his grandest, though not always clear and definite in his own mind, and, hence, the work is marred with some imperfections. It has been attempted in the foregoing essay to develop the complete idea of the Poet — not in his own beautiful poetic form, but in the abstract form of thought.

Let us express the general movement of this drama from another point of view. In it is introduced the Mythological World, the adequate poetic representation of which, however, gives the Epos. The latter has as its mediating instrumentalities those beings of a realm beyond — the god and goddess, the nymph, fairy, elf, angels; or, to present its negative elements, devils, furies, goblins, griffins, etc. These supernatural powers are portrayed as influencing man externally. They, therefore, do not belong to the Drama in its strictness, for it exhibits man as determined through himself — through his own internal being — through motives, ends, passions, thoughts. It is the most adequate expression of self-determination, of freedom, and, hence, it is the highest point of Art. The divinities of the Epos may, it is true, be only these internal determinations of man in an external form, but it is just this form which gives the basis of the essential distinctions of Art. The Epos, therefore, passes away in the culture of nations when they come to a profounder self-consciousness, and the Drama takes its place as a truer and more adequate representation of Spirit. In order to ascertain, therefore, the true position of the mythological element in the play before us, we must be careful to note that it also is transitory; it passes away with the dawn of light, the most perfect symbol of intelligence; when the parties fully wake, in the presence of Theseus, it is no more. In like manner it departs in the history of nations. The Poet has thus introduced an epical element into his drama, but only as a subordinate phase; the action moves out of this purely epical world, where, if it remained to the end, it would not give a true drama. A dramatic composition which employs only these instrumentalities of the Epos is a contradiction — it violates its own fundamental principle. Many dramatists have committed this sin against their Art, and thus debauched it, but Shakespeare always remains true to its highest thought; if he seems at times to wander, it is only to return with additional spoils. The External, though employed by him in all its shapes, he invariably transmutes into the internal.

The views which have been held concerning the purport of this drama have been various, and have, as a general rule, seized some one side and considered it to be the whole. It has been thought to be an intrigue of capricious love, and certainly this is one of its elements, namely, the part of the lovers. It has also been called a romantic drama, as if the mythological world were its single thread, whereas it is only one of the several threads which are woven together into the complete fabric. But the most general explanation seems to be that it is a dream. To this view, however, the objections are so strong that it cannot be reasonably entertained. Granting that the world of fairies is the same as the world of dreams, the above-mentioned explanation leaves two entire movements of the play wholly unaccounted for, namely, the first and the third. More than half of the poem is, therefore, decidedly awake, and transpires in the Real World. In the next place, it is not pretended that the lovers dream these occurrences in Fairy-land; on the contrary, they first go to sleep after all the events there have transpired. They only compare their experiences to a dream. Then, when we have called it a dream, what is explained, since the content of dreams is so various, and their product is not generally a poem like *Midsummer Night's Dream?* Finally, the name of the piece is cited in support of this view; but it may be laid down as a general rule that the titles of Shakespeare's comedies have only the most remote reference to their contents; several have, in fact, names of quite the same signification. It is true that the world of Imagination bears a great resemblance to that of dreams, and it is just this resemblance, and nothing else, of which the Poet speaks. Hence the necessity of seeking a higher synthesis, which will account for every part of the drama, and will combine its diverse elements into a consistent unity.

# TEMPEST.

The great and striking peculiarity of this play is that its action lies wholly in the Ideal World. It differs, therefore, from every other drama of Shakespeare in the character of its mediation. The Poet, in most of his works, portrays the Real World, and exhibits man as acting from clear, conscious motives, and not from supernatural influences. But here he completely reverses his procedure; from beginning to end, the chief instrumentalities of the poem are external; its conflicts and solutions are brought about by powers seemingly beyond human might and intelligence. It should, however, be placed in the ideal class of mediated dramas, in all of which some phase of the Ideal World is the great mediating principle. But in these plays the Real World is also present, and there is in the course of the action a transition from the one to the other. Hence, too, there follows a change of place and time, and the so-called unities must be violated. But *Tempest* has not this double element — with the first scene we are in the magic realm of the island and its influences, which do not cease till the last line of the play. Hence it is more unique, more homogeneous, than any of the dramas belonging to this class; the unities of time and place can be observed, and the action lies wholly in the Ideal World. It is, therefore, the culmination, and, it may be added, the perfection, of this dramatic form.

It is now the duty of the interpreter to translate the

poetic shapes and mediations — in which this play abounds above all others—into Thought.   Thus he gives the same meaning, the same content, which is found in the play; but he addresses the Reason and Understanding, instead of the Imagination.   What Shakespeare expresses in poetry he must express in prose, and, moreover, must supply the logical *nexus* which the imaginative form cannot give.   Hence, above all things, let him not fall into the error of merely substituting one poetical shape for another, whereby nothing is explained and confusion is only increased.   If Prospero is called Shakespeare, or by any other name, what is gained by the change?   The same difficulties remain for Thought as before.   The task is not easy, nor is it likely to give satisfaction at first to the reader; for these beautiful ideal shapes must perish before our eyes and be transformed into the dry, abstract forms of prose.   The contrast is striking, perhaps repulsive; but, if we wish to comprehend, and not merely to enjoy, Shakespeare, there is no alternative.

Let us bring before our minds the three leading facts of the play and grasp them in their true relation.  First, Alonso and his company represent the Real World; but they have arrived at a magic isle, where they are under the sway of unknown external agencies.   Within certain limits they still can act through themselves, but their chief movements are determined from without by the Ideal World — Ariel and his spirits, who constitute the second element. Thus the fact is indicated that the Ideal or Supernatural World is master of the Real or Natural World.   Thirdly, there is Prospero, a being who commands both, yet partakes of both, these principles — the real and the ideal, the natural and the supernatural; he is connected by nationality, and even by family, with those in the ship, but is at the same time the lord of Ariel and of the Spirit World, who fulfill his behests with implicit obedience.

Here appears the twofold nature of Prospero, which is the pivotal point of the drama, and, hence, its comprehension must be our first object. He controls the elements, he is gifted with foresight, he possesses absolute power — yet he in his weakness has been expelled from his throne and country. To be sure, there is the difference of time between his expulsion and his present greatness, but this cannot adequately account for the contradiction. Let us try to explain these two elements of his character, as they have been elaborated fully by the Poet in the course of the drama. In the first place, Prospero must manifest the finite side of his nature. As an individual, he comes in contact with other individuals and things — in general, with the realm of finitude in which he himself is finite. Limitation begets struggle; thus arise the collisions of life. Many men, it seems, have been his superiors in these struggles; his brother is a much more practical man — has dethroned him and driven him off. Such is Prospero the individual, and as such he collides with various forms of finite existence. He has been hitherto defeated in these conflicts. This is the one element. But Prospero also possesses the side of universality; he is spirit, intelligence — which comprehends, solves, and portrays all the collisions of the finite world. It is only through long discipline and devoted study that he has attained this power. His pursuit of knowledge, moreover, cost him his dukedom, and, hence, was the source of his chief conflict — that with his brother. He thus stands for spirit in

its highest potence — the Universal — but he is at the same
time the Individual, and, hence, is exposed to the realm
of finite relation and struggle, which, however, his reason
must bring into an harmonious unity.

But his spiritual activity is mostly confined to a special
form of intelligence — that form which embodies its contents in pictures and symbols, namely, the creative Imagination. Prospero does not employ pure thought, but
poetic shapes and images. He must, therefore, be the
Poet, who has within him the world in ideal forms, and,
hence, possesses over it an absolute power. He calls up
from the vasty deep whatever shapes he wishes in order
to execute his purposes and perform his mediations.
Thus he solves all the contradictions in which he, as an
individual, is involved, and subdues all the influences
which come within his magic circle. For he is this universal power; and in the sphere of ideality — in the realm
of spirit — nothing can resist him. The revenge of Prospero is, therefore, ideal, for certainly Shakespeare would
never have taken such instrumentalities as these spirits to
portray a real revenge merely. Moreover, the play must
end in reconciliation — the harmony of the Individual with
the Universal; for spirit possesses just this power over the
conflicts of finite existence — it must show itself to be
master.

In this way we can account for the commanding position of Prospero in the drama. He is the grand central
figure — the absolute power who controls ultimately the
movements of every person, and from whom all the action
proceeds. The form of mediation is, therefore, external;
but, truly considered, Prospero is no *deus ex machina* —
no merely external divinity brought in to cut the knot

that cannot be untied. The interpretation must always exhibit him inside of the action; the clew is his double nature. As an individual, he is engaged in conflict; but then he steps back, beholds and portrays that conflict, and solves it through spirit in the form of Imagination. He is, therefore, the mediator of his own collisions; thus externality falls away. The solution is, hence, not external, which would be the case if the absolute power simply stood outside of the action and commanded everything ᴛo take place. It is the special duty of the critic to explain these external mediations — of which the play is full — into a clear, spiritual signification.

Prospero is, therefore, the mighty spirit standing behind and portraying the collisions of his own individual life, and of finite existence generally. But this is not enough to account for his activity. He could easily put his experiences and struggles into a dramatic form without invoking the aid of the Supernatural World. The necessity of this element must be seen. If he would give a complete picture of his own activity, he must portray not only the above-mentioned conflicts, but also portray himself as portraying them. In other words, he must depict himself as Poet — as Universal; he must give an account of his own process, and that account must also be in a poetic form. This will push the Imagination to the very verge of its powers, for thus it must do what abstract thought alone can usually do, namely, it must comprehend and portray itself. Hence comes the external form representing it as the absolute master over its materials.

The Drama thus attempts to account for itself in a drama — in its own form. Having swept over the whole field of life and portrayed every species of collision, it now comes to grasp itself — its own process. Thus. it becomes truly universal — a complete totality ; for it takes in the world and itself too.    This play is often considered Shakespeare's last, and it may be regarded as a final summing up of his activity — or, indeed, that of any great poet.    In his other works he has portrayed the manifold variety of collisions, but now he portrays them being portrayed.    Here he reaches, if he does not transgress, the limit of dramatic representation, though not of poetic conception ; he can use only strange, symbolical shapes to indicate his meaning — shapes quite unmanageable for mere ocular, theatrical effect.

It is now time to see the poem springing from the twofold nature of Prospero.    As individual, we must expect to behold him involved in some of the ordinary dramatic collisions.    An analysis will reveal three of them, all in regular gradation of importance.    First, there arises the collision in the Family — Prospero, the father, on the one hand, against the lovers, Ferdinand and Miranda, on the other.    The old conflict is depicted — the choice of the daughter is opposed by the will of the parent.    Secondly, there is portrayed the collision in the State — Prospero, the rightful ruler of Milan, against the usurper, Antonio, supported by the King of Naples, both of whom with followers are on board the newly-arrived ship.    Thirdly, there is the more general collision, which may be stated to be between Rationality and Sensuality — the former represented by Prospero and Ariel, the latter by Caliban, with Trinculo and Stephano.    The Sensual rises up against the Rational in all its forms — in Institutions and even in Art, as well as in Intelligence.    Such is the material for Imagination to work upon.

But the other side must not be forgotten. The Imagination, at the same time, portrays itself elaborating this content. The Poet is not only going to make the drama, but is going to show himself making it. This gives the ideal element, representing Prospero as having the absolute power of mediating all the collisions of his individual existence. Moreover, the above-mentioned collisions of this drama are the general collisions of all dramas; the Poet thus depicts himself grasping and arranging the pure forms of his own deep poetic Art.

The reader is now prepared to summon before his mind the total organization of the play, as the frame-work upon which all the details may be placed in a luminous, as well as in an exhaustive, order. There are three movements, which, however, must not be considered as absolutely separate, but as fused together into one action. The first movement is introductory; it unfolds the wrong done to Prospero, who has been expelled from his kingdom by men here present in the wrecked ship; this wrong occurred before the time of the drama, but is told in it. These enemies of Prospero have now come into his power by means of the Spirit World of his island, whose double character is typified in its two representatives — Ariel and Caliban. So there are here a real and ideal thread, one supreme over the other. The second movement has as its three threads the triple collision with the individual Prospero, which threads are represented by the lovers, the usurping brother, and Caliban, respectively. All have punishment inflicted upon them by the spiritual agencies of Prospero, who is thus the Poet dispensing poetic retribution. Here is a real world of conflict, over which hovers an ideal world of justice, reflecting itself in the stainless mirror of

the Imagination.   The third movement is the Reconciliation, also mediated by the Spirit World ;  the guilty repent,
the injured forgive, and thus discordant strife turns to
the sweetest harmony.   The conflicts of the individual
Prospero are all solved ; Family, State, even Sensuality,
are no longer in struggle with him ;  that real life of his, so
turbid and troubled, has elevated itself into the clear,
placid Ideal, wherein all its Past lies beautifully imaged.
Ariel, thy work is now done ;  hence, " to the elements !''

Such is the happy mediation of the play, which is tinged
at times with deep seriousness.   It is, therefore, intimately connected by its coloring with that class of Shakespeare's plays in which wrong is atoned for by repentance,
and the criminal escapes by " heart's sorrow '' the punishment of death — the legitimate consequence of his
deed.

I. 1.  Let us now take the poem in hand and see
whether these things, with a reasonable interpretation,
can be found in it, or whether they are the absurd subtle-
ties of the critic's fancy.   First comes the tempest, from
which the drama takes its name, the effect of which is to
divide the ship's company into three parts, corresponding
to the three threads above mentioned, and to scatter them
into different portions of the island.   But the peculiarity of
this tempest is, as we learn in the next scene, that Prospero
has brought it about through Ariel.   It is, therefore, not a
tempest which has taken place through natural causes ; it is,
evidently, a poetical tempest.   For certainly Shakespeare
would not have us believe that storms are produced by spirits
ordinarily ; but this one certainly is.   What, then, does the
author mean ? for his procedure here assuredly needs explanation.   I think he tells us — in saying that Ariel, by com-

mand of Prospero, caused the tempest and dispersed the
company — that tempests are called up by the Poet; that
they are a poetical instrument employed to bring about a
separation of parties, and to scatter them into different
places, as here. We are, therefore, led to inquire whether
Shakespeare himself has ever employed this means in any
of his dramas. Accordingly, we find the same instrumentality in *Twelfth Night* and *Comedy of Errors*, used for
the same purpose. The tempest is an artifice of the Poet
for scattering, or possibly uniting, his characters in an
external manner. Here, then, in the very first scene, the
Poet is portraying his own process.

The second scene of the First Act, which now follows,
is the most important one in the play, for it gives the key
to the action. A careful analysis of all its elements will,
therefore, be necessary. First appears before us the
Family, the primary relation of man — here that of father
and daughter, the latter of whom speaks in the first line
of her parent's Art, which she herself, being purely individual, does not possess, but still knows of. For their
relation is a natural one — not spiritual — that between parent and child. She is excited by sympathy for the suffer-
ers, when the father assures her that no one has perished —
in fact, no one can perish — in the vessel. Again we ask
the question: Why this confidence of Prospero that all
will be saved? The prevision in his art, which he speaks
of, is that of the Poet, who ordains beforehand, by the
strictest necessity, the course of the action and the fate
of the characters, and knows what kind of a drama he is
going to write. He lays down his magic mantle — that
is, he assumes the individual relation to his daughter —
and then begins to give an account of his life and con-

flicts as an individual. Here, then, he relates his first collision — a brother, with the aid of a foreign king,. has driven him from his dukedom.

Nor does Prospero conceal the cause of his banishment. He neglected the Practical for the Theoretical ; he handed over the administration of his government to others, and devoted his time to his books, his study, his Art. The logic of this transition is evident. He cuts loose from the Real World, and the Real World retorts by cutting loose from him — drives him off. Where, now, is he? Having severed all his individual relations, he is manifestly left just in his ideal realm. But there is one tie which he cannot break — he is a father. This bond still unites him to finite existence ; or, if he must depart for the ideal world, the daughter must go along. The two, therefore, are put in a vessel together, and reach the magic island. Prospero intimates that it was this relation which saved him ; otherwise, he would have given that final stroke which dissolves all individual relations :

> *Miranda.* — Alack, what trouble was I then to you!
> *Prospero.* —                     O, a cherubim
> Thou wast, that didst preserve me. Thou didst smile,
> Infused with a fortitude from Heaven.

The nature of the transition of Prospero from the Real to the Ideal World is thus made manifest. It differs, therefore, from the idyllic group of dramas, in which there is always a similar transition, based, however, upon the flight from the World of Wrong. It also differs from *Midsummer Night's Dream,* where there is likewise a similar transition, based, however, upon the flight from the World of Institutions, or of Right. But in *Tempest* this transition is based upon the flight from the whole finite world of conflict, of individual relation, of practical activity; and, hence, necessarily lands Prospero in the magic island — in an Ideal World.

It is furthermore to be noticed that both parties have their just and their unjust element. Prospero is wronged — he is dispossessed of his recognized rights by violence; yet he himself is not without guilt. The Real World has a claim upon him as ruler, which claim he has totally ignored. Hence the play must result in reconciliation, and not in the death of the wrong-doers. Prospero, as Poet, must see both sides and represent them in their truth, and cannot avenge himself as an individual. This drama, therefore, will not have a tragic termination; it must, as previously stated, end in the repentance of the one party and forgiveness of the other.

2. Prospero has thus brought the story of his life down to the tempest, embracing the conflicts of his individual existence. His enemies, having been wrecked in the ship, are now scattered over the island and in his power. Now the ideal powers enter into the action of the drama. But behold! Miranda sleeps in the presence of the Spirit World; she is mortal — individual merely; she possesses not the vision and faculty divine. It is no wonder that she cannot choose but sleep in the invisible realm, for eyes cannot help her. But who appears here in this Spirit World? An airy being called Ariel, who seems not to be restrained by any bonds of Space and Time; who flies abroad and performs on land and sea the behests of his master. He was the cause of the shipwreck, we now learn, and he gives a vivid account of his feats in that work. Again an explanation is demanded, and we feel

compelled to say that Ariel is that element of Prospero before designated as Imagination, which thus gives an account to itself of its own deeds in a poetic form. For Ariel controls the elements — is sovereign over the powers of Nature, and directs them for the accomplishment of his master's purposes. In general, he seems to perform every essential mediation in the entire poem. What possesses this power but Imagination? Yet we must not press this meaning too closely, for Shakespeare does not allegorize, but always individualizes; he fills out his characters — whether they be natural or supernatural — to their sensuous completeness. We shall observe that there are many sides given which are necessary to the image, but not necessary to the thought, even when the thought preponderates. Therefore these Shakespearian creations cannot be interpreted as allegories, in which each particular stroke has its separate signification, but rather the purport of the whole should be seized and its general movement.

But this dainty spirit, Ariel, is not wholly satisfied with his lot; he has that absolute aspiration of Intelligence — nay, of Nature herself — namely, the aspiration for freedom. What is meant here by freedom? Merely to get rid of labor and then be idle? We think not; it is rather to accomplish the work in hand — to embody itself in some grand result; this is the toil of Spirit, of the Imagination. The freedom is the realization of its end, when the Imagination has clothed itself in an adequate form, which process, it may be added, can be completed only at the close of the poem; then Ariel is dismissed to the elements. But he never could have been free unless he realized aspiration in an objective form. It will thus be seen that Ariel quite corresponds to that element of

Prospero's character which was called Spirit — Intelligence — or the Universal as opposed to the Individual.

But the Poet Prospero proceeds further; he gives a history of Ariel. Once he was the slave of the hag, Sycorax, who imprisoned him in a cloven pine because he would not perform her earthly and abhorred commands. Here is presented the conflict which is as old as man — spirit against flesh, Reason against Appetite. Moreover, we see its earliest form; spirit is overcome and is subordinate to flesh — to sense. Hence the groans of Ariel from his prison-house, till at length Prospero comes to the island and frees him. Now he is the servant of Prospero, and transforms himself into every kind of shape which Prospero commands, in order to perform the various mediations of the play. He is at once sent off on an errand, the nature of which will soon be seen.

But what is this other shape which now rises upon our view — a monster, half man, half beast? He is the slave of Prospero, compelled to perform all the menial duties; in other words, his is the service of sense. His origin is not left in doubt — he is the son of Sycorax, and the heir of her character. Now we behold the opposite of Ariel in every way — Caliban is sense in all its forms, sensuality included. The peculiarity of their names, too, has been noticed by critics — with a slight transposition of letters, aerial becomes Ariel and cannibal becomes Caliban. But at present, under the rule of Prospero, sense is subordinated — is made to serve. Caliban is, therefore, the natural man whom Prospero has tried to educate, yet without altering his nature — who cannot be anything else but a slave. His knowledge is just sufficient to contest with Prospero the supremacy of the island. The rise of mankind from a state of nature, through language and education, is here indicated. The claim of Caliban to the sovereignty of the island by right of birth, against the right of intelligence, is a rather severe satire upon the principle of legitimacy, which may or may not have been intended by Shakespeare. This antithesis between Prospero and Caliban should be observed, for it will constitute hereafter one of the collisions of the play.

There can hardly be a doubt concerning the main signification of these two figures of the drama. They are not portrayed as human in form, but as unnatural — or, if you please, supernatural; they exhibit one side, one element of man in its excess — Ariel is spirit without sense, Caliban is sense without spirit. They are, therefore, not human, for man includes both of them. Or, to revert to our abstract terms, we behold the two principles of Prospero's character — the Individual and Universal — objectified into independent forms by the Imagination of the Poet. Moreover, the inherent antithesis and hostility — in other words, the collision between these two principles — is also indicated. Prospero has, so to speak, separated himself into the two contradictory elements of his character, and given to each an adequate poetic form, and has also stated their contradiction. But he remains still master over both; they, though opposites, are still his servants — are still the instruments of the Poet who stands behind and directs their acts. Such is their fundamental representation in the play.

Another relation has been indicated in the poem with distinctness, namely, the relation of the race of Caliban to Art. The foul witch, Sycorax, is the representative of the Ugly; she has even lost the human form — " with age and envy grown into a hoop." She came from Argier, a land beyond the pale of culture, where spirit is still enslaved in the bonds of sense. But even there she could not live, on account of her negative character. She is put on the island, which remains a wild, untamed jungle till the arrival of Prospero. The fate of Ariel has been mentioned, as well as his enfranchisement; but at present, under the rule of Prospero, nature is the servant of mind and is the bearer of its forms. Art is, therefore, possible, since the Sensuous is now controlled by the Spiritual: for Art is spirit expressed in a sensuous form.

II. Such is the first movement. The Poet has unfolded all the instrumentalities of his Spirit World, and has brought the story of his life down to the time of the action. Now he is ready to elaborate the collisions of the play in its various threads.

1. The first thread depicts the conflict in the Family. Our Ariel brings to the fair maiden a lover — the Poet never fails to do so. By his mysterious music Ferdinand, one of the ship's company, is led to Miranda. Both fall in love at first sight; the natural unity of sex which calls forth the Family asserts itself on the spot. What else could happen? Ferdinand is alone in the world, Miranda is almost so — only her father is known to her. If man and woman belong together, certainly these two must feel their inseparableness, for there is nobody else to whom they can belong. It is the old climax — admiration, sympathy, love. "They are both in either's powers;" each one finds his or her existence in the other.

But now appears the obstacle, for the course of true love can never run smooth — at least in a drama. The collision so frequently portrayed by Shakespeare again arises

10

for a new treatment — that between the will of the parent and the choice of the daughter. Prospero opposes the match, charges Ferdinand with being a traitor and spy, and lays upon him the menial task of removing "some thousands of logs." But Miranda is present with consolation, and even offers to assist in the labor; the young Prince bravely stands the trial — he is willing to undergo any toil for love's sake. The mutual declaration is made; then follows the mutual promise; the unity of feeling is complete. It is the essence of all love-stories.

The next time we meet with the father, in this connection, he has yielded his objections and sealed their pledge with his consent. But all along we have been aware that his opposition was feigned — that he intended from the start to acquiesce in their marriage. In fact, he was the very person that brought it about. For his conduct he has adduced an external motive — "lest too light winning make the prize light." Still deeper is the design which he cherishes of not only restoring his daughter to his own possessions, but also of making her queen of Naples. But the true internal necessity that his opposition should be feigned lies in his double nature. The Poet, who is none other than Prospero himself, interposes an obstacle — the refusal of the parent;. which parent also is none other than Prospero himself. As father he stands in an individual relation to his daughter and comes into conflict with her; but as Poet he has brought about this conflict, and must solve it by giving validity to the right of choice. Such is the solution demanded by reason, and the one which Shakespeare universally gives to such a collision. Prospero knows, therefore, from the beginning, that his daughter will triumph — in fact, that he must make her triumph. The key to his conduct is that the father or individual and the Poet or Universal are one and the same man.

The right of choice is, therefore, victorious over the will of the parent — a right which, though generally conceded at the present time, was once stoutly contested. Their love has been portrayed through its successive stages — the first predilection, the mutual declaration, the secret plight of troth, the consent of the father. But one thing more remains to be done — the ceremony with full and holy rite must be ministered. Upon this point Prospero lays the greatest stress; he speaks of it no less than three times in different places. Without the formal solemnization of marriage their union cannot be ethical; it can bring forth only the most baleful weeds — hate, disdain, and discord. Lust is not love; indeed, it is the destruction of genuine love — a Caliban cannot truly enter the marriage relation. Moreover, the ceremony gives reality to the Family, which hitherto existed only in the subjective emotions of the parties. Religion (or the State in our time) comes in with its sanction and objectifies their union — makes it an institution in the world.

The marriage rite is, therefore, not a meaningless and unnecessary formality. Yet the origin and primal basis of the Family is love, which the Poet has here portrayed in all its fervor. But left to itself simply, and ungoverned, it degenerates into lust. Our author would teach the lesson, if we understand him, that the ethical element and the emotional element must both be present in true affection; for it is destroyed by the Ethical alone, which is the case when the daughter is wholly obedient, and simply follows the will of the parent, and lets him choose for her.

She thus cannot have much intensity in her love, and, hence, Miranda insists upon her affection, and the father at last yields.    On the other hand, passion alone, without any ethical restraint, is even more fatal to love.    Now, both these elements in their one-sidedness are represented by Shakespeare as antagonistic to the unity of marriage. The truth is, the Emotional must be regulated, restrained, and made permanent by the Ethical; and the Ethical — which now takes the form of devotion to husband or wife, instead of obedience to parent — must be filled, vivified, and intensified by the Emotional.

The marriage is followed by the masque, whose connection with the rest of the play is to be carefully studied, for it reveals more than anything else in the work the special character of Prospero as Poet.    He calls up Ariel, who, it will be noticed, always appears when some important mediation of the drama is about to be performed. For what purpose is he now invoked?    Mark the language of Prospero:

> — "I must
> Bestow upon the eyes of this young couple
> Some vanity of mine art; it is my promise,
> And they expect it from me."

At once there rise up before us the goddesses of the ancient Greek world — the poetical forms of all ages.    These, then, are the spirits over which Prospero has power through his minister, Ariel; this, too, is his Art, which has brought forth all the other wonderful shapes of the poem.    They are the beautiful forms of the Imagination, over which the Poet alone has control.

But let us notice the content of this little interlude; what will be its theme?    Nothing else but what has already

taken place, only in a new form for the lovers, who thus
behold a representation of their own unity. The mainspring of the action is Juno, the spouse of the king of gods
and men; therefore both the type and guardian of wifehood, of chastity, of domestic life. She sends Iris, her
many-colored messenger, for Ceres —

> " A contract of true love to celebrate,
> And some donation freely to estate
> On the blest lovers."

Such is the object of the visit of the two goddesses, which
is still more precisely expressed by each in their songs.
Juno particularly confers marriage-blessing and honor;
Ceres, physical comfort and prosperity. But mark that
Venus and her blind boy are invited to stay away. They
represent unholy lust; they plotted the means whereby
dusky Dis, or devilish sensuality, carried off the innocent
Proserpine, the daughter of Ceres, to the infernal regions.
Thus the ethical element is again emphasized.

The relation of Prospero as parent — as individual —
has now been portrayed, as well as the collision resulting
therefrom and its solution. But he is also Poet, and,
hence, must shadow forth the whole subject in the objective forms of poetry. It has already been pointed out
that his feigning an objection to the love-match resulted
from his poetical prevision, and, hence, that such an objection must finally be abandoned. Thus he has manifested
in himself, and also depicted in the drama, the collision in
the Family. But now, when consent has been given, and
the hindrances smoothed over, a second time he appears
as Poet, as if to leave no doubt of his nature in the mind
of the reader or hearer. He steps back and reproduces,

in a new poetical dress, the substance of the whole story
before the lovers. This little play within the play thus
has the effect of a double reflection of the action.

New beings appear in order to celebrate the contract of
true love; Naiads, whose crown is chastity, and the sun-
burnt sicklemen, whose trait is industry, join in a dance.
But, while Prospero is busy calling up these beautiful
shapes from the Ideal Realm, he suddenly thinks of the
conspiracy of Caliban. A new collision against himself
as an individual has arisen, which demands immediate
attention; the real world rushes in upon him, and at once
the poetical world vanishes. He is thus reminded that
there are other things to be done, other struggles to pass
through, and, finally, other collisions to be portrayed.
But he is highly vexed at the interruption, and in his
anger he utters the doom of the whole finite world, which
sounds like the Last Judgment. It is the most sublime
passage of its length to be found in Shakespeare:

> "And, like the baseless fabric of this vision,
> The cloud-capp'd towers, the gorgeous palaces,
> The solemn temples, the great globe itself,
> Yea, all which it inherit, shall dissolve,
> And, like this insubstantial pageant faded,
> Leave not a rack behind. We are such stuff
> As dreams are made of, and our little life
> Is rounded with a sleep."

It is just this finite world which is so full of conflict and
has caused him so much trouble. No wonder, then, that
he almost curses it, and announces its utter perishability.
But, though the life and works of man, and also the physical globe, are transitory, he is far from saying that mind
—the Universal—will thus pass away. On the contrary,
he now invokes the latter against destruction, for it is the

master over finitude, over the negative powers of the world.
Again our Ariel must appear—"come with a thought."
Why? Only because he is thought. He answers: "Thy
thoughts I cleave to." Why again? Because he cannot
be separated from them. Thus Prospero and Ariel prepare for the conflict with Caliban, the account of which
will be taken up in its proper connection.

2. Such is the first thread; the second is the collision
in the State, which is the central thread of the play. Prospero, as rightful duke, comes into conflict with a usurper
—his own brother—who is supported by the King of
Naples. Again we see that Prospero, in his individual
relation, has fallen into strife and been overthrown. The
history of his expulsion has already been given, and it
must be noticed also that he relates the occurrence as
something long antecedent to the play, and not embraced
in its action, though its necessary presupposition. Such
has been the wrong done to him. But now the universal
element of his nature appears; his enemies are completely
in his power; their punishment is to follow.

The tempest has conveniently scattered the ship's company into groups, in one of which are to be found all the
offenders. But, first, there arises a conflict among themselves. There are three good characters—that is, those
without guilt—Gonzalo, Adrian, and Francisco; opposed
to these are the three wicked ones—Alonso, Antonio, and
Sebastian. The two latter show their hatred, especially
of the honest Gonzalo, by bitter ridicule, while Alonso is
beginning to feel repentance for his deeds through the loss
of his son. Yet a deeper retribution appears to be impending over him. He has aided in dethroning a brother; a
brother now threatens to dethrone him. The same man

whom he unjustly assisted to a crown seems about to punish him.   But his repentance will save him from final overthrow.   So much for Alonso.   Antonio is a much worse
man.   His conduct is consistent; he cannot stop in his
negative career; he must continue dispossessing and assailing the rights of others, for that is the logical necessity
of his character.   Having wrongfully expelled his nearest
relative, he very naturally begins to plot against his greatest benefactor, the King of Naples.   But the poetical
mediator, Ariel, is again on hand to prevent the consummation of the plan; the Poet cannot let the matter end in
that way.   The victims wake with the music of 'Ariel;
thus the design is frustrated.   The main poetical mediation is next to be accomplished — of course through Ariel.
It is reconciliation by repentance.   Repentance means
that man has the power to make his wicked deed undone,
as far as its influence upon his own mind is concerned.
He can free himself from remorse — from the consequence
of his own negative act.   But the repentance must be
complete; it includes the confession of the wrong, contrition adequate to its magnitude, and an entire restoration of its advantages.   Spirit thus becomes again at
peace with itself, and is relieved from its own destructive
gnawings.   This reconciliation is, therefore, a spiritual
process, and, hence, must be accomplished by the representative of spirit — Ariel.

The three criminals are in the presence of Prospero,
who is invisible to them.   They are, hence, in the presence of their own wrong; retribution is at hand.   Again
we urge upon the reader to keep in mind the double nature
of Prospero — as individual he has suffered these injuries,
but as universal he is the Poet, who overcomes and por-

trays them, and, indeed, punishes them with his poetical justice. He, therefore, puts into operation his Spirit World, whose main object is now to excite conscience — to rouse remorse. They are hungry; a banquet is spread before them by several strange shapes. When the King and the rest begin eating, the banquet vanishes. Thus it is indicated to them that a power beyond their consciousness is at work in the isle. Here it is — Ariel, who now drops his invisible form and appears to them like a harpy, the symbol of vengeance. He calls himself Destiny, or a minister of Fate; his function is retribution. He comes to avenge the wrong done to Prospero:

> —" For which foul deed
> The powers delaying, not forgetting, have
> Incensed the seas and shores, yea, all creatures,
> Against your peace. Thee of thy son, Alonso,
> They have bereft; and do pronounce by me
> Lingering perdition — worse than any death."

So far it resembles that external power which the Greeks called Fate, and which even controlled Jupiter himself.

But is there no salvation from the wicked deed? Hear Ariel again:

> —" Whose [the powers'] wraths to guard you from—
> Which here in this most desolate isle else falls
> Upon your heads — is nothing but heart's sorrow,
> And a clear life ensuing."

What a wonderful change! Ariel is no longer the representative of Grecian Fate, but is a preacher of Christian Gospel, whose doctrine is repentance — "heart's sorrow and a clear life ensuing." Man can now avoid the retribution of ancient Destiny. Though Ariel has assumed this shape to the wicked three, yet the reader has all along known that it was merely a poetical form; that Ariel, in reality, is not a minister of Fate, but of Prospero—of spirit, of self-determination.

Thus the three "men of sin" are brought to a consciousness of their crimes; they wax desperate at their guilt, which now reacts negatively upon their minds—"like poison, 'gins to bite the spirits." The innocent three weep over them, "brimful of sorrow and dismay." When the guilty have sufficiently atoned for the wrongs which they have committed, Prospero is ready to grant forgiveness; he declares that their repentance is "the sole drift of his purpose." The frenzy begins to subside after they enter his charmed circle; gradually reason returns, and Prospero, though invisible, tells to their innermost conscience the nature of their crimes and the consequent punishment. All is now plain to them subjectively. But, to remove the last doubt, Prospero presents himself to their eyes looking just as when he was Duke of Milan, and confirms his previous utterances. Alonso, in particular, repents in the most heartfelt manner—surrenders the advantages of his wrong and asks pardon; he makes his deed undone as far as lies in his power. Therefore his son is restored to him; the marriage of Ferdinand and Miranda receives blessing. Thus it is ethically complete, having received the sanction of both parents.

It is evident that the ability which the mind possesses of healing its own wounds—of canceling its own negative deeds—is here portrayed. Spirit alone can reconcile itself with itself and come to inner harmony; for, if it is truly universal, it must have the power to mediate all its conflicts. Therefore the play cannot have a tragic termination, as was before stated. It must end in reconciliation

<br>

— mediation. Prospero himself, in his highest potence, represents this absolute might of spirit, which cannot succumb to any struggle, but must overcome every conflict. Though Shakespeare has, to a certain extent, employed the heathen form of Fate, he has truly expressed the Christian doctrine of Repentance.

3. We are now ready to take up the third thread—the collision between Prospero and Caliban. The character and origin of the latter have already been noticed; it was stated that he represented the natural man—man still immersed in his senses, and not yet elevated to a rational existence. He, therefore, must collide with the world of spirit represented by Prospero, for the reason that it necessarily subordinates him, and even reduces him to a slave. Such is the function of the senses—they are the pack-horses of intelligence; and the physical man, even if he constitute the whole man, must follow the same law. Caliban is, therefore, a menial of the lowest type, and is set to performing the most degrading services for Prospero. His ignorance and utter slavishness to the External are manifest from the fact that he cannot comprehend either the mediations of Spirit or of Nature; he regards them as ghosts and goblins sent to torment him.

But Caliban has not always been in this condition of servitude. Prospero found him on the island, treated him with the greatest kindness, taught him to speak, and admitted him to his own family. The result was an attempt to violate the honor of his daughter. Prospero has now learned the very important distinction that an animal is an animal and must be subordinated—at least not admitted to social equality. There is a difference between a man and a brute, notwithstanding our so-called humanitarians. By ignoring this difference we do not elevate the lower, but inevitably degrade the higher. "I had peopled else this isle with Calibans," is the threat of the beast. Thus passes away the fantastic humanity of Prospero when it comes in contact with the reality.

Such is the man-monster in the family relation; the author is now going to bring him before us in his political, and also in his religious, character. All our countrymen can study the picture with profit at the present time. We have both Caliban and Prospero in our midst. Our philanthropic Prosperos have forgotten the fact that the Sensual must be subordinated to the Rational; the distinction between humanity and animality seems to be quite ignored. The institutions of Reason cannot be subjected to the rule of Appetite, against which they were reared as barriers. Yes, the philanthropic Prospero is at last forced to the exclamation—

> " A devil, a born devil, on whose nature
> Nurture can never stick; on whom my pains,
> Humanely taken, all, all lost, quite lost. "

Such an insight will hereafter lead to the true solution of the Caliban-problem, for mark! this conflict, too, must be harmonized to the peace and interest of both sides.

Caliban, the natural man, is, therefore, in a deadly struggle with Prospero, the rational ruler. The ship also — or the Real World, if you please — has its sensual element as well as the island — the Ideal World. The next thing, therefore, is the appearance of the representatives of this element—Trinculo and Stephano. They, too, have been separated from the ship's company by the tempest, and, from a natural attraction of character, have been brought together with Caliban. Here we see the sensual trio made up from the ship and the island. The two strangers bear the stamp of reality — are men of flesh and blood — belong, therefore, to prosaic life and speak in prose; while Caliban, since he is a native of the island, is strictly a poetical being and speaks in verse. There is also a distinction between Trinculo and Stephano, the former being not so much jester as coward — craven in spirit — with the fear of the External always before his eyes; the latter being a drunkard, the slave of appetite. Caliban represents both persons, for he is mortally afraid of the imaginary spirits, and he swallows with the wildest ecstasy the contents of Stephano's wine-bottle.

Caliban's religion now appears also; he deifies the man who has gratified his appetite. Yet he himself remains a slave, and performs the same servile duties; he will kiss the foot of the new deity, dig pig-nuts for him, and carry all his wood — a task which is so irksome to do for Prospero. But he thinks he has obtained freedom, which to him means the reign of sensuality. The mob seems to have broken loose from the strong hand of Prospero, lust and violence hope now to rule triumphant, and the ominous shout of drunken bestiality falls upon the ear: "Freedom, hey-day, hey-day, freedom! freedom, hey-day, freedom!" It is curious that Shakespeare has endowed two beings so completely opposite as Ariel and Caliban with the same aspiration for freedom. He has thus indicated the two great definitions of that word which have always divided mankind. The one means unrestrained lust and anarchy, the other means liberty through institutions; the one is the realization of sensuality, the other is the realization of reason.

But the political side is still further developed.  Such beings must have some conflict among themselves, which Ariel, our poetical mediator, does not fail to bring about. It only ends, however, in a beating given to the coward, Trinculo, who is innocent.  But they have a common enemy — the present lord of the island — against whom they now conspire.  It is King Stephano against King Prospero — the Sensual trying to dethrone the Rational. Stephano is not without his worshippers to-day.  He represents the demagogue in the political world, who rules the rabble by gratifying their passions, himself being the incarnation of those passions.  He thus unites the worst elements of society in a crusade against all established order and right.  It will be noticed also that not the least attraction for their "freedom" is the fair Miranda; both Family and State are to be subjected to unbridled lust.  But their very nature is turned against them; their innate tendency to theft leads them aside from their purpose, and they are caught in their own toils. Still, they cannot reach Prospero; he is spirit, knows of their schemes, and sends upon them retribution in the shape of dogs and hounds — turns against them their own passions.

He is thus victorious in this final collision; all his enemies are now in his power; he has mastered the conflicts of his individual existence.  Nay, further, he has, not merely punished, but even reconciled, all his enemies. Caliban himself submits, manifests hearty repentance, and is cured of his delusive worship.  Sense thus yields to Reason.  Such is the truly positive function of Spirit — to bring all into harmony with itself, to make all reflect its own image.  It may crush out with its power; but that is a negative result, and really no solution of a conflict. The highest attainment of intelligence may be expressed by just this word—reconciliation. The colliding individuals of the play are now united in spirit, and the harmony is perfect. They all have come to see the nature of their deeds. This is their common insight, and, therefore, their common concord; furthermore, they hasten to make their wicked deeds undone. Hence, when the criminals arrive at this island, their destiny is to rise above their hitherto selfish, individual existence, and become reconciled with the Rational—the Universal.

III. This is already the third movement of the play, which is so completely merged into the second that it has not been separated in the preceding exposition. It is, however, distinct in thought, and in other dramas of Shakespeare it is very distinctly marked off in the dramatic structure. Still, the reader will here behold the three great movements of this class of plays: Disruption through Wrong, Mediation through an Ideal World, Restoration.

Thus Prospero has changed all his enemies into an image of himself, and has made them participate, to a certain extent at least, in his own double character. Each person, through repentance, reflects Prospero, and places himself in unity with him. Nor must his double nature be considered anything strange or unknown; it is found more or less developed in every soul. As a moral, and particularly as a thinking, being, man must solve the conflicts of his individual existence. Indeed, the sum of all conflicts and the greatest of all contradictions is the one above mentioned, which in abstract language was called the contradiction between the Individual and Universal.

Nay, the mightiest of men — for he was a man — whose
spirit, however, raised him to be a divinity — Christ himself — was he not the embodiment of this contradiction?
A celebrated sarcasm was once uttered concerning him:
" Yes, Christ was able to save the whole world, but couldn't
save himself." True, and his chief merit. Christ as
individual was necessarily involved in the struggles of the
world and perished; but as spirit he created it anew, and
made it, so to speak, a different world, for its history
since his time is the history of Christianity. So, too,
Prospero as an individual is overwhelmed with the collisions
of life; but as spirit he has mastered and portrayed them,
and even converted his enemies into his own image.

Prospero's career is now at an end; his work is done
when the reconciliation is completed. He calls up once
more the world of spirits, who have been his faithful
instrumentalities, in order to bid them farewell forever.
He abjures his rough magic — his Art; and soon he will
break his staff — bury it in the earth — and drown his
book. For the present, Ariel is retained, who brings
together the entire company and restores even the ship.
" Then to the elements ;" the play ends — his poetical
activity ceases.

The relation of the play to Shakespeare himself has frequently been discussed. Long ago a critic suggested that
Prospero was Shakespeare. But the mistake has been
that the play was supposed to represent Shakespeare's
individual life. It might be taken as a portraiture of his
poetic, universal life, or that of any great poet. Other
mighty individuals have been suggested in place of Prospero, but in such cases there is merely the substitution of
one name for another, whereby, however, nothing is

explained. We can only say, as we began, Prospero is
the Poet generically, who, in the first place, embodies the
manifold themes of his Art in a dramatic form ; and, in the
second place, portrays himself in the act — portrays himself performing his own process also in a dramatic form.
The Drama can go no further ; it has attained the universality of Thought.

Here also can be found the reason why it is impossible
to give a theatrical representation of this play. What
form shall we assign to Ariel and Caliban? A child for
the one, and a low human shape for the other? Then we
feel the impassible chasm which shuts off the Poet's creation from the stage. The pictorial art is equally impotent
in reaching these conceptions? Why is this? Because
Ariel and Caliban are thoughts more than images ; they are
not only far beyond the realm of sensuous representation,
but even begin to transcend the realm of pure imagination.
Hence we can read them and think them, but cannot image
them with clearness ; they lie too far in the sphere of
unpicturable thought.

If we now put together the beginning and the end of
the drama, we find that Prospero departs from the Real,
passes through the Ideal, and returns to the Real. The
middle stage is alone portrayed in the play. It would
seem, therefore, that Prospero, being forced to abandon
the practical world on account of his devotion to his books
and his Art, solves in his theoretical domain all the contradictions of finite existence, and thus returns in triumph to
the practical world. Thought, therefore, though at first
antagonistic, finally restores action. Here we behold a
phase of the same mighty theme which is treated in *Hamlet* and in Goethe's *Faust*, notwithstanding the great dif-

ference of form between these poems.   But, though this drama touches the Real World at both ends, its action lies wholly in the Ideal World.

*Tempest* stands very high in the list of Shakespeare's dramas; in some respects it is his supreme work.   Its wonderful types, its perfect symmetrical structure, its bright poetic language — but, above all, its profound signification — must always make it the favorite among the thoughtful readers of the Poet.   It has not been adequately appreciated in the past; it is that one of Shakespeare's plays which has yet to find in the future a full recognition of its meaning and importance.   This noblest literary form, invented and perfected by Shakespeare, which no poet since his time has been able to reproduce — namely, mediation through an Ideal World — finds its culmination and perfection in *Tempest.*   Moreover, it is a drama bursting the bounds of Dramatic Art and pointing beyond; theatrical representation utterly breaks down in an attempt to give the shapes here, for they refuse to be seen by the outer eye — only the inner eye can behold them.   The old theater is gone, sunk beyond resurrection; its ghost may still linger, furnishing a place of amusement but no longer inhabiting the temple of culture. *Tempest* plainly indicates the limits of the old Drama; it is also a prophecy of a new Dramatic Form — will the prophecy be fulfilled?

# PART II.

---

# HISTORICAL DRAMA.

# HISTORICAL DRAMA.

## THE NATURE OF THE HISTORICAL DRAMA.

I. THE RELATION BETWEEN THE LEGENDARY AND HISTORICAL DRAMA. — In the Historical Drama a new field opens. The domestic relations of man are placed in the background, and the political element becomes paramount. The Family occupies still a position as an ethical institution, but it is now subordinate in importance to the State. Consequently the species of drama is different, and a different kind of effect is produced. In the Family the emotions of man are at home, and manifest themselves in their greatest intensity; the collisions occurring in it, therefore, appeal in the strongest manner to the feelings. But the State rests more upon intelligence, and is further removed from our daily life and its sympathies, though it must not be thought that the State is devoid of an emotional basis in human nature. Indeed, love of country is capable of absorbing every other activity in certain periods of great national calamity; still, in the ordinary life of men, the Family is necessarily the more immediate institution. The main *pathos* of the Historical Drama will, therefore, be different from that of the Domestic Drama. This difference of substance is necessarily followed by a difference of form.

The form of the Historical Drama lies between pure

Fable and pure History. The Fable is a yielding, flexible material, which the Poet moulds freely to his own conception and gives it a shape corresponding to the thought. It is not trammeled by rigid Fact, by fixed Time or Place, and, hence, its adaptation for creative Art surpasses that of History. The Poet reflects in the Fable the world in which he lives — he portrays the consciousness of his age. With this unstained plastic material he is enabled to show the conflicts of the time in their spiritual purity — free from partisan rancor, from religious bigotry, and from all other disturbing influences. The Artist, therefore, works most truly when he takes the thought of his own time and pours it into the remote mythological form, which may be made pliant to his gentlest touch. But once let the historical form be taken to express the same thing, let an important historical character or conflict of the present time be introduced in its reality, then the flood-gates of prejudice and passion are opened, and the work will be torn to pieces by opposing factions. This is very far from being an æsthetic effect. Most peoples have created a fabulous period before the dawn of History as a dwelling-place for the imagination — it is the paradise of poetic forms, which never have to jostle against the hard reality.

But History has been enacted; its form is given and is inflexible. The fact cannot be bent, and remain fact; in so far as the Poet does bend it, he verges toward fiction — he makes History a fable. The age has assumed that fixed shape; none other can take its place. Men have acted; there they stand, with their names and deeds written upon the parchment. History, being thus crystallized, is far more inclined to break than to bend in a poetic treatment; but its unyielding materials may be considerably softened by going far back in time and approaching the era of Fable. The Historical Drama is, therefore, composed of two somewhat antithetic elements — History and Poetry. But its essential form must remain historical; the fabulous or ideal element may vary from a mere drop to quite the half of the play. There may be only a slight shifting of Time and Place, or there may be a large group of unhistorical characters, with new incidents. Shakespeare's usage differs in different dramas.

But there is a point where the Poet must not vary. He has to portray the conflicts of the age which he undertakes to represent with an absolute fidelity. These conflicts are also the profoundest content of Poetry; hence History and Poetry, in their ultimate thought, come together — have the same fundamental principle. One inner spirit animates two distinct forms, and even these forms are united in the Historical Drama. Still, the Poet looks back through the atmosphere of his own age; he cannot live out of his own time. This fact always determines the coloring, and often the selection, of his theme, yet he ought to show the true spiritual struggle of the epoch which he has chosen to body forth. Shakespeare undoubtedly beheld the Lancastrian period with Elizabethan eyes, though he has given the actual historical conflict of that period. His portraiture of the Past is unavoidably tinged with the consciousness of the Present. Hence the Historical Drama has in it a kind of double reflection, being partly of what is and partly of what has been, which twofoldness is inherent in the species.

The Historical Drama is the Drama of nationality; this is its truest and most exalted function. The institution with which History deals is the State; it subordinates all other institutions and principles. Its expression in Art has demanded a special artistic form, which attempts to reconcile the real elements of History with the ideal shapes of Poetry. The domestic and other species of Drama seek the Fable as their most adequate material, but the Historical Drama looks to the records of the nation and to the deeds of the national heroes. The emotion to which it appeals is patriotism, which elevates the individual into one existence with his country, and Art thus inculcates the noblest devotion of human character.

In the ordinary Drama the deed is brought home to the doer in person, the action of the individual returns upon him in the course of a single play. It is thus complete in itself; reward or retribution is shown in the result. But the historical deed continues for all time to produce its effect; it is thus transmitted far beyond its return to the individual. For the nation partakes of it and carries it forward; and, as the life of the nation endures, the deed of a man becomes perennial in its consequences. The act, though performed by a person, is in truth national, or, possibly, world-historical. Hence arises the necessity of transcending the limits of a single play in order to bring together actions and their remote consequences. Therefore it is that we have the two Tetralogies — the Lancastrian and the Yorkian — each being a series of four plays intimately connected. Or, if we wish to take a broader view, therefore it is that we possess a grand Dramatic Epic of ten plays, portraying and linking together in thought transitional periods of the English nation. Or, if we desire to grasp the complete generalization, therefore it is that Shakespeare has presented to us the colossal outlines of a world-historical Drama of fifteen plays, being forced to such a lofty and comprehensive theme by the grandeur and universality of his genius. Thus he makes the deed run through time almost from the beginning of positive History.

II. Outline of the Historical Drama. —Shakespeare, to a certain degree, wrote his historical plays backward. The epoch nearest in time to his own age is the subject of some of his earliest productions; the blood, fate, and swift retribution so often seen in the Wars of the Roses fascinated the youthful mind of the dramatist. The York-ian Tetralogy, which portrays a period of national disinte-gration, accompanied with horrible crime and butchery, is the least retrospective, the most immediate, of his works; it seeks after strong effects by means which may often be justly called sensational. To the riper age of the Poet belongs the Lancastrian Tetralogy, which exhibits the nation in a constructive epoch, ridding itself of a worth-less monarch, subduing rebellion at home, and conquer-ing its hereditary enemy abroad. He thus goes back in thought as he advances in years. Still later are the Roman Historical plays; the Poet has now transcended the limits of nationality, and necessarily begins to consider the movement of universal history. Patriotic fervor sub-sides into a more calm development of colliding princi-ples, and his stand-point is no longer national, but world-historical.

This is the natural development of the individual mind; it recedes from the Present, seeking the lessons of the Past, and returns laden with the spoils of centuries. The world of to-day is a mystery — indeed, a Babylonian con-fusion — if we cannot trace its constructive elements in that which has been. As the man grows older he becomes more retrospective; hence he keeps looking back further and further in the history of his race to reach eternal principles. To trace the development of the individual Shakespeare we should by all means follow these plays after the order of their composition, which is for the most part backwards in time. As he recedes in the Past he deepens in thought, expression, and treatment.

Still, this is not the highest method of studying these works. History is chronological; its stream cannot be turned back by any individual standing in its course—not even by Shakespeare. Its principles are to be shown by the Poet; the deepest thought of the epoch must be given by him; its profoundest struggle is always his most worthy theme. It is at this point, and at this point only, that Poetry and History meet. It is not necessary that the externalities of a nation or a period be given in their literal fidelity; this is, in fact, impossible. The costume, the language, the general coloring, may all be different from what they really were, but the spiritual conflict of the time must be shown in its verity. If, therefore, the Poet has taken a series of historical themes, they can be truly considered only in the order of history, which is successive in time; thus the thought of each epoch can be seen in its connection with the thought of succeeding epochs. A full explanation of Shakespeare's historical labors will demand something of a Philosophy of History. A slight sketch will show the outlines of his thought in this direction.

Of the Greek historical age the Poet has left us no adequate portraiture, though the scene of action in several dramas is placed in the ancient Hellenic world. *Troilus and Cressida* is a decided approach toward an historical play, but, inasmuch as the subject is fabulous, and was a myth to the old Greeks themselves, it lacks one of the essential distinctions of history. Still, it exhibits the inherent principle of Greece in its political manifestation—the story of the Trojan war was always the best picture of Hellenism. Shakespeare has distinctly stated that the great fault of the Argive host before Troy was lack of subordination—the individual asserted himself too strongly; authority—and, hence, organization—became impossible. This was the prime defect of Greece during her historical period also; she sought an absolute autonomy for state, tribe, community, city, individual. The result was internal strife and jealousy, in which all united action of the nation was generally lost. Thus the army before Ilium is an image of the Grecian world, and is suffering from the same malady which ultimately destroyed Greece; yet much of the special coloring of *Troilus and Cressida* is modern to a degree that makes it appear incongruous. This play has also the peculiarity of being the most reflective of all Shakespeare's writings, though its scene is laid in the most remote time. It also takes its place between the purely legendary and the purely historical dramas, forming a transition from the one and an introduction to the other.

But it is Rome which exercises the strongest fascination over the Poet. Here, too, we have the assertion of individuality—not, however, that which excludes other cities and nations, but that which includes the whole world in the grasp of its ambition. Assimilation was the fundamental principle of Rome; it sought to make all peoples Roman. Its intense nationality assailed nationality, destroyed the same, and therein destroyed itself. Because it was based on conquest, it naturally bore within its own bosom the germ of destruction. The strong national life of Rome subdued all to itself, both within and without; the negative sweep of its career involved the Family at home and the Nation abroad — that is, the Roman State sacrificed the domestic relation, and sought to wipe out the principle of nationality from the face of the earth. But it repaid the ruin which it wrought with infinite blessings. The universal sway of the Roman soldier has long since departed, but the universal sway of Roman spirit still prevails in our laws and municipal institutions.

The series of Roman Historical plays will show various phases of development in the Roman principle. The prologue is *Coriolanus*, which exhibits this people in preparation for the conquest of the world. The drama portrays mainly the internal struggles of Rome, to subordinate which produces so much strength of character. The State gets rid of the mighty individual in *Coriolanus*, and finds an instrument for counteracting his hostility. The State absorbs the Family — even in its supreme female representative, the mother; Volumnia cares not for her son as son, but only as Roman. The State subjects Political Parties, which have to acknowledge it as their ultimate principle. The training is severe, but essential for the assurance of victory; the Roman national spirit must show itself more intense than any other, if its destiny be to subdue all nations.

The world is conquered, and the great transition takes place from Republican Rome to Imperial Rome. The mighty conqueress had absorbed all people into herself, was gradually changed in character, and lost her primitive principle. Unity under one government has been her

policy; this unity must logically be carried into her institutions; the multiplicity of the Senate and the People
must sink into the unity of the absolute Monarch. To
this great revolution are devoted two plays — *Julius Cæsar*
and *Antony and Cleopatra* — which form the culmination
of the Roman Historical series. The former introduces
at once the heroic individual, who has already unified in
himself the whole Roman world. Between him and the
supporters of the old constitution a conflict arises, which
destroys him, though his principle is triumphant. There
is, however, no single individual left who can unite all the
contending elements; hence the play of *Julius Cæsar*
stops with the Triumvirate — a mere breathing-place in
the rapid flight toward Imperialism.

In *Antony and Cleopatra* the transition is completed;
the three men of the Triumvirate are reduced to one, who
is now the Emperor. The career of Rome cannot stop
till all known nations are consolidated into one government, under one law, and administered by one ruler. It
is a world-historical epoch, for the whole world participates in the change. To make the thought of these two
plays complete, the earlier period of Cæsar's life, embracing his struggle with, and triumph over, Pompey, ought to
be supplied. It is manifest that the Poet had mastered
the historical details and thought out the conflicting principles of that time. Thus no link would be missing; the
cycle would be full; the transition from the Republic to
the Empire would be shown in all essential phases. But
any intention on the part of the Poet to write such a
drama cannot be proven.

The result of Roman conquest and civil organization
was the destruction of the nations. The world became

Roman; it was assimilated; a dull uniformity resulted,
which deadened all vigor of mind and body. Nationality
must be restored to the human race, the massive Roman
Empire must be broken to fragments, and each fragment
wrought into a new nation. This is accomplished by the
Northern Barbarians, who fall upon the enervated people
of the South; each tribe takes a slice of territory. It is a
time of social disintegration, in which the youthful Shakespeare found a theme as congenial as the Yorkian Tetralogy. For here *Titus Andronicus* must be placed; although
under protest, it will have to be admitted into the series
of historical plays, and into Shakespeare's dramatic
family.' In particular, his authorship of it cannot be
rejected without undermining the external evidence upon
which the most authentic of his plays repose. At this
point the Roman Historical series comes to an end, having
delineated the Roman world in its early struggles, in its
culmination, and in its close.

The restoration of nationality to Europe is the chief
work of the Middle Ages. This is the next grand world-
historical movement—the rise and development of the
modern nation. The Teutonic tribe adopts the Roman
law and institutions; the result is a wholly new world,
composed of individual States living together like the
members of a common organization. The family of
nations is the friendly title which is often given to it, and
which it, in the main, deserves. Of this family England
may be fairly considered as the worthiest member in its
political development. Nationality is its strongest principle, and, in general, it has acknowledged the same principle for other countries. Still, England has attempted
the subjugation of its neighbors at various times, and

thus has not been wholly consistent. But such attempts have brought in their train great disasters, in which the conquests have been lost and the peace of the land disturbed. The general result, notwithstanding, has been individual freedom and national autonomy. It has, however, taken a long and intense struggle to attain this end.

Shakespeare has also employed his pen upon this greatest world-historical theme — the rise of the modern nation. Moreover, he has taken very naturally the happiest example, England, which was his own native land. Ten English Historical plays are the glorious fruit of his inspiration, and no poet has ever so truly shown the spirit of his country. The English nationality, in its conflicts and in its triumphs, is the central pivot upon which the entire series moves. It has to struggle with its own weak and wicked kings; it rushes into foreign conquest and brings untold calamities upon itself in violating its own truest principle; it finally completes its political enfranchisement by subordinating Church to State. Thus the last fetter of the nation is thrown off in freeing itself from an external spiritual domination.

Nationality is, therefore, the theme and the inspiration of the English Historical plays. They, hence, appeal most profoundly to the human heart, touching its noblest emotions, while they are at the same time true to the supreme political principle of modern times, which is the autonomy of the State. Also, the Roman Historical plays are strongly national, yet with a profound glance into a power above the Nation, namely, the world-historical principle.

III. Collisions of the Historical Drama. — Next we are to consider the conflicts which arise in this sphere.

Nationality has to assert itself against other institutional principles and ethical relations of man. The result is that many things which seem of the most sacred and binding nature are quietly set aside or openly trampled underfoot. The nation demands a supreme sacrifice; what, then, can be excluded? Let us try to separate and carefully distinguish the relative worth of the conflicting principles; otherwise, the Historical Drama — and, indeed, the Historical World — is a mass of confusion and contradiction. The main point is to see everything in its true limitation, and not from a one-sided dogmatism to pass a sweeping condemnation upon the actions of the great characters of history who are engaged in struggles wholly different from those of ordinary life, and who have to violate what is, in order to pave the way for what is to be.

The first of these conflicts begins with the individual, and may be stated as the conflict between nationality and morality. Every person is supposed to have a conscience, which is the guide of action; he follows his ideas of right and wrong in his daily transactions with his neighbor. Veracity, Honesty, Candor, Humanity, are moral virtues whose validity everybody must acknowledge, but a national exigency not infrequently arises which demands their sacrifice. Which side shall be taken? Recollect that the question demands a real opposition; there must be a conflict which cannot be avoided, and one principle or the other has to be followed. If a man rests absolutely in the moral consciousness, then he can find no justification for war, for diplomacy — indeed, for nationality. The most potent instruments for maintaining the independence of the State he cannot employ, since that often involves the deception, plunder, and even destruction of his fellow-men. Such actions are assuredly not moral, and that person alone is a consistent moralist who refuses to defend his country by any species of violence or cunning.

Now, the Historical Drama, if it enforce nationality as the essential and supreme object of human action, will exhibit just this conflict, whose only solution is the subordination of the moral to the national principle. The supposition always is that a case arises in which the two cannot be reconciled; one must be taken to the exclusion of the other. The great statesman, whose eye is always on the Nation, may be expected to show his strongest and most characteristic trait by his choice at the point of conflict in the two principles. So, too, the national hero is national by virtue of his total absorption into his nation. It is not intended to say that every violation of morality by public men is necessary or justifiable; they are too often immoral when there is no need — that is, where there is no conflict between moral and political duty, or where the moral obligation is far stronger than the national necessity.

But the other side must not be left out of sight nor omitted in the Drama. Even the most justifiable violation of morality carries with it retribution — the wrong must bring its penalty; justice is the absolute principle in the government of the world. Such is the tragic destiny of the Great Man; he is bound to fall into guilt in accomplishing the most beneficent revolution, and that guilt is brought home to him in punishment. He suffers for the evil which he has done, yet he had to do the evil in order to realize the infinitely greater good. It has long been remarked that the great historical character is not

12

happy; he is rent asunder by two warring fates, each of which tears off a fragment of his flesh whichever way he may turn. The nation, too, which permits moral violation, even for the sake of its own existence, admits into its bosom a lurking enemy, which can be expelled only after years of pain and struggle. Still, the responsibility must be taken by the individual and by the nation; life and progress often demand the destruction of what is established, with all its fearful consequences.

The second collision of the State is with the Family. Now we enter the institutional world, of which, however, some individual must be the representative. The most obvious form of this collision is the case of the father who is taken to maintain the endangered nation, though his wife and children perish. It is true that, if such were the result universally, the country would be destroyed anyhow. But the real necessity lies in the fact that without the nation the Family cannot exist; for the loss of nationality involves the uncertainty, if not the loss, of all other institutions, while the defense of nationality is their defense. But here comes the sacrifice — the maintenance of the nation calls for that member of the Family by whom alone it is nourished and protected. Thus one particular family may perish; still, the institution of the Family is thereby defended and preserved, for that institution — the State — whose chief purpose is to secure all other institutions, is thereby maintained. But, if the State perish, the whole institutional world follows after, or is saved by the caprice of the conqueror. Hence it is an accident if the Family survives when the nation perishes, and it is also an accident if the Family perishes when the nation survives.

In representing the domestic relation, woman enters the Drama. The Family is her peculiar realm, while the State is the sphere of man's activity. The beauty in the character of the one and the greatness in the character of the other are always to be traced back to their respective institutions; this is, indeed, the ultimate basis of all characterization. But the State and the Family may collide; then we behold, if portrayed in its purity, the most powerful and the most tragic of all collisions — the collision between the principle of man and the principle of woman. Both are right, both are wrong, both must suffer. The solution, however, cannot be withheld — the woman has to be sacrificed; her institution is the lower and must be subordinated, though the full penalty of her sacrifice is burnt into the very flesh of the man.

But this conflict and immolation of the Family takes a peculiar form in the modern European State. The wife of the King is Queen; the mother of the household may be the ruler of the people. The Family is thereby changed in its fundamental nature. The woman is reduced to being a political instrument — her children follow her condition; that is, the State absorbs the domestic relation. Hence the Queen-mother, a compound word which expresses this double character, becomes an important and peculiar element in the history of European nations. Her fate is to be harassed by the struggle between maternal instinct and political necessity — to have her emotional nature sacrificed to some national object. When different members of the same house seek control, the Family is broken up; its union around the mother is lost, and she is often forced to take part against her own kindred. The unmarried princess has in store a destiny equally

tragic.   Political advantage determines her marriage;
the essential element of domestic happiness — mutual
love of man and woman — is disregarded; the emotional
basis of a true union is often wanting.   Again it is the
sacrifice of the Family to the State.

Undoubtedly the male members of the royal house are
compelled to succumb to the same custom, and have to
suffer, but it is the women who are most deeply aggrieved,
for their institution is made to yield.   The penalty follows
hard after; infidelity is the universal trait of kings, and also
it would seem not to be wanting in queens sometimes;
jealousy cannot be absent from such a union.   The kingly
hearth is a domestic curse.   Thus it will be seen that the
royal woman — whether she be mother, wife, or maiden —
is inherently a tragic character, who has to stand in the
eternal cross-fire between domestic love and political duty
or ambition.

Still, let us recognize the rational object of royal intermarriage.   It has been said previously that the modern
European system of States partakes of the nature of a
family, and is often called the family of nations.   To
link its members together in peace and domestic affection,
the different sovereigns seek to form matrimonial alliances
between their children.   Thus it is attempted to transfer
the ties of the Family into the State, and to create a
domestic bond between the nations of Europe.   In this
manner war is often averted, quarrels are healed, and,
above all, the country is strengthened in its independence
by powerful connections.   The fact specially to be noted,
therefore, is that the supreme world-historical principle of
modern times, namely, the principle of nationality, has
seized upon the Family as a mighty instrument of its

realization. But the tragic element remains, notwithstanding; woman is sacrificed — man meets with retribution.

The third principle with which the modern State shows a conflict is the Church. It was the policy of the Holy See to bring together the nations of Europe under one supreme head. Rome wished to be the mother of this large and interesting family of peoples. She thus inherited the principle of unification from the Roman Empire, but her means was now a spiritual power, though physical force was standing prepared in the background. A sort of universal republic floated in the imagination of her illustrious Pontiffs; the common bond of union was religion. Thus arose the great conflict between the Occident and the Orient, whose grand historical manifestation was the Crusades. This was the external struggle of Europe during the Middle Ages; it was the deadly combat between two religions — Christianity and Mohammedanism. This crusading spirit is not omitted by Shakespeare, though it does not give the foundation to any play.

But the internal conflict of the European State with the Church is of far greater significance. Civil authority was continually rasping against ecclesiastical domination, which was everywhere skillfully organized. The Church had made itself, in the strongest sense of the term, an institution, and in many cases it both enacted and administered the law. One or the other — State or Church — must be superfluous, and the world-historical question was: Shall the nation again be swallowed up in an universal Roman Empire? The spirit of modern times could give only one solution — the State felt, and ultimately asserted, its supremacy, though its conflict with the Church was a perennial source of strife till it culminated in the great schism

known as the Reformation.   For the political significance
of Protestantism was the subordination of Church to
State, while the political significance of Catholicism was
the subordination of State to Church.   It is again the
spirit of nationality, which is wrestling with a new enemy.

Nor can the effect of this pursuit of political objects
upon the Church itself be omitted by the Poet.   It lost its
great end, for it subjected its religious purpose to secular
aggrandizement.   It was thus no longer truly a Church;
it was a political organization — an Empire which sought
supreme authority.   It had, therefore, come to contradict
its own principle of existence.   But the spiritual effect,
which should be the chief care of religion, was unfortunate.   Its great men were trained to a diplomatic cunning;
its moralists, too, often indulged in a subtle casuistry
which confused and debauched the honest instincts of the
people; learning and speculation, which it fostered, were
not seldom prostituted to defend hypocrisy and falsehood
for the sake of some political advantage — that is, the
truest and highest content of religion was sacrificed to
the ecclesiastical organization.   Hence came the double
revolt against its domination — from the moral conscience
of the individual and from the political principle of the
State.

The English Historical Drama will necessarily exhibit
this conflict in all its phases, as well as the final triumph of
nationality, of which England is the most worthy representative among modern peoples.   The external struggle
of Christian Europe with Mohammedanism frequently
looms up in the background — particularly in *Henry the
Fourth* — and the King, as the son of the Church, is delib-
erating about some expedition to the Holy Land.   Still,

the internal conflict is enough to occupy his attention; he is the ruler of the State in a far higher sense than he is the son of the Church. The result of the struggle, as indicated in this Historical series, will be that the English people will change its religion and withdraw from the Catholic Republic, a result springing directly from the spirit of nationality.

The fourth conflict is that of the individual State with the world-historical principle, which is the essential ground of its existence. In such a case the State falls into contradiction with its higher self, and bitter is the penalty of the error. It was said above that nationality, in its universal sense, is the political spirit of the modern world; that Europe is a family of nations, whose ideal aim is to live together in independence, yet in harmony. Each country, therefore, must acknowledge the right of other countries to be as valid as its own, and must aid in vindicating that right in case it should be assailed. Now comes the essential insight—it is that a nation, in attempting to subjugate a nation, is destroying the principle of nationality, and thus falling into conflict with the world-historical movement of the modern age, and undermining the very foundation of its own existence. The collision lies between the State individual and the State universal— between national selfishness and national principle. Herein England has been guilty of violation; she has sought foreign conquest, which, as contradictory of her own highest end, has brought forth internal dissension and ruin. The Poet was probably not conscious of this struggle when he treated it, but it exists in History all the same, and is the moving principle in the transition from the Lancastrian to the Yorkian Tetralogy.

Such are the four inherent conflicts of the State — with Morality, with the Family, with the Church, and, finally, with itself. These conflicts are the nerve of every dramatic action; they form the most abiding and the most worthy themes of human interest; they involve every man and every people in their meshes. They have many gradations, which will be more fully detailed when the particular dramas come up for treatment. Here, too, must be sought the ultimate ground of character, for the dramatic individual is the bearer of a principle which he must carry into execution against the opposing principle of other individuals.

IV. More Detailed View of this Last Collision. — We have arrived at the supreme political conflict, which, in its most general form, may be expressed as the conflict of the State with itself. This is the peculiar field of Shakespeare's Historical Drama, though other collisions play into the action. Here the Poet shows his wonderful political sense; quite equal it is to his poetic genius. Here also appears that higher principle which changes, and even destroys, nations; for one of the conflicting sides may represent something greater than the existing national principle, with which, indeed, it may happen to come into collision.

This conflict of the State with itself has two very different manifestations, which should be carefully distinguished in thought. The first is the external collision — one nation against another nation. A State is thus in conflict with a State — that is, with its own essential form, with itself. Such is the contradiction involved in all wars. Whether or not it is possible to avoid war by any political contrivances is a subject which does not belong here; it is sufficient to say that all attempts of the kind have been hitherto unsuccessful. The conflict comes — a people and a civilization pass away forever. This conflict lies in the very limitation of one State against another State; each seeks — and, indeed, must seek — to assert its own individual existence and its own national principle. Finally, the supreme struggle is brought on, in which one of the nations often sinks out of the ken of History.

But the victorious nation, after the lapse of its allotted period, meets with the same fate — it is conquered and disappears. The same mighty principle which destroyed its enemy now destroys it; so the series continues, or has continued in the past. But what shall we call this principle which thus uses the nations as its instruments? Its reality will not be doubted; it is clearly the highest, strongest principle of History. Let us name it the world-historical principle, or even the World Spirit. It calls a nation into existence to execute its behests; this is, then, a world-historical nation. In looking at the past we observe that in antiquity the empires of the Orient — Greece, Rome — were world-historical nations at successive periods. But the main interest for us is the collision which thence arises. A nation armed with this principle goes forth to subdue other nations and subordinate them to the same influence. The result is a struggle between the world-historical principle and the State, which gives the highest possible collision, but, at the same time, farthest removed from the popular feeling and the popular consciousness. Its plainest manifestation is seen in *Julius Cæsar.*

A second phase of the external collisions of the State can hardly be elevated to the dignity of the preceding.

It is when wars are entered upon from national or monarchical caprice, or from some trifling and temporary interest. Thus we have State against State simply. Still, even in the most trivial conflicts some faint reflection of the World Spirit may be often traced. In the petty struggles of non-historical people and tribes, like those of America, Asia, and Africa, there can be, however, but little significance.

But it must not be thought that this world-historical principle is some external power outside of the people themselves. It is, in fact, their own inner development — their deepest consciousness. The nation which perishes, perishes through itself; so the nation which conquers, conquers through itself. When one people makes a higher synthesis than its neighbors, in its institutions and in its thought, that people is certain to be victorious in the end. It has so happened in the past that nationality has not been able to change fundamentally its principle, and pass to the higher one; each nation has seemed capable of realizing only one world-historical thought. Thus a whole people becomes tragic and dies in the defense of national existence. Such are the two leading phases of the external collision of the State.

We next pass to consider the internal collision, which is always more direct and of greater interest to the citizen, as well as more continuous in its effect. Now the State is divided within itself — separates into opposing elements — and at once we behold the phenomenon of *Political Parties*. These are essentially two, but with many shades of difference within themselves. It is a fact which has always excited surprise and investigation. All States — in particular, all free States — have this diremp-

tion in their very nature, though it is sometimes foolishly regretted. But the content—the foundation of the
political party—is the State itself; nay, lies in the very
constitution of the human mind. Some men hold on to
institutions, to customs—in general, to all the realized
forms of intelligence; in their permanence and unchange-
ableness alone public safety and public happiness are supposed to lie. This view, though absolutely true in its
proper limitations, becomes in its extreme one-sidedness
destructive of all progress; the human mind is cramped
in the trammels of a rigid formalism, and freedom of
every kind is annihilated. The protest of the outraged
spirit of man produces a new party, which, in its excess,
seeks to destroy, or to be forever changing, the established
institutions of the State. In the modern political world
these two parties are known as Conservative and Radical;
it is their action and reaction which on the one hand
secures to institutions permanence, and on the other
hand prevents them from becoming fetters to body and
soul.

Class or caste, in antiquity, was the dividing line of
party, and the ame is true at the present time, though to
a different extent among different peoples. The Patrician
was by birth a Conservative, for he wished to retain the
ancient privileges of his order, while the Plebian was by
birth a Radical, for he wished to acquire new rights. To
employ another form of expression, the one side represented the objective—the permanent; the other side represented the subjective—the changeable. Both are not
only necessary to the State, but belong to every complete
individual mind.

The particular issue upon which the parties divide is
very different in different countries, and in the same coun-

try at different times. It may be division of the land, right of suffrage, paper money, etc. But each issue reflects the general spirit of the whole, and each party therein adumbrates its universal character. In reference to the Historical Drama, this particular side must be presented in its full sensuous completeness.

This conflict of parties is a perennial one, and ought to be, for from it comes all political vitality, all true development. But it leads to guilt, and, hence, becomes tragic when it seduces the individual into placing his party above his country. The great example of such a deed and its consequences is witnessed in *Coriolanus*. Both parties must be subordinate to the State — must have their end and design in its well-being. Hence at this point arises the possibility of a collision of political principles, the one of which is embodied in a partisan organization and the other in the State. Such is, perhaps, the tendency of all political parties; it is their belief and their constant instruction — our side must prevail, else the country is ruined. But it may truly be said, if such be really the case, then the country is already ruined. When the government cannot be trusted to either of the great political organizations without fear of its destruction, the nation is already on the point of dissolution; the very statement is a declaration to that effect. But the assertion is seldom true, though each party inculcates it as a fundamental dogma of its existence that "we possess all the patriotism and all the true political principles, while our opponents are the enemies of their country." Such is the main internal collision of the State, wherein party assails country; the solution is that the individual who introduces this conflict is banished or perishes.

But the world-historical principle may work also through

the party as we saw it before working through the State. In such case the result is the destruction of the nation from within, or at least a fundamental change in its constitution. For the World Spirit feeds upon nations; it is the foe of nationality. Hence the world-historical individual appears as the destroyer of his country — of the constitution and the laws. But, in reality, he only carries out what has already been developed in the consciousness of the people.

All social innovations, when they become of national importance, assume the form of a political party. This is, therefore, the means by which the spirit of man rises into institutions — objectifies itself in more perfect forms. A persistent agitation of some social question finally produces a party out of a clique, which then may become the dominant party, and rule the country and make the laws in accordance with its principle. Some class, as the laborers or the property-holders, may succeed in elevating itself into a party, if its claims become a truly national question. Thus every social revolution takes the shape of a political party, and may, therefore, be made one of the elements of an internal collision of the State.

If we now take a glance back and recapitulate what has been elaborated, we find that there are essentially two main collisions of the State with itself — the external and the internal. The former is one individual State against another individual State, either of which may be the bearer of a world-historical principle, or of some finite national end. The latter — that is, the internal conflict — is the Political Party against the State; here, too, a world-historical element may be involved, or some merely partisan or individual object. These phases would seem to comprehend the totality of the relations of the State from this point of view. The Family, too, exists in this play of colliding powers, and may itself fall into conflict with any one or all of them. Thus the poet has an ample store from which he can select to diversify his treatment.

V. CLASSIFICATION OF THE HISTORICAL DRAMA. — This must follow the order of History, which is chronological. Each play is cut off at both ends, so to speak; it is taken out of an uninterrupted stream of events — of actual facts. That which goes before and that which comes after also demand to be recognized — hence the tendency in the historical sphere to a series of dramas. The division into Tragedy and Comedy cannot be applied here, with good results, to the single plays. Each of these usually portrays both success and failure — the happy victory of one party, the tragic end of the other. Hence, in the historical plays, taken singly, there is as a general rule no complete Mediation, as well as no complete Tragedy. Both elements are present, and usually they are not fully blended into harmony.

But, when these separate plays are joined together in their proper groups, then the previous divisions of Tragedy and Comedy (or Mediated Drama) begin to rise up to view again. For instance, the Yorkian Tetralogy is inherently tragic — it ends in the destruction of both the colliding Houses. On the other hand, the Lancastrian Tetralogy is mediated — the termination of the long and intense political struggle is happy. The same may be reasonably said of the group of two Roman Historical plays, *Julius Cæsar* and *Antony and Cleopatra* — the end is universal peace, along with the triumph of the imperial principle, although many illustrious heroes have fallen in the conflict.

If we rise now to still higher generalization, and grasp the separate character of the two great historical series

—the Roman and the English—in their fundamental
distinction, the same thought will come up in the mind:
for the Roman Historical series, ending with *Titus Andronicus*, is tragic, just as the Roman world itself was
tragic, and passed away in a conflict with the surrounding
Barbarians. As its history, so its poem. On the contrary, the English Historical series, taken as a whole, is a
Mediated Drama, in which the end is happy. The conflicts
of the State within and without are reconciled—the outcome is a nation free from all external control. This is
truly the triumph of nationality, of which England is the
great representative.

Finally, if we bring together the two great series into
one thought, we find that they constitute a mighty World-
Drama, with a tragic conflict for the nation in Rome,
which conflict, however, is mediated for the nation in
England. Verily, the ancient world was tragic—was the
true home and origin of Tragedy; Fate, with drawn sword,
ready to smite, was forever hovering over it there in its
Heaven. But the modern world, based upon its Christianity, means the reconciliation of man with himself and
with his God; Love, not Terror, is its principle; Fate
turns its sword upon itself. Hence the true instinct of
the Poet of the modern age has made his World-Drama a
mediated one, passing through deep and dark struggles to
a happy end.

The play forming the transition from the Legendary
Part is *Troilus and Cressida*, which, though founded on a
legend, has such a decided preponderance of the political
element in its composition that it may be ranked as an historical play. The following table will present to the eye
a summary of the classification:

HISTORICAL DRAMA. PART II.

ROMAN SERIES. (TRAGIC.)

- Transition to the Historical Drama. — Troilus and Cressida.
- Prologue. — Coriolanus.
- From Republic to Empire — Mediated. — Julius Cæsar. / Antony and Cleopatra.
- Epilogue. — Titus Andronicus.

ENGLISH SERIES. (MEDIATED.)

- Prologue. — King John.
- Lancastrian Tetralogy — Mediated. — Richard II. / Henry IV. — (Two parts.) / Henry V.
- Yorkian Tetralogy — Tragic. — Henry VI. — (Three parts.) / Richard III.
- Epilogue. — Henry VIII.

In regard to the Dramatic Structure, its two leading elements — Threads and Movements — will remain in the Historical Drama. Of Movements there are two, portraying a rise and a fall — or a culmination of some kind of fortune or misfortune. Much more distinctly marked than the Movements are the Threads; at least such seems to be the general rule. The two States engaged in external war, the two Parties engaged in internal struggle, fall naturally into a representation through two opposing Threads. As the Historical Drama is essentially political, and, hence, portrays a political conflict of some kind, both sides have to be shown in their separate development. Also, besides the political Thread, there may be a domestic or a comic Thread, which must, however, both contrast and harmonize with the leading historical theme. The special application of these principles will be seen in the plays themselves, which are now to be considered.

13

# TROILUS AND CRESSIDA.

The frame-work of this drama is the Trojan war. It has nearly the same limits as the Iliad; for it presupposes the quarrel of Achilles and Agamemnon and the withdrawal of Achilles till the death of his friend, Patroclus, when he again goes into battle and slays Hector. Many Homeric incidents and motives are retained, while many are introduced which would have made the old Greek bard stare with wonder. The famous heroes of the Iliad are brought before us, but we can hardly recognize them in their modern shape; the beautiful plastic outline is not lost, but is subordinated to the inner element of character. The statue is transformed to flesh and blood. Shakespeare has taken these antique ideal forms and poured into them the subjective intensity of the modern world. This is the greatest and most enduring ground of interest in the present drama. The old Greek hero is now moved, not by the god from without, but by himself from within — the divine influence is transmuted into his own intelligence. Ulysses, the favorite of Minerva, no longer meets the goddess upon the highways and addresses her in familiar accents, but communes with his own spirit. In other words, the ancient Epic has changed into the modern Drama. The meaning is the same both in Homer and in Shakespeare, but how different is the form! Yet it must not be forgotten that the outside is Greek, though the inside is Anglo-Saxon; the Hellenic mould is always visible, though it is not the sole, nor even the most prominent, object of interest.

The contrast is certainly striking, and is often so incongruous as to convey the notion of a humorous purpose. In the mouths of these old Homeric personages the Poet has placed the most abstract statement of what may be called his philosophy that is to be found in any of his works. His views of society, of life, of institutions, are here expressed in a language as direct and definite as that employed by the thinker trained to the use of the abstruse terms of the schools. What these principles are, and their influence upon his literary activity, will be discussed further on in the present essay. The reflections are mainly political, but are sometimes psychological, and show a mind most subtly scrutinizing its own processes. Those who hold that Shakespeare was the supremely unconscious poet would do well to study this play till they understand it — if, indeed, it can be fully understood without some philosophical culture and knowledge.

But the strangest and most incongruous element which is foisted into this old Homeric company is the manners of chivalry. It amounts to downright burlesque, and such, beyond any doubt, it was intended to be by the Author. The best passage for illustrating this phase of the drama is the challenge borne by Æneas from Hector. All the heroes seem to be transformed into mediæval knights, each one of whom is ready to prove the supreme beauty of his mistress by ordeal of battle. The climax of humor is attained when the aged Nestor, who has lived three generations of men, comes forward and offers to demonstrate to Hector by proof of arms "that my lady was fairer than his grandam." The principles of honor,

valor, love, hospitality, with which these personages are
endowed, give to the whole action the pleasing aroma of
the Middle Ages.  The reflective element before mentioned, which was injected into the characters of the old
heroes, is serious rather than humorous, but the chivalrous element is purely humorous, and turns them all into
Don Quixotes.  With Shakespeare the age of chivalry is
past, and it is with him an object of ridicule as much as
with Cervantes.  The hoary shapes of antiquity he thus
places in a modern institution, which, however, was already
worn out in his own time and laughed at by the whole world.

Such is the Homeric group which is introduced into the
present drama; but there is also another set of persons
here, whose principle and whose actions are unknown to
the Iliad.  Love is with them the main business — not
war.  The legend of Troilus, Cressida, and Pandarus is
the creation of the later romancers, which was grafted on
the old story of Troy.  It portrays the struggle of the
tender passion in one of its phases — the fidelity of man
and the falsity of woman.  The burning intensity, the
fierce conflicts, the supreme power of love, find their
expression in this part of the fable, which is, indeed, a
later development of human spirit.  Still, the relation
between the two groups must be traced; the Trojan war
was caused by the faithlessness of a woman whose restoration is demanded by the Nation; the refusal calls out the
heroes who are seeking to bring her back by force.
Female infidelity is the theme; in the one case it involves
the Family merely, but in the other case it involves the
State.  Helen and Cressida, therefore, resemble each
other; both perform the same deed, though in different
relations, which also produce different results.

Such are the two threads running through the play. They may be named, according to their leading tendency, the love-thread and the war-thread; though parallel in action, in thought the first is the source of the second. The movements also are two, the division being manifest, not only by a difference in principle, but also by a difference in merit. The first movement, in general, passes from strife and separation to unity. The parted lovers are brought together by the mediation of Pandarus, and are made happy by mutual vows of devotion. In Troy the division of opinion which previously existed is healed; in the Greek host the angry Achilles is wrought upon by the cunning of Ulysses, and seems to resolve to take part again in the war; thus the hostile armies come to internal harmony preparatory to the external struggle. The second movement portrays the passage from union to disruption and conflict. The lovers, on the one hand, are torn asunder by an unforeseen occurrence; Cressida proves faithless, and thus the bond of emotion is broken. The combat, on the other hand, arises between the two hostile forces; after many fluctuations, Hector, the Trojan hero, is slain, and his countrymen cease from their attack and retire to the city; things are left as they were before. The negative termination of the play is striking; Troilus and Cressida are separated, and the foes still confront each other with warlike preparation.

I. 1. Taking up the love-thread and following it through the first movement, we observe that the divine passion has been already excited in the bosoms of the lovers, and moves on speedily to its fruition in the betrothal. Troilus is first introduced to us. He is still young and impulsive; he is completely swayed by his strong and intense emotions. He has met the fair Cressida, though the circumstances are not told; at once we see him literally consumed with the sacred flame. She dances before his mind continually; sighs burst forth unbidden from his heart; every duty or purpose is swallowed up in the whirlpool of his passion. Such is the lover, pure and simple — the Romeo of the world. But Troilus has another trait, which gives him dignity and elevation of character, and which stands in the most direct opposition to his absorption in his feelings. He is a man of action — a warrior second only, if not equal, to Hector, and a patriotic defender of his country. But these two elements of his nature are now in deadly struggle; in his own breast is the conflict between Love and War. Honor and ambition call him to the field, where the destiny of Fatherland is being decided. But passion has seized him in its firmest grasp; its supremacy is declared in the very first line of the play, where, after arming himself for battle, he calls out:

> ' — "I'll unarm again;
> Why should I war without the walls of Troy,
> That find such cruel battle here within?"

Such is the first triumph of Love over the bold warrior; it has tamed him till he is "weaker than a woman's tear," which, notwithstanding the contemptuous expression of Troilus, is an instrument of considerable power. But now there is another combat which he has to wage — fierce, incessant, lachrymose. The favor of the fair Cressida seems very uncertain; her uncle cannot wind up the negotiation with sufficient speed. Troilus, therefore, feels in his heart that most painful of all pangs — the pang of unrequited love. Still, he has hope, though he is very

impatient, and Pandarus keeps alive his imagination by
recounting the charms of his beautiful mistress. At last
the mediator brings about their meeting. Troilus is all
fervor and passion ; he makes the first declaration of devotion, which is followed by that of Cressida. Open, sincere, even unsophisticated, is the youthful suitor, the best
model of the love-hero that Shakespeare has left us. His
emotion is so pure, intense, and direct that its beauty has
no flaw, while at the same time his character rises out of
a mere emotional existence into the region of the noblest
manly activity. It is true that love asserts its mastery
for the time being, still it does not quench his zeal for his
country. But now, as the conflict within him is soothed
to repose by his union, Troilus will be himself again if
jealous Fate will but refrain from interference. Such
good behavior, however, can hardly be expected of it in a
drama. Let the reader, with gloomy foreboding, await
the outcome of the story a few pages ahead.

Pandarus has been just mentioned as the mediating
power between the two lovers. His function is not very
important, since both the man and the woman are touched
with a mutual passion, which is sufficient to bring them
together without any assistance. Pandarus is rather a
busy-body; active, yet harmless. He is certainly not a
villain; the alliance which he seeks to bring about is
worthy; his means can hardly be condemned by the rigid
moralist, though his jokes are a little too free for the modern ear. Assuredly the odious word " pander," which is
supposed to be derived from his name, cannot justly be
applied to his conduct in this drama. Moreover, his
understanding is not strong; the artful Cressida stands
far above all his schemes and makes fun of him, though

he is able to exercise a good deal of control over the
ardent and simple-hearted Troilus.   His name has brought
upon him a legacy of abuse which his deed in no sense
justifies.   There is not an enterprising mother in the land
who does not do as much without a breath of condemnation.

Cressida receives after Troilus a visit from the industri-
ous match-maker, who tries to excite her love and admiration for the youthful hero in every manner possible.
The name of Troilus is continually introduced in the con- '
versation; his beauty, intellect, youth, are the themes of
great praise, but it is his valor which is the main subject
of laudation.   The famous heroes of Troy are made to
pass in review one after another; the noble Troilus is
superior to them all — even Hector is no exception.   But
the adroit Cressida listens to the encomiums bestowed by
her uncle with a complete penetration of their object, par-
rying his questions, tormenting him with a feigned opposition, uttering words of detraction against Troilus, indulging in a wild strain of banter and jest; in fine, she teases
her dear uncle to desperation, and conceals from him completely her real feelings and purposes.   He confesses that
he cannot understand her, while she probes him to the
bottom by her blunt words — "you are a bawd."   Her
character comes out plain in this interview; she is shrewd,
witty, and wanton; no person of the caliber of Pandarus
can touch the depths of her mind — the cool understanding effectually controls the emotions.

Such a woman is now to be seen in love, for she all the
time has cherished a secret affection for Troilus.   What
will she turn out to be?   Her admiration is genuine; in
her monologue, in which she has no motive for conceal-

ment, she says that she sees in the actual Troilus a thousandfold more " than in the glass of Pandar's praise may be." But feeling must be suppressed ; she, therefore, does just what might be expected — she refuses subordination to love. Her argument is without the trace of passion, and is directed against passion :

> " Things won are done, joy's soul lies in the doing —
> Men prize the thing ungained more than it is [worth] —
> Achieved [us], men still command ; ungained, beseech ;
> Then, though my heart's content firm love doth bear,
> Nothing of that shall from mine eyes appear."

That is, consummation dampens ardor, suspense keeps it alive. Led by this specious reasoning, she intends to keep under the rising flame, and make the true love of her devoted suitor her sport and his instrument of torture. The emotion which she feels must be concealed, and converted to a means for some other end besides mutual union. She is the intellectual coquette.

The fundamental distinction between the characters of Troilus and Cressida is now apparent. The man resigns himself to his love ; many great interests are pressing him, but they are brushed aside — his sacrifice is complete. But the woman subordinates her love to her understanding — to her planning and schemes ; she refuses the absolute surrender to the feeling of Family. She, therefore, must be declared to be untrue to the deepest principle of her sex. Her falsity hereafter is adequately motived by this single trait ; love — devotion to the one individual — is not the controlling impulse of her nature. But we must advance to the next stage — the good offices of Pandarus bring about their meeting. It has already been noticed how Troilus, true to character, makes an imme-

diate and unreserved declaration of the most fervent devotion.    But Cressida is also true to her character; she hesitates, suspects, makes abstract reflections of various kinds.
When she does whisper her love she repents — reproaches
herself with having "blabbed," and is forever recalling
what she has said.    "Where is my wit?" she asks; for
wit is her boast — to it she is always trying to subject
her words and actions.    There is no full, free resignation,
but she is continually catching herself and her utterances,
as if her thought had to go back and take a glance at
itself.    Her mind is her pride; she is really ashamed of
her love.    Cressida is best designated by calling her the
opposite of that which Troilus describes himself to be:

> "I am as true as truth's simplicity,
> And simpler than the infancy of truth."

For she is full of falsity and stratagem.    Both take a
vow of eternal fidelity, yet with a wonderful difference of
manner, which is prophetic of the future.

To this love-thread must be added the appearance of
Helen and Paris.    They hardly belong to the action, and the
pretext upon which they are introduced is very slender.
But thereby we are forced to cast a glance into the remote
background of the war, and observe their relation to Troilus
and Cressida.    Their life is a sensual resignation to love;
for its sake all ethical ties are disregarded, even nationality is jeopardized.    But it is the god to whom absolute
submission must be yielded; the song of Pandarus
declares its almighty power as well as its pang.    Paris is
kept out of the fray by the spell of Helen, while all his
guiltless brothers are fighting in the front rank of battle.
So, too, Troilus disarms himself when his heart is sub-

dued—the spirit of love is stronger than the spirit of war. Helen has already manifested the infidelity which Cressida will hereafter manifest; the husband, Menelaus, who seeks to recover his wife by force of arms, is not less devoted than Troilus, the lover. It is the story of women faithless and of men faithful; the ordinary romance is reversed. Thus the famous couple are dismissed; they will not be further employed by the Poet, who must not repeat his theme, and, hence, must pass to the consequences of that memorable elopement, namely, the siege of Troy. But we catch a glimpse of their world, its sweet dalliance and sensual indulgence; there is enthroned the queen of beauty whose might none can resist. Even Hector, it is declared—Hector, the true husband and stern warrior—would yield to the blandishments of this mortal Venus:

—"Sweet Helen, I must woo you
To help unarm our Hector. His stubborn buckles,
With these your white, enchanting fingers touch'd,
Shall more obey than to the edge of steel,
Or force of Greekish sinews. You shall do more
Than all the island Kings—disarm great Hector."

2. We now pass to the war-thread, the structure of which is somewhat complex, and, therefore, must be carefully analyzed. In the first place, there are two sides — the Trojan and the Grecian — which are arrayed against each other in war. But, in the second place, each side has two parties or factions, which are opposed to each other mainly, though not wholly, on questions of policy. These internal differences are now to be portrayed; the characters which maintain the conflicting opinions are to be grouped and designated; the means are to be shown whereby each side arrives at a substantial harmony within

itself.   Such is the first movement — from separation to union.

(*a.*)  The siege has lasted seven years, and still the walls of Troy are standing.   The Grecian princes have lost hope, and seem ready to abandon the enterprise. Failure has to be acknowledged ; there can be no longer any disguise.   It is a situation of despair ; a great national undertaking must be given up, whose abandonment comes next to the loss of civil freedom.   This is the trying political situation.   What is its cause, and what is its cure? The heroes have to address themselves to the dangerous condition of affairs ; their various characters will be manifested according to their conduct in the present emergency ; it is a time which tries men's souls.

The first speaker is Agamemnon, commander-in-chief. He utters the word of hope.   It is true that their plans have hitherto failed, but such is the course of all great enterprises ; something always arises to obstruct them — the realization never equals the thought.   "Persistive constancy" is the supreme test of manhood ; let us not give way to adverse fortune.   The language of Agamemnon is full of dignity and encouragement ; in him center the aspirations of the Greek army — he represents its desire, its purpose, its endurance, but not its intelligence. He does not speak of the cause of the ill success of the war, nor of the remedy for the present evils ; he can attribute them only to the caprice of fortune — a solution which always indicates blindness.   Empty hope, perseverance without reason, good intention without power, he possesses in a high degree ; as leader, he is hardly more than a respectable figure-head.   But it must not be thought that he is out of place.   He brings to his office rank, character, experience, and personal dignity, which, perhaps, could not be found so happily blended in any other chieftain; the brain, however, must be supplied from a different source. Thus Agamemnon, notwithstanding his high position, seems a puppet to a certain extent, for he does not furnish the ultimate moving principle.

Next comes Nestor, "the old man eloquent," who echoes the sentiments of the commander, and enforces them by new arguments and illustrations. In him the orator appears; he adorns his speech with the graces of diction, employing a great profusion of figures and speaking in a vein of strong enthusiasm. The distinction in their styles of address is plainly indicated by Ulysses: The words of Nestor are beautifully ornamented, "hatched in silver," while those of Agamemnon are more strong and homely, and should be held up "high in brass." But the character of the old hero is the interesting point. Nestor is not the man who creates, but is the man who appreciates and gives utterance to the thought of others. The new plan is laid before him; his opinion is decisive. Too old for invention, his powers of judgment have increased with age; none of the passions of youth or the jealousies of leadership obscure his vision; his mind grasps the thing as it is, without the least taint of prejudice. But the thought must first be brought before him — he cannot originate it; the choice of what is best is his strength. Appreciation and expression are the salient points of the white-haired sage of the Greeks.

Now, to complete the triad of characters, we must have the originator — the man of creative intelligence. Here he appears, and is on the point of speaking. Ulysses — for such is his name — is the supreme personage of the drama; the proportions of his intellect are truly colossal.

He understands the difficulty at once, and sees the remedy. Above all human beings, he possesses insight and invention; he clearly comprehends the causes of the existing evils and knows their cure. He will not be content to utter innocent platitudes — that fortune is fickle, that men must be patient, that reverses show the true worth of the warrior. Failure has overtaken the expedition; there is some good reason for it, and he intends to go to the bottom of the matter. The disease, however deep-seated, must be discovered, and then the medicine can be applied. Such a discussion will lead Ulysses to examine the whole organization of the Greeks before Troy, and his argument will draw in the general principles of all social institutions, and even of individual conduct.

Such is the representative group of the one party in the Grecian army; it is the positive, patriotic party, which believes in prosecuting the war to a glorious termination. This element is common to the three, but the fine gradation in their characterization should be distinctly noticed. Agamemnon is the embodiment of all the lofty impulses of the grand national enterprise, and, hence, is truly the leader of the people; but his limitations are his feelings — faith, hope, perseverance, good intention, cannot take the place of knowledge. Nestor rises higher; he has appreciative intelligence united with the golden gift of persuasion. He first repeats the somewhat empty exhortations of Agamemnon, but, when the deeper nature of Ulysses opens its treasures for his judgment, he yields an unhesitating assent. The apex is, of course, occupied by Ulysses, whose crowning gift is, as before said, creative intelligence.

Let us now listen to what such a man has to say about the nature of the existing evils and their remedy, for certainly his words will be worthy of attention. "The spe-

cialty of rule hath been neglected "— the individual has
not performed the particular function allotted to him;
there has been no subordination — and, hence, no organization — in the Grecian army. To illustrate his principle,
Ulysses goes through the physical and intellectual universe :
the same law of harmony prevails everywhere. The plan-
etary system, with its central power, " Sol, in noble emi-
nence enthroned and sphered," is a striking example,
which is here elaborated in great detail. But it is the
social fabric — the institutions of man — in which the
necessity of degree, of subordination, is most plainly
manifested. Without it the whole realized world of right
would crumble to ruin; there would be no security for
the weak, no respect for age or consanguinity; Astraea
would again take her flight to the skies :

> " Strength should be lord of imbecility,
> And the rude son should strike his father dead ;
> Force should be right ; or, rather, right and wrong —
> Between whose endless jar justice resides —
> Should lose their names, and so should justice, too."

Ulysses sees plainly that subordination is the primal law
of institutional life ; each person must fill his place in the
community and must freely submit to what is above himself. But why not let institutions perish? Then man
perishes. The individual is reduced to the wild beast of
nature, with all its voracity ; he will at once proceed to
devour his own species. This ultimate reduction is also
stated in all its force and abstractness by the old Greek
thinker, or, rather, by Shakespeare :

> " Then everything includes itself in power,
> Power into will, will into appetite ;
> And appetite, an universal wolf,
> So doubly seconded with will and power,
> Must make perforce an universal prey,
> And last eat up itself."

Such is the logical outcome of "this neglection of degree;" it is the destruction of institutions, and the destruction of institutions is the destruction of man. The result springs from the most severe dialectical process: The individual is resolved into appetite, and appetite, being universalized, must consume all, which includes itself. No words could more distinctly prove that the Poet was in the habit of *thinking*, in the true sense of the term — that is, of testing every principle by the form of universality. If this were written by a poet of to-day, it would be laughed at by many a critic as a specimen of pure German transcendentalism. That the inference before mentioned is not far-fetched, note again the language with care. Man becomes mere appetite, which is an *universal* wolf; this wolf must, of necessity, make an *universal* prey, till it finally comes back to itself, and at last *eats up itself.* With what absolute precision is the negative result drawn; with what remorseless rigor is the whole philosophy of sensualism burnt to ashes in two or three short sentences! And must the confession be made? Be merciful, oh ye gods; the statement has the very manner — or, if you please, the very knack — of the Hegelian Dialectic, the most terrible of all metaphysical goblins. Having said this, let us pray, now or never — "Angels and ministers of grace, defend us."

There is such a determination on the part of many writers to reduce the greatest and wisest of poets to the same dimensions as themselves, that any attempt to exhibit his thought is met with a storm of ridicule. Here is the lurking egotism: To be sure, Shakespeare is the supreme genius of the world, but I can exhaust him at a single hasty reading; to be sure, his intellect is most profound, but I can probe it to the bottom at a glance.

It is so flattering to human vanity, and so easy compared
with the tediousness of study, to say: I did not see that
meaning when I read the play, and, therefore, it does not
exist at all. But the fact remains that Shakespeare
gives many indications of being acquainted with former
systems of thought; his allusions to Plato and Aristotle,
even in his earliest works, would show that he had already
in youth delved in the richest mines of ancient speculation. His power over abstract expression can be seen in
all his writings, but it is the great and abiding interest of
this drama that he gives the most direct and purest statement of his views of nature, man, and society. That
there should be striking coincidences of ideas, and even
of method, between the greatest thinker and the greatest
poet, without either's borrowing from the other, is most
credible; both have the same ultimate thought, though
its utterance is, in general, very different; each expresses
the deepest and subtlest principle of his age — the
one employing mainly the abstract forms of thought, the
other mainly the poetic forms of imagination.

Such is the argument for the institutional world put
into the mouth of Ulysses by Shakespeare. Never did
thought defend more sternly and successfully the choicest
acquisitions of the race. Still, to careful students of the
Poet the doctrines are not new. Though he has nowhere
else expressed them so completely, they really form the
ground-work of all his dramas, and are the inspiration of
his poetical activity. Why is Shakespeare the greatest of
poets? Not because of his language, or of his imagery,
or of his constructive ability, or even of his characterization; these are all very wonderful, indeed, but they have
been reached by lesser minds. His supreme greatness

lies in his comprehension and embodiment of the ethical
— that is, institutional — world; its profoundest collisions
he penetrates with his inevitable glance; he knows, too,
their mediation and final solution. It has been the object
of these essays, as the reader doubtless has perceived, to
drop all minor points of view and hold the eye unswerv-
ingly upon this one element. It is truly the Shakespearian
world, into which a person must be initiated if he would
wish to stand face to face with the great bard. If we
suffer the mind to lose itself in the externalities of his Art
— in the words, in the figures, in the versification, or even
in the characters — we can obtain but a very partial and
very cloudy reflex of the total man.

A further observation may be added. The importance
of this institutional element is not confined to the study
of Shakespeare; it is the deepest moving principle of that
which is vital and permanent in all literature, from the
Homeric Epos to the modern novel. Men will cherish and
hold on to what is highest in themselves, and the work of
Art must adumbrate something which is of eternal interest; such are the conflicts in the Family, State, Society,
and institutions generally. Criticism would do well to
pay attention to them if it would rise out of the realm of
mere subjective opinion to the dignity of a science, for
thus it abandons caprice and fastens itself upon the most
objective realities.

Ulysses has now laid bare the evil under which the
Grecian army is suffering; its logical consequence also
has been unfolded. But these words are still general.
Who are the authors of this present state of affairs? This
question brings us to the other party of the Greeks.
Achilles, the mightiest warrior of them all, has withdrawn

from active participation in the conflict and stays in his tent, mocking their discomfiture. The motive is offended vanity; he has grown "dainty of his worth;" he has not obtained the position which he thinks that his merit deserves. He also disapproves of the manner of conducting the war — there is too much strategy and too little fighting. An additional motive is given later — his tenderness for one of Priam's daughters, Polyxena. To Achilles is joined Patroclus, his friend, who here appears as a merry mocker, caricaturing the leaders of the opposite party. But his humor has nothing malicious or bitter in it; his chief object is to make the weary hours fly more swiftly by some amusement.

Ajax, too, has turned sore-head, and refuses to fight; his grievance also seems to be mainly unappreciated merit, though he is infected with the example of Achilles. Ajax represents mere physical strength without brain; he is an immense mass of muscle. The difference between him and Achilles is that the latter has also bodily dexterity, and is possessed of more mind, though this is not excessive. Still, both maintain the side of force against the intellectual direction of the war, as upheld by Ulysses. To Ajax is joined Thersites, one of the most prominent characters of the play, whose utterances have impressed some critics so strongly that he has been considered to represent Shakespeare's own opinions concerning the Trojan war and its heroes. The main purport of the whole drama has thus been found in his sayings. Thersites reflects the negative element of the Grecian enterprise; he sees the weak side, and only the weak side, of everybody and everything; in this field lies all his intellectual shrewdness. ·He is, therefore, the supreme fault-finder;

his speech is nothing but biting satire; his "gall coins slanders like a mint." He cannot comprehend that which is universal and supreme in such a national undertaking; but he has the keenest eye and the sharpest tongue for the petty faults and foibles of the leaders, who are, after all, only the instruments for the accomplishment of a great principle. Ajax sets him to reviling the chiefs of the opposite party, though little of his abuse of them appears in the play, for Thersites evidently appreciated the intellect of Ulysses; but upon Ajax and Achilles he pours the full flood of his bile. Thersites and Patroclus are both attendants, and, to a certain extent, take the place of clowns; but the latter is a sportive humorist, who can laugh at the ridiculous phase of a cause which he at last dies for, while the former is the pure satirist, whose soul is blasted with its own curse, and who can have no principle to die for. He is, therefore, an arrant coward.

Such are the two parties which have developed themselves in the Grecian army. It is the struggle between the hand and the head — between force and intellect. Ulysses states the difficulty: The carefully elaborated policy of the leaders is called cowardice; wisdom is counted no member of the war — brain is to be governed by brawn:

> —"The still and mental parts
> That do contrive how many hands shall strike
> When fitness calls them on, and know by measure
> Of their observant toil the enemies' weight —
> Why this hath not a finger's dignity,
> They call this bed-work; mappery, closet-war."

And so withdraw from the field of battle. These are the public reasons which Achilles and Ajax give for their course, though their private, and doubtless more potent, reason has already been stated to be a lack of due appreciation of their deserts.

But now comes the remedy, for intelligence here, too, must assert its supremacy and control in some way these men of muscle ; they must be won.  Ulysses will be equal to the emergency ; the challenge just received from Troy furnishes the opportunity.  His plan is to divide the opposite party.  Ajax can be secured by a little flattery, which is at once administered with astonishing effect, for it even turns him into an enemy of his fellow-grumbler, Achilles.  But the latter is a far more difficult case to manage, for he is not stupid, and really knows his own worth.  No extravagant laudation can catch him ; indeed, he has long been used to it, and must have yielded ere this if such means were sufficient.  On the contrary, the extraordinary marks of admiration which are still shown him by the Greeks serve to keep alive his haughty pride.  Therefore the opposite method must be employed with him — instead of praise, neglect.  Since it is applause which ruins him, Ulysses proposes to elevate another man over him :

—"By device let blockish Ajax draw
The sort to fight with Hector; among ourselves
Give him allowance for the better man,
For that will physic the great Myrmidon,
Who broils in loud applause, and make him fall
His crest, that prouder than blue Iris bends."

How clear the diagnosis and how suitable the medicine !  It will be noticed that Ulysses always takes Nestor into counsel ; the two then control Agamemnon.  Nestor is the man of supreme appreciation.  He, too, had his plan, for he first advised that Achilles be selected as the antagonist of Hector, but he at once abandons his own scheme

when he hears the better one of Ulysses. He is not good
at origination, but his judgment is without a cloud —
without a trace of personal vanity.

The plan is carried into execution. Achilles is passed
by without the customary marks of respect from the
Greeks; he notices the slight and muses on the fickleness
of popular favor. While in this mood Ulysses passes
before him, perusing a book with great intentness. A
strange book was that for camp-reading in Homeric times.
Ulysses cites from it the remarkable statement that man

> "Cannot make boast to have that which he hath,
> Nor feels not what he owes, but by reflection."

What can this mean, asks the horrified modern reader,
with the metaphysical bugbear rising in his imagination.
But Achilles, though rather lean in intellect, clearly understands the passage, for he illustrates it with a striking and
appropriate comparison; indeed, to him "this is not
strange at all." Wonderful men were those old heroes!
The seed has fallen on good ground, and Ulysses enforces
the same doctrine a second time with a much stronger
turn of expression:

> —"No man is the lord of anything,
> Though in and of him there be much consisting,
> Till he communicate his parts to others;
> Nor doth he of himself know them for aught
> Till he behold them formed in the applause
> Where they are extended."

The metaphysical deluge is again upon us. Is there,
then, no plan of salvation? But the matter keeps getting
worse. We might have pardoned that former abstruse
discussion on institutions, for it was a theme so dear to the

Poet; yet now he plunges remorselessly into the deepest psychological question known to philosophy. But what has the devout man to do except to struggle after, with the prayerful hope of soon touching bottom? Ulysses here states the doctrine of reflection, and, what is more strange, he uses for its designation exactly the term employed in modern systems of thought. Man cannot truly possess anything unless his possession is reflected through others: nay, he cannot truly know anything till his knowledge is reflected back to himself through others. Then both possession and knowledge are real—objective; otherwise, they are idle figments of the brain.

All this reasoning, however, only prepares the way for a practical application of the doctrine to Achilles, who is thus caught in the web of his own principle. He has retired from active warfare. Can he be surprised, then, if he finds himself no longer reflected in the applause of the Greeks, but that Ajax has taken his place? The case is clear; all past fame is lost unless rescued by present activity. The controlling motive of his character is now reached, and to it is added the stinging reproach that he, the great warrior of Greece, submits to be the lover of one of Priam's daughters. Ulysses departs; and it shows the character of Patroclus—that he has before urged, and now again urges, these same views upon his friend. Patroclus is at bottom a patriot, though he must have his joke at the expense of the leaders. The opposition of Achilles is manifestly broken, though he does not directly say that he will return and take part in the war. But afterwards he is present with the other Greek leaders at the intended combat between Ajax and Hector, and there challenges the Trojan hero.

So harmony seems again to be restored in the Greek
army. It is the brain of Ulysses which is everywhere
seen in these transactions; the feat is purely intellectual.
When the fighting comes he steps into the background, and
the interest diminishes. The great error of Grecian discipline — lack of subordination — he exposes; the breach
between the leaders he heals by winning Ajax and then
Achilles. Such is the one side in this war. We are now
ready to pass over to the other side, and take a glance at
its internal condition.

(*b.*) The Trojans have also two parties within their
walls; the division springs from a question of policy,
namely, the surrender of Helen. A message has been
received that her delivery to the Greeks will end the
war. Upon this subject we are now to hear the delib-
erations.

Around Priam, who presides and who seems rather to
favor the surrender, is gathered the wonderful group of
his sons. Hector advises to give her up. The hazards of
war are uncertain; many lives have been lost, and, moreover, Helen is worthless in character. It can be seen that
Hector advances the ethical view; caprice and passion
cannot sway his judgment; the Good is something real,
and not an individual whim; "value dwells· not in the
particular will." This last expression again sounds like a
technical term of the schools, and vividly recalls *der
besondere Wille* of German philosophy. But the strongest
argument of Hector is based upon the right of the Family,
of which the abduction of Helen was a gross violation;
"the law of nature and nations" demands to have the
wife restored to the husband. The religious element of
Troy — represented by the priest, Helenus, and the proph-

etess, Cassandra — urge the same view of the question
after their own peculiar methods.

But Paris and Troilus are strongly opposed to her surrender. The former claims that he had the consent of
them all for his act. Still, if this were not the case, he
would cling to his prize, for his controlling principle is,
not moral goodness, but sensual love, which has its com-
pletest embodiment in the beauty of Helen. Troilus
argues decidedly in the same direction. His own relation
to Cressida renders him susceptible of the passion which
now darkens his judgment; but he has also another and
better motive — the maintenance of the majesty of the
King, his father, and of the dignity of his country. To
this last aspect of the subject Hector finally assents,
clearly against his notions of right. National honor, but
chiefly personal glory, quench the claims of conscience.
Retribution will overtake both, in accordance with the
nature of their deeds, as we shall see hereafter. So the
great warrior is won, the two parties have fused, and
Troy is substantially united in the determination to keep
Helen.

Here ends the first movement with its two threads, both
of which have a tendency toward unity. The war-thread
which has just been developed has, perhaps, the most
purely intellectual tinge found in the works of Shakespeare. So much reflection and so little action, so much
deliberation and so little passion, cannot be pointed out
elsewhere in his dramas. Then there is Ulysses, the
supremely intellectual hero in a far higher sense than
Hamlet. For Hamlet's mind is defective, if not diseased;
it is forever caught in its own cobwebs, and cannot march
forward to the deed. But the thought of Ulysses, so pro-

found yet so transparent, never destroys itself, but proceeds by necessity to realization; it must find itself reflected, to use his own term, in the world around him.

II. But now the character of the whole drama begins to change; the thought becomes more jejune, the structure more fragmentary and confused. The second movement, which commences here, is far inferior to that which has preceded, and grows worse till the end. But the two threads can still be followed, though their demarkation is by no means as plain and sharp as it was in the previous movement.

1. The love-thread, which portrayed the happy culmination in the emotional union of the pair, Troilus and Cressida, is now to exhibit their separation — both external and internal, both in space and in spirit. Calchas, the father of Cressida, who has performed many important services for the Greeks, demands that she be exchanged for a noble Trojan prisoner and brought to the Greek camp. The request is granted; Cressida has to leave Troy and Troilus; Diomed is sent to bring her to her parent. The parting scene of the lovers manifests anew their characters. Troilus feels the possibility of Cressida's desertion; she will be unable to resist the grace and flattery of her Grecian suitors. To be sure, she spurns the imputation of infidelity, but devotion has never been her supreme principle; hence her readiness to change individuals. The chivalrous bearing and sweet compliments of Diomed seem to touch her favor, even in this scene, where she is taking leave of Troilus, who shows decided marks of jealousy — not without cause. She passes to the Grecian camp, where each hero gives her a kiss in turn, though Ulysses, the wise man, passes judgment upon

her character. That judgment is very severe; it implies
that she is without modesty and without fidelity.

She is already in love with Diomed; the tie of affection
which bound her to Troilus is broken. The latter comes
from Troy and beholds with his own eyes her faithlessness,
and hears with his own ears her declaration of desertion.
The struggle is a most intense one, but he gives her up
and slips "the bonds of Heaven." She says that her eye
leads her mind — her love is for the last man whom she
looks upon. The sensual side of her nature is here most
strongly emphasized, whereas in the first movement her
striking trait was the cool understanding which held control over her emotions; this is not a contradiction, perhaps,
but certainly a difference. There is no retribution for
her act; judged by Shakespeare's usual method, her
treatment is incomplete. But Troilus has tasted a little
of his own advice before the Trojan council. He would
not permit the wife, Helen, to be restored to her husband;
the advocate of violent separation is himself separated
from her whom he loved. Still, the fact remains that the
faithful man is punished and the faithless woman goes
free.

2. The war-thread is next to be carried forward from
the point where it was left. The hostile sides, having
come to internal unity, are prepared for the external fight.
Diomed is the messenger, and while he is among the
Trojans he has occasion to give his opinion of the war.
It is an intensely satirical view; both Paris and Menelaus
equally deserve Helen, since they make no "scruple of
her soilure," and the whole commotion is only a scramble
for a strumpet. Diomed, like many a soldier since his
time, evidently wishes that he had not enlisted, and damns

the war. It has been already noticed that Thersites holds the same view; "nothing but lechery, all incontinent varlets," is his unvarnished characterization of the struggle and the heroes. But Diomed is a warrior and a chivalrous gentleman, while Thersites is the universal fault-finder and base coward. These two persons represent, in the main, the satirical element which some critics have found in the entire play, notwithstanding its far more elevated positive characters.

The single combat between Ajax and Hector now takes place, in the true mediæval fashion. But there is not satire here, in the proper sense of the term, for satire selects the weaknesses, the finite elements, of an individual, society, or great enterprise, and holds them up to scorn and indignation. There is, however, burlesque in the entire account of the challenge and the duel, for burlesque puts its content into an alien form, as in the present instance the old Homeric personages and occurrences are thrust into the manners of chivalry. But, notwithstanding this humorous coloring, the collision of the two nations is genuine and earnest. The combatants meet; after a little fencing, sufficient to clear the honor of both, Hector refuses to fight Ajax, since the latter is his cousin. Hector, though of the loftiest courage and generosity, is without pride; he is the antithesis of Achilles. He will not shed the blood of his own family, even if hostile; though the disgrace of the surrender hangs over him, he offers to throw down his weapons and to embrace his "father's sister's son."

So ends the first combat. Hector visits the Grecian princes; he receives knightly welcome and sumptuous entertainment. He there is greeted with a challenge from

Achilles, who, however, will first honor him with the most gracious hospitality. There is a vein of incongruity running through these scenes which, added to the merry bantering of the chieftains, produces a ridiculous effect. But the challenge of Achilles is countermanded by a secret letter from Troy. Love in his case, too, triumphs over war; his "major vow" is the pledge sworn to Polyxena. Thus the persuasive words of Ulysses are lost; the strongest motive of Achilles is here, not wounded pride — as we would certainly have inferred from the previous movement — but his passion for Priam's daughter.

But there is still another change in the motivation — his friendship for Patroclus is more powerful than even his love, since the death of Patroclus rouses him to go to battle, in which he slays Hector, though in a manner most cowardly and wholly inconsistent with both his previous position and character. It will thus be seen that the most elaborate and most profound part of the play — the reconciliation of Achilles through the dexterity of Ulysses — is without a purpose; it is a colossal instrumentality which produces no ultimate effect. On the contrary, a motive almost unknown, and certainly not developed in the drama, is dragged in from Homer to determine the result. Also, there is a change in Hector; the most noble, generous, and humane of all the chieftains, Grecian or Trojan, perishes, though there is an attempt to justify his fate through his disregard of the entreaties of parents, sister, and wife, and of the omens of Heaven. But the deeper ethical retribution was prepared long before in the Trojan council, when he surrendered conviction mainly to desire for personal glory; the result is, he is destroyed in its pursuit. But the parting scene at Priam's palace is clearly the motive intended here, and thus produces a new discrepancy.

The termination of this drama resembles a goodly ship going to pieces amid the breakers; gradually it splits asunder, and nothing is seen but the disconnected fragments floating on the surface of the angry waters. The play is literally wrecked. The characters become different, and even inconsistent; the great preparations of the first movement are inadequately carried out, or entirely dropped; the action and the structure are confused; unnecessary parts are introduced, and necessary parts are omitted. To name the work has given great difficulty; it is not comedy, tragedy, history, or mediated drama; inasmuch as the true end is wanting, there can be no complete proof for any designation. As it stands, the war-thread terminates in the death of Hector, which must pass for tragic, though Hector is not the leading character of this thread. But the love-thread ends in mere separation, which is no solution at all, as there is no requital for the deed.

There is always a strong impulse to think out for ourselves some worthy termination of the work — to construct anew this noble dramatic temple from its ruins, in accordance with the established principles of the Architect. The usual method of Shakespeare is to reward the fidelity of the woman with a restoration of her estranged lover — Julia, Helena, Hermione, Imogen; but the fidelity of the man to a treacherous or unreciprocating beauty is compensated by bestowing upon him another mistress, who will be faithful, as is seen in the first and second loves of Romeo, and in the case of Duke Orsino. The devoted Troilus deserves a change of individuals. Certainly none of the characters of this thread have a tragic motive. On the whole, the tendency seems to be toward mediation, though that tendency is by no means fulfilled. So much for the love-thread. The course of the war-thread might be: Achilles, under the influence of the intellect of Ulysses, is reconciled with the Greeks; goes forth to meet Hector and slays him; the restoration of Helen follows, with peace between the contending peoples. Thus the national collision is solved, and in the first movement of the play there is much to indicate some such conclusion. In this manner the present negative end is brought to a positive reconciliation in both the threads, namely, war ends in peace, and fidelity is rewarded with fruition. To reconstruct Shakespeare is an act of temerity, but it may be permitted to his faithful readers to think as complete what he has without doubt left incomplete.

The purport of the whole play has been supposed to be satirical and also humorous. That both these elements are present in it must be at once granted, but they are subordinate. The collision is serious — between nations, and on both sides there is violation and justification — a wrong and a right. The Greeks vindicate the Family, but assail the State; while the Trojans vindicate nationality, but violate the Family. It is a genuine conflict in these institutions, and not a delusion. Moreover, the leading characters on both sides are imbued with deep earnestness. The satirists and merry-makers, in one form and another, are found in all conflicts of society, and, hence, they are not absent even from the tragedies of Shakespeare. To account for the marked inequality in this drama, conjecture has not been idle; the weak part is variously supposed to have been written by the Poet in his youth, or in a bad mood, or not at all by him, but by some other playwright or playwrights. It is, perhaps, immaterial which view is adopted; they have all quite the same degree of probability, and rest upon equally good evidence.

# CORIOLANUS.

*Coriolanus* is essentially a drama of Political Parties. Internal dissension, through partisan organizations, is shown in a variety of forms; also, other elements, as foreign war and the domestic relation, intermingle in the action and diversify its incidents and coloring. Moreover, the warring principles of the two parties are aristocracy and democracy — the conflict which has always in History been most prolific of political strife. The main characters are graded according to their partisan bias and intensity, for the essence of the conflict is party versus country. Finally, the heroic figure of the drama is a person who cannot subordinate his hatred against a party to his love for his country. Great as is Coriolanus, Rome must get rid of him, and all like him, before she can conquer the world.

It will be seen that the action exhibits two distinct movements — the one of which terminates in the banishment of the hero, the other in his death. Coriolanus is portrayed as the great defender of his country, but also as the greater enemy of the plebeians; partisan rancor leads to his expulsion — to his separation from Family and State. Herein both sides commit wrong. Such is the first movement. The second movement shows Coriolanus passing over to the enemies of his country, in order to ruin it and thereby ruin the opposite party. Patriotism is subordinate to partisan hate; even attachment to his own

15

class cannot outweigh his desire for revenge. His nation and his order, therefore, cannot mediate his hostility to a party, but his family can, though at the cost of the life of himself, one of its members.

On the other hand, the two threads which run through the whole play are the political and domestic, in their manifold relation and interaction. The political thread is shown in both its internal and external manifestations, namely, in partisan dissension and in foreign war; while the domestic thread — the Family — has its various sides represented in the mother, wife, husband, son, father, neighbor, and friend.

I. 1. Taking up the first thread, we find that at the very beginning of the play the key-note is struck — internal dissension through parties. The people are riotous — not without cause, for they want bread; they also recognize their chief enemy among the patricians to be Caius Marcius (Coriolanus). But even among the people is heard the voice of moderation — a citizen appeals to them to remember his services to the country. The demagogue, too, is present, who thrives on sedition and whose tendency always is to subordinate State to Party. Thus the one side is shown in its excess. Marcius now comes before us as the representative of the other extreme. He reproaches the populace with cowardice, insubordination, and fickleness, employing an intensity of language which could only provoke wrath, and even descends to mocking their personal habits — nay, he is ready to destroy them utterly:

> " Would the nobility lay aside their ruth
> And let me use my sword, I'd make a quarry
> With thousands of these quartered slaves, as high
> As I could pick my lance."

Here is manifested the wrong of Coriolanus; he seems to think that nobody has even the right of life except his party. It is clear that no State can exist with such contending elements in its bosom; one side must be eliminated.

But as we saw a moderate man among the plebeians, so also there will appear a mediator of patrician blood. This is Menenius, an old man of noble stock, but beloved by the people. His object is conciliation; his stand-point is the common country of both high and low; he reaches the people by his homely anecdotes. The fable of the belly and members treats of the necessity of harmony in an organization; each member must fulfill its function, and yet be subordinate to the purpose of the whole. Still, Menenius insists more strongly upon the central or controlling principle, as a good patrician should do; the people are to be cared for like an eternal baby. But they are determined to have established rights, and the special power of the tribunes to enforce them. Just now they are asserting the right to live against the right of property; they must have something to eat, though the corn belongs to another. It is the old story of all revolutions — a vested right has become a great fetter and a great wrong. The extreme principle of Coriolanus is to maintain what is established and to destroy the innovators; Menenius would also maintain the ancient system of things, with a paternal guardianship of the people. But the latter will be — indeed, are already — an integral, not an accidental, element of the body politic; they have secured certain privileges and the means for enforcing them, and thus participate also in the established institutions of the country.

But this internal conflict must now cease in the presence

of the external one — the war with the Volscians. Here, again, there are two contending elements, each of which must be brought before the reader. The Volscian State is faintly sketched; it does not differ essentially from the Roman. We are told of a Senate and Senators; there is a hint of a system of espionage. But the main figure on the Volscian side is Aufidius, who is portrayed quite as the counterpart of Coriolanus, though with a personal jealousy which is foreign to the character of the latter. There is no world-historical principle at stake — the whole war has the appearance of a predatory foray, though Rome is, of course, defending the existence of the State, which has been attacked from without.

To turn now to the Roman side, we find that the campaign has been so arranged as to display the valor of Coriolanus in its most colossal manifestation. The army is in two divisions, though the hero is apparently a private soldier. The division in which he is present attacks the Volscian town. The Roman soldiery, made up of the common people, flee, while he maintains the contest single-handed; through his prowess mainly the town is taken. The contrast is here evident. Coriolanus possesses in the highest degree the patrician virtue of personal courage, which is not so highly developed in plebeian blood. But this is not the end of his heroic feats. He passes to the second division of the Roman army, distant "not a mile," which has just been driven back. With his presence victory returns, and for the sixth time he vanquishes his valiant foeman, Aufidius. We now see the clear outlines of his character; his chief trait is declared to be personal pride — strength of individuality — which he is ready to assert against every restraining power. With this pride

the institutions of his country will conflict. The question
is: Which principle must be subordinated?

He is received in Rome with great rejoicing; his family
and his friends crowd around; the Senate gives him a
public reception. But he is too proud — for it is hardly
modesty — to hear his own praise; he seems almost to disdain recognition from mortals. In the general joy, party
is forgotten by the plebeians, and he is elected consul.
But he despises the means; the humiliating ceremony in
presence of the people to which he is forced by them has
excited his disgust and wrath; party spirit is again aroused
and his election is revoked. Coriolanus cannot submit to
an institution — his individual will is supreme. This first
discipline of office — the suppression of his personal caprice
and the submission to the established custom — cannot
be endured by him:

> " What custom wills, in all things should we do't
> The dust on antique time would lie unswept,
> And mountainous error be too highly heaped
> For truth to o'erpeer."

Hence on this side he is as revolutionary as the plebeians. The two parties thus reach the same point — the
destruction of the institutions which restrain their tendencies. The patricians, however, as the true conservative
element of society, seek to conciliate both sides and to
retain the ancient laws and customs of the nation.

The next step of Coriolanus is to attempt to unite his
order into a violent party, and to take away the tribunate
and other privileges of the people. He appeals to the
nobles with powerful arguments, but his effort is in vain.
It is not their principle; indeed, it is the duty of authority
to prevent the State from dissolving into its elements.

Here is the point where Coriolanus separates from his order — the one subordinates State to Party, the other subordinates Party to State. Thus a new conflict arises. Coriolanus turns against his order, and falls back upon his own individual will — his pride — which he will assert against both parties, and even against the State. What is the result? He must leave, since such a man cannot be mediated; family, friends, class, are all brought in, but they cannot reconcile him with the existing order of things. He suffers the fate of the heroic individual amid institutions — he is banished.

2. We now pass to the domestic thread, which mingles with, and finally determines, the political thread of the drama. The Family, in its various elements, is brought before us in a series of marked characters, representing its different relations. Volumnia, the mother of Coriolanus, is the typical Roman matron, who has subordinated her maternal instincts to the feeling of nationality. The death of her son she even could rejoice in, did it occur on the field of battle in defense of his country. Still, she is a patrician in the strongest sense of the word, though she does not carry it so far as to allow class-pride to conflict with her love for the whole Roman nation. There is no place for her husband here; hence the Poet has most judiciously omitted all notice of him. Moreover, Coriolanus is clearly his mother's son, in the sense that he has inherited many of her qualities. Alongside of Volumnia, whose highest principle is nationality, is placed Virgilia, the wife, whose domestic tendencies and whose deep feeling of Family constitute a strong contrast to her mother-in-law. She will not even stir out of the house till her lord return from the wars. She is quiet and unobtrusive; her world

is in the domestic emotions — in the love of her husband and child. Little as is said of her, we nevertheless behold the clear outlines of the ethical female character, which never fails to subdue the strongest men. Coriolanus has thus chosen a wife of a nature quite the opposite to that of his mother; both together control, finally, his will and his emotions. The little boy, the image of his father's disposition, is added to make the Family complete. The hereditary principle here involved is worthy of notice. Character descends at one time through the mother, at another time through the father; the more intense individuality perpetuates itself. To this group of relations is joined another woman from the outside, the friend and neighbor, Valeria, who manifests none of the earnest traits peculiar to the other two women, but is distinguished by a light-hearted, gossiping tendency, which has but little to do with the sober realities of State and Family.

When the news is brought concerning the battle, the mother thanks the gods that her son is wounded, but the wife is horrified at the thought. At last, when Coriolanus returns in all the glory and honor of his prowess, amid the acclamations of the people and patricians, the domestic relations of the hero are again introduced and characterized. First of all, he kneels to his mother; respect and obedience to her he regards as the supreme duty. Then he addresses his wife, who is silent, though weeping tears of joy at his triumph. The delicacy of the delineation must be felt by every reader of taste and penetration. The mother now sees her strongest wishes, her wildest fancies, realized — her son has come to be regarded as the savior of his country. One thing remains — the highest honor of the State, the summit of a Roman's

ambition, is yet to be conferred upon him.    How he
destroys his prospects by his headstrong passion and
pride, and by his hatred of the plebeians, has been
already narrated.

The family relation is introduced the third time, in
order that its attitude may be portrayed in this conflict
between Coriolanus and the people.   As the end is now a
political one, the mother alone appears, for she has a political purpose throughout the play.   What will now be her
conduct toward her son?   Will she side with his extreme
partisan views, or will she be in favor of conciliation?
Any one who has carefully observed her character hitherto
will have no difficulty in deciding which of the two courses
she will take.   Volumnia has her deepest principle in the
love of country, though she is patrician to the core, and
hates the plebeians as a party.   At this point she and her
son separate; it becomes manifest that the ultimate controlling trait of each is' different.   Even Coriolanus is
mistaken about this element of her character; he is astonished that his mother does not approve his course — she
who was wont to heap the most opprobrious epithets upon
the people.   Therefore he imagined that she as well as
himself hated the plebeians more than she loved her country.   Volumnia urges reconciliation; she advises him to
dissemble his feelings — policy is her watch-word; her
highest personal ambition is to behold her son the chief
man of the State.   Still, he is obstinate; finally she intimates that he dishonors her — that death must be the
result of his conduct.   She also strikes the true distinction between them:

> "Thy valiantness was mine, thou suck'dst it from me;
> But ow'st thy pride thyself."

Coriolanus yields, for the filial bond was the strongest in his nature; to it everything else was subordinate. He seeks the people; a word causes him to lose his temper; his mother, after all, fails to mediate his partisan hate and subordinate it to the good of the country.

Such is the first general movement of the drama. It portrays Coriolanus in his transition from being the hero of the external conflict to being the victim of the internal conflict, with the attempted mediation of the Family. The difficulty is, Coriolanus cannot pass from the soldier to the citizen—from war to peace; the man of a different class, or of the opposite party, he regards as a public enemy—as a Volscian; he transfers the intensity of the military struggle to the peaceful rivalry of the political struggle. Now, as party organizations are inherent in the very nature of the State, it is evident that such a man must be ejected from the State as incompatible with its existence. His political enemies, it is true, are not without guilt, for they seek to take every advantage of his weaknesses. Still, the blame must attach mainly to him. Now, what will such a person do in his banishment? His mother fears his disposition as well as his dark intimations; she desires Cominius to accompany him in his exile in order to keep him out of any alliance hostile to the country. How different is she at present from what she was when Coriolanus went forth to the Volscian war! Now she seems utterly broken down, for her son is disrupted from the State and her hopes are crushed forever —that is, in separating from Rome he has separated from her highest end, while he was fulfilling that end when he was in the war.

II. 1. The second general movement of the drama

exhibits Coriolanus in conflict with his country, and the successful mediation of his Family, though involving his own destruction. The main stress must, therefore, be laid, in this part, upon the external collision of the State, since the existence of the latter is threatened from without, as its repose was previously assailed from within. Coriolanus will pass over to the enemies of his nation, for such a course lies in his stand-point, as hitherto developed. His hate of the opposite party is greater than his love for the whole country; hence he can readily sacrifice the latter to the former. A patrican State, or no State at all, is the maxim of his conduct. Thus he was really not a true Roman; he did not accept the Roman constitution as developed up to that time, for that had already become a mixed government of aristocracy and democracy. Or, to state the same thing in different language, his pride has carried him into conflict with the highest institutions; that heroic individuality which shone forth with such grandeur in the Volscian war is now manifested on its negative, destructive side, for it asserts itself against the demands of patriotism. Such is the inner connection of these two movements.

(*a.*) Coriolanus, in disguise, first seeks out his greatest foe, Aufidius. Why should not they be now reconciled, since the object of their enmity has become the same — since both seek to destroy Rome? Before entering the house, Coriolanus, in a short soliloquy, seems to comprehend the true nature of his conduct; he intimates in a general way that his sudden separation from friends and country has no good ground, and that his sudden friendship for Aufidius is equally destitute of a reasonable foundation. Still, he will not, can not, retrace his steps. There is a feast in the mansion of Aufidius; the servants are busy with preparation; the host, after some delay, is brought in to Coriolanus. The latter reveals himself, announces his desertion of Fatherland, and then gives his motive and his purpose:

> — " In mere spite,
> To be full quit of those my banishers,
> Stand I before thee here.
> — I will fight
> Against my cankered country with the spleen
> Of all the under fiends."

Revenge is above life, above country. Aufidius, in the impulse of the moment, receives his new guest with the strongest expressions of gratitude and love, and offers on the spot half of his commission. Of this generosity he will afterwards repent.

The Volscian army is mustered and sets out for Rome. Coriolanus has become its idol on account of his soldierly qualities; war is just the element in which he is seen to the best advantage. Moreover, a change in his demeanor is noticed; he has quite laid aside his former insolence, and can even descend to flatter the Volscian commonalty. The reason is manifest — he is ready to subordinate his most intense personal feeling in order to acquire the means of accomplishing his revenge. But Aufidius, among his own countrymen, has been cast into the background; his jealous nature, which before showed such ugly traits, is excited anew; a conspiracy is formed for the destruction of the new-comer. When Coriolanus yields to the entreaties of his mother and spares Rome, an adequate ground of accusation is furnished, the old Volscian enmity is again stirred up, and he falls a victim to that people whose interest he had, no doubt, betrayed.

(*b.*) We now pass to the Roman side as portrayed in this thread. The city is quiet after the departure of Coriolanus, though the nobility are vexed at the result. The plebeians are now the object of the deepest hate of his mother; she curses the tribunes for their conduct toward her son. Still, with all her provocation, she does not allow her enmity of the common people to overcome her love of country. The strongest and most severe test has been given; her ultimate principle is manifest. The citizens are congratulating the tribunes on their victory, when there arrives startling news. Coriolanus has gone over to the enemy and is marching against Rome. A second messenger confirms the information; now commences the reaction. The tribunes begin to see the consequences of their conduct. First, the reproaches of the patricians are tauntingly uttered in their presence; but, secondly, their supporters — the people — are much more violent against them; in fact, their death seems imminent. Still, they have committed no crime which deserves a tragic fate; after being badly frightened, they are spared.

But the Volscians are at the gates of Rome; resistance is no longer possible there must be some speedy relief, else the city will be taken. Cominius, the old companion in arms, goes out to mollify Coriolanus; the effort is fruitless. Then Menenius, the dearest friend of Coriolanus and of his family, succeeds in reaching his presence after much difficulty. The old man with tears beseeches him to pardon his own countrymen, and tries to excite in his breast some affection for country. But class, friends, and Fatherland are subordinate to his revenge; to his partisan hate he seems ready to sacrifice all ethical institutions. Even his family he abjures: wife, mother, and child I know not, says he. But he does not comprehend fully his own nature; this form of mediation, after the failure of all others, is now to be tried.

2. Hence the domestic thread is introduced at this point in order to save the State from the impending danger. The various members of the family of Coriolanus appear before him in the Volscian camp. The internal struggle begins with great intensity in his bosom; he melts at their sight. Still, he will not "be such a gosling as to obey instinct." His wife speaks first of their sorrow caused by his conduct; but Coriolanus shows the deepest element of his character when he kneels in humble reverence before "the most noble mother of the world." She, on the contrary, offers to bow down to him with a sharp reproach of filial disrespect, an act of humiliation which seems to startle Coriolanus as the utter perversion of the true relation of persons. It is clear from these passages that his strongest instinct is reverence for his mother, and thus the outcome of her embassy must be the obedience of her son. Still, the struggle cannot be settled at once; the idea of "capitulating again with Rome's mechanics" comes up to his mind in all its repugnance. After the wife, the child, and the friend have done their part in softening his emotions, the mother takes up the argument and presents it with telling emphasis. It is the Family pleading for country with one of its members, since it must perish with that country. How dire is its wretchedness:

> "Making the mother, wife, and child to see
> The son, the husband, and the father tearing
> His country's bowels out."

Here the domestic relations are stated in full. But this is not all; the conflict extends into religion — their prayers are a contradiction. The highest principle of Volumnia has been stated to be nationality; if she cannot mediate her son with her country, she will seek death from his very act:

> " Thou shalt no sooner
> March to assault thy country than to tread
> On thy mother's womb
> That brought thee to this world."

Here we have the strongest and most terrific image of filial violation. Strange to say, the wife, Virgilia, now utters the same sentiment; her mild nature has been absorbed in the colossal will of the mother. That is, his family, in all of its relations, will be swept away in the destruction of the State. The only exception is his boy, another genuine Coriolanus, who will not submit to be trampled upon by an enemy. Still her appeals are not answered; she begins to despair of success. Then, with lofty contempt, she turns away, disowning her motherhood:

> " This fellow had a Volscian to his mother."

And all his other domestic relations are denied to him. This is too much for Coriolanus. His strongest tie he can allow to be severed; he might even contemplate his mother dead; still he would be her son. But disowned — denied to be her offspring — that cuts deeper than her death. He yields, Rome is saved, but he declares to his mother that he will probably have to die for his act. To which declaration she gives no answer — country is, with her, above son; its salvation being accomplished, she and the rest of her relatives return to receive its gratitude. Family has thus mediated the conflict of the State.

We thus find that Coriolanus did finally meet with something to which he yielded. Pride is the word employed by the Poet, and his various transitions may be regarded as so many phases of his pride — of his refusal to subordinate his individuality to any external power. First, his pride conflicts with Aufidius and the foreign enemies of Rome, and makes him the heroic and patriotic soldier of surpassing valor. Second, his pride conflicts with the plebeians, an internal party of Rome, and makes him the violent partisan. Third, his pride carries him to the extent of conflicting with the State, and makes him the enemy of his country. Fourth, his pride submits to the Family — in particular, to his mother; here, then, it has found its limitation, a limitation which is hinted on the very first page of the play. There a citizen says that Coriolanus had, first of all, as the motives of his actions, the desire to please his mother, and then pride.

The final solution of the drama, namely, this mediation of the external collision of the State through the Family, seems to be not wholly satisfactory. Wars are not thus ended, generally; the domestic element is not the reconciling principle of the nation. The difficulty lies in the original fable, and makes it indeed a fable — unnatural, impossible, but perhaps affecting on account of its very one-sidedness. When we reflect that the Roman Family was almost wholly merged in the man and in the nation, we may account for Volumnia, but Coriolanus is still a mystery, or at least an exception. Still, given these characters, with their relations as here indicated, this drama is a consistent and most skillful piece of workmanship, and is at the same time adorned with the fairest poetic coloring.

# *JULIUS CÆSAR.*

This drama may be said to exhibit the Ethical World of Shakespeare in its highest form, as well as in its most accurate gradation. Three typical characters are brought before us participating in the revolution of a great epoch. Domestic life is placed in the remote background, where, however, in the person of Portia, it shines through the tempest of political strife with a divine beauty. We now behold the Poet rising to the serenest elevation of historical insight, in which the nation is only a transitory element in the great movement of Universal History.

But, first, it would perhaps be well to enumerate some of the elements which belong to this Ethical World of Shakespeare. Those most obvious and most commonly recognized are the Individual, Family, and State. These elements have their limits against one another; hence they fall into conflict, and one must be subordinated to the other — that is, the individual may assert himself against the demands of Family or State, or the Family may come into collision with the State. It is evident that there must be a gradation of rank in these powers; one must be above another, else strife and confusion can only result. But, above all these, there is a fourth principle, which has not the taint of finitude which rests upon the others. For even the State — to which every individual must bow and every principle yield, whose absolute supremacy is expressed in the fact that its safety is the highest law —

seems, notwithstanding, to be exposed to the might of the destroying angel. The past is strewed with the wrecks of States — the empires of the Orient, Greece, Rome, the Middle Ages, have arisen and passed away; and so we must acknowledge a Power above the State which calls it into being and also puts an end to its existence. What this Power is we need not now discuss — we only wish to recognize and name it. Let us call it the Spirit of the World's History; or, more concisely, the World Spirit; or, in the language of religion, God in History. Only let us not imagine that it is some far-off Power, wholly external to man, whose arm descends and smites him to the earth without his knowing whence it cometh or whither it goeth.

Furthermore, all these principles can be vitalized only through the individual. Taken alone, they are mere abstractions, and of no force; but when a man goes forth armed with them, and makes them the basis of his action, they move the world. It is only in this way they can collide and form the foundation of a drama. An individual thus becomes the bearer of some grand ethical principle, and can come into conflict with another individual who is fulfilling the same destiny in a different sphere. For instance, a person may assert the right of individual conscience — certainly a valid principle — against the majesty of law, which is the command of the State; or, like Antigone, may prefer duty toward Family to obedience to civil authority; or, finally, there may be a still higher collision — that between the defenders of the State on the one hand, and the supporters of the World Spirit on the other. Such is the collision between nations struggling for independence and their conquerors — the collision of Carthage

# 242    JULIUS CÆSAR.

with Rome, of the Pole with the Russian, of the Hunga-
rian with the Austrian.  We feel for the fallen nation; we
may even weep over an heroic people defeated and pros-
trate.  Still, in the end we are compelled to say: It is
just; the World Spirit, whose right it is to judge the
nations, has decided against them.

Now, it is just this collision which Shakespeare has presented in *Julius Cæsar*.  For Cæsar is the representative
of the World Spirit; he appears upon the stage of History
as the destroyer of his country's liberties; hence the great
conflict of his life was with the State.  It is, indeed, this
fact which has caused him to be calumniated by nearly
twenty centuries of writers and speakers.  But note that
Shakespeare does not join in this cry of execration.  To
him Cæsar's career is not political, but world-historical;
not limited to a single State, but having the World as its
theater.  To him Cæsar stands at the head of that eternal and infinite movement in whose grasp the nations are
playthings.  But, on the other hand, let us not forget that
this movement was nothing external to Rome—it was the
movement of Rome herself; the Roman Constitution was
sapped perhaps before the birth of Cæsar.  He only
carried out the unconscious national will; he saw what
Rome needed, and possessed the strength to execute it,
and this is his greatness—and, in fact, the only real
political greatness. . That one man can overturn the form
of government permanently, against the will and spirit of
a whole people, is preposterous.  That such was not
Shakespeare's view is shown by the termination of the
play—the conspirators are overthrown and the supporters of Cæsar are unsuccessful.  But this will be more
fully pointed out hereafter.

The State has also its representatives in this conflict — Cassius and Brutus, more especially the former. They were the bearers of the spirit of the old Roman Constitution, and were strong enough to destroy the individual Cæsar, but by no means the movement which he represented. The thought of Cæsar remained, and Octavius simply steps into his place, conquers, and has peace — shuts the temple of Janus for the first time in generations. That is, Cæsar's revolution is accomplished, and the Roman people acquiesce.

With this explanation we may now consider the leading incidents of the play. The first scene introduces us to the necessary background upon which the whole drama is painted — the Roman people. Shakespeare has most truthfully depicted the populace as fickle and faithless, without any substantial fixity of purpose within itself. Hence we hurry into the next scene to find the element which gives consistency and stability to this mass. Here the two great men of the time appear, like gladiators, each one bent on the destruction of the other. Cæsar has arrived at the summit of his greatness; he is ready to receive the crown and be called king, whose functions, indeed, he already performs. This fact is to be particularly noted, as it will answer many objections that have been raised against the play. The critics are much troubled because Cæsar does not say or do anything great, and declare that he is inadequately portrayed. But the Poet represents him at the consummation of his deeds, and as the founder of a new order of things; greater he could not well be.

To be sure, a drama might be written which would exhibit Cæsar at an earlier period of his life — in the bloom of his activity, energy, and military genius. But such a drama could never present the collision which Shakespeare intended, nor in the faintest degree exhibit the ethical ideas which lie at the basis of this *Julius Cæsar*; for in the present work it is absolutely necessary that Cæsar, as the representative of the World Spirit, be assailed, and that his assailants perish. Equally devoid of insight is the reproach of another critic — that Cæsar comes upon the stage only to be slain; for the play assumes Cæsar in the plenitude of his power. This is its first presupposition.

The second presupposition is the deep hostility of Cassius to the government of Cæsar. These are the two gladiators who, in this second scene, leap forth stripped for the fight. Cassius is in ability only inferior to Cæsar, and Cæsar is perfectly aware both of his hatred and of his talents. Cassius is first shown in the play overcoming the scruples of Brutus and alienating him from the party of Cæsar. With what skill does he introduce the subject! with what logical force are all the motives adduced, until Brutus, partly by the most delicate flattery and partly by adroit appeals to his moral nature, is completely won! A further proof of Cassius' ability is that he essayed Brutus first of all, for the name of Brutus was the greatest and most venerable in Rome, going back even to the expulsion of the Roman Kings; and Brutus himself was, perhaps, the most respectable character in Rome, and, consequently, of the greatest influence among his fellow-citizens. With him, the conspiracy might be a success; without him, it was impossible.

In the third scene we have Cassius working upon an altogether different character — Casca. This man is the desperado of the conspirators, a man possessed of the greatest physical courage, but without an iota of moral courage. He will rush upon an enemy and stab him, but turns deathly pale at a clap of thunder. Whatever is human he is ready to meet, but that which he conceives to be divine or supernatural is a source of the direst terror. This man Casca, Cassius must have; no respectable man could have been found who possessed equal audacity. In fact, every conspiracy or vigilance committee has just such an instrument, whose function it is to do work which no decent man is willing to perform, but which must be done. When we observe that Casca was the first one that stabbed Cæsar, we know exactly where to place him. Cassius needs this man, and it is curious to note with what consummate tact he proceeds. Knowing the weak side of Casca's character to be his superstition, he brings all his force to bear upon this single point. There is only one result which can follow — Casca joins the conspiracy.

Thus far we are all admiration for the intellect of Cassius, but several things have transpired under his direction at which the rigidly moral man must shrug his shoulders. He has, no doubt, taken advantage of the weakness of Brutus and Casca, and deceived them both; he has declared that to be truth which he himself could not have believed, especially to Casca; he has laid a most unrighteous snare for poor Brutus by writing him anonymous letters, which the latter took to be calls from the people; finally, he designs the assassination of a human being — an act which can hardly be justified from any purely moral point of view. Further on in the play we shall find many other deeds of an equally doubtful nature. How, then, is Cassius to be understood? Shall we take the common statement — that this is a case of great intellect without any moral perceptions? But, if we look at another side, we behold a character of the noblest stamp — of surpassing brightness. With what energy does he strive to restore the old Roman State! with what industry does he collect every fragment of opposition to the mighty Cæsar! with what readiness does he die for his country! To be sure, he knows the might of place and pelf, but he uses them only as instruments to his great end.

There is simply one clue to his conduct. His highest end was the State, and everything which came into conflict with this end had to be subordinated. It was a time of strife and revolution; the ancient landmarks of society were swept away; the prescribed limits of order were obliterated. No man ever saw more clearly than Cassius the finitude, one-sidedness, and inadequacy of the merely moral stand-point in such a period, and, consequently, he proceeded to disregard it entirely. Suppose he did deceive or assassinate a man, provided he thereby saved the State? In fact, what is war but lying, cheating, robbing, and killing for one's country? And the man who can do these things most successfully, and on the most gigantic scale, is the hero — is the great general. To be sure, all this is done to our enemy; but that can be no justification; the moral obligation lies between fellow-men, and not fellow-countrymen. When Cassius no longer has this end in view, he is as moral as any man would require — in fact, an exemplary character. His abstinence is especially contrasted with the debauchery of Antony; he is moderate

in desires, meager in shape, a great student and observer
of men — all of which point to a temperate and steady life.

His chief characteristic, then, is the subordination of
moral to political ends. He is the statesman ; his thought
and activity find their limits in the State ; his world is his
country. His point of view is hinted by himself :

>—" In such a time as this it is not meet
>That every nice offense should bear his comment. "

His reasoning is: To be sure, Lucius Pella has taken
bribes, but that offense can by no means be balanced
against his services and abilities, or his influence ; therefore let it pass, for we need the united efforts of all
against the common enemy. A distinguished American
officer once expressed this subordination of moral to political duties in the following toast :  " My country — may
she ever be right; but, right or wrong, my country."
This is, perhaps, only the *feeling* of patriotism ; but the
insight of Cassius was deeper, for he comprehended *intellectually* that the right of the State is superior to any individual right of conscience, whenever these rights come in
collision.

But the cyclus of characters, in order to be complete,
must have its moral representative. This is Brutus. The
Poet has treated this character with such evident delight,
has thrown around it such a halo of virtue, that it seems to
be the leading one of the play. The honor, sincerity and
nobleness of the man, the purity of his motives, his unim-
peachable integrity in a corrupt age, the perfect fulfillment of every duty of the citizen, are brought out in their
most glowing colors ; even his family relations are introduced to crown the moral beauty of his character. All

the virtues of private life seem to center in this man, and
we heartily join in the encomium of Antony:

" This was the noblest Roman of them all;
His life was gentle, and the elements
So mixed in him that Nature might stand up
And say to all the world: This was a man. "

But alack the day! he was called upon, or thought he was
called upon, to act in times of revolution, when all the
ancient prescribed landmarks were swept down, and when
even the clearest and most logical head could scarcely find
its way out of the confusion.    Now, what does this man,
of the keenest sense of honor, of the most truthful nature,
proceed to do?    First, to desert, and then to assassinate,
his dearest friend.    His motive, he says, was the general
welfare, but immediately thereafter declares that Cæsar
had as yet done nothing hostile to the public good.    And
so this contradiction runs through all his acts and sayings.
It is evident that he had violated the fundamental principle of his nature — his profoundest intellectual conviction.
As far as his insight goes, the act is wrong.    Cassius can
consistently do such a deed, for his stand-point is the
State ; and in its preservation everything — men, property,
and principles — are to be submerged.    But poor Brutus!
what is his next step?    He tries to justify the deed.    Listen
to his soliloquy, for nothing can more completely show
the inadequacy of the moral point of view, and it is,
besides, a fine specimen of moral reasoning not unknown
in our day:

" It must be by his death; and for my part
I know no personal cause to spurn at him,
But for the general. He would be crowned;
How that might change his nature, there's the question."

It would seem that he was not aware of the great change
which had actually taken place in the Roman Constitution,
and does not know that the formal coronation of Cæsar
would produce no alteration in the real condition of things.
This fatal lack of all political sagacity in the leader would
destroy any party or any cause. To continue:

> " It is the bright day that brings forth the adder
> And that craves wary walking. Crown him — that,
> And then I grant we put a sting in him
> That at his will he *may* do danger with. "

Possibility is here made the basis of action. That all practical wisdom is based on directly the opposite principle
need hardly be stated. Moreover, all crimes can easily be
justified in this way, since a man has only to plead some
indefinite possibility.

> " The abuse of greatness is when it disjoins
> Remorse from power; and, to speak truth of Cæsar,
> I have not known when his affection swayed
> More than his reason. "

From this it would appear that Brutus thought that Cæsar
was still a good man and unworthy of death. It was only
what Cæsar might become that can furnish any defense for
the deed.

> —" But 'tis a common proof
> That lowliness is young ambition's ladder
> Whereto the climber upward turns his face;
> But when he once attains the topmost round
> He then unto the ladder turns his back,
> Looks into the clouds, scorning the base degrees
> By which he did ascend; so *Cæsar may*.
> Then, lest he *may*, prevent. "

Possibility is again announced as the basis of action. The
logical nature of this category is not very difficult of com-

prehension. In the Possible the Real and the Unreal are not yet differentiated; therefore it cannot have any determination. But action is something determined, and, since the Possible has no such element in itself, the subjective mind alone can make the necessary determination. Everything is possible, and just as well impossible. Who is to determine? Only the individual, and he must also act on this determination. Thus subjectivity asserts its absolute validity, and this is what is meant by the subjective or moral point of view, which in this play is represented by Brutus.

> —"And since the quarrel
> Will bear no color for the thing he is,"

(what he now is cannot justify our act—another declaration that Cæsar had as yet done nothing which merited death,)

> " Fashion [state] it thus: that what he is, augmented
> Would run to these and these extremities;
> And, therefore, think him as the serpent's egg,
> Which, hatched, would as his kind grow mischievous,
> And kill him in the shell."

If you cannot find a real crime, draw on your imagination and you are sure to discover one. It will be noticed that in the foregoing soliloquy no charge is made against any act of Cæsar's. And yet the world has generally held that it is not moral perversity which utters these declarations—nay, that it is moral greatness.

What, then, is the matter? *Brutus is not able to subordinate the various spheres of ethical duty when they come in conflict.* He recognizes them all, to be sure, but not in their true limitations. Hence, when they collide with one another, he becomes a mass of confusion, strife, and contradiction. Herein lies his immeasurable inferiority to Cassius, who clearly comprehends these limitations and acts upon them. It is intellectual weakness — the inability to rise out of merely moral considerations in political affairs. The trouble is with Brutus' head — not his heart. He intends to do the right thing, only he does not do it. He acts not so much in opposition to, as outside of, his real intellectual convictions; for mark! he is not all inwardly convinced by his own specious reasonings. He gets beyond his intellectual sphere — is befogged and lost.

So, after all, we see that intellect is necessary to the highest moral action. We have had much talk of late concerning the cultivation of the intellect to the neglect of morality. But it seems that Shakespeare has here contrasted these two sides of human nature in the most effective manner, decidedly to the disadvantage of the latter. For Brutus is a man of intense moral susceptibility, yet of small mental caliber; the result is that his mistakes and (what is worse) his transgressions are appalling. Shakespeare has thus illustrated a truth which it will do no hurt to repeat nowadays — that the content of a moral act can be given only by intelligence, and that the cultivation of intellect is in so far the cultivation of morality in its true sense. Hence our public schools are our best — and, indeed, are fast becoming our only — moral teachers. To be sure, submission does not always follow insight; men often know the right, but do it not. Still, we can hardly ascribe this to their knowing it, nor should we assert that they were better off if they had not known it. For in the one case there is a possibility of their becoming good men; but, if they have no comprehension of the good, it is impossible.

In ordinary times of civil repose, we should say of Brutus: What a noble citizen! No one could be more ready to fulfill his duties to his family, to his fellow-men, and to his country. But it must be recollected that these duties were the prescribed usages, customs, and beliefs of his nation; they were given to him—transmitted from his ancestors. But, when prescription no longer points out the way, such a man must fall, for he has no intellectual basis of action. Still, the morality of mankind in general is prescriptive, and does not rest upon rational insight; they follow the footsteps of their fathers. Hence it is that most people think that Brutus is the real hero of the play, and that it is wrongly named. But this was certainly not Shakespeare's design, for it was very easy to construct a drama in which Brutus should appear as triumphant by having it terminate at the assassination of Cæsar, with a grand flourish of daggers, frantic proclamations of liberty, and *"sic semper tyrannis."* Shakespeare, however, takes special pains not to do any such thing, but to show the triumph of Cæsar's thought in the destruction of the conspirators. Still, Brutus remains the favorite character with the multitude, because they do not, and can not, rise above his stand-point, and to-day he is often taken as the great prototype of all lovers of liberty.

The effect of intellectual weakness combined with strong moral impulses appears, then, to be the meaning of this character. It is amazing to observe its contradictions and utter want of steadiness of purpose; nor are they at all exaggerated by the Poet. This man, who could assassinate his best friend for the public good, cannot, when a military leader, conscientiously levy contributions for his starving soldiers; "for," says he, "I can raise no money

by vile means.'' That is, he would sacrifice that very
cause, for which he committed the greatest crime known
to man, to a moral punctilio. This may be moral heroism, but it is colossal stupidity. Furthermore, in every
instance in which Cassius and he differed about the course
to be pursued, Brutus was in the wrong. He, out of
moral scruples, saved Antony, against the advice of Cassius; this same Antony afterwards destroyed their army
and with it their cause. Moreover, the battle of Philippi,
the fatal termination of the conflict, was fought in disregard of the judgment of Cassius. And, finally, he dies
with a contradiction upon his lips, for he says that Cato
was a coward for committing suicide, and then declares
that he will never be taken captive to Rome alive, and
shortly afterwards falls upon his own sword.

Perhaps, however, he came to the conclusion that his
country needed his death, for he said in his celebrated
speech: ''I have the same dagger [which slew Cæsar] for
myself when it shall please my country to need my death.''
This oft-quoted and favorite sentence seems to be usually
regarded as expressing the very quintessence of moral
sublimity and heroic self-sacrifice. But one naturally asks
who is to be judge whether his country needs his death
— the country or himself? If the country, then he would
be a criminal publicly condemned, and there would be no
necessity for his dagger, since his country would furnish
him both instrument and executioner free of charge. But,
if he was to be the judge himself, why did he commit such
villainous acts that, in his own opinion, his country needed
his death? All this was intentional, no doubt, on the part
of Shakespeare, for it comports too well with the contradictory character of Brutus to admit of any other suppo-

sition. One imagines that if the old bard could have fore-seen all the frothy vaporings and mock-sentimentality to which this innocent absurdity has given rise, he would still be laughing in his grave. Such is the *true* irony of the great Poet, so much insisted on by some critics, which portrays the finitude of individuals, classes, and even whole historical periods, so adequately that they themselves take delight in the picture.

This difference in character between Brutus and Cassius must lead to a collision, and accordingly we have the celebrated quarrel in the Fourth Act. Here we see the respective stand-points of the two men fully exhibited. Brutus is haughty, insulting; he plumes himself upon his moral integrity, and though it seems that he was ready to take — and, indeed, asked for — some of the money which Cassius had raised by "vile means." Cassius, on the contrary, keeps restraining himself, though exasperated in the highest degree, and ultimately leads the way to reconciliation. No personal feelings can dim to his eye the great end which he has in view; nothing must be allowed to put it in jeopardy. Hence the quarrel, which would otherwise doubtless have terminated their friendship, if not have ended in a personal encounter, is healed as speedily as possible. There is a mightier collision pending which hushes all lesser strifes.

A further contrast to Brutus is Antony. This loose reveler is true to his friend, Cæsar, and avenges him, but the rigid moralist abandons and slays him. Antony is, moreover, a man of pleasure, and acts from impulse; Brutus pretends to be a philosopher and to be guided by fixed principles. "I am no orator, as Brutus is, but a plain, blunt man, that love my friend." Antony's highest

end was personal devotion to one whom he loved; he in
no wise comprehends the movement of either Cassius
or Cæsar. Thus both Antony and Brutus are quite on
the same spiritual plane, and, hence, Antony can justly
reproach Brutus for his faithless conduct with a cogency
which the latter can by no means answer:

> " Witness the hole you made in Cæsar's heart
> Crying *long live, hail Cæsar!*"

Yet Antony does most ample justice to the motive of Brutus, and seems to place all worthiness of an action in the
motive — a point of view, it need hardly be said, purely
moral and subjective:

> " This was the noblest Roman of them all;
> All the conspirators, save only he,
> Did what they did in envy of great Cæsar;
> He only in a general honest thought
> And common good to all made one of them."

These lines are often quoted as Shakespeare's actual opinion of Brutus; but they are spoken by Antony, to whom
they appropriately belong, and to nobody else. It is by
no means certain that Shakespeare's own views are to be
found always in the utterances of his characters. The
dramatic Poet expresses his convictions in the action, in
the collision, and, above all, in the catastrophe. Judging
by this standard, we should most decidedly aver that the
above lines did not express Shakespeare's personal opinion.
Both Antony and Brutus, therefore, have quite the same
intellectual stand-point, though differing much in their
outward lives; but the one was true to it, the other was
not. Brutus ought to have acted as Antony — to be
faithful to his deepest convictions, and to have remained

friendly — or, at least, indifferent — to Cæsar. Cassius alone can *intellectually* slay Cæsar.

Such appears to be the general purport of this play. Much might be said upon its formal excellence — the poetic beauty, rhetorical finish, and unusual clearness of the language, making it a favorite with many who read nothing else of Shakespeare; also the logical arrangement of the parts and the happy consecution of motives might be more fully unfolded; but all this we shall leave to our reader to follow up at his leisure. Some of Shakespeare's fairest gems of characterization are found in the minor personages of the play, as Portia, the absolute type of wifehood, and Lucius, the faithful slave; but their principle is plain and need not to be specially developed. Moreover, all the mediations employed are deserving of the most careful study, on account of their truth and profundity, as when, for example, in the Third Act the Poet makes popular oratory the means by which the tide is turned against the conspirators, and thus assigns to it a place as one of the chief political instrumentalities in the ancient and modern world. Also, those curious supernatural manifestations — as the cry of the soothsayer, " Beware the ides of March," the appearance of the ghost of Cæsar, the presence of a lion in the streets, the wrathful signs of the heavens — seem to demand some rational explanation; as well as the strange anthropological phenomona — as the presentiments of Cæsar and Brutus, and the dreams of Calpurnia and Cinna the Poet. Here is a side which Shakespeare always elaborates in full, and which makes a setting for his Ethical World. But the object at present is to bring into prominence this Ethical World of Shakespeare and the great significance of its collisions, for these same collisions are taking place to-day, and, indeed, their true solution constitutes the comprehension of, and mastery over, the practical world.

To recapitulate, there are three leading moments in the drama: First, Cæsar in the consummation of his world-historical career—on the pinnacle of his power and glory; second, the reaction of the State against him, headed by Cassius; third, the negation of this reaction through the restoration and absolute validity of the Cæsarean movement. Hence we see that Cæsar is the real hero, and that the piece is justly entitled *Julius Cæsar.* We also see that the collision is between the World Spirit and the Nation, and that in this struggle three typical characters participate, forming a complete cyclus of characterization. Cæsar represents the world-historical stand-point, Cassius the political, Brutus the moral. Cæsar perishes: the ancient national sentiment rises up for a moment and destroys the individual, for, being of flesh and blood, an assassin may rush upon him and stab him to the heart—but his thought is not thus doomed to perish. Next to him comes Cassius, whose great mistake was that he still had faith in his country—a pardonable error, if any, to mortals! He did not, and perhaps could not, rise above the purely political point of view; to him the State was the ultimate ethical principle of the Universe. Hence he did not comprehend the world-historical movement represented by Cæsar, but collided with it and was destroyed. He is, indeed, a painful, deeply tragic character; with all his greatness, devotion, and intelligent activity—still finite and short-sighted. The mistake of Brutus is that he had anything to do with the matter at all—that he took a part—or, at least, a leading part—in this revolution. The col-

lision lay wholly beyond his mental horizon; hence he
represents nothing objective — is the bearer of no greatest
ethical principle, like Cæsar and Cassius.   He presumed
to lead when he was intellectually in total darkness, trust-
ing alone to his own good intentions.   We do not blame
him because he was ignorant, but because he did not know
that he was ignorant.   Every rational being must at least
comprehend its own limits — must know that it does not
know.   We may laud the motive, but lament the deed;
still, man, as endowed with Reason and Universality, cannot run away from his act and hide himself behind his
intention, but must take the inherent consequences of his
deed in their total circumference.

Brutus is, no doubt, the sphinx of the play, and has
given much trouble to critics on account of the contradictions of his character.   He seems both moral and
immoral — to be actuated by the noblest motives for the
public good, yet can give no rational ground for his act.
Indeed, we are led to believe that his vanity was so
swollen by the flattery of Cassius that it hurried him
unconsciously beyond the pale of his convictions.   Still,
Brutus was undoubtedly a good citizen, a good husband,
and a good man.   But any one of these three relations
may come into conflict with the others.   Which, then, is
to be followed?   If a man has not subordinated these
spheres into a system — which can be done only by Intelligence — he cannot tell what course to pursue.   Sometimes he may follow one, sometimes another, for in his
mind they all possess equal validity.   Hence such a
person can only be inconsistent, vacillating, and contradictory in his actions; and such a person was Brutus —
a good, moral man, who recognized all duties, but did not

comprehend their limitations, and, hence, fell beneath their conflict.

To the foregoing account of the leading characters and of the main principles at issue may now be added a few details of structure. The general action of the play lies between the triumph of the individual Cæsar and the success of his friends of the Triumvirate. The spirit of the old Roman Republic rises up against him and destroys him, but his principle, as the world-historical principle of that age, cannot be destroyed. The Triumvirate is but a transitional stage in the change from Republicanism to Imperialism, a change which will be fully accomplished in the following play of *Antony and Cleopatra.* There the principle of Cæsar is firmly established, unaided by the mighty individual Cæsar. But, to reach this consummation, a long and fierce struggle must be passed through.

Two distinct movements may be seen in the drama of *Julius Cæsar.* The first unfolds the internal conflict at Rome — the Republican conspiracy against the Imperial autocrat; it ends in the death of Cæsar on the one hand, and the flight of the conspirators from Rome on the other, which flight is brought about by the popular oratory of Antony. The second movement portrays the external conflict — the war between the two sides, ending in the battle of Philippi. Moreover, there are two threads running through the play, made up of the two opposing parties. The one thread is that of Cæsar and his adherents, the other is that of Cassius and Brutus. Around these central figures all the other characters may be grouped.

Rome had conquered the world. The stern spirit of the Republic could suffer no limitations; it was impelled by an irresistible impulse to reduce to its sway all the nations of the globe. Whatever was not Roman had no right to be; existence could only be purchased by submission to the Roman principle and by adoption of Roman institutions. The national spirit which gradually arose in the small hamlet along the banks of the Tiber was simply illimitable; hence it sought to sweep away the boundaries of nations, and could be satisfied only by the absorption of all other peoples. Assimilation was its strongest and most abiding principle; the world must become Roman. It is this colossal strength and intensity of nationality which gives to Rome her eternal charm and inspiration. But just here, too, we must look for the one-sidedness and imperfection of her deeds and character. Though the Romans, of all peoples that have ever existed, were the most intensely national, their whole career is, on the other hand, but one continued assault upon nationality; in the conquest of other countries they were logically destroying their own principle.

Hence, when the world was subdued, republican Rome was no more; when she had obliterated the bounds of nationality she had obliterated herself. The process is manifest; the conquered peoples which were incorporated into her life changed her character; the world absorbed

Rome quite as much as Rome absorbed the world. Not captive Greece alone captured her conqueror, as a Roman poet sings, but all other conquered States assisted. Hence she was changed — was no longer Rome; she could not extend her conquests — her republican vitality was gone. Thus we pass to the Empire, whose chief destiny will be, not to conquer, but to hold together; not to bring about an external addition of territory, but an internal organization of the manifold nations, and their consolidation through laws and institutions.

Now, it is just this transition from republican to imperial Rome which Shakespeare has made the subject of his two greatest historical dramas. The theme is not merely national, but world-historical — in it the whole world participates; for it was then under the sway of Rome, except an outlying circle of unhistorical peoples. On the plains of Pharsalia the old system of things was permanently overthrown; the Empire was essentially established in the complete supremacy of one man. This first phase of the conflict, which ends in the triumph of Julius Cæsar, is not given by the Poet, though it would almost seem as if he had entertained some such design. The struggle with Pompey is always hovering in the historical foreground, and the party of Pompey is one of the colliding elements in both these later Roman plays. The character of Julius Cæsar, which is so inadequately portrayed in the drama of that name, would thus be exhibited in its full development and amid the greatest exploits of the hero. Other slight indications might be pointed out which lead to the same inference; [still, it would be rashness to assert positively that Shakespeare ever intended to complete the missing link.] As it is, the Roman Trilogy is a matter of conjecture, and we should gladly accept the two dramas which have come down to us upon this subject.

The play which goes by the name of *Julius Cæsar* presupposes the hero as having attained the summit of his power and glory; he is really the sole supreme authority in the State, though a formal recognition to this effect has not yet been embodied in the laws and institutions of the country. The crown is offered to him, but he hesitates. Now the embers of the old republican spirit of Rome begin to glow anew; the supporters of Cæsar's old antagonist are not idle. The result is a conflict between imperialism and republicanism — between the new and the old. Brutus and, preëminently, Cassius stand as the representatives of the ancient Roman constitution; they succeed in assassinating the autocrat, and seem for a moment almost to have won. But they, in their turn, fall before the reaction — the principle of Cæsar, even without his personal guidance and prestige, is far stronger than the old Roman principle. The Triumvirs, his friends and supporters, avenge his death; republican Rome is defeated by her own citizens; the Cæsarean movement is restored, and will now pass on to its complete realization.

Such, in general, is the collision in Shakespeare's *Julius Cæsar.* It is clear that the play does not give the full solution of this great world-historical problem; the Triumvirate was but a brief phase of the transition to imperialism. The three must be reduced to one; such is the tendency of the world. It is logically impossible that this neutral order of things should endure. Hence another drama becomes necessary in order to portray the completion of the movement. That drama is *Antony and Cleopatra,* whose theme is, therefore, the reduction of the

Triumvirate to the Empire. The principle of Rome was stated to be assimilation of nations; hence it cannot suffer itself to be divided into three, or even two, nations. The intimate connection—not only of thought, but also of treatment—between *Julius Cæsar* and *Antony and Cleopatra* has often been observed; incidents, motives, characters, are often merely touched upon in the former play in order to prepare for their full development in the latter play.

The material is very large and almost unwieldy, and it will aid us in obtaining a complete survey of the whole subject, if the various collisions, both of State and Family, are pointed out separately. [These constitute the basis of all dramatic action, and are always the pivotal points of interest and development.] In the play of *Antony and Cleopatra* they are, in general, the following: First, is the collision between Rome and the yet unconquered portion of the world. It is still the glimmer of that spirit of conquest which shone with such intensity throughout the life of the old republic. But now it has become feeble and unimportant, though by no means extinct; [the Poet has given to it only one short scene, besides several allusions scattered through the drama. Indeed, the Roman generals dare not conquer too much, on account of the envy of their superiors; the zeal of the soldiers is quenched in the fear of degradation. Thus Ventidius is afraid of winning too great military glory by his defeat of the Parthians. The second collision is within the Roman Empire—between the Triumvirate and the younger Pompey. Here we behold another renewal of the struggle, which was temporarily ended on the plains of Pharsalia, which was rekindled by Brutus and Cassius,

to be again extinguished on the plains of Philippi. It is
the struggle between republicanism and imperialism. But
the old Roman consciousness has passed away forever;
again the star of the republic sinks beneath the horizon,
and will rise no more. The second Pompey is destroyed
by the second Cæsar, the representative and heir of the
Empire. The third collision is within the Triumvirate, and
is the essential one of the play. Lepidus, the peace-
maker where no peace is possible, is speedily eliminated;
then the struggle between Antony and Octavius breaks
forth in its full intensity. The former seems satisfied
with the threefold division of the world, and, above all,
desires to be let alone in his Oriental enjoyment. But
Octavius has the thought of unity as his deepest principle
and as his strongest ambition; he thus is the representative of the world-historical spirit and conquers — must
conquer. Such are the three political collisions of this
drama, each one of which becomes more intense as it
becomes more narrow: The external collision of Rome
against the rest of the world; the internal conflict of the
old Roman principle against the Triumvirate; finally, the
disruption of the Triumvirate and the triumph of the
imperial principle.

Amid these purely political elements is mingled the
domestic collision of Antony — his violations of the ties of
the family. He has abandoned his first Roman wife for
the unethical relation to Cleopatra. After a time, however, he leaves the latter and returns to the Roman Family with new resolutions; but his second Roman wife he
also deserts and returns to Cleopatra. Thus he abandons
both the Roman State and the Roman Family for an Oriental country and an Oriental mistress; it is clear that he

can make no claim to being the champion of the destiny
of his country, which he has thus forsaken. Rome has
already subordinated the Oriental world, but Antony goes
back to it; hence his fate is clearly written in its fate.

This enumeration gives the principal factors of the play,
though by no means in their true dramatic order. But
the material of the work is so multifarious and complicated that the mind must have some guide to which it can
turn when it gets lost in the labyrinth of detail. The
universal complaint is that *Antony and Cleopatra* is wanting in dramatic simplicity, and the complaint is certainly
well founded. To the less careful reader or spectator
its movement seems confused — at times chaotic — and
there is hardly a doubt but that the Poet has undertaken
to compass too much in the limits of one drama. Still,
it has his language, his thought, and his characterization
in their highest potence. We shall now pass to consider
the organization of the play as a whole, and attempt to
unfold its various parts, stating their meaning and relation.

There are manifestly two main movements, though
other divisions are possible, according to the stand-point
of the critic. The first division exhibits the various conflicting elements of the Roman World, and ends in their
apparent reconciliation. It has three distinct threads or
groups of characters, each of which has a locality of its
own. The central figures of these groups are, respectively, Antony and Cleopatra, Octavius, Pompey. The
second movement shows the disruption of the truce and
the struggle of the hostile principles and individuals, till
their final and complete subordination to one man —
Octavius. Here there are essentially two threads — that

of Antony and Cleopatra on the one hand, and that of
Octavius on the other; the minor groups are more or
less intimately connected with these leading personages.
The elaboration of this scheme will show all the elements
of the work in their proper order and signification.

I. 1. The first thread of the first movement may be
called the Egyptian thread, and is the fullest in its portraiture, as well as the most interesting. The first speaker
is an old Roman soldier, who strikes at once the key-note
of the drama. He complains in bitter scorn that the
illustrious warrior, the "triple pillar of the world," has
sacrificed his great historical destiny to sensuality. But
here come the pair; what is their conversation? They
are talking of love, whose power Antony expresses in the
strongest language. It is illimitable — subdues all; it
demands "a new heaven and a new earth." Note must
be taken that this is not the ethical affection of the Family, but sensual love. Here is indicated the strongest
principle of Antony's nature; he will often fluctuate
between his contradictory impulses, but in the end will
always return to the "Egyptian dish." Just now he is
feeling some satiety and shame, which he seeks to disguise
carefully from Cleopatra.

She, however, with a true instinct of the situation, suspects him, and we shall now behold the successive waves
of jealousy, anger, affection, despair, which heave and
surge through her nature. The fundamental trait of Cleopatra is passion — passion in all its forms and in its fullest
intensity. As love, as hate, as irascibility, as jealousy, it
has the same colossal manifestation. There is absolutely
no ethical subordination in the woman. She recognizes
no duty, submits to no institution. She seems to have

admiration for the heroic element of Antony's character, and, with the true instinct of her sex, she adores his courage; but her love for him springs mainly from his boundless capacity for revelry and sensual indulgence, in which she participates along with him. Corresponding quite to the degree and intensity of her passion, the Poet has portrayed her power of fascination — indeed, the one arises from the other. It is curious to note how the greatest personages of Roman history have, in turn, submitted to her spell: Pompey the Great, Julius Cæsar, and now Antony. The contrast is apparent; it would seem as if the adamantine Roman character must always sink before this gorgeous Oriental enchantress. But she is destined to meet with her master. The cool and wary Octavius sees her; she tries her sorcery upon him without success, and then — dies. It is her destiny that, if her charm be once withstood, she, like the Sirens of old, will destroy herself. [Her attractiveness, therefore, does not consist in youth, in grace, in figure, in personal beauty; it lies in the sensual intensity of her whole being, which appears to set on fire all who dare look upon her. Such is the central principle of her character.

At first she torments Antony with her suspicions, because she sees the conflicting principles in his bosom. Her sarcasms are directed against the " married woman" Fulvia, wife of Antony, and also against Octavius, who, a " scarce bearded " youth, undertakes to dictate to the old warrior. Her purpose is manifest; she wishes to sever Antony from all Roman connections. Hence she tries to engender a conflict which may lead to a separation of the Orient from the Roman Empire; at least she is seeking to detain Antony by every means in the East. But she

sneers also at his domestic relation, and, above all, desires
to detach him from the Roman Family. The purpose
which runs through all her conversation is to break off the
two main ethical relations which still have some power
over him, namely, those of family and country.

But Antony is resolved to go; the death of Fulvia
causes him even to long for a Roman wife, and the political occurrences demand his immediate presence in Rome.
Now comes the separation; it is what might be expected.
To follow her through the careenings of her passions is
unnecessary. [As the cynical Enobarbus intimated, she
dies instantly — dies twenty times and more.] But Antony
holds fast to his purpose with a Roman firmness, amid all
her extravagant ado, which for a time leads us to hope
well for his future. Again we behold her during the
absence of her lover. Imagination, excited and intensified by the deepest trait of her nature — by her passion —
now controls her. His image is always present to her
mind; it surpasses all the memories of the other Roman
heroes who yielded in times past to her enchanting wiles.
Next we behold her under the influence of bad news;
word has come that Antony is married — again has allied
himself to the Roman Family. Her passion now reaches
its climax in the form of anger; she becomes simply
irrational in her rage; she beats the innocent messenger,
and even prepares to kill him. Her seeming justification
is that she is subject to moral self-control no more than
the elements.

"Some innocents 'scape not the thunderbolt!"

But she bethinks herself. She knows the power of her
sensuous attractions; she, too, knows their deep hold

upon Antony. What, then, are the years, the beauty,
the disposition, of Antony's new wife? "let him [the
messenger] not leave out the color of her hair!" By
patient questioning she discovers that the personal graces
of Octavia must be far inferior to her own, and, above
all, is wholly wanting in fervid intensity of passion:

> "She shows a body rather than life,
> A statue than a breather."

Cleopatra is so well satisfied — indeed, delighted — with
the result of the examination that she now rewards the
messenger with gold. She has the most unerring instinct,
which tells her the deepest principle of Antony's nature;
she knows that Antony must, in course of time, turn
away from the cold and unattractive Octavia, and go back
to the enjoyment of sensual love, which he can find in
the highest manifestation only in her. This inference is
not, and can not, be falsified by the event. Antony returns
because he must obey that which is strongest within him.
Such is Cleopatra — the embodiment of all that which is
most fascinating to the senses of man, and at the same
time the victim of her own powers of fascination. For
she is tortured with her own passion even more than she
tortures; her gift, so painful and fatal to others, is equally
painful and fatal to herself. Her world is a carnival of
enjoyment — no ray of duty or of ethical devotion enters
there; physical agony is the sole retribution which comes
home to sensual indulgence.

2. We can now go back and take up the second thread
of the first movement. The two colleagues of Antony
are at Rome, the true center of the nations at that time;
their conversation turns upon the man who has sacrificed

his Roman destiny to Oriental indulgence. We catch a glimpse of the Triumvirate, with the relation and character of its three members.

Octavius is the man of cold understanding, who has grasped his ultimate end with clearness, and who pursues it in politic disguise, but with inflexible determination. Already we can see his grand purpose looming up in the future; we also see that he plainly comprehends the conflict which he must pass through in order to attain his object. His great obstacle is Antony, who surpasses him in every quality except the greatest, namely, the mind to grasp, and the will to accomplish, the world-historical destiny of Rome. This is for Octavius the highest end; to it everything else is subordinate. For this reason his character has often excited moral aversion. He sacrifices his colleague; his sister, whom he seems really to have loved, is thrust by him into a short and unhappy marriage to further his policy; he disregards the most sacred promises; in fine, all the emotions of man, and all the scruples of conscience, he subordinates to his great purpose — the union of the nations in one empire. He himself says in one place that he is seeking universal peace — the harmony of the whole world in a single government. He is one of those world-historical characters whose fate it is to be always condemned for trampling upon moral considerations when they collided, not merely with his own subjective purpose, but with the absolute movement of humanity, which he represented.

But Antony, in this fundamental trait, is the contrast to Octavius. He is one of the triumvirs; he is a great soldier, with heroic elements of character; he was the victor at Philippi; he was the friend and supporter of Julius

Cæsar. His opportunity is really greater than that of Octavius. But he has not the clear ultimate end; he is not at one with himself; his deepest controlling principle is enjoyment — gratification of the senses — though he is capable of enduring the most terrible hardships of war. Hence he falls into the lap of Orientalism, yet struggles to return to his Roman life and destiny; but he finally relapses completely, and thus loses the great opportunity. Between these two men — Antony and Octavius — the struggle must arise. The question is: Which one will unify the Triumvirate? From the very beginning the Poet has elaborated the dramatic motives so forcibly that the result is plainly foreseen.

Now there remains the third triumvir — Lepidus. He is the peace-maker, though peace is impossible; he tries to compromise two contradictory principles which are on the point of embracing in a death-struggle. Conciliation is possible between individuals, but not between principles. If one principle be truer — that is, more universal than another — the former must subordinate the latter; for, otherwise, it is not more universal. The higher truth must realize itself — must make its superiority valid in the world; this means always the subsumption of what is lower. [ Lepidus, therefore, has no perception of what is going on around him; he placed himself between the two jaws of the world, and is speedily ground to death. His basis is the peaceful continuance of the present condition of affairs — of the Triumvirate — which is in reality a fleeting phase of the great transition to imperialism. A man with good intentions, but with a weak head, amid a revolution — what is in store for him but annihilation?

The first utterance of Octavius is a complaint against

Antony; he is disgracing his office and his country by his
conduct in Egypt; he has insulted his colleagues; but,
above all, he has permitted, through his inactivity, the
enemies of the Triumvirate again to muster their forces
and threaten Italy.  In other words, he is faithless to his
high calling and to the destiny of Rome, which is the most
serious thought of Octavius.  Here is seen plainly the
difference of their characters and their ends.  But Antony
has shaken off the Egyptian enchantress — has come to
Rome ; the two rivals are brought face to face in order to
settle their quarrel.  Antony answers the complaints of
Octavius with such success that they are seen to be mere
pretexts for the most part; still, the old veteran asks
pardon of his youthful confederate, and thus tacitly points
out the superior to whom he acknowledges responsibility
and submission.  In this act the destinies of the two men
are truthfully foreshadowed.  But Octavius is not yet
ready to strike the final blow ; he must first unify all the
rest of the Roman world against his antagonist.  He,
therefore, consents to conciliation ; and, to tie the hands
of Antony for a time, he gives his sister in marriage to
the latter, as suggested by his wily counselor, Agrippa.
The tether works well; it holds Antony till both Lepidus
and Pompey are overwhelmed, and their territory absorbed
by Octavius.  But now they are reconciled, and hasten
to unite their powers against the common foe of the
Triumvirate.

Such are the transactions of Antony at Rome; their
nature and consequences are now foreshadowed in two
very different ways, through two very different characters — through Enobarbus and the Soothsayer.  Enobarbus
is a most wonderful delineation; he is the mirror which

reflects the results of the deeds which are enacted by the high personages of the drama; in particular, he adumbrates the conduct of Antony, his friend and companion. His chief trait is, therefore, intellectual sagacity; he foresees with the clearest vision and foretells with the most logical precision. But he possesses at the same time the reverse side of human nature in colossal magnitude; glutton, debauchee, sensualist, he seems immersed in the very dregs of Egyptian license, and when he is absent his memory is filled with Egyptian orgies. The two extremes meet in him — the keenest intelligence and the grossest sensuality; the mediating principle between them — namely, moral subordination — seems not to exist. He is the peculiar product of an age of corruption, in which even mental cultivation aids in blasting the character. He appears to have anticipated the main consequences from the beginning; he tried to keep Antony in Egypt; then he sought to prevent the reconciliation with Octavius. He also intimates that the marriage will in the end intensify the enmity which it was intended to forestall. For he knows that Antony will return to the Egyptian Queen; his highly-colored account of her appearance when "she pursed up his heart upon the river Cydnus" indicates the power of fascination over the senses, and the deep hold which she must consequently retain upon Antony. Enobarbus manifestly thinks that his master ought to go back at once to Egypt, though his appetite seems to favor such a decision quite as strongly as his judgment.

Such is the intellectual reflection of Antony's conduct and destiny; now follows a second reflection of the same through a wholly different medium, namely, through the prophetic emotion. Its bearer is the Soothsayer. This

man, too, urges very strongly the return to Egypt — the
reason whereof he says he has not in his tongue, but in
his feeling, in his instinctive perception of the future.
Antony is warned that the dæmon, "thy spirit that keeps
thee," cannot resist the might of Cæsar; it becomes
afraid in the presence of the latter.    Antony feels the
truth of the declaration, resolves to go back to Egypt, and
gives the true ground — "in the East my pleasure lies."
The Soothsayer thus utters in his peculiar form that which
has already been told; the principle of Antony is subordinate to the principle of Octavius — the higher end must
vindicate its superior power.    This is not only known,
but is now felt; the Poet has indicated the same result
both through intelligence and through feeling.    The Triumvirate is, however, reconciled within itself, and must
turn its attention to its external foe.

3.  This is Pompey, who is the central figure of the third
thread of the first movement, which thread may now be
taken up and traced.    Pompey, from the first, exhibits
no great strength of purpose, no firm reliance on his principle.    He stands as the representation of the old republican constitution of Rome, in opposition to the tendency to
imperialism; he cites as examples of admiration those
"courtiers of beauteous freedom," pale Cassius and
honest Brutus, who drenched the capitol,

> — "That they would
> Have one man but a man.  And that is it
> Hath made me rig my navy" — etc.

He has also a personal ground — to avenge the fate of
his father.    But he is clearly not the man to be at the head
of a great political movement.    He has, moreover, a

scrupulosity which makes him sacrifice his cause to a moral punctilio. Such a man ought never to begin a rebellion whose success is not his highest principle. His main hope is that Antony will remain in the East; but, when the latter returns and is reconciled with Octavius, Pompey becomes frightened at their hostile preparation and compromises for a certain territory — that is, he really joins the Triumvirate in the division of the world, and thus utterly abandons the principle which he represented. Logically, he is now absorbed in the new idea by his own action, and he disappears as a factor of the drama.

His position is wholly due to the fact that he was the son of the great Pompey; birth, the most external of grounds, makes him leader. But by the side of him is seen the genuine old Roman republican, to whom the cause means everything, though he is called a pirate by his enemies. This is Menas, who sees and condemns the folly of the new treaty; who reflects the weakness of Pompey as Enobarbus reflects the weakness of Antony. Now comes the supreme moment of Pompey's career. All three of the triumvirs are on board of his galley, holding high festival in honor of the peace; the rulers of the world, the enemies of his principle, are, as it were, bagged and placed at his disposition. Menas urges upon him immediate action with the greatest vehemence; but no, his "honor" will not let him, the nature of which honor is seen in his declaration that he cannot advise the doing of the deed, but he would applaud it if it were done. Menas now deserts, for he to whom the good old cause is the highest principle of existence cannot endure to see the destiny of Rome and of the world sacrificed to a moral scruple. However great may be our admiration of Pompey's motive, it destroys his world-historical character; both he and Antony are, therefore, alike in surrendering their grand opportunity, though the one yields it to sensual love and the other to conscience. Pompey, hence, keeps his agreement, but Octavius, who subordinates both emotion and morality to his great political purpose, breaks that same agreement when his plan is ripe, and slays his confederate in return for the latter's fidelity and conscientiousness. The character of Brutus in *Julius Cæsar* is in this respect repeated in him.

Now, if the moral test be the sole and absolute test of the deed under all circumstances, it is manifest that Pompey is the hero of this play, as Brutus is, by the same criterion, the hero of *Julius Cæsar*. But if there be a national — indeed, a world-historical — duty as well as a moral duty, and if these duties come into irreconcilable conflict, in which one side must be subordinated to the other, the question can by no means be so easily dismissed. The solution of Shakespeare is plain, and it is the same as that of history. The national or the world-historical principle always subsumes the moral, because it is the truer, the more universal. [ This very drama is condemned by certain critics because it is said to have no noble — that is, moral — characters, and because it represents the political principle as triumphant. The complaint is frivolous; the Poet has written from the complete reality, and not from a one-sided abstraction, which, however valid in its sphere, has limitations which it ought not to transcend. The ultimate criterion of these critics is the moral one, which is certainly not that of the Poet.

Indeed, there is just this struggle between the moral and political elements going on at all times in all countries. The purely moral man is in a condition of chronic disgust at public life and public men ; he generally judges by altogether too narrow a standard, and is, hence, unjust. But the public man is also too apt to sacrifice moral considerations to some supposed expediency, when, in reality, there is no conflict of duties. The relations of the individual in society must ordinarily be controlled by morality ; this is just its function. But in revolutions — in periods of political disintegration — the collision between principles arises in its fullest intensity. One side must be chosen ; still, the choice is a violation which calls forth a retribution. In our own recent struggle we all thought it our duty to sacrifice every moral tie to the imperiled nationality, if the two conflicted. In that prolonged and intense effort the moral consciousness of private and public life disappeared, for it was immolated ; though the nation was saved, the Nemesis of violated morality still scourges us ; this is the real price — the spiritual price — and not the blood or the treasure spent, which we paid, are now paying, and shall continue to pay for our national existence.

In the final scene of this thread, when the banquet is portrayed, we behold the fate of all the leading characters foreshadowed in the most subtle manner. Here are collected the representatives of the main conflicting principles of the drama — Antony, Pompey, Lepidus, Octavius, with their chief subordinates. They indulge in a drunken carousal, symbolical of the mad confusion of the period. Who will keep his head clear and retain his senses amid the wild revel? Lepidus first yields to the wine, and is carried out; the others sink into an Egyptian debauch; but the cool-headed Octavius never for a moment loses his self-control, and when he finds himself touched with the wine he hastens away from the company. No sensual pleasure can conquer his understanding; he will remain master.

Such is the first general movement of the play, ending in the reconciliation of all the colliding characters. The Triumvirate is restored to internal harmony; Pompey is admitted to a share of its authority; Antony is restored to the Roman Family and State. Even external conquest breathes for a moment. Nothing is settled, however; principles have been compromised, but they are as antagonistic as before.

II. Suddenly comes the disruption. The Poet does not portray it in full — he merely indicates the result. Cæsar and Lepidus united to destroy Pompey, then Cæsar turned upon Lepidus; which important events are all announced in one short scene. Antony leaves Octavia; next we find him with Cleopatra. Such is this rapid separation which introduces the second general movement of the drama. There are now essentially but two threads, namely, the two antagonists, with their respective adherents. Of this last movement there are three distinct phases — the first defeat of Antony, his second defeat and death, the death of Cleopatra.

1. Antony, when he fully comprehends the inexorable purpose of Octavius to subordinate him also, takes his departure from Octavia. She is the true Roman wife, who is by no means devoid of deep emotion, but it is the quiet, pure emotion of the Family; her feeling is confined to the bounds of an ethical relation, and herein she is the direct contrast to Cleopatra, whose passion is hampered by no limitations. She tried to perform her duty to both

husband and brother; but that husband had as his deepest
impulse sensual, instead of conjugal, love, and that brother
had as his strongest principle political supremacy, instead
of fraternal affection, even if he possessed the latter also.
Octavia, with the most beautiful devotion, tried to conciliate the conflicting individuals, but was sacrificed by
both. Thus the Family sank before the thirst of passion
and before the thirst for power.

The Poet, having elaborated the motives of all that is
to follow, passes at once to the scene of the struggle
which is to decide the fate of the two colliding personages. The infatuation of Antony is brought out in the
strongest colors; he fights a naval battle against the advice
of all his soldiers, from the commanding officer down to
the common private in the ranks. The ground of his
conduct is the control exercised over him by Cleopatra.
Then during the crisis of the fight she flies; Antony
follows. The result is utter defeat by sea, universal
desertion by land. His Oriental connection has thus
brought to ruin his world-historical opportunity; he has
sacrificed everything Roman — even his Roman courage.
The internal struggle now begins. He feels the deep
degradation of his behavior; the memories of his Roman
life again awake in him; he seems ready to reproach the
cause of his fatuity; but the weeping enchantress by her
presence subdues him more completely than Octavius had
done in the battle just fought, and again his deepest trait
asserts itself:

> "Fall not a tear, I say; one of them rates
> All that is won and lost; give me a kiss —
> Even this repays me."

But even a stronger evidence of his love is given. He

suddenly comes upon Thyreus, the messenger of Cæsar,
toying with the hand of Cleopatra. There ensues a fit
of jealousy so violent that he totally forgets his generous
nature and orders the man to be whipped. The thought
of her infidelity crazes him; he has loved her more than
the whole world in the literal sense of the expression,
✓ since he has sacrificed the world for her sake. What if
another shares with him the possession? The strongest
element of his nature revolts. But a declaration of Cleopatra lulls his wrath; again harmony prevails. Now,
however, their union is threatened from without by the
approach of the victorious Octavius — a conflict which
must arouse all his dormant energy.

Octavius is true to his aim throughout these scenes; his
cool calculation is never disturbed by a whiff of passion
— his politic cunning is everywhere paramount. His
enemy is surrounded by a net-work of espionage, while
his own movements are artfully concealed. He acts with
a celerity and secrecy which are incomprehensible to
Antony; his insight into the real situation is never
clouded for a moment. He orders the battle to be fought
at sea, with every advantage in his favor. His impertur-
bable understanding, which grasps clearly the end in view
and the means to reach the same, shines through all his
actions. After the victory he will grant no terms to
Antony, who must be entirely eliminated from the world
in order to produce unity. But Cleopatra he attempts to
detach by specious promises; he has no faith in her
fidelity, and but little trust in women under the most
favorable circumstances. She seems to listen to his pro-
posals; her conduct is at least ambiguous; two opposite
impulses divide her purpose.

2. We pass on to the second phase of the second movement, embraced in the Fourth Act. Antony now has a new motive for action — his union with Cleopatra is in jeopardy. His heroic character returns in its fullest intensity; he fights, not to save an empire, but to preserve his relation to the Egyptian Queen. It will be noticed that the deepest principle of his nature is assailed; he might dally away the world, but he cannot surrender the tie to Cleopatra. Again we behold all the noble elements of his nature in full play — his generosity, his warm-heartedness, even to servants — his activity, his heroism. Nor is the other side of his character omitted; there must be a final debauch before departure for the battle-field. Still, there is the dark reflection of the future; music in the air is heard by the common soldiers, who express their feelings in ominous words; their belief is that the god Hercules, tutular deity of Antony, is now leaving him — his cause is lost beyond hope.

A second battle is fought; a temporary advantage is gained on land, but the Egyptian fleet yields to the foe — traitorously as Antony supposes, and as also we may suppose. The internal conflict now arises more fiercely than ever; she to whom he has sacrificed a world has betrayed him. What agony could be more intense? She appears before him, but neither her presence nor her language can assuage his revengeful anger this time; she has to leave him. But is his love entirely gone — that which was the strongest principle of his nature? She will put the matter to proof, the test being death — absolute separation. Accordingly word is sent to him that she is no more; that she died with his name on her lips. He answers the test in the fullest degree — separation from her means death, which he at once proceeds to inflict upon himself. Other motives, too, influence his resolution — as the sense of shame, the fear of dishonor, the loss of his opportunity; but the main impelling power which drove the last blow was the thought of being forever disjoined from Cleopatra. Thus his deepest principle asserts itself with an absolute supremacy. He had already sacrificed an empire and a world-historical destiny for his love; it is easy and consistent now to give his life in addition. His career is made up of a series of external conflicts on account of his passion, and internal conflicts with his passion.

3. The third phase of the second movement is embraced in the last Act. Cleopatra is now the central figure. The difference between her and Antony is seen in the fact that she is willing to survive him, but he was not willing to survive her; separation does not mean death in her case. There is, however, no doubt about her love for Antony, but there is as little doubt about her readiness to transfer it to another person. She has been making provision for the future — she has been laying plans to catch Octavius in her toils. He comes into her presence; but he is not charmed; his cool head cannot be turned by sensuous enchantment. This seals her fate. She has met her master; she has found the man who is able to resist her spell. The proof is manifest — she learns that Octavius intends to take her to Rome to grace his triumph. This secret is confided to her by Dolabella, who seems to be the last victim of her magical power. That power is now broken; nothing remains except to die. Still, she shows signs of a better nature in this latter part — misfortune has ennobled her character:

"My desolation begins to make a better life."

The heroic qualities of Antony, now that he is gone and she can captivate no new hero, fill her imagination; she will go and join him in the world beyond. Her sensual life seems purified and exalted as she gives expression to her "immortal longings." Her deepest trait is, however, conquest through sensual love; she will live as long as she can conquer; when her spell is once overcome she will die, dwelling in imagination upon the greatest victory of her principle and upon its most illustrious victim.

The fate of the immediate personal dependents of Antony and Cleopatra is connected with that of their master and mistress. The relation is so intimate that they die together; the devotion of the servants will not permit them to survive. But Enobarbus is the most interesting of all these subordinate personages; his character, too, undergoes a change in this second part. His sharp intellect has foreseen, and tried to avert, the consequences of Antony's folly, but without avail. Now begins his internal conflict. Should he follow interest and desert a fool, or preserve fidelity and cling to his fallen master? It does not surprise us that he goes over to Cæsar; that he was led by his sagacity and not by his moral feeling. He saw the rising star of Octavius, and followed — but bitter is his disappointment. The conqueror will not trust a traitor. Enobarbus finds out that he has " done ill;" his intelligence has failed utterly. But this is not all. The generous Antony sends his treasure after him with kindly greetings. Now he calls himself, not fool, but villain; the moral elements — as honor, gratitude, fidelity, conscience — burst up in his soul with terrific force. This mediating principle, which was previously so inert, is now supreme, asserting itself over both pleasure and intellect. He repents

of his conduct, but is not reconciled; he slays himself—
an irrational act, but one which shows that remorse was
stronger than existence. So intense is his anguish that
he will not retain a life without moral devotion.

Octavius has passed his final and supreme conflict,
which the Poet seems to make the most difficult, as well as
the most glorious, of all the conflicts in the drama. . This
victory is greater than the victory over Antony, who
had already been subdued by Cleopatra; now the mighty
conqueress is herself conquered. The man who can resist
the fascination of the Orient is the true Roman—is the
ruler capable of maintaining and perpetuating the Roman
principle and the Roman empire. Even Alexander was
absorbed by the East, and his realm passed away like a
cloud. Octavius can spend a tear of pity over his illustrious foes, but his emotions never clouded his judgment
or hindered the clear, definite pursuit of his political end.
When the play terminates we feel that a great epoch, with
its external and internal throes, with its weak men and
mighty heroes, has passed away. All the struggles are
overcome, not by temporary compromises, but by the
subordination of the lower to the higher principle. The
world finds unity, peace, and law in the Empire. This
epoch is, therefore, the true date of Imperialism.

# TITUS ANDRONICUS.

It is not necessary to say much about this play. Its chief interest is certainly not æsthetic, but, from a biographical point of view, it derives some importance as indicating a very early and rude phase of the Poet's mental development. Since the biographical method is not followed in these essays, each drama must be regarded according to its own intrinsic worth, and not in its relation to the author. Two questions of some interest may be briefly noticed — the authenticity of the play, and its proper dramatic classification.

*Titus Andronicus* has often been declared not to be a work of Shakespeare's. The wish is here father to the thought; only internal evidence can be adduced in support of such an opinion, for the statement of Ravenscroft seems utterly untrustworthy. The external evidence is altogether too strong; many plays whose genuineness is not questioned are not so well authenticated. The testimony of Meres, and the insertion in the First Folio, are two facts which must be accepted, and which carry along with them an irresistible conclusion. Conjecture has sought to explain them away into a slight revision on the part of Shakespeare; so it may be, but alas! so, too, it may not be.

The second doubtful point is concerning the position of *Titus Andronicus* among the historical plays. Its right to such a place, though claimed by some critics, may be questioned. Its historical setting is manifest — the action occurs in an historical State, in an historical period, amid a great historical conflict; yet the story, as such, seems to be wholly legendary. But the political element equals, if it does not overtop, the domestic element; this is the essential test of an historical play. Tamora, the Gothic Queen, avenges upon Andronicus the defeat of her nation, as well as the slaughter of her son; also Aaron, the Moor, manifests the hatred of race, and his union with Tamora hints the union of the most diverse conquered peoples against their conqueror.

The most satisfactory way, therefore, is to consider this play as the termination of the Roman Historical series. For Rome herself was tragic — retribution came at last from those outlying barbarous peoples against which she had committed so many wrongs for hundreds of years. It was necessarily a scene of pure human butchery, the like of which, in quantity and degree, was probably never seen before or since — that of mad savagery turned loose upon its oppressor. Hence, after all that may be said against it, the play of *Titus Andronicus*, with its accumulated horrors, gives a true reflex of the end of Roman History.

# KING JOHN.

*King John* strikes the key-note of the whole series of
English Historical plays, namely, nationality. Its very
beginning utters a defiance against France, the hereditary
foe of England. The glory and supremacy of Fatherland
constitute the theme; there is a glow of patriotic exulta-
tion, which makes many verses shine like diamonds, while
the spirit of the whole work is one grand outburst of the
love of country. There is in it the intense consciousness of
English greatness, English freedom, English manhood.
The style, though varied, is always an exalted reflection of
its thought and feeling; the poetic fervor rises at times to
a sort of national ecstasy. Other strong passions of the
human soul are portrayed in the play, but they are all
subordinated to supreme devotion to country. Such is the
atmosphere which we here breathe, and which nerves the
spirit with a new inspiration. Indeed, there is a special
character introduced as the representative of nationality
— a character which gives tone to the entire drama. It is
Falconbridge, whose story is the golden thread which both
illumines and holds together the other parts of the action.
Following his career, we are perpetually reminded of the
theme which furnishes life and unity to the work.

In reading *King John* the chief disappointment seems
to arise from the fact that nothing is said of the Great
Charter. It would appear almost necessary that the great
Dramatic Epos of English History should begin with the

struggle from which England dates her liberties, and to which she points as the origin of her first and most important constitutional document. Thus the rise and growth of the English constitution would be the subject of the English Historical plays. But in *King John* the Great Charter is not even mentioned, and the nobles who revolt proceed on grounds very different from those recited in that famous instrument. It is clear that Shakespeare did not attach as much importance to the covenant at Runnymede as we do, if, indeed, he knew of its contents at all; the discussions and conflicts of a succeeding age first disturbed the dust on the venerable parchment. The struggle for individual liberty, which the Great Charter was supposed to guarantee, had not yet arisen, though its mutterings were plainly heard by the last of the Tudors. Under the Stuarts it broke forth and resulted in the Great Civil War. Then the origin of rights became the theme of warm discussion and diligent investigation; they were traced back to ancient grants and charters with that peculiar reverence for precedent in every Anglo-Saxon bosom — a reverence which will never accept a new idea unless dressed up in old, worn-out garments.

Personal liberty, in its universal sense, was certainly not the essential point in the conflict between King John and his barons; that conflict arose between the rights of the nobility and the rights of the crown. The people, as such, occupy no prominent place in the Great Charter. But in the time of the Stuarts the struggle lay between the people on the one side, and the crown and nobility on the other. Had the Poet lived earlier or later, he might have taken one or the other form of this collision; as the case stands, he takes neither. The age of Elizabeth was not a struggle between the throne and the barons, nor between these united and the people. The elements of the nation were in harmony, hence it was a period of internal peace and national development. But there was a dynastic conflict with a foreign State, and a religious conflict with a foreign Church. The consciousness arising from this condition of affairs is precisely the foundation of the present dama; hence its theme is, primarily, the Right of Succession to the crown. Must the title vest absolutely in the eldest of the line? Is it necessary or just that the heir should always be monarch? Here the answer will be given by Shakespeare. Secondary, but important, is the conflict with the See of Rome. The Poet cannot live out of his own time, in any true sense of the term; he writes his play, though it be historical, from the standpoint of his age.

The action will show the nation upholding the king, both against the legal heir of the throne and against the Church, as long as that king, in so doing, maintains the right and supremacy of the State. It will also show the nation falling off from the sovereign when the latter abandons his national principle and seeks to support his authority by violence and by external power. Thus there will be a transition from the true monarch of the people to the unfit occupant of a throne. The consciousness which underlies the whole fabric is that the right of a nation to a ruler is superior to the right of an heir to the crown. A kingdom is not a mere piece of personal property, subject to the laws of inheritance, or even of possession. Such is the conflict, plainly indicated; it is the universal right of the State against the individual right of the heir or of the possessor.

19

The drama has two well-marked movements—the one portraying the external struggle of the nation, the other portraying its internal struggle. Each movement has also two threads—the English and the foreign—and upon these threads the action takes its course. The first movement shows the king in conflict with the two extraneous powers—France and the Church—the political and the religious enemy. Both unite against England—the one supporting the right of Arthur as the legal heir to the throne, the other asserting the claim of Papal domination. King John steps forth as the defender of imperiled nationality; the people support him; he wins a complete victory over his combined enemies. This victory is brought about chiefly by Falconbridge, the type of the English national hero. Such is the first movement; the nation supports the king against the heir and against the Pope. The second movement now begins; it will show the change of character in the monarch, and the consequent disruption of the country internally. As long as John maintained the honor of England abroad, and took nationality as his guiding principle, he retained the unswerving allegiance of the English people. But he has the misfortune to capture the true heir, and at once he plots the young prince's murder to secure his throne. Thus, by his own act, he makes title of supreme importance; and, as he has not the legal title in himself, he logically destroys his own cause. He abandons his national principle for the principle of inheritance, which he had himself previously nullified. His title is now questioned, since it is his own deed which calls attention to its defect. Revolt of the nobles follows; disaffection of the people shows itself in dark forebodings. Then comes foreign invasion added to domestic strife, and, finally, an ignoble submission to the Church — that is, the victory which ended the first movement is completely reversed. John is no longer the true ruler, though he may now be the true heir after the death of Arthur; the nation is assailed from within and from without, and seems on the point of succumbing to the foreign political and to the foreign religious power — to France and to Rome. Nothing now remains to the king — who has sacrificed his most glorious national attribute, namely, the maintenance of the independence of England against all foes, internal and external — but death. Still, the nation cannot perish with him; the national hero, Falconbridge, again comes to the rescue of the drooping country; the enemy is worsted and retires, the nobles return to loyalty, a new king is crowned, and England is once more free from dissension and war. The very last speech of the play echoes the spirit of the whole; it is the exultant declaration of this same Falconbridge, the embodiment of English nationality, wherein he utters a parting shout of triumph and defiance:

> " This England never did, nor never shall,
> Lie at the proud foot of a conqueror,
> But when it first did help to wound itself.
> Now, these her princes are come home again,
> Come the three corners of the world in arms,
> And we shall shock them. Naught shall make us rue
> If England to itself do rest but true."

I. 1. We can now proceed to the detailed elaboration of the plan which has just been outlined. Let us follow out the English thread of the first movement. The beginning of the play ushers in at once the national conflict between France and England — a conflict which is continually reappearing throughout this whole series of historical dramas; hence the little scene here given is a kind of introduction to all which is to follow. The pretext on the part of France now is the claim of young Arthur to the throne. The simple legality of this claim is unquestioned. It is admitted by Queen Elinor, by Falconbridge, and, indirectly, by John himself; indeed, the pith of the play would be destroyed by a denial of it. But the assertion of Arthur's title by France is assailing the autonomy of England, since a foreign potentate thus dictates who shall be her ruler. A legitimate king who owes his throne to external support cannot be the true representative of the State; thus there arises a struggle between the right of inheritance and the right of the nation.

John is now forced, as it were, into becoming the defender of his country, and, hence, the bearer of nationality. This is his only claim — and, indeed, it is the highest claim — to the throne; but he will lose sight of it — he will prove unequal to his lofty position. England is ready to ratify his title if he have the mettle of a ruler. It is at this point that we see the defect of his character; he starts well, but breaks down. The poem, however, must have a man without this flaw — a true and persistent representative of the national spirit — in order to supply what is wanting in the King. Here he comes, just after the defiance given to France; it is Falconbridge, to whose origin and personal qualities a long scene is devoted — not without purpose.

Let us scan him closely, therefore, and note every essential peculiarity with which the Poet has endowed him, for his character and actions belong not to History. The traits, physical and mental, which he manifests are so pro-

nounced that the Queen-mother at once recognizes the
young stranger to be the son of her son, Richard Cœur-
de-Lion, whose exploits in the Holy Land had made him
the English national hero. The descent of Falconbridge
is finally established by the confession of his own mother.
Thus both his ancestry and his character point him out as
the heir and supporter of English nationality. But the
circumstance which is dwelt upon with special emphasis is
his illegitimacy. The use to which the Poet puts this incident is in every way noteworthy, since it would seem to be
a perilous fact to meddle with in a drama.

The object is manifestly to sever the heroic individual
from the ethical relation of the Family in order to conse-
crate him more exclusively to the State. Falconbridge is
first introduced to us disputing the claim of his legitimate
brother to the paternal estate. His title to the property
is based upon the fact that he is the elder son, which fact
would ordinarily make out a clear case of right; but his
sonship is questioned, and, what is more, is wholly dis-
proved. He manifestly does not believe in his own claim;
he very soon abandons it and accepts sonship derived
from the great King Richard, outside of the pale of the
Family. Thus he is declared the heir of that man
whom the nation delights to call its hero, and now he
will begin life anew as the champion of nationality. The
frail-bodied, weak-spirited brother takes the inheritance
of the Family, while Falconbridge himself is adopted into
the great national family of the Plantagenets. The English humor which previously added such a healthy flavor
to his English good sense now overflows his whole being,
yet he is imbued with a hearty earnestness in every fiber.
He takes pride in his birth; he would not choose any

other if he could. Legitimacy only is derived from the Family; his institution, the State, is something more exalted and more worthy of a great character. His origin, therefore, is national — as near as such a thing is possible — and not domestic; his career must be national, and not domestic.

In other plays the Poet has introduced the Bastard, but has endowed him with a character altogether different. In *Lear* and in *Much Ado About Nothing* he is portrayed as the natural villain, in hostility with the whole Ethical World. Since both Family and State disown him, deride him, oppress him without any fault of his own, he turns against them both and tries to destroy them. Such is the logical result of illegitimacy amid social institutions — their victim becomes their bitterest foe. But in the present play the Bastard is rescued by being elevated into a national existence, which is the more intense and vigorous because of his total separation from the domestic bond. He thus can have an institutional — and, hence, a truly national — life. Such is the meaning of his adoption into the Plantagenets — the royal family is national rather than domestic; but even in it he is still not legitimate.

The third character of this English group will express a new relation between Family and State. It is now a woman — Elinor — usually called the Queen-mother; that is, both queen and mother. Thus there are united in her person two relations — the political and the maternal — which are always incompatible and often in collision. On the French side is her counterpart, Constance, who also is, or aspires to be, Queen-mother. Each is the real power behind the throne, and each without doubt justly blames the other for the troubles which have sprung up;

both have equal hate, yet both show a touch of horror at
the war. The effect of this political relation of the mother
upon the Family is now seen — its members are torn asunder with the passions of civil strife; Elinor opposes the
claim of her grandchild, Constance goes to war with her
son's kindred. Elinor is now Queen-mother, but, if
Arthur possesses the crown, then she will no longer be
Queen-mother, but Constance will be. Thus political
ambition is the motive which drives her to disrupt her
own family — to violate the right of her own grandson, a
right which she herself acknowledges to be valid. Domestic life is impossible in such a condition of affairs; the
tender maternal relation loses its sweetness and beauty;
its vital warmth is deadened by a political relation.
Womanhood, too, drops its highest, most glorious, principle — devotion to the Family; its purity is sullied with
rancor and intrigue; the female emotional nature turns to
gall and becomes the source of the most bitter passion.

It is not to be denied, however, that a rational ground
can be given for introducing the domestic into the political relation in the case of royal families; indeed, such a
procedure is inwoven into the very fabric of the customs,
laws, and institutions of modern Europe. Still, it means
the sacrifice of the woman in the subordination of Family
to State, for thus her world is destroyed or plunged into
an atmosphere poisonous to its organization. Such is the
English thread, with its three prominent characters, though
others will be added hereafter. Each of these, it should
be noticed, manifests some phase of the conflict between
the domestic institution and the political institution.

2. We may now pass to the French thread and notice
its leading personages. Here, too, we find a Queen-

mother, as was before stated — a woman whose ambition has kindled a war between France and England. She is ready to sacrifice nationality to the claim of her boy and to her personal advancement; in general, she tries to immolate the State on the altar of her family. This is not political wisdom; for, if she conquered, her child could not be truly king — the ruler of an independent people. She would destroy the nation in acquiring its scepter; she thus is defeating her own end. But she is thereby made the unconscious instrument of French aggrandizement, and, when she is no longer needed, she is quietly set aside. Her character is full of the deepest pathos and passion; the pith of her delineation lies in the perpetual struggle within her bosom between the mother and the queen; her soul is cut in two, and she surges from one side to the other in a tempest of grief. As queen she exposes her child to the perils of war and diplomacy, but as mother her heart breaks when he is taken prisoner. It must be granted, therefore, that motherhood was the deepest principle of her nature, though it was covered over with so much ambition and selfishness that it required a great calamity to make it burst up through the hardened crust on the surface.

The Duke of Austria, the next figure, is the result of an historical confusion of two different persons, but his character stands forth clearly outlined, though verging toward caricature. He is the intended contrast to Falconbridge, who hates him as the supposed slayer of Richard the Lion-hearted. The son is thus marked out as the avenger of his father's death, wherein, however, there is little honor, since the Duke is a notorious coward. But retribution is visited upon the destroyer of the English national hero, in spite of history and chronology, and patriotic feeling is satisfied. The fact that the Duke of Austria espouses the cause of Arthur is sufficient to brand it with the hostility of England.

Next comes the French rulers, father and son, whose contrast lies chiefly in their moral natures. The King is a man of conscience; his actions proceed from his convictions of duty; his ground for maintaining the title of Arthur is justice. He is also deeply religious in his feelings, but the essence of religion for him lies in its moral significance, and not in devotion to an ecclesiastical organization. With the latter, indeed, he will collide in the course of the play. He considers himself to be the guardian of right, violated in the person of a helpless boy, and his commission he holds

> " From that supernal judge that stirs good thoughts
> In any breast of strong authority,
> To look into the blots and stains of right.

The character of the man in other situations can leave no doubt concerning the sincerity of these words; it is the religious conscience which speaks in him and directs his actions. He, therefore, will develop a twofold conflict with the influences of his own party, besides his struggle with John. He is not a mere politician — hence he will collide with the political selfishness which is seeking to control the French expedition; nor is he a mere devotee of the Church — hence he will oppose its violation of good faith and moral rectitude. Conscience thus arrays him against the policy of the Dauphin and the policy of the Legate.

His son, Lewis the Dauphin, is of quite the opposite char-

acter; the moral element is simply cut out of his spiritual
nature. He is a most obedient son of the Church when
the Church falls in with his schemes of aggrandizement,
but he sets aside her authority without the least hesitation
if she oppose his designs. He is restrained by no delicate
scruples of truth or honor from gaining a personal advantage; his plighted faith is merely a means of deception.
He, therefore, disregards the conscience of his father
on the one hand, and the authority of the Church on the
other hand, if either should happen to stand in the way
of his personal ambition; he is a self-seeker in politics
and a hypocrite in religion. He has no great national end
to excuse or sanction his ethical violations; his object is
an individual one, to which he is ready to sacrifice both
principles and institutions.

To complete this foreign group of characters we shall
go out of the way a little, and consider here the Legate
of Rome, Pandulph. Our mother, the Church — for this
is the image which she loves to employ, and by which we
love to designate her — transcends her religious function
and seeks to control the political movements of the time.
Her heavenly raiment thus becomes spattered with ter-
restrial mud; her religious yearnings are strangely inter-
mingled with secular aspirations. Now, Pandulph is the
embodiment of this tendency — a political clergyman, or
a clerical politician. In him the Church-mother, like the
Queen-mother before mentioned, seems to have lost something of her maternal instincts, for she is continually falling out with her dear children and beating them sorely.
It is true that they often deserve a whipping on account
of their naughty behavior, but she appears to be not
wholly impartial, for she is rather inclined to spare the

favorite transgressor. Her representative is Pandulph, who is the master of cunning and casuistry — the one of which enables him to overreach in politics, the other to hunt down any moral scruples. He will have to face a double — indeed, a triple — conflict; as he asserts the supremacy of the Church, he is forced to assail and suppress the claims of the State, Family, and Conscience.

Let us now pass to the story of the play and behold these characters in action. Before the walls of Angiers the French and English armies are drawn up and the struggle begins. The two Kings declare the grounds of their conduct; John asserts the right of national self-control without foreign interference; Philip maintains the right of inheritance, though he thereby has constituted himself the judge of another nation. Then the two Queen-mothers take up the dispute; the hot words fly like sparks; both indulge in a display of the fiercest passion. Their talk descends to billingsgate, that smoking falchion of female indignation; the culmination is that each charges the other with the highest vice of her sex — unchastity. Thus alongside the war of men we have the more furious, yet less bloody, war of women. The effect of political interest upon the Family is here seen to be the destruction of domestic harmony. Another pair of natural enemies —Falconbridge and Austria — show their teeth in this interview, but do not yet bite.

The town of Angiers is in a state of anxious inquiry; it has forgotten to which of the kings it owes allegiance, and is wholly unable to decide the question. Here they both come with sweet words of persuasion, but the arguments of each are so strong against the other that the town concludes to obey neither. That little community has reduced the science of politics to its ultimate proposition — we belong to the winning side. The monarchs themselves must first settle which of the two is the more powerful, for towards him its loyalty has no bounds. But the proposal angers Falconbridge; it seems to him to be an affront to nationality — his deepest principle. He, therefore, suggests that both armies reduce Angiers, and then they will have something to fight for. As the case stands, the exhausted victor would probably not be able to take the prize after it was won. The recusant town is on the point of being punished for lack of patriotic devotion, but its political cunning does not desert it in the hour of need, and again it is ready with a new proposition. This is nothing less than a marriage between Blanche, the niece of King John, and Lewis, the son of King Philip, which makes the gates of the town fly open "with swifter spleen than powder."

The matter is speedily arranged; John divides the English territory in order to furnish the requisite dower, and herein shows his lack of national feeling. But, above all, eager is the heart of the crafty Elinor, Queen-mother, who thus wins a complete triumph over her rival, Constance. The King of France also yields to the political situation, after uttering one deep sigh of conscience and causing provision to be made for Arthur. The chief sacrifice, however, is the sweet and innocent Blanche. She is a Princess; domestic life for her is impossible; she is to be offered up to the Moloch of the State. She accepts her destiny with resignation, though she tries to infuse into her situation some of the warmth of conjugal emotion; still, her royal birth tears her from the hearth in order to make her an offering. It is again the sacrifice of the Family to political considerations. The Dauphin takes the Princess for her lands, though he, in the hollow fashion of the court, gives an extravagant declaration of love. The object of such an alliance is manifest; it is to banish the conflict of the State by interposing the Family —to supplant national enmity by domestic affection. The bulwark, however, is very imperfect; the demands of the State usually swallow up the ties of the Family, and a political marriage is sure to become a domestic curse. Such is the inherent nature of the present situation.

Let us next see what are the elements of opposition to this union. First, Falconbridge objects most decidedly —and he represents the spirit of the English nation. The agreement dismembers the territory of England; it violates national honor; it brings submission without a struggle. Indeed, both Kings have disregarded the principles upon which they began the war. John took arms to maintain the integrity of his country, which he has now divided; Philip, "whose armor conscience buckled on," has yielded the claim of Arthur for the sake of his own interests, though he tries to a certain extent to rectify his wrong. In reflecting upon these matters, Falconbridge is disgusted and angered at the political chicanery of both sides; he, for a moment, seems on the point of abandoning his great principle of nationality, and substituting self-interest or "commodity." But this was merely a temporary fit of spleen; it is his first lesson in politics, and he will get over it like other people since his time. Though he here says, "Gain be my lord," he remains afterwards true to his lofty end, and continues to the last to be the truest representative of the nation.

The second person whose opposition to the marriage may be expected is Constance. She sees her son's interests sacrificed, her own rights ignored, sacred oaths disregarded; all her hopes are at once crushed into despair. The intensity of her anguish throws out words that burn like molten iron; her passion turns to a wild frenzy. It is manifest that her political ambition is so ingrained into her very nature that to part with it is next to death. The question now arises in the mind of the reader or hearer: Which side of her double nature is the stronger — the queen or the mother? Her grief at present results from not being queen, for she is still mother — still possesses her boy. The severest test is soon to be applied. Constance will lose her little son in the approaching battle; she will then be no longer mother. Her conduct in that situation must tell which is the deeper principle of her character. But now it is her political disappointment that lashes her feelings into a tempest of passionate utterance.

The third opponent of the alliance with England — and, hence, of the marriage of Blanche and the Dauphin — is Pandulph, the representative of the Church, which has excommunicated King John for disobedience to its mandates. The Church thus asserts an authority above the State; it is also an organized power, with mighty instrumentalities for enforcing its will. Now comes the conflict between the religious and the political institutions. King John boldly proclaims the independence of the nation:

> —" No Italian priest
> Shall tithe or toll in our dominions;
> But as we under heaven are supreme head,
> So under heaven that great supremacy,
> Where we do reign, we will alone uphold,
> Without the assistance of a mortal hand."

This is a most emphatic statement of the political significance of the Reformation, which brought about the subordination of Church to State. Pandulph, on the contrary, asserts ecclesiastical supremacy, absolves the nation from its allegiance, takes away kingship; in fine, he seeks to destroy utterly the civil relation between monarch and subject. He proclaims that the assassin of John is to be "canonized and worshiped as a saint;" a monk will hereafter seek to obtain this most holy laurel.

The Legate also commands the recent agreement to be broken, and the French army to be employed against the English heretic. Let us now watch the father and son — Philip and Lewis — acting in accordance with their different principles. The son is without conscience. He sees in the present turn of affairs an opportunity for personal advantage greater than those which the fulfillment of the marriage contract offered — he uses the Church as a means. At once he becomes very pious, and insists upon obedience to Pandulph's order. To be sure, he violates good faith, and endangers the new-born Family to which he has pledged his sacred fealty; but these are moral considerations, which have not the weight of a feather against his self-interest.

Passing to the father, we observe one of the most profound collisions to be met with in the works of Shakespeare. Philip possesses a powerful — indeed, controlling — principle in conscience. Good faith, amity, oaths, are spiritual elements which he cannot disregard. But here is the Church, which commands him to break them; and the Church, too, is a principle which he acknowledges most devoutly. What is he to do? Philip hesitates to obey the mandate of Pandulph, and maintains the right of moral obligation as revealed in the human heart. It is the great function of the Church to foster and enforce the moral conscience of man; but the Church now has a political end, to which it subordinates its religious end. It is thus in contradiction with itself, and is really destroying the purpose of its existence. The King of France, therefore, asserts the internal spirit of the Church against its formal authority.

But Pandulph is just the man — who has been trained by a rigid scholastic discipline — to meet and put down such cases of rebellious conscience. His argument goes to enforce the submission of private judgment to ecclesiastical control, and to assert the supremacy of the external organization of religion to its internal behests. Most subtly does he point out the contradiction between these two principles:

> "It is religion that doth make vows kept;
> But thou hast sworn against religion
> By what thou swear'st against the thing thou swear'st,
> And mak'st an oath the surety for thy truth
> Against an oath."

The form also is most happy; the bald, logical utterances of scholastic divinity echo from every line; the vein of fine-spun casuistry, confusing the head and misleading the heart, gives a suspicious subtlety to the whole speech. But it is far from being a mere sophistical jingle of words; on the contrary, it is a genuine statement of the right of religious authority against the right of individual opinion. There is, however, a most important suppression in the argument of the Legate. It is that the prime duty of religion is to quicken the conscience of man; and when the organization of religion — the Church — for its own purposes seeks to deaden that conscience, its right of existence has ceased. Philip is manifestly not convinced, but withdraws his opposition, and henceforward drops out of the play.

The mandate of Pandulph causes still another struggle —it threatens the disruption of the Family, here represented by the Lady Blanche. The agreement whereby her marriage took place is broken —broken by order of the Church which makes marriage a sacrament. Which shall she follow? Husband or kindred? It tears her heart asunder to decide. Blanche differs from the other women of the drama in having no political ambition; she is the true woman — devotion to the Family is her whole nature. But the Family is now at war with itself; so must she be. Both Church and State sacrifice her to their purposes. She was born to be an offering; her lovely form is mangled in the conflict of nations; the last note that we hear from her is a wail of agony over her situation.

If we now sum up the collision in which the Church is involved, we find it to have three phases — the collision with State, Family, and Morality. A political supremacy is the ultimate object of the See of Rome. In carrying out this object it comes into conflict with the entire sphere of ethical relations. It compels the individual to fight against his nation; to disregard his domestic ties; to surrender his conscience. Now, since religion must have these ethical principles as its only true content, it has reached a condition of absolute self-contradiction — its organization has turned into the bitterest foe of that which it was created to secure. The opposition between form and spirit is carried to the point at which they entirely fall asunder, and a breach is inevitable. But the

Church, for the present, triumphs over all its obstacles — it subordinates State, Family, and Conscience to its designs; the schism within it has not yet sunk into the mind of Europe.

This great conflict is not portrayed by the Poet with partisan bigotry and malice, but it is shown in its simple purity — in its true colliding principles. The old play of *King John*, which Shakespeare probably took as the foundation of the present work, is full of Protestant rancor and one-sidedness. But here each element is given in its validity as well as in its inadequacy. The result is curious: Shakespeare has been claimed to be both a Catholic and a Protestant, but he is neither; he is the Poet who sees in every great struggle two conflicting principles, each of which has its truth and its error, its right and its wrong, yet one of which is supreme. His oath to his genius is: I shall show both sides as they are, by the eternal gods.

No doubt here is witnessed the same contest logically which is known in history as the Reformation. That movement was a protest of Conscience, Family, and State against the crushing formalism of the Church. The result of it was that it established, in a part of Europe, at least, the subordination of Church to State; it justified the Family by abolishing celibacy; it generally upheld the right of private judgment in regard to matters of Conscience. But, on the other hand, the Church is not without its strong justification, and Protestantism is not without its serious weakness. The Poet has taken the precaution to throw the struggle into a period long antecedent to the Reformation, and thus exhibit purely the principles at issue, without exciting the blinding passions of theological controversy which the real event would awaken. Nor are the principles confined to Englishmen. King Philip of France is a Protestant, uttering the protest of Conscience in a far higher sense than King John.

The two armies now fight the battle. England is victorious on all sides. Nationality is asserted triumphantly against France and the Church. The hero of the fight is Falconbridge; it is his spirit which animates the English hosts. The greatest result of the victory is that Arthur, the claimant of the throne, is taken prisoner. But this is the supreme misfortune of John, and constitutes the turning-point of his destiny. Arthur abroad, supported by foreign foes, is an external danger which unites all England under the banner of the King; but Arthur a captive, at home, is the object of royal suspicion and popular sympathy.

II. The trouble now becomes internal — this is just the transition to the second movement. As long as the enemy of the nation supports the heir, the nation supports the usurper in the external struggle; but, when the struggle ends, the usurper must not assail the heir, who also has his right. This is just what John proceeds to do; hence arises the internal struggle. The theme is nationality against inheritance; the former is supreme, yet the latter has its validity. From disruption within to national restoration will be the course of the second movement, ending in the coronation of a new monarch. Here also are the same two threads as before.

1. The English thread may now be taken up and followed through to the end. John orders Arthur to be put to death, thus abandoning his first support — the nation — and seeking to obtain by crime the title. But thereby

he really loses his only claim, for he is not truly a ruler
now; and, moreover, he acknowledges by his conduct the
superior right of Arthur. But the young prince is not
murdered; he perishes in attempting to escape from
prison. His character is that of pure innocence and
sweetness, to which childhood is added; still, fate has
made him the center around which gather foreign war
and civil dissension. The life of a guiltless boy thus
seems to threaten — at least to disturb — the life of a
nation. He would like to divest himself of the struggle
by forgetting his origin and turning shepherd, but royal
birth makes him a sacrifice. Still, he must be got rid of,
and, as he had done nothing worthy of death, the Poet dis-
poses of him by accident. The pathos of his situation
results from the sight of an innocent and amiable youth
thrust between the shears of national destiny.

There is here a question about the character of Hubert,
Arthur's keeper. Did he intend to put out the young
prince's eyes, and then yield to the piteous entreaties of
the latter? Or was the whole transaction designed by him
in order to "fill these dogged spies with false reports?"
Hubert afterwards says repeatedly that he never entertained the thought of murdering the child, and we must
. accept his statement or consider him guilty of prevarica-
tion. To burn out the eyes, and to kill, are not the same
thing; perhaps Hubert intended to do the former, but not
the latter. In this manner all his declarations and acts
may be reconciled. The question has two sides; still, it
comports best with the whole text to consider him a man
of noble instincts under a rude exterior, whom even
Arthur loved, though his jailer. The King has simply
made a mistake in judging of Hubert's character by his

rough appearance — a mistake which Hubert resents both
in deed and in word; for he saves the young prince, and
declares to John in person, who had really entrapped him
into the promise of murder before he knew it.

> " Within this bosom never enter'd yet
>    The dreadful motion of a murd'rous thought,
>    And you have slander'd nature in my form;
>    Which, howsoever rude exteriorly,
>    Is yet the cover of a fairer mind,
>    Than to be butcher of an innocent child. "

This passage doubtless gives the true explanation of his
character, and is the test by which everything else said or
done by him is to be measured.

A great change is now to be observed in the King. He
becomes suspicious in mind and dilatory in action; he is
plotting to secure the title which springs from birth, and
he gives the nation over to discord from within and to
invasion from without. He has done a great wrong;
guilt destroys his mental repose and undermines his outward activity. His opposition to the Church has also
turned into an abuse; he plunders it for money, instead of
resisting its political encroachments. The struggle, both
with Arthur and with Rome, has been pushed beyond the
limit of right into the realm of violation. Such is generally the case with the conqueror; he knows no bounds,
and he ends by subverting in victory the very principle
which he fought to establish. The psychological change
and the political change exactly correspond — one reflects
the other.

Now comes the reaction against him, which shows itself
in two forms — internal strife and foreign invasion. Of

the troubles at home, the first is the revolt of the nobles, whose chief representative is Salisbury. The wrongs committed by the King make them disaffected, and, finally, the death of Arthur drives them into open rebellion. Thus, however, they fall into as deep a violation as the King — they become the assailants of the nation. Moreover, their conduct is partially based upon a mistake about the manner of Arthur's death. Their wrong is manifest — they would sacrifice the independence of their country to their moral indignation. Conscience now turns against nationality, as, in the case of the French King, it turned against the Church. This is the most modern of all collisions to be found in Shakespeare, for it belongs, in its full development, to our own time; it gives an expression of the conflict between the individual sense of duty and the authority of institutions. But, in the scope and intensity which it has in the present age, it does not belong to the Shakespearian world.

The second internal trouble is the dangerous commotion among the people. These acts of John they feel to be destructive of peace and justice; this feeling they express, not in the form of an abstract proposition, but they take the manifestations of Nature for their language. At once the whole physical world becomes the mirror of the political world; the storm, the sun, the moon, the bird, are omens which prognosticate the revolutions of society and the destiny of the individual. Such is the employment of the supernatural appearance by the Poet; it is a mode of expression for what lies vaguely in the feelings. It is not mere superstition; it tells the truth, though darkly and remotely. In this very play Shakespeare puts into the mouth of Pandulph, the man of intellect and not of emotion, a full explanation of his method:

> "No natural exhalation in the sky,
> No scape of nature, no distemper'd day,
> No common wind, no custom'd event,
> But they will pluck away his natural cause,
> And call them meteors, prodigies, and signs,
> Abortives, presages, and tongues of heaven,
> Plainly denouncing vengeance upon John."

The culmination of this popular feeling is found in the prophet who foretells, in wild and often frenzied utterance, the consequences of national wrong. Here he is, too — Peter of Pomfret, who has declared that the King will deliver up his crown " ere the next Ascension day at noon," and who goes through the country " with many hundreds treading on his heels." It is merely a way that the people have of declaring their deepest conviction that retribution will be visited upon the violator of right, and that the conduct of John merits dethronement — even death. This judgment they read in Nature, and hear from the mouth of the Seer; the justice of this world is the religion of the next.

The King has thus alienated the three estates of his realm — Clergy, Nobles, Commons. He sees the result and tries to make his deeds undone. He seems to repent bitterly of the supposed murder of Arthur; he seeks reconciliation with the indignant lords. But in these retractions he proceeds, not from principle, but from weakness; it is not so much repentance for a great wrong as terror at a great mistake. Then follows his cowardly submission to the Church, in which he surrenders to Rome national independence without reserve. This is the completion of his downward career; he has totally reversed his first patriotic position; he has declared by his act that he is not the sovereign of free England. But the nation will not perish; it has a guardian in the person of Falconbridge, who still is ready and able to protect it against all its enemies, both foreign and domestic. The King's submission is shown to be utterly fruitless. It does not rid the country of the foreign invader, for Pandulph cannot force the Dauphin to retire; nor does it secure John even against the religious enemy, for a member of the plundered clergy administers to him a fatal draught of poison. Such is this impressive history; it shows the fate of the ruler who begins by maintaining nationality and then sinks to its surrender — he destroys his own authority and logically deposes himself.

2. We may now take up the French thread of the second movement, beginning just after the English victory. It is first to be seen how Constance will endure the captivity of her son. Hitherto she has been the politician, but at present she will manifest the mother. It is not the loss of the throne which now seizes hold of her mind; her ambition is sunk in the terrific violence of maternal grief. She wants to die — rejects all comfort, refuses the religious consolation of the future state, and ends in madness. Most awful, yet deeply significant, is that passage wherein her sinking reason leads to a disbelief in the restoration of her lost child in Heaven. Only through the imagination can she bring back her pretty Arthur, but to take his image for reality is insanity. Over the rest a veil is drawn; we merely learn of her death afterwards in a fit of frenzy. Hers is a most profoundly tragic female character, in which the conflict between the political and domestic relation is expressed with a Titanic intensity.

But motherhood wins the triumph, yet it is a triumph which costs both reason and life.

The next move on the part of the French is the invasion of England, which is strongly urged by the Legate. He has clearly fathomed the character of John, and partially that of the English people. His sagacity tells him that the King will murder Arthur and thus excite disaffection. His argument seems so plausible that the Dauphin is convinced and makes the expedition, but the conscientious father, Philip, does not appear to have taken part. It will be noticed that Pandulph in these discussions rests his foresight upon general principles, and not upon instinct; he is the man of understanding, and not the prophet. He states the exact ground of French success and of English misfortune; it lies in the captivity of Arthur, which is thus the turning-point of the drama.

The revolted English nobles come to the aid of the invader. Their moral conscience has driven them to abandon their country and desert to its foe. They, when surrounded by French soldiery on every side, feel the torturing contradiction of their conduct; Salisbury, in deep distress, gives utterance to the struggle in his bosom. It causes him sorrow to " heal the inveterate canker of one wound by making many;" he feels the bitterness of having to "step after a stranger" here in his own Fatherland, and to follow the " unacquainted colors" of the ancestral enemy of his people. So the moral man becomes aware of guilt in carrying out his one-sided principle, and conscience has fallen into an utter contradiction with itself. The cause is not left in doubt. He has not been able to see that his duty to the nation is first and supreme; and this is his contrast to Falconbridge. Hear his de-

•

fense and judge of it—evil must be done that good may
come :

> " For the health and physic of our right,
> We cannot deal but with the very hand
> Of stern injustice and confused wrong."

Thus morality has surged over to the support of its direst
foe — the so-called Jesuitical maxim.

But the full consequence of the deed is yet to come.
These nobles are traitors; hence the thought is near that
they may betray one side as well as another. To the
French, therefore, they are objects of suspicion, which is
increased by Salisbury's strong expressions of grief at the
state of his country. The Dauphin, too, is by nature
inclined to suspect a moral person as not subservient to
his purpose. The result is : As they betray, so they are
betrayed; their action is about to be brought home to
themselves. They are warned in season and escape,
returning with deep thankfulness to the nation even
under that king whom they had before deserted. Let the
conscientious but wrong-headed men learn a lesson and
be saved, this time at least, saith the Poet.

But now we are to have a final exhibition of the Legate
and the Dauphin. John submits to Rome; Pandulph
orders the French army to withdraw. The Dauphin, from
the obedient son of the Church, becomes, in a breath, its
most refractory child. What is the matter? His political
interest now conflicts with religious authority, and he, in
his turn, has come to refuse subordination to Rome; he
is just where John was before. The Dauphin has no conscience; the Church is employed by him simply as an
instrument. But Pandulph is truly a comic figure; here
his deep policy has swallowed itself. The State which he

invoked to subject State to Church very naturally refuses to be subjected itself. This is just the old struggle over again — the Legate is exactly where he began. Such is the outcome of the political authority of the Church; it shows indeed a comic retribution. When the end is supposed to be gained, it is simply lost. Pandulph vanishes, and Lewis declares for battle.

England, therefore, must look for defense to her own stalwart arm; an Italian priest cannot secure natural autonomy. Now is the time for the hero to enter and assert his principle. On the spot he appears, uttering the defiant voice of the nation against France, the Church, and domestic traitors. Falconbridge was deeply disgusted at the submission of John, but that could not taint his devotion to his country. His moral indignation also was intensely aroused when he beheld the dead form of Prince Arthur lying upon the rocks, but he never entertained the thought, for that reason, of deserting to the hereditary foe of his native land. In all his actions there is seen the same adamantine fidelity to England, and his extravagant laudation of her valor and greatness comes from his innermost soul. As opposed to the ecclesiastical, domestic, and moral person — all of whom are represented in the drama — he is national. This does not mean that he wantonly disregards these other principles, but, in case of a conflict between them and the nation, he goes with the nation.

Under his leadership England triumphs a second time over France, and the kingdom is brought back to internal harmony. Corresponding to this national restoration is the death of the sovereign who was unable to uphold the principle of his country. A new king must begin the

new epoch; he is the son of John, and, hence, the conflict between inheritance and possession, which opened
the play, is now solved.  But, at the same time, it is
announced in thunder-tones that the heir must be a ruler;
that he must truly represent the deepest national aspiration; that the loss of birthright shall follow like destiny
upon his desertion of nationality.  It is the same lesson
both in the case of Arthur and in the case of John — the
right of succession is valid within its limitation; but,
when it conflicts with the right of the nation, it must be
set aside.  Such has always been the fundamental principle of the English people, though to maintain it has cost
many an intestine struggle.  The final solution came by
taking away from the king political power, so that he could
not be the supreme representative of the nation, and
leaving to him the empty right of inheritance.  But this
revolution was destined to take place long after the time
of Shakespeare.  The play ends — the last person to leave
the stage is Falconbridge; there he stands, speaking to
future England and inspiring it with his own lofty spirit
of nationality, as he utters words which stir the breast
like the trumpet-call of battle.

# RICHARD THE SECOND.

In *Richard the Second* the fundamental theme is the right of revolution. We behold a king deposed, and the grounds of his deposition declared in the most explicit manner. It is manifest that the Poet intended to justify the change of rulers, and thus to show when revolution may be necessary for the welfare — perhaps for the existence — of the nation. The whole action is the story of a king who loses the essential attribute of kingship, and, hence, loses his crown. In English History the royal authority has been often claimed to be of God; Shakespeare boldly puts this religious element also into the conflict, and makes it subordinate to the national principle. Though Richard asserts the divinity of his office and its superiority to any human control, he is still hurled from his throne by the people of England. There is no disguise, no softening of the collision — it is the divine right of Kings against the temporal right of the State. The latter is supreme — is, indeed, the most divine of all things.

Let us note the connection between this and the preceding drama. In *King John* we see the monarch making good his defective title by his determined support of nationality. He maintains the independence and honor of England against her stalwart enemies — France and the See of Rome. Thus he is the true ruler, and receives the unquestioned loyalty of the people. But he loses his

lofty principle of action, namely, the defense of nationality; he submits abjectly to the Church, and the country
suffers the ignominy of a French invasion.  The change
in his conduct and character is complete; he is no longer
King, indeed, and we may suppose his violent death anticipated dethronement.  The main point to be noticed is
that John failed to support nationality against the external
powers which sought to subject it; he could not, therefore, remain the representative of the free nation.

In *Richard the Second* it is not a combat without, but a
struggle within; it is not the attitude of the king toward
foreign States, but his attitude toward his own subjects.
The issue is wholly internal, and now the right of the individual becomes the paramount object of interest.  But
Richard, as well as John, violates the principle of nationality, though in a different manner.  The English State
can not and ought not to be placed under the yoke of an
external power as long as its supreme end is to secure the
liberties of the subject.  The government which most
adequately maintains the rights of the individual will be
most strongly pillared in the hearts of the people.  The
depth and intensity of national feeling must in the end
repose upon the excellence and purity of national institutions, whose highest object may be stated to be the security of the Will of the Person in all its manifestations.  Let
this be destroyed by a government, then such a government is not worthy of its independence, and the people
are not fit to be free.

Here lies the violation of King Richard — he assailed
the truest principle of nationality by committing wrongs
upon the subject.  He refused to be controlled by the
law; the institution of which he was the head, and whose

end is to secure to every man his rights, was perverted
by him into an instrument of the most arbitrary extortion.
The very ruler was thus destroying the State, was assailing in its most tender germ the principle of nationality.
From being the means of protecting person and property,
government in his hands has become the most potent
engine of their destruction. Such a king must be put out
of the way; the struggle cannot be avoided. The question is: Shall the nation or the sovereign endure? The
answer is given in this drama by the deposition and death
of King Richard the Second.

But the conflict cannot end here. There are two sides
— both have their validity; each party has committed a
violation. The title of Richard is unquestioned; his right
to the crown is asserted by that same law for the defense
of which he has been deprived of the throne. The
wrong of Richard has been punished by the loss of his
kingdom, but his punishment has begotten a new wrong,
which, by the same inexorable logic, must call forth a
new retribution. Such a result will take place, but to
portray it will far transcend the limits of a single drama.
Hence arises the necessity of the Tetralogy, or series of
four plays; two such Tetralogies now follow in regular
sequence. It ought also to be observed that the king
who succeeds Richard is not the next in line of succession. Thus the right of inheritance is doubly violated —
the second time without any guilt on the part of the true
heir. After two generations of men, and after the original violators have lain long in their tombs, the penalty
will come — the most terrific struggle known in English
History, the Wars of the Roses, will break out concerning
the right of inheritance, and sweep the descendant of

Bolingbroke from the throne, and his entire family into the grave. Thus we pass from the Lancastrian to the Yorkian Tetralogy.

But we have at present to consider the Lancastrian Tetralogy, whose logical frame-work should be carefully examined. King Richard is deposed — in undermining the law he has undermined his own throne, which rested upon the law; the consequence of his deed has been visited upon him. But who is to succeed him? Here it is naturally the man who has been most deeply wronged — who, in his own person, most adequately represents the majesty of violated justice. Thus a subject has revolted from the king and made himself king; he has obtained the crown by acknowledging and maintaining in arms the right of revolution. The new king has, therefore, called into existence the principle of his own dethronement, and has enforced it as a basis of action for the entire nation. For the conviction of the people must go along with their deed; that deed has been dethronement, and, hence, their conviction is now grounded upon the right of deposing the legal sovereign.

This is the difficulty of all revolutions; they are aimed at the stability of institutions — hence they cannot be very stable of themselves. A revolutionary government is logically a contradiction in terms, for its purpose is to upset government — to destroy that which is established; hence its success depends entirely upon the speed with which it abandons its own principle. Having seen the right of revolution, we now behold the wrong of revolution — a wrong which will be brought home to every country that attempts revolutionizing, even from the most justifiable causes. A nation has to endure the penalty of violation, although that violation may be absolutely necessary to preserve a higher element of national existence. It is a genuine conflict of principles ; both sides are right, both are wrong, yet in different degrees ; the ultimate test of their relative worth is the universality of their principle. The chief characteristic of the Historical Drama is that it rises above the guilt and punishment of the mere individual, and shows the guilt and punishment of whole nations and whole epochs, thus manifesting how the deed in history returns to the land with a whip of scorpions, even after the lapse of generations.

(The deposition of Richard, therefore, will not end the conflict ; revolution has been let loose in the country, and must, in its turn, be put down. It was stated that the act of Bolingbroke is in its nature contradictory of itself ; that the dethronement of the king, applied as a general principle, must mean his own dethronement.) The logic of the situation at once begins to disclose itself ; the very men who aided him in acquiring the crown are just as ready to take it away again) Indeed, they must claim this to be a right of the subject. Thus the government of Bolingbroke inherits rebellion and revolution, which must be put down by force of arms — that is, he is forced to turn around and undo his own work, counteract his own principle, stamp out the doctrine of revolt by which he ascended the throne. If he is successful, he will restore the nation to harmony, confirm the succession in his family, and solidify the shattered institutions of the land. This is the great work whose accomplishment is portrayed in the First and Second Parts of *Henry the Fourth*, a truly national poem, whose theme is the restoration of England to internal peace and greatness. There-

21

fore, if *Richard the Second* showed the right of revolution and its success, *Henry the Fourth* shows the wrong of revolution and its defeat. Still, there is one deep, underlying principle to both these works — it is the right ✕ of nationality, which at one time hurls the monarch from his throne and at another time tramples into dust the standard of rebellion.

The English nation, united within and confident of its strength, feels an aspiration for its ancient glory. There is nothing to do at home; the national enthusiasm cannot be restrained. Moreover, it finds in a new king a man of heroic mould. Just across the channel are situated the fair domains of France, the hereditary foe of the nation, and a large portion of these domains once lay at the feet of England. The play of *Henry the Fifth* is the last of this first group; it exhibits the spirit of nationality bursting its limits and going forth to subjugate other peoples. It is an epoch of national glory; England has become the proud conqueress; she seems poised on the very pinnacle of fame and prosperity. Thus ends the great Lancastrian Tetralogy, passing off the stage in a blaze of success and patriotic fervor. But at the same time it must not be forgotten that just here can be traced the source of the unutterable calamities which followed, and which brought on the overthrow of the Lancastrian dynasty. For England, through foreign conquest, is really destroying herself; she is assailing the independence of other nations, and therein is undermining her own principle of nationality, as well as opposing the world-historical movement of modern times, which is to maintain the autonomy of the individual State. She, therefore, is guilty of the deepest wrong against the spirit of the age and against the family of European nations, as well as of a crime against herself; hence bitter will be her retribution. But these considerations will be more fully developed when the Yorkian series comes up for treatment.

The drama of *Richard the Second* may now be unfolded in its details. Its purely poetic merits are of the highest order; in radiant glow of imagery and in fiery intensity of expression it is unsurpassed. It possesses also the national exaltation of the English Historical Drama generally; it lightens with passages of combined patriotic and poetic enthusiasm. Indeed, the leading character may be justly called a poet, whose own misfortunes inspire utterances of deep passion, mingled with the most brilliant hues of fancy. There is a lyrical coloring diffused over the entire work, and, as a drama exhibiting action and characterization, it can by no means be esteemed as highly as when it is considered simply as a beautiful poem.

The action exhibits a double change; it is a stream with two currents sweeping alongside of each other in opposite directions. It shows how to lose a realm and how to acquire a realm; it passes on the one hand from kingship to deprivation, and on the other hand from deprivation to kingship. It will, therefore, be manifest that the drama moves on two threads, having as their respective centers of interest the monarch dethroned and the monarch enthroned. The cause of this reciprocal change of situation is the wrong done to the subject by the king; a subject then defends his own rights, which is the right of the nation against the sovereign, and therein makes himself the representative of nationality. He thus takes the place of the king, since the latter is at the head of the

State, whose highest function is to secure justice, and not
to be the instrument of wrong. That subject, therefore,
who, in his own person, supremely represents justice, and
vindicates it when assailed, is in truth the ruler of the
people. The present drama will simply show this thought
working itself into reality.

There are also two movements in the play — the first of
which shows the guilt of the king, the second his retribution. Each movement carries along within itself the two
threads above mentioned — that of Richard and that of
Bolingbroke. The one falls, the other rises; at the point
of crossing, in their descent and ascent, lies in general the
dramatic transition. First we are made acquainted with
the crimes and follies of Richard — the murder of his
uncle, the supremacy of favorites, the banishment of Bolingbroke, the expedition to Ireland. The counter-thread
unfolds the scheme of Bolingbroke, his banishment and
his return, together with the disaffection of the nobles and
commons. The second movement exhibits the downward
career of Richard to dethronement and death, as well as
the execution of his favorites, while at the same time
Bolingbroke ascends the throne with the general consent
of the realm. Thus the guilt of Richard is punished by
that person upon whom he has inflicted a most wanton
injury; hence wrong and its retribution make up the whole
action.

I. At the beginning of the play the two threads run
together for a while, and then separate. The duel shows
the opposing sides, though Richard seems to be playing
the part of a mediator. He calls upon his uncle, the venerable John of Gaunt, to bring forward Harry Bolingbroke, Duke of Hereford, who had challenged Thomas

Mowbray, Duke of Norfolk. The two combatants at once appear, and each gives his statement of the case. Bolingbroke, who is the son of Gaunt and cousin of Richard, makes a number of charges, which seem to be in the nature of indefinite surmises, and which he himself did not seriously entertain; but there is one most emphatic accusation which manifestly embraces the whole ground of the challenge — his uncle, Gloster, was murdered by Mowbray. This deed of blood calls for justice, and Bolingbroke swears that he will be the avenger of his relative. Herein he declares his principle, which he will afterwards carry out in its extreme application. Mowbray easily answers the other charges, but the death of Gloster he hurries over with an ambiguous expression, in striking contrast with his general candor and plainness of statement. Something is the matter, and we shall watch sharply for the true explanation in the future course of the drama.

Richard tries to conciliate the fiery duelists by a little humorous banter, and then by an exercise of royal authority. But both refuse obedience in the most unequivocal manner. Herein we catch a slight glimpse of a principle which was supreme among the feudal nobility. Honor was above everything; if it collided with authority, the latter must yield; the king had no right of command in its realm. The individual alone is the monarch there, and is responsible for both word and deed. Life belongs to the sovereign and would be readily given at his bidding, but not honor; hence arose the duel, which was a trial above the law. Richard cannot reconcile the combatants, and so appoints a day for the fight.

But, before we proceed to the final result of the contest, we are fully initiated into the motives of all the prime

actors. The truth comes out plainly; Richard is himself
the cause of Gloster's murder, and Mowbray was at most
only his instrument. The entire situation clears up at
once; Bolingbroke is striking at Richard through Mowbray; already the wily politician snuffs the future revolution in the air. Hence throughout this duel the real combatants are the King and Bolingbroke. Here, too, is
shown the difference between young manhood and old age
—between son and father. Gaunt refuses to stir for the
punishment of his brother's murderers; though implored
by the widowed Duchess of Gloster, he can only leave
vengeance to God, who will, in His own good time, bring
retribution upon the offenders. Gaunt clearly sees what
the conflict involves. Justice invokes him to slay Richard,
yet thereby he will fall into guilt himself; his age and
disposition lead him to shun such an entangling collision,
and leave the wrong to Heaven for rectification. But the
son, Bolingbroke, is ready to undertake the struggle,
whose consequences will keep him busy the rest of his life.
For he can right the wrong only by doing a wrong, which,
in its turn, will call for its penalty.

The preparations for the duel are made in magnificent
style; the two combatants leap forth with an eager delight
for the fray, and utter mutual defiance. But, just as they
are about to engage, the King stops the encounter and
declares against both the sentence of banishment. Here
Richard appears in his best light; he says that he will not
suffer civil strife in his dominions, and that he will remove
all cause for internal war. In such combats he beholds
the "grating shock of wrathful iron arms," and he
darkly forebodes the bloodshed which will hereafter result
from feudal turbulence. The young monarch — for he

always appears as a youth — does not lack intellectual
vision; he will repeatedly manifest the clearest insight
into his surroundings, and foresee results far in the future
with the inspiration of a prophet. But there is no action
corresponding to his intuition; he can neither control
himself, nor does he know how to employ instrumentalities
to control others. His attempt to subordinate the principle of honor to authority is worthy of success, but his
means are utterly inadequate. When we reflect, too, that
he was well aware of the ambition and character of
Bolingbroke, we fully comprehend how unable such puny
hands were to wield the massive tools of government.

Let us now see in what manner the two noblemen conduct themselves under decree of exile. Bolingbroke
receives the sentence with a sort of defiant submission.
His actions seem to declare that banishment is one of the
means of accomplishing his political ambition; he goes
but in order to return. The parting interview with his
father is somewhat frosty, and suggests dissimulation. It
does not, indeed, appear that Bolingbroke had already
laid out consciously the complete plan of his future
career, but political instinct was urging him all the same
toward the throne. Mowbray, on the contrary, overflows
with the sorrow of hopeless separation; his punishment is
more severe, though less deserved, than that of Bolingbroke, and he plainly insinuates ingratitude against Richard — doubtless with good reason. His beautiful lament
has for its burden the loss of the English tongue, which
he must now forego in a strange land; it is a sentence
which condemns him to a speechless death. His function
in the play is thus accomplished; he will appear no more.
Though there are some later allusions to him, his part in

the murder of Gloster is not cleared up by them, and the first suspicion hangs over him to the last.

With this duel begins the strife which only ends with the Wars of the Roses. It is the prelude which opens a great epoch of internal struggle — a struggle which lasts nearly three generations, and forms in Shakespeare the theme of two dramatic cycles. Its intensity shows the strength of the disease; the baleful virus of personal animosity and insubordination had permeated the entire body politic. Long will be the fever, deep and oft-recurring the throes of the malady, until the poison is eliminated from the system, and the strong arm of the Tudors, in suppressing individual license, will assail individual liberty, whence will arise a new and almost as lengthy a conflict. But this period lies beyond the work of the Poet. At present we are to witness the transition from feudalism, in which the quarrel of two noblemen could involve the peace of the whole realm, to the modern world, in which the State has brought into subordination the turbulent, though powerful and high-born, subject.

Nor should we fail to notice the redeeming trait of these people; they all are fired with an intense feeling of nationality. Whatever else they may do, they never forget that they are Englishmen. Both the exiled nobles express the same attachment to country; Richard glows with it, and the aged Gaunt on his death-bed sings the praises of England in an unrivaled strain of poetic exaltation. Nationality is the grand swelling theme, in which all discord is swallowed up. This is the sound germ which will sprout into a healthy and vigorous tree when it is fully developed. Thus distinctly appears even now the national consciousness of England, which is her unifying principle amid all dissension, and the course of her history will be to unfold it into institutions which will give to it an absolute validity in the real world.

1. The two threads of Richard and Bolingbroke, which have hitherto run together, here separate, and will not unite again till the situations of the two men are reversed. We can now take up the part of Richard and follow it through to the end of the first movement. Bolingbroke has departed, but his designs are not unknown to the King, who has "observed his courtship of the common people," and noted with just suspicion his great popularity. "Off goes his bonnet to an oyster-wench" — an act of condescension whose motive can easily be discerned. Richard draws the conclusion with absolute precision; Bolingbroke acts " as were our England in reversion his, and he our subjects' next degree in hope." The monarch has unquestioned power of insight — here he states the whole difficulty of the future. But what does he do? He furnishes an opportunity to his enemy by banishment; certainly he takes no steps to act in accordance with his knowledge. Indeed, he appears to defy his own judgment by resorting to the most odious abuses of which government is capable, namely, favoritism and extortion.

Richard has almost foretold his own fate; it will now be announced to him in the most emphatic terms by the way of warning. It is the old devoted John of Gaunt, now lying at the point of death, who tells him that his abuse of kingship will dethrone him; that the spilling of kindred blood will receive its recompense. Richard answers the dying patriot with vituperation — even with threats. Next he proceeds to his crowning act of wrong towards the subject — he confiscates the property of the banished Bolingbroke. This deed also is not accomplished without a warning; even the weak-spirited York utters a protest:

" Take Hereford's rights away, and take from time
His charters and customary rights;
Let not to-morrow, then, ensue to-day;
Be not thyself; for how art thou a king,
But by fair sequence and succession?"

This passage states in the most direct manner the logical nature of Richard's deed. The same law which secures to Hereford his property secures to the King his crown. If the King, therefore, disregard that law, he is destroying his own authority. Here we have the thought of the whole play — sovereign and subject have the same fundamental right; if the former tries to ruin the latter, he is really trying to ruin himself, and will succeed in the attempt. Richard thus is strangling his own authority, and — when we consider that the person who is in this manner elevated by his wrongs into being the representative of the cause of right is the powerful and popular Bolingbroke — there can be only one result.

Such is the crowning deed of wrong done by Richard; now follows his crowning deed of folly. He quits England at the critical nick of time, and makes an expedition to Ireland, leaving as governor during his absence the Duke of York — aged, imbecile, and not firmly attached to his interests. The strong outlines of the King's character are now before us. There is a divorce between his intellect and will of a peculiar kind; he possesses foresight, he comprehends results, but he seems to think that a monarch's conduct is above all guidance through the judgment. What he knows need not direct what he does; his

action is quite the contrary of his thought. Ordinary
mortals may be controlled by their intelligence — but is he
not sovereign and above all control? Sunk in pleasure,
poisoned by flattery, he has come to believe that in his
case there is no responsibility for the deed. This is the
Richard of prosperity; adversity will soon show a new
phase of his character.

2. Going back and taking up the thread of Bolingbroke after his banishment, we may observe all the tendencies which conspire to bring him to the throne. In the
first place, the circumstances are favorable — events which
he did not control catch him up and carry him forward in
their current. But, in the second place, the greater part
of the governing influences he did set in motion; though the
time was ripe for a change, he caused himself to be chosen
as its leader. This deep political purpose is everywhere
manifest, and still deeper is his political instinct, which
sets him on the right course without his knowing why. It
is often very difficult to draw the line between consciousness and unconsciousness in his action, but both his conscious and unconscious methods of working are equally
well adapted to the end in view. Nor does the character
require any such distinction; indeed, it would be spoiled
thereby, for Bolingbroke is to be portrayed as the natural
politician whose impulse is as good as, or better than, his
reflection. Kingship hovered before him — perhaps darkly
— when he challenged Mowbray in order to reach Richard.

He hastens to make the issue; he intends to reap every
possible advantage of the murder of Gloster, for whom he
appears as the avenger, knowing all the while who is the
guilty man. Profound, too, is his dissimulation; profounder, indeed, than he wills it to be, since it is the very

marrow of his nature. To conceal, and at the same time to carry out, his design are the two conflicting objects which must be united in his action. His courtship of the people has partially revealed him, though without any evil result, owing to the character of his adversary. But we are mostly left to hover between his instinct and his intention, in seeking to explore the dark depths of his spiritual being. He never soliloquizes, thus manifesting, to a certain extent, an absence of reflection and of self-conscious purpose.

Favored by the people, aided by the nobles who see in his wrong the possibility of their own, Bolingbroke soon comes back to England. The whole manner of his return indicates that it is the result of a deep-laid, well-executed conspiracy, though its details are left wholly to surmise. His hand of cunning is seen in every movement, though that cunning is often purely instinctive. The King is absent in Ireland; the odious favorites run away; the impotent York is left to weather the storm alone. The latter is a character that is half and half — on both sides and on neither; the type of senile indecision. He sympathizes with Bolingbroke, yet will adhere to the King; too weak in body on account of his age for the rough activity of war, he is much too weak in will to prop a fallen kingdom. He has no money, no forces; he goes to his revolted nephew and gives him a sound lecture on the sin of rebellion and ends by declaring his neutrality. The old man, therefore, can do nothing; thus the last hope from any English source vanishes. Next we hear that the Welsh have dispersed on the rumor of the King's death. It is manifest that Richard cannot control instrumentalities; every implement for his defense falls from his hand harmless to the ground, while Bolingbroke manifests the most subtle appreciation of each means of success.

His main supporter among the nobility is Northumberland, who will hereafter play a leading part in the reign of King Henry the Fourth. Northumberland is the representative of rebellion; his life is made up of factious opposition to authority. His principle is thus hostile to all government; he embodies the feudal insubordination to law; his pleasure is in being a king-maker. Such is the chief instrument of Bolingbroke — an instrument which is manifestly as dangerous to his supremacy as to that of Richard. Here we see the future peril which will spring up in the realm, and there is suggested the new conflict which arises from the present conflict. Bolingbroke will first use the rude weapon of rebellion, and then break it to pieces. Indeed, the family of Percy are all here — Northumberland, Hotspur, and Worcester — aiding the revolt, a family which will have to be eliminated from the State.

Bolingbroke, in most unequivocal manner, places himself at the head of the national movement and centers it in himself. He sees precisely the strong point of his cause, and gives it a forcible expression:

> " If that my cousin King be King of England,
> It must be granted I am Duke of Lancaster.''

His right is the same as that of the King; he is really upholding the law of the realm. But, since he is not allowed to vindicate his claim by judicial process, there remains to him the way of revolution:

> — "I am a subject,
> And challenge law; attorneys are denied me,
> And, therefore, personally I lay my claim
> To my inheritance of free descent."

But he purposes much more — in fact, all that lies in his deed; for, if he be the supreme arbiter of the State, then he can only be its ruler. Accordingly he proceeds at once to the work of reform; he condemns to death Richard's favorites — "those caterpillars of the commonwealth." But towards the men around him he keeps up his dissimulation; he declares that he has come only for his rights. To the King also he professes the most devoted loyalty, yet at the same time prescribes the conditions of his submission. So profound is his concealment that even his most trusted and active supporter, Northumberland, is not fully assured of his future action. Bolingbroke, therefore, has secured the favor of the nation by maintaining that the king is to guard, and not to violate, what is legally established, and that the king himself is not above the law, but its creature. Such is the deepest political principle of the English nationality, and with it the subtle Bolingbroke is careful to place himself in harmony.

A subordinate thread is the reflection of the whole struggle in an unconscious form — in the dim, nebulous forebodings of the soul. First is the Queen; she feels that something is out of joint, yet she does not know what it is. She only knows that there is a dull presentiment of evil weighing down her spirits. It is the deep instinctive nature of the wife to feel beforehand what is going to happen to the husband with whom she is so closely bound up in emotion. Moreover, the Queen has seen the throes of the kingdom; she has heard the prophetic warning of the dying Gaunt, as well as the earnest protest of the aged York. She draws the conclusion, and the correct conclusion — not with her intellect, but with her feelings. In

like manner the Welsh, the superstitious men of the mountains, have been thrilled with the premonition of impending disaster, and read it in blazing letters inscribed on the
face of heaven.   So, too, the gardener has felt the throb-
bing pulse of the time, and, as he looks upon the sprays,
weeds, and flowers of his own little commonwealth, he
beholds the various manifestations of the political world.
Each has thus a special way of expressing that which is
wildly rocking and heaving in the soul of the nation.

II.  Such is the first general movement of the play.
The threads of Richard and Bolingbroke again strike
together, and cross at this point ; the one man is mount-
ing towards kingship, the other descending to death.   In
the second movement, which will now be unfolded, both
their characters will develop latent phases.   Richard is to
be stripped of his infatuation, and is to be brought to see
that even a monarch is held accountable for his deeds at
the bar of eternal justice.   Bolingbroke will gradually
work out of his ambiguous position, and assume both the
title and the authority of ruler.

1.  Taking up the thread of Richard and following it
through the second movement, we shall hear poetic strains
of enchanting melody, as one wave of misfortune after
another rolls the young King towards the final goal of his
destiny.   He truly becomes a poet now — like the fabled
swan, singing his own death-song.   It is a new and unexpected phase of his character, yet by no means inconsistent with what we already know of him.   Calamity has
opened the sluices of the soul ; that sensuous nature of
his, which was before sunk in self-indulgence, now comes
upon the grim reality of life and is stricken into throes
of passionate despair.   Its utterance partakes still of this

sensuous element in the man, and its theme is the noblest
theme of Tragedy — the Nemesis of the human deed.
His intellect, whose penetration was previously noted,
remains with him yet, and now rises out of the slough of
pleasure on the many-colored wings of the imagination,
and looks far down into the future of England with a prophetic insight.    The odious tyrant, the ignoble sensualist,
the contemptible weakling of the first movement, thus
develops the most exalted side of his character, and
becomes a personage with qualities highly attractive and
ennobling, if not heroic.

But before he begins to descend he is to be placed on
the very pinnacle of kingly infatuation; this is his belief
in divine right — a dangerous doctrine for English monarchs, as English history abundantly shows.   He imagines
that his presence will be sufficient to put down rebellion,
that his will is God's will, and that he simply cannot lose
his throne by any deed.

> "Not all the water in the rough rude sea
> Can wash the balm from an annointed king;
> The breath of worldly men cannot depose
> The deputy elected by the Lord."

The outcome of this doctrine is manifest:   The king is
not responsible for his action;   he is above the great law
of retribution.    Moreover, his energy is sapped by such a
faith; against every soldier on the side of Bolingbroke he
imagines that "God for his Richard hath in heavenly pay
a glorious angel."   The justice of a thing, the moral
quality of an act, do not concern the sovereign who rules
over eternal right as over the meanest subject.    Early
authority, false education, and, above all, poisonous flattery, have inflated him into an immense puff-ball, to be

blown off his throne by the first rude wind of adversity.
Even the Bishop of Carlisle reproves his extreme reliance
on a power external to man, and declares that "the means
that Heaven yields must be embraced." The good Bishop,
though a dignitary of the Church, believes that fate
is not religion, and that self-determination in man is the
true faith in God. The imagination of Richard has, however, a picture for the situation; he, like the sun, need
only appear, when the clouds of revolt will of themselves
disperse before his majestic presence. Such is the summit of his delusion.

Reports of misfortune come in rapidly from every side.
He hears that the Welshmen, his main support, have scattered in every direction. The King grows pale at the
news, but recovers himself when he thinks of his uncle,
York. Word is next brought that both old and young,
men and women, have gone over to Bolingbroke, and that
the favorites have been executed. Finally, when it is
announced that York has joined the rebels, the last prop
is taken away; universal revolt has wrested England from
the scepter of Richard. What now will be his conduct?
His intellect will fully comprehend the situation — his
imagination will dress it up in all the brilliant colors of
poetry; but his will, his power of action, his ability to
recover himself, lies paralyzed within him, smothered in
the delicious fragrance of his own soul.

A man who relies entirely on external power must fall
into despair when everything goes against him — when
that external power shows itself hostile. In express contrast to the religious resignation of Richard stands the
prelate, Carlisle, who reproves this very element in him

and tries to spur him forward to an energetic defense of his cause. Alongside of the worthy Bishop is the secular man of action, Aumerle, who also seeks to rouse the King from his supineness. But Richard can only fluctuate between the two extremes of his nature — between fatuitous reliance and unmanly despair; there is no internal vigor to buoy up his sinking soul.

Let us take a rapid survey of his acts as he steps down from kingship into the grave. He repeals the sentence of banishment against Bolingbroke — all whose "fair demands shall be accomplished without contradiction." In the presence of his rebellious subject Northumberland he utters his own humiliation — indeed, declares his own dethronement. Then Bolingbroke appears in person; Richard clearly foresees what is coming; his surrender is absolute: "What you will have I'll give, and willing, too." Of course this is an invitation to take the crown, even if there was no such intention.

But the deeper he sinks in despair the brighter becomes his song; from the ashes of action glows the intense fire of poetry. His fancy has the profusion and brilliancy of a tropical garden; it blooms almost to bewilderment and exhaustion. Still, the spiritual necessity is obvious; he must find relief from his sorrow by casting it out of himself into images — into a long and somewhat labyrinthine gallery of pictures. Such of old has been the need of the bard — in fact, of man; suffering makes the poet and the reader of poetry. Nor must we pass over the prophetic insight which Richard here shows; he, too, knows the consequences of revolution; his intellect is unclouded by misfortune. Rebellion is a monster which eternally begets itself, and whose sweetest food is the blood of its warmest supporters. Tell Bolingbroke, says the inspired King,

> — " He is come to ope
> The purple testament of bleeding war;
> But ere the crown he looks for live in peace,
> Ten thousand bloody crowns of mothers' sons
> Shall ill become the flower of England's face;
> Change the complexion of her maid-pale peace
> To scarlet indignation, and bedew
> Her pastures' grass with faithful English blood."

The crown is next brought, and Richard hands it over to Bolingbroke in person, uttering himself the salutation of the new monarch: "God save King Harry!" Thus he crowns with his own hand the usurper, and, as he truly observes, has become a traitor to himself with the rest, for he has given his "soul's consent to undeck the pompous body of a king." But this is not all; he must acknowledge the justice of his deposition — confess his guilt and its merited punishment. "His weaved-up folly" is to be raveled out to the last thread; the believer in divine right is now brought face to face with the opposite right — that of dethronement. He has lost his dignity; he will not keep his name; he is no longer himself. A looking-glass is brought which shows his former face. Its image is flattery; he is not King Richard, and he dashes it to pieces. He has come to see his follies as they are; he has atoned for his wrongs. Deprived of every kingly honor, he is brought to behold his deed in all its nakedness. The world of illusion in which he before lived has vanished, and the world of reality dawns upon his wondering eyes. Responsibility for the deed crushes into his soul, and a new consciousness has arisen; "I see the very

book indeed where all my sins are writ, and that's myself. "
Verily they are burned into his flesh in colossal letters,
which can be read in their true meaning by the most
unlearned man who looks upon them.

But this is not the end yet. Stripped of his regal robes,
he is still to be stripped of his personal freedom ; he cannot be permitted to roam through the land as an ordinary
person. Royal birth, as it heaps up responsibility, heaps
up punishment. He is thrust into prison in order to separate him from society, like a criminal ; but he has also to
be torn away from the Family, whereby the Queen, too, is
hurled into the vortex of suffering. And more yet ; his
deprivation must be made complete — so he is deprived of
life. He is brutally slain in prison. He exhibits courage
at the last moment ; if he had done so before, he would
have commanded more respect, but he would not have
been Richard. The hope of life makes him a coward ;.
the certainty of death nerves him to his first act of resistance. There in confinement we see him occupied with
his fancies — "studying how I may compare this prison
where I live unto the world." However remote may be
such a comparison, still he will "hammer it out." He
possesses not fancy merely — his speech is not a string of
images merely — but the whole conception is poetic, and
he is gifted also with the higher quality of imagination.

As king, Richard is an utter failure ; as poet, he is a
complete success. And it is this fact which not only
reconciles us to him, but arouses a warm sympathy with
his misfortune. Retributive justice looks ugly when smiting down this beautiful form with its inexorable mace of
steel. A weak, sensual tyrant would have been a repulsive object to both the moral and the æsthetic sense ; but

clothe him in the brilliant robes of the poet, and, though
he still must remain morally offensive and be punished
according to his guilt, he becomes a true theme for tragic
Art. The internal conflict of Richard begins with his
descent, and corresponds to the external conflict; as he is
hurled down from without, he suffers within, singing in
his descent with deeper and deeper glow till the light goes
out in the darkness of death.

2. The second thread of the second movement is Bolingbroke's, whose career to the end of the play is now to be
glanced at. He has hitherto concealed his real purpose,
but the time has come when it must be revealed to
the world, and also to himself in a certain degree. The
weakness of Richard, who tells him to take the crown,
could only confirm him in his secret design. But he was
not able to do otherwise, for what security will he have
against a repetition of the injury? Here, then, is the
difficulty: Bolingbroke is compelled to do a wrong against
the king in order to secure the right of himself and of
the subject. The penalty must come; the consequences
of his violation will be visited upon him, and still more
upon the nation which assisted, or at least acquiesced.
This is, indeed, the greatest of all difficulties — the tragic
difficulty of the world — wherein a man cannot turn to do
a great right without at the same time falling into a great
wrong, for which he is bound to endure the punishment.
Bolingbroke gets his property, and obtains restoration
to his country, but to make them sure he must have
supreme authority. This act is the precursor of the Wars
of the Roses.

The deeds of Richard's reign are to be undone. The
death of Gloster is investigated; it is not clear who was

his executioner, and the matter remains undecided. Duelists again appear, as at the beginning of the play, but
their differences are made "to rest under gage." Bolingbroke accepts the crown ; the only voice heard in protest
is that of the brave, clear-headed Bishop of Carlisle, who
here presents the side of the wrong done by dethroning
Richard. A subject cannot pass sentence on his king ; it
is a violation of human law, and still more of divine law.
The noble prelate also utters a prophecy of the terrible
consequences of the usurpation ; the blood of England
shall manure the ground ; kindred shall war with kindred ;

> "Disorder, horror, fear, and mutiny
> Shall here inhabit, and this land be called
> The field of Golgotha and dead men's skulls."

Thus Bolingbroke has his wrong and its retribution held
up before him, and the Poet gives the motive for the plays
which are to follow.

A slight reaction begins ; a conspiracy in which both
clergy and laity are represented ,is formed to get rid of
the new king. The plot is discovered through the care-
lessness of Aumerle by his father, the Duke of York,
who at once sets out to inform the monarch. The interest
of this little scene lies in the conflict between father and
mother — their son is a traitor. The father, maintaining
the principle of the State, will bring to punishment his
own child ; the mother, maintaining the principle of the
Family, will conceal his act and protect him. All three
ride a race to the abode of the King, who adroitly pardons the son, even against the prayers of York, who
shows himself to be an unnatural parent in his superlative
loyalty. This form of the domestic collision might be

made the basis of a whole tragedy, but it seems not to have been touched upon by Shakespeare in any other play.

The conspiracy is broken up; the lords, spiritual and temporal, who were engaged in it lose their heads, except the bold Bishop of Carlisle; Henry Bolingbroke is firmly seated on the throne of England. But the death of Richard he did not purpose; though he wished him dead, he loves him murdered — the fear of retribution is stronger than the hate of the royal person. The wrong of Bolingbroke is now complete, and he has become fully conscious of it. He declares in deep contrition at the end of the play his own guilt, whose stain he intends to wash off by a voyage to the Holy Land.

This is, indeed, a prophetic drama. Three leading characters have now prophesied the troubles which are to result from the present usurpation, and thus have pointed to the succeeding plays. The precise nature of the conflict is also foretold: Northumberland, who has deposed a king, will try to do so again; the rebel must then be subordinated to authority. Richard the seer has seen and uttered both the essential circumstances, and the true logic of the future situation:

> "Northumberland, thou ladder wherewithal
> The mounting Bolingbroke ascends my throne,
> The time shall not be many hours of age
> More than it is ere foul sin, gathering head,
> Shall break into corruption; thou shalt think,
> Though he divide the realm and give thee half,
> It is too little, helping him to all;
> And he shall think that thou, which know'st the way
> To plant unrightful kings, wilt know again,
> Being ne'er so little urged, another way
> To pluck him headlong from the usurped throne."

# HENRY THE FOURTH.

The entire poem of *Henry the Fourth*, with its two parts, has as its theme the restoration of England to internal harmony. Revolution has been invoked as a principle by the nation; the result is that government itself is in danger of perishing. The forces of society must now be reversed, and made to act in just the opposite direction; the conviction of the people, which has been nurtured to the point of rebellion, must be converted to faith in authority. It is the nature of revolution to be forever revolutionizing, and thus prolonging itself into an infinite series of political upheavals which must end in the destruction of the whole institutional world. We now are to behold a man who can be, not only a rebel chieftain, but also a civil ruler, and whose deepest trait of character is the capacity to transform revolution into the stability of government. We are also to behold a nation which will support such a man in his great endeavor, and whose wonderful political instinct has led it from internal peace to rebellion, but will now lead it back again from rebellion to internal peace with entire safety. It is a picture which every man of every country can look upon with profit and delight, since it exhibits in their full validity the two highest, yet often contradictory, duties of the citizen — the duty of revolt and the duty of submission.

In *Richard the Second* was seen the right of revolution; the King undermined his throne in undermining the law,

upon whose observance it was founded. But in *Henry
the Fourth* we behold the wrong of revolution; the King
has to put down by force the seditious element which has
sprung up from the seeds of rebellion. The subject,
however, was too extensive for a single play; the Poet
has, therefore, made of it two dramas, both of which have
the same fundamental thought. The First Part of *Henry
the Fourth* ends with the defeat of the rebels in open battle; in the Second Part they are overreached by a treacherous diplomacy. When the monarch dies, the kingdom
is at peace and is quietly transmitted to his son, who
becomes King Henry the Fifth.

The First Part of *Henry the Fourth* is to be treated as a
play complete in itself, for such the author undoubtedly
intended it to be. The most obvious division of it is into
the threads, of which there are two. It is not easy to
name them, but they may be called the elevated or serious
thread, and the low or comic thread. They are distinguished, not only by their subject-matter, but also by
their form. The one clings to palace and touches only
the high affairs of State; the other descends, not to the
hovel, but to the brothel, and portrays the negative
phases of society. The one is written in the most imaginative verse, the other in the bluntest prose. Moreover,
the first thread separates itself into two antagonistic
groups, which center around the King and around Percy,
respectively, between whom is the great conflict of the
play. The second thread is that of Falstaff and Prince
Hal. The latter has fallen off from the family of his father
and become the associate of thieves and libertines. He
is, however, the connecting link between the two threads.

The action has also two movements, of which the first shows the disruption in the State by the conspiracy of the Percys ; in the royal family, by the estrangement of Prince Henry ; in society generally, by the debauchery of East-cheap. It is a time of general disintegration, from which a new nation is to be born. The reaction which is portrayed in the second movement begins with the reconciliation of the Prince with his father. The regal household is now united and becomes a type of the country which is to be ; even the most depraved classes are whirled into the struggle for nationality by the irresistible spirit of patriotism. The end is that rebellion is defeated and destroyed in the persons of its two most formidable representatives, Hotspur and Worcester. Keeping these outlines in mind, we may now proceed to fill them up with the details of the action.

I. 1. In the very first words of the play the monarch congratulates himself on the termination of civil war, and expresses his delight at the future prospect of national harmony. Everything seems to have settled down for the moment into a state of peace. But he has no repose within ; there is the consciousness of guilt resting on his spirit, as well as the fear of punishment. He has committed a great wrong in the dethronement and death of Richard, and he knows it ; remorse is tearing his soul to pieces. But he has another conviction, which costs him quite as much agony as the throes of conscience — his large observation of life, and, above all, his recent experience with King Richard, have taught him that the first law of this world is the law of man's responsibility for the deed. He has, therefore, the strongest faith in retribution, and it is that faith which haunts him till death, and

makes him see in every misfortune the signs of divine
vengeance visited upon him for his sins.

The supreme question, therefore, with Henry Bolingbroke is: How shall I free myself from these burning
pangs of conscience and obtain reconciliation? He
accepts the way which his age had pointed out — he will
make an expedition to the sepulcher of Christ in order to
gain the precious boon of absolution. Already at the
end of *Richard the Second,* when the feeling of guilt first
broke utterance from his soul, he had proposed a voyage
to the Holy Land to wash away the stain of his crime.
But even here, into this most sincerely and deeply religious part of his nature, the politician intrudes; afterwards
he declares on his death-bed that it was his policy to lead
the restless and turbulent spirits out of England and give
them occupation in a crusade against the Infidel. A
double character he bears throughout; it is the result of
a conflict between the demands of conscience and the
demands of the State — between the moral and the political man. He has a strong instinct to be an upright —
indeed, a religious — person; but let him once hear
the cry of the nation, then he will employ dissimulation, falsehood, violence — in fine, he will subordinate
every principle to the end which he deems to be national.

Another point is worthy of a glance. We see here
looming up in the background the great struggle of
Europe with Asia, the world-historical conflict of the
Middle Ages. It took a religious form — Christianity
against Mohammedanism. All the countries of the Occident were as one nation against Oriental supremacy, and
England, as a member of the European family of peoples
— though lying remote from the scene of the conflict — is

nevertheless touched with it, and must show a slight adumbration of its intensity in her great Historical Poem.

But even while he is talking, the King receives news of warfare nearer home, and a national struggle with surrounding countries seems on the point of breaking out. It is announced that the Welsh have been victorious in the West, and have taken prisoner the English leader, noble Mortimer; "the tidings of this broil brake off our business for the Holy Land." Still again comes startling news from the North; the Scots have made a fierce foray on the English border under the ever-valiant Douglas, who, however, has been defeated by the invincible chieftain, young Harry Percy, called Hotspur, son to Northumberland. Thus we drop at once from the remote European struggle into the national conflict — England against her next neighbors, Wales and Scotland. Here is indicated the supreme effort of the English nation in an external direction — that is, the consolidation of Albion, the elevation of England to Great Britain. For it is the true destiny of the sea-girt Isle to be comprehended in one nationality — to be brought under one government; the triad of separate States, warring with one another and struggling for mastery or for independence, must be reduced to unity and peace.

Still, it is not an external conflict with other peoples which is going to be considered in the play; it is an internal conflict which is impending, and where signs begin at once to show themselves. "What think you, coz, of this young Percy's pride?" asks the King of his counselor, Westmoreland. The haughty warrior, Hotspur, has refused to surrender his prisoners to the sovereign, except the one captive prince of royal blood, Mordake, Earl of

Fife. An act of defiance it was assuredly; but when we learn that Hotspur, according to the custom of war in such cases, had a right to the captives with the single exception mentioned, the affair wears a different aspect. The King has demanded more than his just dues. What can the adroit contriver mean? He must be seeking a quarrel, and now finds a pretext. The suspicion at once darts through the mind that he has already determined to humble the great house of Percy the first moment that he is securely seated on the throne.

This suspicion is confirmed by the hostile feeling of the court against Worcester, another Percy, who, says Westmoreland to the King, is "malevolent to you in all aspects." Now comes the struggle; the audacious Hotspur must be called to an account for his refusal of the prisoners, and the King is forced to "neglect his holy purpose to Jerusalem." Thus we come at the pith of the play. Its theme is not the conquest of heathendom, nor the subjugation of neighboring countries; its purpose is to show the subordination of the rebellious spirit of the time, and the complete restoration of the country to internal concord. To this end the king-makers and revolutionists must be put down, and the supremacy of civil authority maintained by every appliance of force and diplomacy.

Such is the national phase of affairs as presented at the beginning; but now we are to look at the domestic conflict in the royal family, wherein the King is beheld acting the part of a parent. At the mention of Percy's son, Hotspur, he is reminded of his own son, the wayward Prince Harry, who stands in the most unfavorable contrast to the young lion of the North, for the latter is

" a son who is the theme of honor's tongue." It is a most painful thought for the monarch ; he wishes " that it could be proved that some night-tripping fairy had exchanged in cradle-clothes our children ;" he would like to have Hotspur for his son, inasmuch as " riot and dishonor stain the brow of my young Harry." The alienation between father and son is complete ; the young Prince seems to give no promise of worth and talent corresponding to his high position. Herein is the greatest mistake of the King, who, so shrewd in political management, utterly misapprehends the destiny and character of his own child.

The ground of this error in judgment lies deep in the nature of the two persons. The dark, devious subtlety of the father was the reverse of the open, transparent conduct of the son ; neither could fully appreciate the other. Both, however, were needed at the time — the crafty diplomatist and the bold striker. Without Prince Harry, the King could probably not have succeeded in the present emergency. He had to do with men altogether different from the weak-willed Richard ; the impetuous Hotspur would be apt, at a single dash, to break through all the fine-spun webs of political cunning. But the Prince was the equal of Hotspur in chivalrous bearing and martial fire, and wás his superior in prudence. The estranged son must, therefore, be added to the father before the struggle between government and rebellion shall be brought to a successful issue ; neither can be dropped without failure to the cause.

Now the disruption which the King manifestly intended to force takes place. The conflict must come — the sooner the better. Here is the whole family of rebels — the Percys — the living representatives of insurrection. Worcester is the plotter of the house ; he is the man of polit-

ical cunning, and herein he resembles the King. The
latter is charged by him with ingratitude — a charge most
true! The sovereign gives him the answer of power:

> " Worcester, get thee gone, for I see
> Danger and disobedience in thine eye."

The second Percy, Northumberland, is next addressed by
the monarch. He is more the mediator than the aggres-
sor; he seeks to avoid a struggle whose danger he seems
to fully comprehend. Thus his action is uncertain and
paralyzed throughout the whole play — quite different from
what it was in *Richard the Second.* He is at present
trying to pacify the King concerning Hotspur's denial of
the prisoners — an impossible task, could he but see into
the workings of the royal brain. The good Blount, friend
of the King, not comprehending the latter's plan, offers
also to be a peace-maker. Hotspur is induced to make a
sort of apology for a hasty speech, but he still proposes to
keep the prisoners; thereupon follow strong words and an
angry separation. A volcano of impulse is that young
Harry Percy; he will after the King, and ease his heart at
the hazard of his head. But he is restrained by his father
from going, though not from talking; in his wrath he lets
out secrets which it is important to treasure up.

The family of the Percys is in a state of deep repentance
for their past actions; having been traitors to the last
monarch, they are not trusted by the present monarch.
Their wrong is now the subject of bitter confession.
Richard, whom they were the chief means of deposing,
in their memory is "that sweet, lovely rose," for which
they have planted "this thorn, this canker, Bolingbroke."
They have also lost their fair name among men for the

sake of the very person who has openly discarded them.
Still further, they are now forced to make choice between
a new rebellion or an abject submission. The important
question is: Will they maintain their old principle of
revolt, or resolve upon its abandonment?

On another point the political action of the two hostile
parties may be compared. The house of Percy has allied
itself with Mortimer, Earl of March, the true heir of the
English throne, whom Bolingbroke had set aside. It was
a bold stroke of policy, and excited the just suspicion of
the King. He refuses to ransom Mortimer, who has been
taken prisoner by the Welsh, being delighted to keep out
of the kingdom such a dangerous competitor. Both sides
are manifestly seeking every political advantage, and each
is well aware of the designs of the other. But the period
for secret intrigue has passed; the conflict must now be
settled by an appeal to force.

The wily Worcester, the planner of the rebels, unfolds
the scheme, which is certainly skillful. Let the Scotch
be sent home without ransom, and thus we shall win the
aid of Douglas through favor to his captive son. Let
Glendower, too, be gained, in order to give assistance to
the claim of Mortimer, his son-in-law. Then Northumberland "shall creep into the bosom" of the Archbishop
of York, and other nobles who have grievances are to be
persuaded into joining the conspiracy. The plan is clear
—the internal enemies of the King are to be united with
the external foes of the nation, and both are to be hurled
against the throne. The crime of the Percys is now
exposed — they are ready to introduce the foreigner into
their domestic quarrels; they do not hesitate to sacrifice
their country to their party. Nationality is not their

ultimate principle, and, hence, the nation will rise up and smite them to the earth. Of course Bolingbroke was defending his own title and his own interests, but, then, the defense of them coincided with the defense of the institutions of the country.

We are now astonished at learning that this scheme was not a sudden device springing from the present interview, but had long been meditated. Worcester declares that it has already been " ruminated, plotted, and set down," and that it merely awaits an opportunity for fulfillment. The actual state of the case is, therefore, that the two cunning contrivers on both sides have been maneuvering for a position all the while; each is watching the movements of the other, and now the battle is to be fought, being forced by the King. Worcester at once calls into the field his man of action, the bold Hotspur, to whose impulsive temperament he could not hitherto intrust the great secret. Hotspur is on fire at the word, and longs to dash into the fight.

We next behold this young chieftain in his family. His wife, Kate, has observed his strange conduct, and insists upon knowing what is the matter. He seems so completely occupied with his own thoughts that he neglects his domestic duties, and hardly pays any attention to what is transpiring around him. His reply to his wife is couched in a strain of humorous banter; still, he loves her, for he teases her. But that intense soul of his leaps out in every act; when awake he moves about in a kind of trance, and when asleep he is at once charging upon the field of battle. His imagination is as vivid as the flash of lightning; he calls up the great enterprise and rushes through all its circumstances; the outer world dwindles to

naught amid the more striking pictures of his own mind.
It is the impetuous, nervous character which throws itself
into its purpose and quite loses its being in its fierce
determination. The same intensity is witnessed in his
intellect and in his action; the word which he employs and
the deed which he does glow with the same spiritual fire.
He can truly throw his soul with its flaming energy into
all his undertakings. It is no wonder that his wife
becomes jealous even of his dreams, and of the images
which withdraw his life from her intercourse and from
every occupation.

But here we are introduced into the meeting of the leading conspirators, in which their ambition and their crime
are unfolded. Now we first catch a glimpse of a most
notable character, "that damned magician, Glendower."
He is filled with all the superstition of the mountains of
Wales; at his birth the front of Heaven was full of fiery
shapes and the earth did shake; supernatural signs have
marked him as extraordinary; no man born of woman
can hold him pace in deep experiment. The Poet clearly
makes fun of his claims, but in respect to Glendower
himself there is a mixture of motives. He wishes to
inspire awe among his credulous countrymen by such
mysterious stories, yet, to a certain extent, he believes
them himself. The line between imposture and credulity
is left uncertain, yet both are undoubtedly present in his
composition. He manifests the wild Celtic imagination
which falls into gross superstition; most characteristic,
too, are his love and cultivation of poetry; he is thus the
conscious maker of mythical lore. In antagonism to these
qualities stands Hotspur, with his English understanding,
who ridicules all supernatural gifts, and who interprets

the wonders of nature into physical causes. But, chiefly, he expresses the most violent dislike of poetry:

> "I had rather be a kitten and cry — mew,
> Than one of these same meter ballad-mongers;
> I had rather hear a brazen canstick turn'd,
> Or a dry wheel grate on an axle-tree;
> And that would set my teeth nothing on edge,
> Nothing so much as mincing poetry;
> 'Tis like the forc'd gait of a shuffling nag."

A most poetical description of the hate of poetry! Hotspur, above all men, is indulging in that which he thinks he despises. He employs throughout the play the most imaginative and intense speech, yet does not know it; but, chiefly, his character and his figure are poetical in the highest degree. He is the instinctive man of action; the deed is his poetry — his creative act; he is the poet in an old sense of the word—the doer. He does not like this artificial singing of a great action as distinct from the performance. Yet, as was said, he has a most vivid imagination, bursting into living pictures; still, it never saps the foundation of his strong common sense, and never degenerates into superstition—into the belief that the figments of his own brain are some divine, supernatural appearance. A poetical figure he is indeed, hating poetry with a most poetical hate.

Now, this man, decked in youth and beauty, gifted with the noblest graces of soul and body, is doomed; he has his sentence written upon his forehead, where it may be read of all men; he cannot subordinate himself to the authority of the State. He is, in fact, the very embodiment of the spirit of insurrection in its most enticing features. There he rides along, lightly reining his fiery

steed; what a glowing, heroic appearance! Yet that eye
of defiance is turned upon the most sacred interest of
humanity. In him the individual is beheld in all his glory
and perfection, yet also in his supreme weakness. Hotspur will not submit to the institutions of the world; he
dashes madly against them — but they are made of something harder than adamant. Beautiful, noble, strong as
he is, he must be swept into nothingness, along with every
man who cannot subordinate himself to the Higher.

But the great crime of the rebels against the State is
yet to be told — it is the division of their country. They
meet and parcel out its territory; Hotspur takes a share,
also Mortimer and Glendower. The spirit of revolt has
now reached its logical result — the dismemberment of
England. When it cannot control the whole, it seeks to
break the nation into fragments. This is the supreme sin
against nationality; rebellion has committed its greatest
violation in the disruption of the country. The man who
undertakes to rescue the land and punish the offenders
may be justly called the savior of the people. Here it is
King Henry the Fourth who plants himself in the breach,
most gallantly sustained by his son Prince Henry; both
are thus the supporters of the spirit of nationality against
the spirit of division and destruction. This is their
eternal merit, which raises them far above their own short-
comings and far above all the glories of their opponents.

2. It is now time to go back and take up the comic
thread, which is so different in style and subject-matter
from the one which has just been considered. Both threads,
however, present great violations — the first of institutions,
the second of morals. The character which connects
these two threads is Prince Henry; indeed, he is the colos-

sal figure which spans the four dramas of the present
series, and may be justly called the hero of the Lancastrian Tetralogy. The estrangement between him and his
father has been mentioned; he has fled from the court and
goes down among the people — yea, among the lowest
people. He will be ruler one day. Beginning at the foot
of the ladder, he is going to climb to the highest round;
he is going to see all, and be all, that his subjects are. It
is a dangerous undertaking for everybody except the
genius. Let you and me not make the attempt — we can
easily fall to the foot of the ladder and roll into the mire
of the ditch; but can we get up again? A hazardous
experiment; let us not try it.

Prince Henry becomes the associate of thieves and
drunkards, and worse; but it is noticeable that little or no
taint seems to be left upon him. He is not a thief; he
can hardly be called wicked or dishonorable. He stands
here wonderfully aloof from even his own deed. It is a
strange situation. What he does is felt to be outside of
his true nature all the time. His controlling impulse now
seems to be the love of sport; it makes no difference how
wild or foolish may be the adventure, he is ready. Entertainment he is bound to have — too little solicitous, according to modern notions, about the means and about the
kind.

But the deeper possibility of his character is also hinted
at here in the beginning. He is aware of the foulness of
these men who surround him; he knows, too, the waywardness of his own life. Hence his present career is the
result of deep purpose; his act is through and through a
conscious one, but we must not for this reason think that
he took no pleasure in its performance. He declares in

his soliloquy at the beginning that he employs this method in order to " show more goodly and attract more eyes " after the reformation of his conduct, which he most sincerely intends. He feels already an absolute adaptability to his situation. When war comes, he will be the supreme soldier; when he ascends the throne, the supreme ruler; but now, in the tavern, he is the supreme reveler. This is enough concerning him for the present; let him rather develop himself along with the action of the play.

The chief means which the Prince employs for his amusement is the most entertaining character in all Literature — the jolly Fat Knight, Jack Falstaff. This is quite the pith of their relation — Falstaff furnishes the fun. Quite impossible is it to analyze him in much detail; that humor of his — fine, mist-like, intoxicating moisture of the spirit — is apt to evaporate in the process of decomposition, and leave something very dry. Certain general statements may, however, be made. Falstaff is the embodiment of sensual gratification; there is no moral subordination in him for the control of appetite. His intelligence is of the quickest and keenest, but not profound or comprehensive. It is not great enough to make him a villain; its superiority lies in its rapidity and dexterity. Then there is that stupendous capacity for every kind of animal pleasure, for the eye clearly figured in his enormous body. He has himself indicated the connection: " Thou seest I have more flesh than another man, and, therefore, more frailty."

Falstaff, therefore, has the highest quality and the lowest quality of man rolled up together in his character, without the mediating principle of morality. He possesses the brightest intellect on the surface, but the most brutish sensuality is lying at the foundation. There the two elements are, interpenetrating throughout that unwieldy bulk, furnishing a most rare incongruity — enough to cause inextinguishable laughter among the happy gods. But it must be confessed that there are not a few people for whom the characterization transcends the limits of the Comic, and the spectacle becomes disgusting — the head of man on the body of a swine. Nor is it difficult to see that the person who holds to morality as the supreme principle can take little pleasure in Falstaff, for the Poet has left out just this quality, and made the omission the main ground of the comic contrast and incongruity.

Still, the Fat Knight, as he has an observing, keen intellect, knows of morality as a guiding principle of mankind. Whatever else may be said about it, he is well aware that it is a belief or a custom in the world, and that it has passed upon him the severest condemnation. At times he talks of adjusting himself to its behests, and of becoming an honest man in the estimation of society. But the truth is, he has no moral instinct — no feeling which impels him to a change of life. He speaks of religious duty, yet he cannot be serious about the matter if he do his best; he often declares that he will repent, and is called by one of his companions Monsieur Remorse, but his resolution sounds like a jest, and he quickly passes from " praying to purse-taking." Repentance with him can only be a matter of knowledge, or of observation; it does not descend into his emotions and drive him amid tears to undo his guilty deeds, and remould his foul, contorted character. Falstaff cannot, therefore, truly repent. He has no moral instinct; his possessions are — intellect on the one hand, senses on the other. His spontaneous impulse always tends downward into the slough of sensuality.

But his chief pretense was the pretense of courage, and the question has been much discussed whether or not Falstaff was a coward. The critics have arrayed themselves in two opposing lines of battle on the subject, and it must be granted that not a little can be said in favor of both views. Either side, by itself, is wrong, and of course one-sided; the truth is the harmonious synthesis which can be seen by going back to the central germ of the character of Falstaff. Courage was the pride of the country, and especially of the noble class; he well understands that it is the virtue in the highest esteem. But, again, he has no inner impulse to courage, nor to any other virtue; intellect tells him that it is a very desirable possession, yet a courageous instinct he assuredly has not. Thus at times he seems to be brave enough, perhaps, but his tendency is to unmitigated cowardice. He naturally gravitates towards the slough, though his understanding holds him up a little.

But the most difficult point in his character is centered in the question: Is Falstaff conscious or unconscious in his conduct? Here, again, two diverse opinions may be, and have been, held, both being founded on good reasons. It has been maintained on the one hand that he — pursuing his own deep purpose — is the consummate actor, and on the other hand that he unwittingly falls into his monstrous lies and contradictions. The truth is, both elements are present, yet it is hard to draw the exact line of demarkation, as in the case of so many of Shakespeare's characters. Yea, in regard to the mighty Poet himself, who can point out the boundary between his conscious and unconscious procedure? Many rules of his Art he kept before his mind, distinctly formulated, and followed them; indeed, we can, in some cases, trace their growth from dim impulse into clear knowledge. He had far more system than people generally will allow; he mostly knew what he was about. Still, it must be granted that he possessed an enormous reserve of poetical instinct, which sometimes heaves up like a new-born mountain — from whence, one knows not; but he had also an intellect equally great in its realm. The most that one can do is to examine his works, discover their law — for it must be discoverable — and, pointing it out to others, say: Open your eyes; there it is. That he was aware of the law of his own composition is often probable, always possible, never capable of absolute demonstration; but, still, he wrote by it — that is the certainty. Let us find it first, if we can; afterwards we may hunt for the line between his consciousness and unconsciousness.

In regard to this question about Falstaff, turn back to his spiritual principle as already given, and the key will be found. He has a keen intellect. He must be aware, for instance, that his portentous lies will be found out; that, in fact, on the spot they deceive nobody. He is entertaining the Prince; he is acting with great success, one thinks. But also he is entertaining himself; his pleasure is in falsehood — he revels in it as in the most delicious luxury; a lie is sweeter to him than a cup of sack. As before remarked, there is no moral instinct in him; even his wit is the slave of his senses. Now we may comprehend the man. The comic character is one that pursues an absurd end — some delusion or insubstantial specter. Falstaff is in himself the essence of all delusion and untruth — a rational man, yet acting with conscious irrationality. Not only does he know what he is, but he wills to be what he is; true only in his falseness, he has attained a serenity which marks the culmination of

Comedy, namely, the voluntary comic character. Thus
all his contradictions may be fully harmonized and
explained.

Around Falstaff is gathered a wild company — the merry
lads of Eastcheap, who serve mainly to fill up the background of the picture. They compose the dangerous
class in a community; it is the negative element of
society. These people are in bold opposition to laws and
institutions; they live in open violation of all that conscience and duty demand — thieving, lust, gluttony,
drunkenness, debauchery of every kind, are their common
traits. They hardly deserve to be separately mentioned,
though the Poet has individualized them all in a few bold
strokes. The thought is near that this social corruption
is the result of the political diseases of the last two reigns
— is the moral consequence of revolution and rebellion.
Institutional violation in the higher classes, sinking down
upon the common people, bursts the barriers of self-
restraint, and lets in the flood of moral violation over the
whole country.

But even this group of the lowest vagabonds, the
nethermost layer of society, is to be absorbed into the
great struggle for nationality which is about to take place.
The means for uniting them with their country and elevating them into a patriotic activity is Prince Harry, who
is down there with them, and knows them. The startling
news of rebellion breaks in upon their revels, just after
that wild and inimitable adventure at Gadshill; word is
brought that Hotspur, Douglas, and Glendower are up in
arms against the government — three such enemies as the
world could not pick out again, as frightened Jack intimates. Still, the sport must not be interrupted; the

Prince acts with Falstaff a play whose theme is his interview with his father, the King. What can be said of such conduct at such a time? It seems like hopeless fatuity, but the end shows rather that it is the most perfect presence of mind. The fact is also to be noted that the Prince shows he fully understands the moral perversity of Falstaff's character, and applies to "that bolting-hutch of beastliness" the most pungent epithets. Falstaff feels the sting of the reproaches and defends himself: "If to be old and merry be a sin, then many an old host that I know of is damned." He also well knows his strong hold upon the Prince through his powers of entertainment: "Banish plump Jack and banish all the world!" This banishment is now what is going to take place gradually; already, beneath his merry exterior, the Prince is meditating a separation and a complete change of life.

The time has arrived when the scene which was given in caricature is to transpire in reality — father and son are alone together. Both show their true characters in this trying interview. The King, with the consciousness of his guilt ever weighing him down, beholds in the waywardness of his child the punishment of Heaven. Out of his own blood he fears that a scourge is breeding which will avenge the crime against Richard: "As thou art to this hour, was Richard then when I from France set foot at Ravenspurg." This is the hideous picture which rests on the air wherever he turns his eyes. The image of retribution could not be stronger or more direct. Here, too, is the manifest instrument at hand—the valiant youth, Harry Hotspur, who has filled England with the fame of his deeds. The contrition of the King breaks open the

hard political crust which covers his soul, and through the
crevices we see the red fires glowing beneath, intensified
by his belief in a divine judgment for the wicked deed:

> — " Thou dost, in thy passages of life,
> Make me believe that thou art only mark'd
> For the hot vengeance and the rod of Heaven,
> To punish my mistreadings.''

But even from this most solemn hour of his life, and from
this most sincere utterance of his heart, political cunning
cannot be excluded.  Accordingly, in the same breath he
begins to give the young Prince a lesson in artful dissimulation; he tells with evident relish by what shrewd stratagem he won the crown, and by what foolish guilelessness
it was lost by Richard.  His chief complaint is that his
son disregards all these subtle maxims of deep policy, and
is too open, free, and familiar with the people.  Such are
the two men; it is no wonder that they could not get along
well together.

The father and son are, however, reconciled; this is the
turning-point of the drama, as well as of the Prince's
career.  He says nothing about adopting the crafty political maxims inculcated by the parent — he clearly will
have nothing to do with them; but an open, free-handed
fight with the gallant Hotspur can alone sate the hunger
of his ambition:

> — " For the time will come
> That I shall make this northern youth exchange
> His glorious deeds for my indignities.
> Percy is but my factor, good my lord.''

All the honor which Hotspur has hitherto obtained, Harry

will take at a single blow. His soul fires at the thought
—he is a new man; with new endowments, he leaps into
his saddle like a winged warrior from the clouds:

> " I saw young Harry — with his beaver on,
> His cuisses on his thighs, gallantly arm'd —
> Rise from the ground like feather'd Mercury,
> And vaulted with such ease into his seat
> As if an angel dropp'd down from the clouds
> To turn and wind a fiery Pegasus,
> And witch the world with noble horsemanship."

Such is the first movement of the play. The great
rebellion has unfolded into reality; the King on the one
side, and the Percys on the other, have rushed to arms
and are preparing for the final desperate struggle. But
the royal family is now united; father and son combined
present an unconquerable front to the foe, and the people,
even to the very dregs, are with them.

II. The second movement is next to be developed. In
general, there are the same threads as before, but that of the
comic characters is more intimately connected with that of
the King, since Falstaff and his associates are absorbed into
the great national struggle and carried along in its current.
The thread of the rebels, therefore, stands at present in
direct conflict with the two preceding groups. Following
in these lines, a rapid survey is sufficient, as the motives
have already been fully elaborated.

1. (a.) King Henry is informed of every movement of
the enemy; he organizes his army and hastens forward to
the field of battle. But first he seeks the way of reconciliation; he offers to redress all the grievances of the
Percys and grant them pardon for past offenses. Now
follows a discussion in which both sides state the ground

of their action.  Hotspur to the messenger, Blunt, and
afterwards Worcester to the King himself, seek to justify
their course on account of the treatment they have received
at the hands of the monarch.  Here the Poet explains the
collision of his own play; the one party charges treachery and ingratitude, the other insubordination and rebellion.  Now, both accusations are true; both sides have
committed great wrongs — both, too, have a justification
for their conduct.  The King has been guilty of perjury,
dissimulation, ingratitude; in fact, he was the first to per-
petrate the crime which the Percys have learned from him,
and for which he is now seeking to punish them.  It
is his own deed which rears its hideous shape before
him:

> " We were enforc'd for safety's sake to fly
> Out of your sight, and raise this present head;
> Whereby we stand opposed by such means
> As you yourself have forg'd against yourself;
> By unkind usage, dangerous countenance,
> And violation of all faith and troth
> Sworn to us in your younger enterprise."

But their own crime is greater — they are compassing
civil war and national murder.  Rebellion is the charge of
the King against them, and it gives him the supreme advantage.  He is thus the supporter of the nation, since the
Percys revolt, not for a national, but for a personal end.
Still, the King, in executing his great purpose, falls again
into guilt.  In his conduct we witness the old conflict
between the political and the moral points of view; the crisis has arisen in which moral obligations stand directly in
the way of the life of the country.  It was the first national
duty to exterminate the Percys, together with their prin-

ciple; only thus could revolt and anarchy be suppressed; the State, to be at all, must be supreme. Rebellion was a fiend still darkly lurking in the land; it had been victorious in the previous reign, and it is yet a power in the government which threatens to be greater than the government.

To be sure, Henry owes to these same Percys his throne, but that cannot alter the national situation: it is his political necessity to put them down without mercy, though it be an act of faithlessness and ingratitude. If Henry wishes to play the moral hero — if he wishes to sacrifice the destiny of the nation to his individual scruples — he has no business sitting on that throne; let him step down and out. You and I might prefer the part of the moral to the national hero; we might let a country intrusted to our hands go to destruction rather than violate a single ethical precept, *but we would not be without guilt.* It is an ugly choice, but it has to be made, and made, not with half-hearted indecision, but with unquenchable, flaming energy. It is a choice which creates the Great Character in poetry, and decides the Great Man in history. Still, an ugly choice, for whichever side be taken, it hurls the chooser into violation and consequent retribution.

No peace is, therefore, possible without the eradication of the element represented by the Percys; the two diplomatic men see that diplomacy is at an end.

Here, now, speaks up the valiant Prince Henry when there is to be a fight. He proposes to settle the difficulty by single combat, in order "to save the blood on either side," and so he challenges the antagonist always before

his eyes — young Hotspur. Thus the two champions are
picked out for a personal struggle, but this could not possibly be any permanent settlement of the national conflict.
Their encounter, therefore, does not take place in the
form of a private duel, but it will transpire in the general
engagement, which always selects its own heroes.

(b.) The group of revelers may now be looked after.
Falstaff has obtained a charge of Foot; Bardolph is sent
off as a messenger; Poins is also employed. It is the
Prince who gives them all some occupation; they can perform some service for their country. Thus the lowest
class of society, whose spirit is negative to civil order, is
infused with a noble motive; the immoral man may still
be fired with the feeling of nationality. Elevation there
is in that, and much hope, when the sunken individual can
offer his life for the Higher — can sacrifice himself, not to
the Beast, but to the God within him. So the wild revelers
of Eastcheap are removed to a new field of activity; their
Prince has bound together the high and the low, the good
and the bad, in the one great purpose of national unity
and supremacy.

But Falstaff shows the two contradictory elements of
his character throughout this part also. His shrewdness
does not fail him, nor does his sensuality. There on his
march is seen the inevitable bottle of sack; but his roguery
has opened the richest vein of peculation in what may be
called the "substitute business." He says himself that
he has "misused the king's press damnably." The result
is, he has collected a band of ragamuffins of whom even he
is ashamed; "unloaded all the gibbets" along the road;
they are the cheap purchase of conscript money. The

instrumentalities of government become, in the hands of
Falstaff, the means of the foulest corruption; whatever
he touches seems at once to be infected with his own
moral taint, leaving out the one supreme exception already
mentioned. Still, it is such a soldiery as best corresponds
to such a character; it were bad to place under him a
body of substantial citizens. Thus we catch a lively
glimpse of Falstaff as Captain.

Again, just before the battle, we have another short look
at him, saying over what he calls his catechism of honor.
It is only a new phase of his double nature. Here in the
two armies before him he beholds the principle of honor
in all its intensity, culminating in the two heroes, Prince
Henry and Hotspur. His intellect comprehends its power
among men; he would like to possess it on certain
accounts, but he has no impulse of honor in his soul; it
can give no gratification to the senses; it is "insensible
even to the dead." His conclusion must follow: "Therefore, I'll none of it." It is a mistake to consider his
attitude toward honor as the central point of his character; it is only a single manifestation alongside of others
which possess equal significance.

Finally, on the field of battle he must be seen; here
he comes all alone in a way that looks very much like
skulking. In excuse of his solitary appearance he says
that he has led his ragamuffins "where they are peppered;
there's not three of my hundred and fifty left alive."
He is, therefore, the sole survivor, except possibly one.
This monstrous lie, so characteristic of Falstaff in laud-
ing his own valor, has been cited by simple-hearted com-
mentators in proof of his courage — a joke as good as any

24

of Falstaff's own. Prince Henry comes rushing along
and reproves his idleness, when he begins lying again.
Douglas darts upon him for a fight; he falls down and
pretends to be dead. But his crowning falsehood is when
he picks up the lifeless body of Hotspur as a trophy and
carries it to the Prince who had slain him, claiming a great
reward. Here he knew that his lie could not deceive, but
his impulse to tell it and act it is all the same. His cunning framed the monstrous plot; he has no feeling of
shame, honor, or truth to suppress its execution. The
central thought of his character may be mentioned once
more. He possesses the keenest intellect on the one side,
the most beastly senses on the other, without the correct-
ing principle of morality.

2. It remains for us to glance at the thread of the
rebels in the second movement. The characteristic of it
is internal disagreement and separation, while on the side
of the King the tendency has been to unification and harmony. Hotspur, Worcester, and Douglas are on hand
ready for the conflict, but Northumberland and Glendower are wanting. The great question is: Shall a battle be risked under the circumstances? There are two
diverse opinions, but the intemperate Hotspur carries his
point against the cool-headed Worcester, after warm discussion. Here is seen the inherent result of rebellion:
It cannot be united in itself; it must ultimately rebel
against itself. Northumberland craftily slips out of the
conflict, which from the beginning was against his judgment, and leaves his son to perish. Glendower, with
equal guile, stays away, hindered by unfavorable prophecies. The cause of the malcontents is thus sinking through

its own logic; but the cause of united England has unified its supporters — in the family and among the leaders of the King there is no withdrawal, no discussion.

But the culmination of the struggle is the combat between the two youthful heroes, Hotspur and the Prince. Each represents what is truest and noblest of his party; each possesses the most brilliant and attractive qualities of mind and body. But one must perish, for they are the bearers of contradictory principles which will endure no compromise. The Prince recognizes the irreconcilable hostility of their deepest natures when he says that our England cannot brook the double reign of Harry Percy and the Prince of Wales. Hotspur falls, and deserves to fall. Never was there a more glorious embodiment of honor, valor, chivalry; he rises up before us as an ideal shape, endowed with all the gorgeous fascination of the knightly character, and in his death the star of the Middle Ages seems to have gone down forever. But he had a trait which blasted all the noble fruitage, and which made it necessary for the tree to be dug up by the roots — he knew no subordination to country. The Prince is the great supporter of that which Hotspur assails; hence he stands forth as the national hero. He has slain the mighty man of the opposite side, the supreme embodiment of defiant rebellion. All the personal glory which clung to Hotspur from his former successes now passes to him, together with the additional honor of his present victory. The drama concludes; the Prince of Wales stands out in colossal lineaments as the triumphant champion of nationality; his father looks forth from the background while Percy is lying at his feet — young Harry is now the man of the future. Once more, at the very end, the same chord is

struck which we heard at the beginning — a chord which
rolls and echoes through the whole work, unifying its multifarious music into one grand symphonic utterance:

"Rebellion in this land shall lose his sway."

---

The inferiority of the Second Part of *Henry the Fourth*
to the First Part is universally conceded.  Several of the
most attractive figures in the latter play disappear now
entirely; others fall off in strength of delineation; while
the grossness increases both in quantity and degree.  It
must be confessed that the texture of the whole is woven
of coarser materials than that of the First Part.  The
structure of the work also is less happy.  There is ample
variety, but this variety is by no means fully transfused
into unity.  In the elevated thread there is an attempt to
compass too much; hence occur gaps and omissions which
hurt the total effect.  In the low thread a detail of scenes
and persons is given which borders on the repulsive; too
much is here brought before us, instead of too little.  Still
further, the two main threads might be made to have a
more intimate connection.

Nevertheless it is Shakespeare's, in a high, though not
in the highest, sense; characterization, wit, imagery, language, betray the hand of the master.  The structure, too,
is Shakespearian, though by no means so decidedly marked
as in some other plays.  Two general movements may be
distinguished in the total action.  The first movement
portrays the elements hostile to the existence of social
order; this hostility has here two forms — the one being
an assault upon the political fabric, the other being an

assault upon morality. Rebellion seeks to undermine authority without, and sensuality to destroy manhood within; the realm of institutions and the realm of conscience are equally assailed. The destructive sweep of this movement thus includes what may be called the objective and subjective worlds in some of their most important phases. The second movement shows the restoration of both the institutional and the moral elements in the accession of a King who has elevated himself to be their chief representative. The whole action, therefore, exhibits the transition from a period of political disintegration and social corruption to the new era of national happiness and elevation embodied in the new Monarch.

It will be noticed, too, that in this play also there are two threads running alongside of each other, which were previously called the elevated or serious thread, and the low or comic thread. In the first is depicted the political struggle; hence it separates into two parties the supporters and the opponents of the government. The second thread has as its central figure Falstaff, and portrays the moral depravity of the time. In the end, Prince Henry renounces Falstaff and adheres to the Chief Justice, an adviser of quite the opposite character. This indicates not only a change in the Prince, but also a change in the period — a change from corrupt practices to fair dealing on the part both of individual and of government. Rebellion is not to be put down by wanton violation of good faith, such as Prince John was guilty of; private character is not to be typified in Falstaff. King Henry the Fourth is too deeply-infected with the time; he cannot pass into the promised land. He was tainted with political crime

in early life, and with moral violation in his later years.
He, therefore, cannot introduce the coming epoch.

I. 1. Picking up the first thread as divided into its
opposing parties, let us proceed to consider the rebels, of
whom there are two groups — one around Northumberland
and one around the Archbishop of York. Northumberland lies at his castle pretending to be sick, but is really
waiting to hear the result of the battle at Shrewsbury.
Rumor at first flatters him with a favorable report, but
soon turns bitter with truthful news. His son, Hotspur,
has been defeated and slain; his brother, Worcester, is a
prisoner; the cause of rebellion is lost. At once he
throws off the disguise of sickness, and is ready to rush
headlong into danger. His first impulse is to unite with
the other malcontents and continue the war, but, when he
has had a little time to cool off, he easily lets himself be
persuaded by his wife and daughter-in-law into taking
flight for Scotland. He never seems to have entered
heartily into the rebellion against Henry the Fourth; it
was clearly against his judgment. Hence his activity was
paralyzed — not so much from cowardice as from lack of
confidence in the enterprise. His part was by no means
a manly one, yet it can hardly be called treacherous; he
had the foresight to look for reverses and save himself.
Quite different does he appear in *Richard the Second;*
there he is the boldest and most active among the supporters of Bolingbroke. The change is to be accounted
for by his distrust of the success of this second rebellion.

The three Percys have now run their course; they are
the Rebel Family in the fullest sense of the expression,
and represent one side of the conflict which forms the
leading theme of the Lancastrian Tetralogy. They are

all filled with the spirit of rebellion, yet each manifests it
in a different phase. Worcester is the crafty intriguer,
whose delight is in plotting — plotting for the pleasure of
the thing rather, since sound discretion would have dictated the opposite policy. But he was met by a man —
Henry Bolingbroke — compared with whom he had not
learned the rudiments of political cunning and dissimulation. The noblest of the Percys is Hotspur — open,
generous, chivalrous; he is quite the reverse of his uncle,
and even of his father. His counterpart on the other
side is the young Prince Harry. Northumberland has
clearly the soundest head of all the family; he is not vic-
timized by his own cunning like Worcester, nor by his
own rashness like Hotspur. His character falls between
the two, and his fate is that of a man who cannot support,
and who cannot refuse to support, a hazardous enterprise.
It is worthy of notice that the two sons, Hotspur and
Prince Henry, resembling each other in many respects,
have characters quite opposite to those of their fathers.

The second group of rebels is gathered around the Archbishop of York. They are discussing the question of
continuing the war; some have hope, others are doubtful.
When, however, the statement is made that the King's
forces are divided and his coffers are empty, the Archbishop boldly decides on fighting. His grievance seems
to be mainly personal — the death of his brother; but he
introduces a new element into the struggle, whose power
is by no means to be despised. He gives the sanction of
God to rebellion; " he turns insurrection to religion " by
virtue of his holy office; he governs, not merely the bodies,
but the souls of his followers. Hitherto the conflict was
only political; now the Church is drawn into it, partially

at least, and resistance to the State receives the approval
of Heaven.   But this element, too, must sink before
nationality, which is here asserted above all other principles.   The clergy were hostile to King Henry the Fourth
from the beginning, and formed conspiracies against him;
hence religion, as sanctioning rebellion, must pass under
the yoke.   Had there been full coöperation between the
political and clerical insurgents, the trouble would have
been far more serious; but revolution has always an inherent tendency to revolutionize itself.

We now pass to the side of the King.   Not much is
told of his preparation against the remaining army of the
revolters.   The general disposition of his forces after the
battle of Shrewsbury is, however, indicated; a part moves
against the French, a part against Glendower, whose death
also is rumored, but the main work falls to the share of
the troops under Prince John and Westmoreland, who are
sent against the Archbishop and Northumberland.   It is
this last division of the royal army which is of any interest for us hereafter.   Prince Henry, notwithstanding his
recent services, does not participate in the final struggle;
he is passing through a different ordeal — through a spiritual fire, which is to burn him into moral purity.   It is
also well that he has no share in the monstrous breach of
faith through which the rebellion comes to an end at the
hands of Prince John.

But what of the King?   We are introduced into the pala-
tial chamber at night; there he sits, worn, haggard, diseased, seeking in vain a little repose through sleep.   The
poorest of his subjects enjoys the sweet boon of which
he is deprived; care and remorse are feasting on his very
soul; he can rest no more.   The internal struggle now

rises into prominence — indeed, takes entire possession of the man. The fear of retribution glances out startled from that pallid face, from that feverish eye: broken in mind and body, he gazes terrified at every occurrence, expecting that his turn has come in the revolution of the times, which "make mountains level and the continent melt itself into the sea." He looks backward and beholds: How rapidly have men risen and then sunk down forever into night; are not we sinking, too? "The body of our kingdom — how foul it is; what rank diseases grow, and with what danger, near the heart of it?" But what most troubles him is that prophetic warning of Richard's to Northumberland, now turned out true: "The time will come that foul sin, gathering head, shall break into corruption." Here it all is. Nor should the reader forget to note that this is the most important of all the links binding together the Lancastrian Tetralogy. Yet into this most serious of all possible moods the dissembler thrusts himself; as, when speaking of his seizure of the throne, the King says, in repentant strain:

> — "God knows I had no such intent,
> But that necessity so bowed the State
> That I and greatness were compelled to kiss."

Still, we must remember that he was not fully aware of the depth of his own guile; the line between conscious intention and unconscious impulse is hard to be drawn in his character. He was, however, a dissembler by nature; he did not need to think to be one. Thus that deed of wrong done to King Richard is the specter which is haunting him day and night, and which makes him writhe in the agony of terror, and sweat, as it were, huge blood-drops of remorse.

Now follows a most important passage. Warwick, in trying to comfort the excited mind of the King, is led to account for Richard's wonderful gift of foretelling, the future. Here is stated the rational principle of all prophecy, and, at the same time, the innermost thought of this Tetralogy:

> "There is a history in all men's lives
> Figuring the nature of times deceas'd;
> The which observ'd, a man may prophesy,
> With a near view, of the main chance of things
> As yet not come to life; which in their seeds
> And weak beginnings lie intreasured.
> Such things become the hatch and brood of time;
> King Richard might create a perfect guess
> That great Northumberland, then false to him,
> Would of that seed grow to a greater falseness,
> Which should not find a ground to root upon,
> Unless on you. "

Men must work out their character — must follow their deepest principle. Let this principle be once accurately observed and understood, then their future conduct may be well predicted. "These things are necessities"— governed by the most rigid logic. Rebellion being given as the fundamental principle of Percy's nature, what he will do can easily be prophesied. Indeed, the King himself has all along been acting upon such a view, and, hence, he has determined to put down the insurgent family. The trouble with him, however, is that he has deposed a monarch; therefore the same inexorable logic perpetually threatens his deposition. Note again that the passage just cited is, perhaps, the most significant one in the entire Tetralogy, which has its logical movement stated here by the Poet himself.

Such is the first thread of the first movement, with its two parties and their respective tendencies. The insurrection, though reinforced by the sanction of religion, is falling to pieces through lack of combined action; it is destroying itself. On the other hand, King Henry the Fourth is harassed with the consciousness of his own ethical violations, and is terrified at the universal corruption of the times. Political wrong has begotten moral profligacy, which is now to be unrolled before our eyes in a series of wild pictures and embodied in a kind of hero.

2. This is the second thread of the first movement, to which we now pass. Falstaff is the central figure; he has returned from the war to the city, and is going to make up in carousals for the time spent in the hardship of a campaign. Moreover, he has brought back with him military fame, which he proposes to put to the best advantage. Prince Henry seems to have voluntarily resigned to him the credit of having slain Hotspur, and tells him in the preceding drama:

> " Come, bring your luggage nobly on your back;
> For my part, if a lie may do the grace,
> I'll gild it with the happiest terms I have."

Falstaff, of course, accepts the false reputation and makes use of it to escape many a difficulty. Through it he will elude the grasp of justice and replenish his empty purse. He keeps sinking deeper and deeper into the slough of sensuality, while Prince Henry is rising out of it into a new life.

At first the Fat Knight appears before us in a rather unamiable mood. He is angry at the Prince, whom he backbites for having made sport of him; the two are manifestly separating. Next Falstaff berates the tradesman with whom he can get no credit; this is one among a number of hints which indicate a conflict between the shop-keeper and the gentleman; chivalry is clearly on the decline in these " costermonger days." But here comes the Chief Justice, about to call him to account for the Gadshill robbery, and for misleading the Prince. Falstaff shows his usual dexterity in defense; it is, however, the report of his "service at Shrewsbury" which rescues him. He is also supposed to be on the point of setting out once more for the field of battle, but he really has no such intention at present.

Sir John is now seen in his domestic relations with his hostess. He refuses to pay his board-bill, and she causes him to be arrested; thence results great turmoil, with second appearance of the Chief Justice. The complaint of the hostess is pathetic: "He hath put all my substance into that fat belly of his." But she has still a stronger indictment against him, namely, a breach of promise of marriage. The Chief Justice commands the satisfaction of the wrongs, but Falstaff knows his cue well: "I do desire deliverance from these officers, being upon hasty employment in the King's affairs." Thus the employment of such a man by the State becomes the means of protecting the vilest profligacy. It is also seen how the social corruption of the period was fostered by the civil troubles, and how morals are often ruined by politics. Supposed services rendered to the country in time of danger are made to cloak villainy and disarm justice.

Next Prince Henry appears on the scene. He manifests a dissatisfied state of mind; he confesses himself to be indeed sad. The cause seems to be twofold — the sickness of his father, and his own public infamy. Sorrow meet for repentance has touched the young man with its fire. "My heart bleeds inwardly," says he. But nobody would believe any tears of his to be genuine; even Poins, his intimate companion, would think him a hypocrite were he to weep. Association with Falstaff has ruined his good name; it is time to change his course of life, he feels. But there must be one more wild adventure before the close of his gay career. He and Poins are going to disguise themselves as tapsters, and observe Falstaff in his revels at Eastcheap, where several things will be found out.

The scene at the Boar's Head Tavern will not abide much handling. It is the world of sensuality in its grossest forms; Falstaff is its supreme hero. The immoral elements of society concentrate here in unbridled debauchery; it is a perpetual carnival of swinish passion. Man and woman are both present, outcasts from the institutional relations of life, yet of necessity joined together in some common principle of existence. It is the Perverted Family which now stares us in the face. Let us also, only for a moment, look at its representatives in the two females. There is the hostess, of whom Master Tisick, the deputy, said that she was in an ill name, and we may well believe Master Tisick. She is ignorant and coarse in the extreme, yet not without a touch of sympathy and love. Far more worthy of note is Doll Tearsheet, who possesses wit and culture, but not virtue. Sir John takes particular delight in her company, as she furnishes food both for his intellect and his sensuality. She is, indeed, a sort of female Falstaff, with the same mental endowments and moral defects. Here, too, in this Perverted Family there rises many a throb of noble emotion: "Thou'lt set me a weeping, an thou sayest so"—the tears flow at parting.

Of course no such a revel is complete without a brawl, which is here produced by the intrusion of Ancient Pistol, the swaggerer, whom Doll cannot endure for his "fustian." A strange development of literary taste in a place of that kind, one reflects. But a main result of the Prince's disguise is, he hears how Falstaff calumniates him behind his back. Thus the breach between them is visibly widened. This adventure at the Boar's Head corresponds to the adventure at Gadshill in the First Part of *Henry the Fourth;* both are similar in plot, yet quite different in their surroundings and their purpose. The former shows the violation of the civil institution, the latter of the domestic institution.

But now we are to see Falstaff's violation of the civil institution in a new phase — a phase which is always certain to make its appearance in a time of protracted war. The recruiting service is seized upon by the corrupter as a means for getting money; men are impressed as soldiers who buy themselves off by bribing the officers. The result is that the State obtains no troops, and the people are everywhere demoralized. Already Falstaff has been engaged in this business; he said in the First Part of *Henry the Fourth* that he had "misused the King's press damnably." He now goes into the country and begins his villainous work, sowing the whole land with the seeds of corruption. It is a very vivid, yet very true, picture — that one of Justice Shallow and his court. Thus the right arm of the nation is paralyzed for warlike effort without, and its heart within is eaten away by the vulture of profligacy.

Such is the career of Falstaff, before his return to the army, in his relations to society. His attitude is seen to be negative toward the whole Ethical World. He is the universal corrupter; the destructive sweep of his deeds throws down quite every barrier erected against license and passion. The Poet has shown him in three essential phases: His disregard of the moral obligations of the Individual, his pollution of the Family, his prostitution of the State. Yet he is not the somber villain — he is still an amusing companion; the sparkle of his wit throws a sort of light upon his dark actions. But he is descending; the bestial side of his nature is increasing: his intellect is not what it was, but is growing dim in a sensual chaos.

Thus the first movement comes to an end. It has shown the nation struggling with Rebellion: a monster which has always two heads — violence without and corruption within; a flame-breathing monster, which not only lays waste the land with fire and death, but also emits a subtle, malarious poison, which long infects the system of the survivors. Yet it is a monster which must sometimes be waked up in order to destroy what is worse; but, when once fed to fatness by success, hard it is to kill him — a task which King Henry has undertaken to his infinite sorrow. Indeed, it is an impossible task for this monarch; he has himself inhaled too much of that poisonous breath, for did he not first nourish rebellion? Both the monster and the King will die together — both are now dying. This part of the action alone remains to be considered.

II. The second movement shows the transition from the Old to the New — from moral and national disorganization to the restored country under a new monarch. The elevated thread is made up of two main incidents — the end of the rebellion and the death of King Henry the Fourth — both passing away together and leaving behind

a ruler who never was tainted with political wrong, and
who has washed away his moral delinquency.

1. The rebels under the Archbishop of York are standing arrayed against the royal troops under Prince John.
Before trying the appeal to arms, messages pass between
the leaders of the opposing forces; there result two con-
ferences in order to bring the difficulty to a peaceful conclusion. Now follows a discussion of the merits of both
sides, maintained by men who are ready to support their
principles with their lives. It is an interesting discussion
— one that must give the collision lying at the foundation
of this Tetralogy. Here we see stated the two conflicting
elements which began with *Richard the Second* and are just
now lowering on each other in armed hostility — the right
of revolution, the right of authority; first one side, then
the other. To carry the mind back more readily, a son of
that famous Mowbray, whom fierce Bolingbroke challenged
long ago, is here, eager to fight his father's foe. The
whole subject is thoroughly gone over again, wherein we
need not follow the speaker; it would be only a repetition
of what has been already said. At last, a full satisfaction
of grievances is promised and accepted; the army of the
insurgents is dismissed; peace is the joyful word.

Suddenly the rebel leaders are seized and hurried to the
"block of death," on the charge of high treason. Prince
John tries to hide his action through evasive language, but
an unwarrantable breach of faith it remains to the straight-
forward mind. It has not even the excuse of policy; the
men had laid down their arms, and nothing was to be
gained by their death. We feel that this Prince John has
inherited the worst side of his father's character; that
under his rule the moral perversity of the time could not

be healed. This must be accomplished along with the suppression of the rebellion. Prince Henry is the one who possesses the double gift; we need no longer wonder why he was kept out of the second expedition. He is the hero of open and honorable warfare, as at Shrewsbury; not of treacherous and cruel artifice, as at Gaultree Forest.

The rebellion is ended; the nation is now united within itself; the great work of the reign of Henry the Fourth is about completed. One thing remains to harass him — the possible discord in the royal family, owing to the supposed waywardness of Prince Henry. The domestic difficulty will next be settled between father and son. Warwick again comes in with his words of solace, which should be quoted in full as the true theory of the Prince's character:

> "The Prince but studies his companions
> Like a strange tongue; wherein, to gain the language,
> 'Tis needful that the most immodest word
> Be look'd upon and learn'd; which, once attain'd,
> Your highness knows, comes to no further use,
> But to be known and hated. So, like gross terms,
> The Prince will, in the perfectness of time,
> Cast off his followers; and their memory
> Shall as a pattern or measure live,
> By which his grace must mete the lives of others,
> Turning past evils to advantages."

So says Warwick, whom the Poet has before employed as an interpreter to explain what might be misunderstood in his play. But even Warwick is by no means convinced of the truth of his own statements; he spoke to quiet the sick King. Nobody, therefore, in England at that time expected anything good of the Prince; he is a character not comprehended, and, indeed, not comprehensible by most men to-day. For are not good and evil held to be

25

two absolutely distinct Universes, between which there is
not even a thinkable connection? Like the old Florentine
Dante's, the Prince's road to Heaven lies through Hell.
Already we have noticed some signs of regeneration in
him.

There he stands now beside the bed of his dying father,
with tears flowing; a softened heart at least, one may say.
There, too, is the crown, symbol of the authority to which
he will soon succeed; it calls forth many a sober reflection,
but, at the same time, the fiercest resolution to retain it on
his own brow. The King rouses from his stupor; the last
misunderstanding, with sharp upbraidings; then forgiveness and reconciliation between father and son. But the
old politician cannot leave the world except in a haze of
policy; it was his deep-laid scheme "to lead out many to
the Holy Land," so that they would not "look too near
unto my state." His last advice is: "Therefore, my
Harry, be it thy course to busy giddy minds with foreign
quarrels," lest the monster, rebellion, may suddenly come
to life again. Harry being overwhelmed just now with
sorrow, let us answer for him: "Thou cunning old fox,
wilt thou not get out of this world in a hurry! Too much
has England already had of falsehood — a soul-consuming
dragon, worse than rebellion. Thy Harry will march out
against a foreign nation, but with far different motives.
Take note that the vulpine breed shall no longer sit upon
a throne, but shall be hunted into its dark burrow in the
bowels of the earth, amid the gloomy forest." The King's
final, very curious, stroke of policy is to die at Jerusalem
in the heart of England, and thus fulfill his vow.

2. The Falstaffian thread may now be resumed, and
continued to the end. It shows the Fat Hero in war,

after his remarkable career among peaceful people. His capture of the Knight Coleville is a piece of extravagant burlesque in the genuine Quixotic vein. It is, doubtless, the true method of portraying such a character on the field of battle. Falstaff as a soldier is a wild burlesque; let him be shown so. We have seen in his previous conduct the utter disregard of all ethical principles; how can he be expected now to fight for them, especially for the State of whose essence his whole life is one violation? But the rewards of courage and patriotism are what he wants. If he can get them by loud pretense, does it make any difference in the enjoyment of them? So he claims at once the recompense of valor — that is, something which he can appreciate. Fictitious courage serves as well as genuine, and is far less dangerous; this is Falstaff's theory of the matter, nor can a man easily be brought to fight for that which is not in him.

Sir John has now reached quite the summit of his delusion; from it he is soon to be suddenly hurled down. His eulogy on sack makes appetite not only the controlling, but the creative, principle of intelligence; man's spiritual nature is just inverted thus — quite Falstaff's own condition. His deceit practiced on Shallow is an act of poetic retribution — the rich desert of a knavish simpleton. But, when Sir John imagines that his harvest has come with the accession of the new King, the time has arrived when he must be undeceived by the most emphatic declaration:

> " I banish thee on pain of death,
> As I have done the rest of my misleaders,
> Not to come near our person by ten mile."

Yet, if "you do reform yourselves," as I, the Prince,

have done, then we shall "give you advancement." A new England will that make, indeed, if thoroughly carried out; the whole element represented by Falstaff must now sink out of sight or be regenerated. What else is said here but that, political rebellion being dead, moral corruption must die, too, or be buried alive in some dark cavernous retreat? Truely a New Epoch will now begin under a New Ruler.

The problem of Rebellion, which has occupied the King in both parts of *Henry the Fourth*, is now solved. Two methods have been tried — open battle and treacherous diplomacy. The spirit of insurrection is subdued, but the struggle has been prolific of every kind of moral violation. This, too, has now been banished out of the royal presence and out of the royal conduct. Thus we are prepared for a changed country, changed objects of national ambition, with a changed King. There must follow a new drama, whose heroic figure is to be King Henry the Fifth.

# HENRY THE FIFTH.

We have now reached the last play of the Lancastrian Tetralogy. *Henry the Fourth*, with its two parts, was occupied with the internal affairs of England : it portrays the great national transition from revolution triumphant to revolution suppressed—from civil discord to domestic harmony. The dynasty has been changed and the country has acquiesced. A great ruler has spent his life-time in this long, wearisome, and painful struggle, the right of which and the wrong of which have torn his mind with their ever-recurring contradictions. But the work is done, and is well done ; England is now a unit within herself, and not a mass of warring fragments ; the spirit of rebellion has been extinguished in the blood of its noblest and most powerful representatives ; no such personage as the gallant Hotspur will again arise to make it attractive with beauty and chivalrous daring.

The result is that a new national life has appeared, whose vigor is pulsating through the whole land with unparalleled energy. England is fired with the hope and ardor of youth ; her inward impulse is driving her forward to some higher destiny ; a narrow, insular existence has become too limited for her mighty aspiration. The nation is loudly calling for a great enterprise abroad, wherein it may realize this new spirit by enlarging the country with new territory, and may give expression, by deeds of valor, to the awakened impulse of nationality.

But the nation is chiefly fortunate in the present turn of affairs on account of having a leader, a man who embodies, in the full sense of the word, the national regeneration. Henry the Fifth is now seated on the throne; he, along with his country, has passed through the political and the moral fire which burns, yet purifies; both are one in character and aspiration. The father, Henry the Fourth, could hardly have been the successful leader of a foreign enterprise; his great vocation was to put down domestic revolution—to effect which, cunning as well as violence had to be employed. The function of the subtle politician has ended with his life; the immoral taint which infected his character must also be cleansed from the land. Henry the Fifth steps forth, the warlike champion and purified man; he has overthrown Hotspur on the one hand, and has cast off Falstaff on the other; both conquests are equally necessary to make him the true representative of his people — the outer and inner conquests of an heroic soul.

England, therefore, is seen marching under his leadership to the subjugation of a foreign foe. Nothing remains to be done at home adequate to the national ambition which is bursting forth on all sides; the pent-up energy must find a vent outwards. In what channel will it thrust itself? Just across a narrow strip of water lies France, the hereditary enemy of the nation; on France, therefore, the storm will be likely to fall. Many an old score is now to be settled between the two peoples. Each has always been a barrier to the other; cannot that barrier be swept down by us, the English? No, not permanently, so one may give the answer here; for it is just that barrier that makes you both just what you are — two distinct nations,

England and France. Remove it, and England will suffer
in the end quite as much as France; indeed, if she be
successful in breaking down all national boundaries, she
will lose the very thing which she is so vehemently maintaining, namely, nationality.

But this reflection lies beyond the play — in fact, beyond
the consciousness of the Poet. To him, Henry the Fifth
seems to be the supreme type of the national hero, and
the conquest of France the highest national object. Thus
the Lancastrian Tetralogy comes to an end; it portrays
the truly constructive epoch of English History according
to the conception of Shakespeare, showing the glorious
rise of the country from rebellion at home to the subjec-
tion of its ancient enemy abroad. Herein, therefore, the
loftiest pinnacle of nationality is reached, and the poetical
work must conclude. The Yorkian Tetralogy was written first, though it follows the Lancastrian in historical
order; the Poet has, in consequence, not developed the
inner ground of the Wars of the Roses. The play of
*Henry the Fifth* is, hence, the culminating point of the
English Historical series.

The structure of *Henry the Fifth* is without its like in
Shakespeare. The employment of choruses or prologues
to precede every Act, as is the case here, is unknown in
any of his other works, if we except the doubtful play of
*Pericles.* The object of these choruses seems, in the
main, twofold; they announce the subject of the Acts
which are to follow, and mark with some care the large
gaps of time which are to be passed over by the mind.
Thus they try to connect somewhat more closely the
disjointed parts of the drama. The Poet himself clearly
sees the loose texture of his work; he is full of apologies,

which imply his own judgment of its main weakness. He appears to feel that he has transcended quite the limits of Dramatic Art — the theme is too extensive for representation on a petty stage; he seems almost afraid of turning it into ridicule. Hence he is continually begging the spectator to use his imagination and forget the apparent caricature. In no other play is he seen to struggle so hard with his artistic form as here; he surges and frets against its bounds on every side. The great exploits of his hero are in danger of appearing farcical on the stage.

The whole action is of the moving, spectacular kind; it is a series of historical pictures selected from one great campaign, with a chorus to explain the general movement and to supply the omitted links. The play, therefore, is closely tied to the external realities of place and time, and is governed to a less extent than usual by an inner controlling thought; hence criticism, whose function it is to unfold this thought, has no very profound task at present. The result is that *Henry the Fifth*, judged by the Shakespearian standard, must be considered as one of the lesser stars of the Poet's dramatic constellation; it is lacking in unity, in concentration, in organic completeness. Still, it must not be esteemed too lightly. As the play moves in the external details of history, much has to be omitted, since the dramatic form is too narrow; such a manner of treatment demands the fullness and diversity of the Epic or of the Novel. The dramatic work must compress all into the one central, glowing point; only those events are to be taken, and only those things are to be said, which embody directly the thought.

As might be inferred from its spectacular character, the play has no inherent division into movements; indeed,

the structure indicates that it is made up of five separate
pictures, each of which is preceded by an explanatory
prologue. Yet the entire action tends to one supreme
event — the battle of Agincourt — in which single effort
the conquest of France was accomplished. The drama
may be externally divided into two movements. First,
the preparation at home on both sides, comprising the
first two Acts; secondly, the conflict and its results, ter-
minating in the overwhelming success of Henry the Fifth.
England, united within after a slight ripple of opposition,
prepares herself for the struggle, passes over to the territory of her enemy, subjugates the country, and tries to
confirm its possession by an alliance of marriage with the
royal family of France.

The division into threads is, however, strictly maintained; they were called in *Henry the Fourth*, and still
may be called, the elevated or serious thread, and the low
or comic thread. The first subdivides itself, according to
nationality, into two groups — the French and the English
— between whom lies the conflict, which is the main theme
of the play. Here we must seek for the political elements
which control the work. England claims the right to the
throne of France, and makes good the claim by force of
arms. The second or comic thread has not less than four
groups; there are the remnants of the old Falstaffian
company; the three English common soldiers who have
the little intrigue with the King; the group of officers
representing the several British nationalities — Welsh,
Scotch, Irish, English; to these must be added the French
Princess in her conversation with her attendant, Alice,
and with the English King. The superabundance here is
manifest; it branches out into so many directions that the

unity of the work is in danger of being lost — the central thought seems not to be able to control the dramatic luxuriance springing out of the subject.

I. 1. Beginning with the English side of the first thread, we notice at once the remarkable change in the life of the King. He is no longer the wild Prince Harry of Eastcheap, companion of thieves and revelers, but he has become a religious man; he has truly received the new birth, which has left "his body as a paradise to envelop and contain celestial spirits." The caprice of youthful wantonness, "hydra-headed willfullness," has been completely laid aside, and there has been a full submission to the established order of the world. It is clergymen who are speaking; they praise especially his holy demeanor, and wonder at his sudden reformation. Indeed, the play throughout exalts the piety of the King as one of his main characteristics, and there is, perhaps, no other personage in Shakespeare's dramas who comes so near being a religious hero. The associate of Falstaff has, therefore, fully redeemed his promise of amendment.

His intellectual gifts, which were never dim, seem to be wonderfully brightened and quickened by his moral change. "Hear him but reason in divinity," says the admiring Archbishop, "you would desire the King were made a prelate;" he speaks of matters of policy with the knowledge and skill of the veteran statesman. But, when he comes to his supreme vocation, "list to his discourse of war, and you shall hear a fearful battle rendered you in music." Still greater is his genius for action; he is the true practical man, who strikes boldly, yet at the same time thinks. In fine, he is the all-sufficient hero in whom intellect and will, the speculative and the active principles

of man, are blended in the happiest harmony. Neither
of these powers paralyzes the other, as is often the
case, but each supports and intensifies the other to a
supreme degree. And also he is the stronger and better
for having passed through a wild period in his youth.
"Wholesome berries thrive and ripen best, neighbored by
fruit of baser quality," says the worthy Bishop of him, a
clerical authority to which we may reasonably submit,
though not without some surprise at the source.

Next there is revealed the chief object of his ambition,
the object for which his whole career has been a long
preparation — in fact, the object in which the Lancastrian
Tetralogy culminates, namely, the conquest of France.
But he will not proceed to it without being first assured
of the justice of his cause. Accordingly he calls around
himself his learned religious advisers, who state in full
the grounds of his claim, and vindicate his title against
the French doctrine, of succession. The Clergy thus
requite his favors to the Church; they even urge him to
conquest, who needed no incitement; the Archbishop of
Canterbury addresses him: "Stand for your own, unwind
your bloody flag," and bids him take as a pattern his
noble ancestors who once did "forage in blood of French
nobility." So speaks the primate of all England, the
chief apostle of peace and good-will among men in the
British isles.

It is manifest that the nation is for war; it is not merely
sustaining, but even pushing, Henry to the struggle. Yet
he is fired with the same ambition; he, therefore, most
truly represents the spirit of the country. The Nobles
are with him, the People have been always with him, now
the Clergy have become the most urgent advisers of an

invasion of France. All classes are in harmony; then there is the furious energy resulting from a common aspiration. It is a national enterprise, at the head of which is marching the national Hero; the outlook is ill for the object which offers resistance to their purpose.

The King organizes rapidly his powers, wisely leaving a bulwark against the Scot "who hath been still a giddy neighbor to us." Then the reply of France is heard; to a denial of the royal claim is added a wanton insult. More impatient, then, is the cry for war. Yet even here in England there is manifested a slight reaction against the general tendency of the nation; this reaction culminates in a conspiracy against the life of the King. Still some embers of revolt remain and give out sparks; thus the old spirit of insurrection will once more appear. Three nobles, most intimate friends of Henry, were ready to thrust a dagger into his heart; but the plot is discovered and the conspirators punished. It is only a momentary gleam, passing into speedy darkness. Rebellion has been put down in the previous reign with vigor and vengeance; it cannot rise now, for other business is on hand to occupy the life of Henry the Fifth. But, after his death, will not the spirit of rebellion dart up again in the face of his successor, and will not the question of title arise once more for settlement? But let us suppress the premonition which the event excites. At present, after this slight reaction, the union is firmer than ever; England — consolidated, as it were, into one body — is eager to be hurled across the channel into the heart of France, shouting with her monarch the popular war cry:

"No King of England if not King of France."

The French group, on the other hand, are introduced discussing the threatened invasion. Their Monarch, with the circumspection of age, manifests no little anxiety; he recalls the many examples of English valor enacted on the soil of his own realm. But the Dauphin, with the impetuosity of youth, is eager for the conflict, having no fear of England now, because " she is so idly kinged." But the clear-headed Constable gives a well-timed warning to the young Prince; he has carefully noted the great transformation of King Henry's character, whose

> — " Vanities forespent
> Were but the outside of the Roman Brutus,
> Covering discretion with a coat of folly."

Of course the French emphatically reject the claims of England, and the messenger departs with the declaration of war. Thus we are prepared for the shock of armies which is to follow — two great nations are about to grapple in a terrific struggle — though the English predilection of the Poet has given a distinct hint of the result. Such is the faint outline of the leading French characters.

2. Passing now to the comic thread, we behold the Falstaffian group without Falstaff. At the first view this omission seems quite surprising, since the Poet has distinctly promised the reappearance of the jolly Fat Knight, at the end of *Henry the Fourth.* Why he is dropped can be only conjectured; but it is manifest that the Poet changed his mind only after mature deliberation. A little reflection on the part of the reader will fully justify the same conclusion; in fact, the dramatic possibilities of the character had been exhausted in the previous plays — nothing could well be added to the portraiture. Besides,

some repugnance to Falstaff must have been manifested
by the more decent and moral portion of the audience,
inasmuch as there are not a few persons of the present
day who cannot endure his appearance and behavior.
Personally, we would like to have seen his enormous bulk
again on the stage and heard some of his monstrous lies,
but, upon the second thought, it is well as it is ; we, too,
like the Prince, have had enough of his society for our
own good, and should now consent to a permanent separation.    Only the death of poor Jack is told ; it looks as if he
had experienced a hard struggle in his last hours, wrestling with repentance ; and we repeat involuntarily the sigh
of Prince Henry on the field of Shrewsbury: "I could
have better lost a better man."

The remaining members of this comic group are brought
forward from *Henry the Fourth*, and need not be characterized in detail.    It is still the reverse side of society —
the immoral element — in the present case transmitted to
a happier era from a period of civil discord.    Its importance is much diminished ; still, it is here, following in the
track of war, and the whole company is about to cross the
channel with the army, not for the purpose of patriotism,
but of plunder.    The contrast to the general feeling of
the nation is most clearly seen in this group of debauched
camp-followers.    Every great enterprise, however right-
eous it may be, always has such vermin clinging to it on
the outside, and trying to reach its vital juices, but they
must be brushed off with the strong hand of merciless
justice.    The fate of these people in the present undertaking will be the same as that of the external enemy —
the French.

II.  In the second movement of the play, which now

follows, the scene changes to France, where the struggle
at once begins. The key-note is struck by the King in
his famous address to his soldiers — the fierce blast of the
English war bugle :

> "Once more unto the breach, dear friends, once more,
> Or close the wall up with our English dead."

The sublime theme of the speech throughout is nationality,
of which Henry is the most glorious representative in English History. The same spirit permeates this entire series
of plays; here is its culmination. Hitherto England had
been able to master her internal difficulties : now she is to
measure herself with another nation, which it is her weighty
enterprise to conquer. If she succeeds, then the English
nationality has won the laurel among peoples. The strong
appeal is, therefore, to Englishmen, their glory and superiority; it is a battle-prologue, nerving for the conflict
which is to follow.

1. Great stress is laid by the Poet upon the behavior
of the two armies just before the struggle comes on. The
haughty confidence and fatuitous arrogance of the French
are brought out in the strongest colors. It is, indeed, the
only tragic ground of their fate ; they seem to defy Heaven
itself to keep them from their prey ; on the pinnacle of
insolence they are placed, to be hurled down by an aveng-
ing Nemesis. Even the cautious Constable gives way to
arrogant boasting. A herald is sent to King Henry
demanding ransom before the battle is fought; the common soldiers play at dice for English captives that are not
yet taken. To the entire French army the victory seems
to be won before the engagement; their camp is a scene
of wild frolic and impatience. Very necessary and skill-

ful is this motive of impious arrogance, in order to detach the sympathy of the hearer or reader from the side of the French, for they are really defending their nationality, while the English are assailing it; their cause is in every way the more rightful. Indeed, the English are not only committing a wrong against a neighboring nation, but against themselves; they are logically destroying their own supreme principle in the present conflict, namely, nationality. All of which is felt by the Poet, and its effects artfully guarded against by introducing an old Greek tragic motive — human arrogance humbled by a leveling Nemesis.

In the strongest contrast to the action of the French is the conduct of the English; from the noble down to the private soldier there is a feeling of humility — indeed, of depression, though not of despair. They all think that the result will be very doubtful; gloomy forebodings haunt them; still, the staunchest resolution pervades the host. But there is one Englishman who is animated by the most exalted hope, who sees in the present emergency the greatest opportunity of his life or of his century — it is King Henry himself. He moves around among his soldiers, giving a word of encouragement to all; he is full of religious fervor — prayer is often on his lips; nor, on the other hand, does he forget even in this most trying hour of his life to play a good joke on a common soldier. He still has some of the former Prince Hal peering out of his conduct; he has not lost his sportiveness. Once, however, in a sudden fit of anger, he gives the most cruel order that every soldier should slay his prisoners — a fact which can be reconciled with his general character only by reflecting that his highest principle is the victory and supremacy of his nation, and whatever jeopardizes this supreme end must be removed at any cost. The day of Agincourt is won; King Henry the Fifth comes out of the battle the greatest of English national heroes; at one blow he utterly overwhelms and subjugates the ancient enemy of his country.

For France naught remains but submission; one people passes under the yoke of another. It has already been frequently stated that such a condition of affairs violates in the deepest manner the principle of nationality; there can result from it only perennial strife and calamity to both States. To avoid the difficulty inherent in the situation, to cement the bond between the two nations by domestic affection, the Family is now introduced into the political relation. Henry marries Catherine, daughter of the French King; but the royal woman is not here, as is often the case, made a sacrifice to the State. The famous wooing scene shows that their marriage had its true basis of love, notwithstanding the strong comic features. But the domestic ties of the Monarchs cannot control the destinies of two great people; the Family is a very imperfect bulwark against the Nation. The political object of the present matrimonial alliance is manifest from the beautiful expressions of the Queen-mother, who gives the true ground of royal intermarriage, in her earnest appeal to the happy pair:

> " As man and wife, being two, are one in love,
> So be there 'twixt your kingdoms such a spousal
> That never may ill office or fell jealousy,
> Which troubles oft the bed of blessed marriage,
> Thrust in between the paction of these kingdoms,
> To make divorce of their incorporate league,
> That English may as French, French Englishmen,
> Receive each other.''

26

2. The comic thread of the second movement breaks
up into four distinct groups. The first is composed of the
old associates of Falstaff; they now meet the fit retribution for their deeds. The immoral company seems to be
pretty much wiped out in the course of the war; Nym
and Bardolph have been hung; "Nell is dead in the
spital;" Pistol, ranter and coward, steals back in shame
and punishment to England. Thus debauchery from its
first prominence in *Henry the Fourth* is quite brought to
an end under the heroic King at the same time with his
great national victory.

A second and new comic group is made up of representatives from the four British peoples — Welsh, Scotch,
Irish, and English. They are all working for the common
cause, though they have their little bickerings among themselves; they show how the heroic King had united every
kind of subjects in his great foreign enterprise. In com-
pliment to the birthplace and blood of Henry, the pedantic
but valorous Welshman, Fluellen, is here the leading figure.
The comic effect rests mainly upon the pronunciation of
the English tongue in a different fashion by each of these
persons, thus indicating with a laugh the checkered variety
of speech and men in the English army — a motley gathering, but with the deepest purpose.

Another group is that of the three English soldiers,
quite sober when talking together of the prospect of the
battle, and not at all very comic figures at any time. But
the King comes along in disguise, and they converse with
him reprovingly; the result is, he exchanges gloves with
one of them in token of a future settlement. From this
incident springs a little comic intrigue, which ends in the
King discovering himself to the soldier, who is overcome

with confusion, but who receives a reward for his manly behavior generally. It is such a simple story as would be told among the common people of their beloved leader.

One more comic group can be distinguished, of which the French Princess, with her broken English, is the chief character. She makes the fourth person employing a brogue in the play. This slender comic instrumentality is quite worked to death; the tendency thereby is to drop down into a farce. These four groups, composing the second thread, have no very rigid central thought: they manifest rather the appearance of capricious diversity. Yet they all celebrate the internal or domestic triumphs of Henry, while the great battle of Agincourt, given in the first thread, celebrates the external or national triumph of the heroic King. It will hardly be questioned, however, that four comic groups here are too many; confusion results from excessive multiplicity always, and the feeling of the artistic Whole is obscured — or, even lost — in a labyrinth of details.

Such is the conclusion of the Lancastrian Tetralogy. Indeed, the present play, as was before said, may be considered as the culminating point of the whole Historical Drama of Shakespeare; it delineates the ideal ruler in his personal, civil, and military character, and it portrays the ideal England in harmony at home and in supremacy abroad. This Tetralogy is, in the highest sense, a positive work, having a happy outcome; it begins with a revolution and passes through to final reconstruction. A Drama of the Nation it may be called, as distinct from the Drama of the Individual; for here it is a nation which, after many conflicts and obstacles, reaches a happy destiny. But there is a dark, concealed background to these bright skies; there is a violation which will demand retribution. A time of negation and destruction will follow, and this brings us to the Yorkian Tetralogy.

With *Henry the Sixth* we enter upon what has been hitherto called the Yorkian Tetralogy — the series of four plays ending with *Richard the Third*. The violation of nationality committed abroad now returns home — the conquest of France produces the civil dissension of England. It is an age of terror — a tragic age — which has also a tragic termination. Both the contending Houses of York and Lancaster pass away, and England finds peace in a new dynasty.

*Henry the Sixth*, though one of the least important of Shakespeare's works, seems to be most written about, judging by the number and length of the dissertations on this play. For its authorship is uncertain, and with uncertainty begins learned conjecture, multiplying itself a thousandfold, and never quite reaching anything certain — for then conjecture would be at an end. This whole field we shall avoid, not feeling any sure footing in it; and to grade probabilities is a wearisome and, to most readers of the Poet, an unprofitable task. So much, however, may be said: In *Henry the Sixth* we find some of Shakespeare's earliest and crudest work, and some which it is difficult to believe to be his work at all.

---

The general subject of the First Part of *Henry the Sixth* is the loss of France through the internal dissensions of the

English. Henry the Fifth, who had conquered the enemy abroad and united all factions at home, is dead ; when his strong grasp is once released, the repelling elements begin to fly asunder. The House of Lancaster, which had established and maintained itself through the ability of its rulers, now furnishes a totally incompetent monarch to the throne of England — a monarch incompetent at first through immaturity of youth, and incompetent always through weakness of character. The mighty work of the previous Lancastrian Kings begins to undo itself; the last and most glorious exploit — the conquest of France — is necessarily the first act in the great drama of retrogression; the battle of Agincourt, around which English national pride especially entwined itself, is now to be lost on account of the incapacity of the head of government.

The First Part of *Henry the Sixth* is not a great play ; even that Shakespeare was its author is denied by many good judges of the Poet's writings. But let this question of authenticity be dropped at once. The organization is rather loose, yet might be worse ; the action is not controlled by a strong inner thought, but moves through a series of pictorial scenes in an external fashion ; liveliness it has, though only playing over the surface. That deep, central flame which fuses all the materials of the drama into oneness — of which the events are merely the fiery outbursts — is wanting here, though there is much activity and struggle. The play, however, has one general purpose to which it seeks to give utterance ; this purpose, as already stated, is to show the loss of the French territory through English dissension.

The clearest and best point in the structure of the present work is its division into two threads, which may be called the external conflict and the internal conflict. The scene of the first thread lies in France; it portrays the struggle between the French and the English. The former are fighting for national independence, the latter for the subjugation of their neighbors. This is a contest in which England must lose, and ought to lose, for she is really violating her own deepest principle, namely, nationality. The second thread will show the means—internal strife will paralyze her efforts; the hatred of parties will turn from the enemy abroad to the opponents within. The reader, for his own advantage, may note the inherent relation between these two threads—war upon your neighbor seems ultimately to mean war upon yourself.

The movements, which the reader may possibly inquire after next, are not very distinctly marked; the turning-point may be considered to be where Burgundy goes over to the French, and thus unites his nation against the invader. Yet the whole action only exhibits occurrence after occurrence sweeping away the English conquests. The two threads, however, proceed with perfect distinctness through the entire play. A short summary of each may now be given.

The first thread, as it shows a conflict, is divided into two sides—the French and the English. The French are striving with success to redeem their country from a foreign yoke; town after town, and province after province, are falling into their hands. They have in these wars their heroic character—the supreme representative of the struggling nation. But it is not the King, not a nobleman, not even a man; it is a poor shepherd's daughter named Joan of Arc, now far more famous than the greatest monarch of that age. Truly she is a remarkable

appearance—in the history of the world a glowing point
of light which darts up and illumines an epoch. Many
sympathetic pens have told her story in prose and in verse ;
she is, indeed, a noble, poetical form—a woman bursting
the barriers of class and of sex, and representing the
nation ; a woman in arms inspiring her countrymen by
word and example to the great deed of national liberation.
It is a rare phenomenon—perhaps the single instance of
its kind in History.

Shakespeare, or the author of the First Part of *Henry
the Sixth*, has not taken much advantage of the imposing
figure of Joan of Arc ; he has rather left her character
and her mission in a state of perplexing doubt. When
the French speak, full justice is done to her wonderful
power ; she is divinely sent ; she has beheld in a vision
the one thing needful in the present emergency ; she is
inspired of Heaven to be the deliverer of her country.
But the English ridicule her claims ; they even assail her
womanly honor, which she, among the French, is represented as having kept unstained ; and, finally, they burn
her for a witch. English feeling, perhaps, dictated such
a portraiture. Between these two opinions the character
fluctuates ; it has no unity in its development, but sways
from one side to the other, finally resting under an English
cloud of suspicion. Still the main fact cannot be obscured
— a woman of humble station rises to be a national heroine, heroic above all men of that age ; the champion of the
Family has become the champion of the State.

We now turn to the side of the English, in order to see
what offset they have to the wonderful Maid of Orleans.
A national hero appears also among them, but of quite
a different kind. It is Talbot, a man trained to the

use of arms, of great experience in war, and of noble
rank. He is mainly the courageous soldier, whose very
name puts the French to flight. There is in his actions a
wild daring which magnetizes the troops under him into
huge masses of fiery valor; this wild daring, coupled with
a chivalrous, open-hearted devotion to his country, is his
characteristic trait. The Soldier meets the Maid; there is
much fluctuation in the conflict, but the English poet
cannot disguise the fact that the result is general defeat.

But the crowning glory of Talbot's career is the manner
of his death. He is a sacrifice to the hatred between two
party-leaders, who were also generals in this unfortunate
time — York and Somerset; neither will send aid to Talbot in his perilous situation at Bordeaux. He perishes;
the English national hero becomes the victim of English dissension — an ominous emblem of England herself. But to his patriotic devotion is now added a new
trait of character — parental love. His young son, John
Talbot, has just come to France in order to receive under
his father's eye a military training; when destruction
lowers from every quarter of the sky, the parent beseeches his boy to escape — from out the rugged breast
of the soldier is seen to leap the pure fire of domestic
affection. But the son is a Talbot; he will not fly from
the enemy; his father is going to stay and die — so will he
if he be truly a son. The youthful hero, after performing
deeds of valor, comes into a dangerous situation, from
which he is rescued by the parent. Again the latter begs
his only son to escape and preserve the name of his
family; but the answer is perfect in its logic:

"And if I fly I am not Talbot's son."

That is, the sole proof of sonship is to remain with his

father in battle; if he run off, he has not the blood of
Talbot in his veins, and the family cannot then be preserved through him, though he should escape.

Such is by all means the most powerful portion of the
play; it is an incident which is worthy of the highest
inspiration. There is portrayed in the hardy bosom of
Talbot a conflict between the parent and the soldier, right
in the midst of the battle raging around — a truly tragic
theme in the best sense of the word. Father and son
perish — both heroes; with them English supremacy in
France perishes; the heroic stock of England has degenerated into factious partisans; the old conquerors — Salisbury, Bedford, and finally Talbot — have been killed, one
after another, till a peace substantially acknowledging
French independence has to be made.

We pass now to the second thread, portraying the internal conflict of England, which runs parallel with the external conflict given in the first thread. There are two sets
of partisans, with very different objects in view. The
one set is struggling for the control of the weak-minded
Monarch. Henry is a cipher in the government; two
great lords, Gloster and Winchester, are fighting for the
substance of regal authority. They defame each other
on every occasion; the presence of the King himself cannot restrain their mutual abuse; their adherents always
have a brawl whenever they meet in the streets, disturbing
public order and requiring the interference of the Mayor
of London to preserve the peace. Both men seem to be
animated merely by a vulgar desire of power; neither
stands as the advocate of any great national principle.
Winchester is a churchman, and pleads the rights and
immunities of his organization; hence Gloster is made to
appear as the enemy of the Church — indeed, of religion

itself. Still, there is little depth to Winchester's piety or to Gloster's skepticism; a pretext was needed by both to cloak their ambition — this is what determined their religious attitude.

But in these disputes the utter incompetency of Henry stands out in the strongest light; he can not unify his counselors at home — much less is he able to lead his army abroad. He has but to go back to the time of his grand-father when he will find a legitimate King — Richard the Second — deposed mainly on account of incapacity. His own dynasty, the Lancastrian, has no title to the throne ex-cept the ability to rule ; what then must happen in his case?

Look now to the second set of partisans for an answer, at present under the leadership of York and Somerset, respectively. York is not seeking the control of an imbe-cile King, but of the kingdom itself. He is the rightful heir of the throne, being descended from those whom the Lancastrians had set aside. In him the right of inherit-ance again comes up. since now the right of ability can no longer be claimed for the usurping house. Thus begins the civil conflict known as the Wars of the Roses ; the whole question of hereditary title to the throne must be fought over again. Each leader collects around him-self a band of retainers whose violence can hardly be restrained ; Vernon and Bassett are types of the mutual hate of the two parties — a hate which can be quenched only with blood. But the present drama does not pro-pose to treat of the Wars of the Roses ; the beginning is only indicated, to be fully carried out hereafter.

We now see that the national spirit engendered by the Lacastrians is lost, and with it has perished every reason-able ground for the continuance of their dynasty. France, the great foreign conquest, is gone from their grasp; the crown, unsupported by a strong ruler, must fall back into the hand of the true heir, who is here on the spot ready to assert his right. The play, therefore, leaves us with this new conflict ready to burst forth. To make it join closely with the next play, the betrothal of Henry with Margaret is introduced, which event finds its whole significance in the two Parts which are to follow.

———————

In the Second Part of *Henry the Sixth* the struggle is wholly internal; France has been lost to the English, and, hence, there is no French thread required to show the foreign war. The strife which England brought upon a neighboring people has turned back into herself; from her own hands she receives the punishment for the wrong done by her to another country, whose right of existence was as good as her own. National retribution is the fundamental principle of this whole Lancastrian Tetralogy — one party is swept off by a second, which, in its turn, is destroyed by a third; thus they rise and fall; every class of men seems to be infected with a corruption whose sole cure is death. The present play shows the transition from the loss of France to the first opening of the great dynastic quarrel — the Wars of the Roses. English dissension, which previously had defeated the English armies abroad, now raises its hand against England herself upon her own soil.

There are two movements, which are very plainly marked, and which present distinct phases of the conflict. The first is the struggle among the Lancastrians them-

selves — between those who agree in supporting the throne
of King Henry the Sixth, but who, in other respects, are
the bitterest enemies. Here there are naturally two main
threads, made up of the opposing parties, the one side
being headed by Humphrey, Duke of Gloster, the other
by Queen Margaret. The result is that Gloster's party is
annihilated, but the Duke of York, who has all along been
waiting for his opportunity, at once springs up with a
new and far more dangerous party. This is the second
general movement of the play; the struggle is no longer
among the Lancastrians themselves, but between the
Lancastrians and Yorkists; the conflict has deepened
into a fight against the supremacy of the reigning house.
The present government means foreign defeat and civil
dissension — it is, indeed, no government; hence its title,
which rests upon the capacity of the ruler, is called in
question by the true heir. The threads are now the two
Roses — the parties of York and of Lancaster.

Beginning at once with the first movement, we notice
that the one party at court is grouped around the brother
of the late King, the protector of the realm — Humphrey,
Duke of Gloster. His power is evidently declining; the
marriage of King Henry with Margaret, and, above all, the
concessions made in consequence of that event, were contrary to his policy, and meet with his strongest disappro-
bation. Gloster represents the old national spirit of
England; he cannot be brought to yield the English
claim to France by any measure. This marriage, coupled
with the surrender of Anjou and Maine, he looks upon as
the disgrace of his country. He manifests, in this drama
at least, the feeling of true patriotism; he will do nothing
against the King; he cannot be seduced into ambitious

thoughts, though he is next in succession to the throne. In general, he, amid a crowd of depraved self-seekers, upholds the principle of nationality.  His character here will be noticed to be different from, though not inconsistent with, what it was represented to be in the First Part of *Henry the Sixth*, as love of power, which seems to be his leading trait there, may exist along with patriotic devotion.

At his side is placed his wife, the Duchess Eleanor, a haughty, indiscreet woman, whose strongest passion is ambition.  She is a germ of Lady Macbeth.  She tries to excite the thought of revolt in her husband, but he puts her down with an emphatic reproof.  But that which gives her most prominence is the fact that she is the special object of Queen Margaret's hatred.  The wife of the Protector and the wife of the Monarch thus manifest mutually the strongest jealousy; the two women fill the court with strife, for both are seeking the same thing — authority. Each plots the overthrow of the other, but Margaret possesses the far subtler character.  The Duchess is beguiled into dabbling with sorcery in order to discover the future destiny of the King and his friends; she is suddenly arrested and banished.

The Yorkists also lean to the side of the Duke of Gloster in this first movement, though not without much ambiguous dealing.  Richard, the Duke of York, is, indeed, playing for the crown; his general scheme is to let the Lancastrians eat one another up, when he will step in and seize the prey.  At first he proposes to " make a show of love to proud Duke Humphrey;" then he goes to the aid of the other side.  Full of treachery and deep dissimulation is his character.  It is hard to see wherein he is any better than the ruling powers; in some respects he is clearly worse. No improvement in the affairs of England can come through him; the same moral and political rottenness will continue, and the fiery process of war must go on till both sides be exterminated. Nor need the further reflection be withheld here — his whole generation, if they inherit his character, can never remain long in possession of the throne. His children will destroy one another till his line be extinct; then there may be some hope for peace to England.

But other Yorkists are different. The Nevills — Salisbury and Warwick — cling to the Duke of Gloster, and are ready to punish his murderers. They are also strongly national, and have been deeply chagrined at the policy toward France. But the main event of their history now is their conversion to the House of York. Richard traces his title back to the third son of Edward the Third, while the Lancastrians are derived from the fourth son of that monarch. The argument is conclusive — both the Nevills hail Richard as England's King. The great king-maker, Warwick, whose career hereafter will become most prominent, already anticipates his future destiny:

> " My heart assures me that the Earl of Warwick
> Shall one day make the Duke of York a King."

Passing now to the side hostile to the Duke of Gloster, which is the second thread of the first movement, we observe that its leader is no longer Cardinal Beaufort, but Margaret, the English Queen. This woman remains henceforward the central figure of her party; France has not only reconquered her provinces from England, but the latter is now subjected to the domination of a French Princess, whose domestic rule will be far more fatal than

foreign defeat.   Margaret is essentially a will-character;
her intelligence, though of a high order, is not her supreme
trait;  that in which she is chiefly deficient is a moral
nature.    She is not faithful to the Family — she loves
another man than her husband ; like so many royal women,
domestic instincts are swallowed up in political ambition.
As ruler of the State, her career is still less commendable
than as wife; she is going to control affairs even at the
cost of the existence of the country.   No great national
purpose is seen in her conduct, or in that of her advisers ;
to have matters her own way is quite the sum total of her
policy.   The weak King, her husband, she despises.   But
she is determined to govern ; this brings her at once into
conflict with the "good Duke Humphrey," the Protector
of the realm ; the result is that Humphrey is deposed from
his office, arraigned for high treason, and finally murdered
in the most treacherous manner.   With him was destroyed
the peace of England, and, indeed, the Lancastrian tenure
of the throne ; the last man of that House worthy of rule
has been butchered by his own kindred; the ·Lancastrian
Family is rapidly putting an end to its own existence.

The group of men around Queen Margaret are animated
with her principle ; they are pursuing a selfish ambition to
the detriment of their country.   No spark of nationality
illumines, even faintly, a single action of theirs ; the fact
is, they are united against the national man, Humphrey,
but they would all desert and betray one another with the
same readiness for the sake of personal advantage.   The
faithless cannot be faithful, even to their kind.   Suffolk
enjoys the distinction of being the Queen's paramour,
though he never controlled her as he had expected to do
when he brought about the royal marriage.   The church-

man also appears in this group — Cardinal Beaufort, formerly known as the Bishop of Winchester; but his importance is much diminished; he has been supplanted in his leadership by a woman. The result of his career is given in a terrific death-scene; a guilty conscience tears away reason and life together. Thus another relative of the King, and staunch supporter of the House of Lancaster, is removed.

King Henry, the helpless puppet around which all these crimes and intrigues are spinning, is the express contrast to his Queen. He absolutely possesses no power of will. His intellect, however, is not by any means so defective; he often shows insight into the true condition of affairs; he tries also to soften the rancor of parties — not by decisive action, but by amicable exhortation. His moral instinct is pure and true; he cannot be brought to believe in the guilt of his uncle Gloster. Of his religious nature, Margaret and others even make fun, coupling it with his utter weakness of resolution. King Henry is, therefore, supremely contemptible; he is not a man, since he lacks the will of a man, while his wife, as if to set him off more prominently, possesses a masculine energy of character.

The party of Margaret is, therefore, triumphant; her chief enemies are dead or banished; peace would now seem possible. But behold there arises a new conflict — deeper, more intense, more terrific than before. The Queen has really undermined the Lancastrian dynasty; its national purpose has perished with Gloster. With the might of destiny there comes up the rival claim of York, and finds many supporters. For the Lancastrians are legally usurpers; their sole title was their fidelity to the spirit of the nation, which accordingly supported their

27

House.   But this title has perished in an imbecile ruler, in
foreign defeat, and in domestic strife ; the same reasons
which brought them to the throne can now be urged to
drive them from the throne.

The second movement of the play has for its theme this
struggle between York and Lancaster.   There are three
phases of the conflict shown here.   First, the Pirates are
evidently in the interest of Richard ; their captain gives
an excellent statement of the points at issue, and denounces
violently the reigning House.   They capture Suffolk on
his way to France ; the favorite of Margaret meets with a
speedy death at their hands.   The service of the Queen
has thus brought its penalty, but there are more men of
guilt still to receive their doom.

The next move against the Lancastrians is Cade's insurrection.   Richard, Duke of York, expressly declares that
he originated it and employed John Cade, of Ashford, as
"a minister of my intent."   But the people were full of
angry unrest and ready for a revolution.   This rebellion
is peculiar on account of its extreme leveling tendency ;
it reads like the accounts of some popular outbreaks of
recent times.   The Poet, with much humor, shows the
extravagant dreams of the lower classes in a period of
social upheaval.   It is curious to note the manner in
which the insurrection was put down ; the cry, "to France,
to France, and get what you have lost," is sufficient to
change their whole purpose.   After all, the strongest
feeling of the English people is the conquest of France.
There seems to be no direct coöperation with York ; the
revolt ends without having accomplished anything of
significance towards the settlement of the great question
between the two Houses.

But the third assault upon the Lancastrians is headed by the Duke of York himself. He had been given the government of Ireland; now he returns with an army for the purpose of maintaining his right to the crown. The battle of Saint Albans takes place; King Henry — or, rather, Queen Margaret — is defeated and compelled to fly from the field, with the loss of Somerset and Clifford. This engagement, however, is not decisive; it rather places the two sides — York and Lancaster — on an equal footing. The throne is not to be won by a single victory or lost by a single defeat — that is, the contest between the Two Roses has just begun; to reach the end another drama must be written.

In the previous play the conflict between the Houses of York and Lancaster opened, but nothing was decided. The two parties are still quite equal; both are willing to compromise their extreme claims. The Third Part of *Henry the Sixth* shows, in general, the transition from this condition of balanced chances to the overthrow and annihilation of the Lancastrians; the crown passes to the Yorkists. The change is one of the bloodiest scenes in History, to which characteristic the play is true in the fullest measure. It is war and bustle from beginning to end — a carnival of barbaric butchery; every character seems to delight in smearing himself with gore; even the language bears often a furious and sanguinary aspect. A red, volcanic fire breaks fiercely from all sides; one towering form after another is swept down and burnt up in that molten stream of vindictive passion. But these outbursts are, in the main, confused, irregular, uncertain;

the Titanic forces of Nature are manifestly at work here; the result is not a well-ordered work of Art—not a work of beautiful, though colossal, proportion, but a mass made up of immense fragmentary boulders.   In other words, the elements of the grandest poem are here, but these elements are not fused into a harmonious unity.   There is often the mighty Shakespearian expression; often the mighty Shakespearian conception of character; but the whole gives the appearance of terrific struggle—of chaos trying to organize itself, and, in spite of all effort, remaining, to a great extent, formless.

Of course the structure of such a drama cannot be of a high order.   There are merely the two hostile parties, which constitute the two threads running through the action; these join in battle, then separate to give utterance to their feelings and opinions, after which they begin the conflict anew.   The play is thus a series of battle-pieces, with short intervening pauses; fortune fluctuates from one side to the other, evidently working to destroy both sides.   For any division into two movements there is no adequate ground; one event seems to be quite as important as another.   But, if the reader thinks it desirable, he can consider the defection of Warwick as the turning-point of the drama, though logically that incident can hardly make good any such claim.   Clearly, the whole structure, if not of the lowest, is of the lower organic type.

After the defeat of the Lancastrians, recounted at the end of the previous play, Richard, Duke of York, and King Henry make a treaty settling the disputed succession.   But no peace is possible; the extremists in both parties control; their death is the only peace.   Margaret

on the one side, the sons of Richard on the other, force
the violation of the compact. A French Fury is thus the
guiding spirit of the Lancastrians; she is driving them
rapidly into the jaws of Fate. Note also the sons of
Richard; they are the future rulers of England; this
whole war is made in their interest; can any hope of
national regeneracy be seen in them? More vindictive,
worse in every respect, they are than their father, who is
bad enough. Fate cries out — they, too, must be got out
of the way before peace can return to distracted England.
Let the mills of the gods now begin grinding.

Another battle takes place; Richard, the father, is slain
— slain by butcher Clifford, whose father had previously
been slain. Blind Nemesis is smiting right and left in
the field, gigantic, vigorous, having much work yet to do.
Blind she is, verily, for she crops the innocent, sweet youth
Rutland — the innocent son of York, not the guilty ones.
A piteous spectacle it is — an offenseless child ground to
death with the wicked. The last time defeat had overwhelmed the Lancastrians; this time the Yorkists experience disaster. It is well; both races must be deracinated
from the soil of England.

Edward — guilty, licentious son of York — succeeds to
the leadership; still, much work for retributive Nemesis,
presiding Goddess of this Lower World. Another battle;
now it is the turn of the Lancastrians to be defeated — indeed, already a second time; defeated they are; a blow to
the right, then a blow to the left — all will be felled at last.
Butcher Clifford is here slain, with many others; a father
kills his son, a son kills his father. The Family, too, is
disrupted and destroyed in this strife of parties; man
has become like the fabled swine — ignorantly consuming

its own farrow. But Edward is now crowned a king; the House of York has vindicated its title; the usurping, wicked, effete line is driven away. Cannot a little peace be now granted to this land? No; Nemesis must finish her work.

Poor King Henry has, therefore, lost his throne, which it is his curse to have possessed. His regal dignity he would gladly put aside: "Methinks it were a happy life to be no better than a homely swain." In a tempest, tied to the rudder, which he cannot move, but which always moves him, he well may be weary of the place of Governor. A most amiable, deeply religious man, yet without will — how can he control the raging elements? An angelic nature, indeed, is his, by destiny allotted to rule over demons; he stands out in spotless white raiment mid the soot and flames of Tartarus. Yet he possesses intelligence; he knows the result of this strife going on around him; he sees that the present wretchedness comes from past wrong:

"I'll leave my son my virtuous deeds behind,
And would my father had left me no more."

Also, he possesses a prophetic insight — he foretells to the Yorkists the destruction of their House through its own members, and he beholds in young Richmond the future redeemer of England. A person of a quiet, contemplative nature, born perhaps to be a holy prophet — but, alas, he is King — King of the infernal regions, with countless fiends to be tamed or strangled. Why does he not fly off and leave the Stygian pool? A domestic bond holds him; his other half — or, rather, his whole — is Stygian queen, and clutches him fast to subserve her purposes. A hapless sight is that—an Angel linked to a Fury. The Fury, too, has a will—has all the will; white, angelic Henry is dragged through murky Pandemonium, and to his honor comes out unstained. Still, the act of a man who cannot act is not likely to be ever very wicked.

The House of York is next seen disintegrating within, for it contains elements which can never be harmonized. The marriage of King Edward it was chiefly which caused a double disaffection—that of the brothers and that of Warwick. The latter now revolts, unites with his most bitter enemy—Queen Margaret—and invades England. The Yorkists meet with defeat; their turn has again come; Nemesis is still busy. Edward is taken prisoner; proud Warwick triumphs—is the great king-maker, greater than the king. A power thus rises in the State mightier than the State; the caprice of an individual changes dynasties. Warwick is really the embodiment of disorganization; he overturned the Lancastrians, now he overturns the Yorkists. A great colossal character he is, the natural outgrowth of the age; in him the spirit of insubordination and rebellion is manifested in its gigantic dimensions. But the mighty figure must be cast down; let his own principle be applied to himself; he once destroyed the supporters of the worthless Lancastrians—destroyed just what he now is himself. Nemesis will bring his deed back to him, swooping from above on speediest wing.

King Edward escapes from captivity; his brother Clarence, who had gone over to Warwick, returns to his ancestral party. Still another battle; whose turn is it now to lose? Lancastrians, answers Nemesis, keeping the account with the most rigid accuracy. Warwick falls; the great king-maker is unkinged by death; his deed has returned.

The Poet will hereafter remould his character, with many improvements, in Hotspur; so Henry the Sixth will essentially be reproduced in Richard the Second, both being incompetent rulers, though the one is good and the other is bad.

But why should these Lancastrians be permitted continually to fight their lost battles over again? Let them be annihilated; then the contest can be brought to an end. King Henry is assassinated in prison by Gloster; his son also is cruelly butchered in cold blood. All the branches of the House of Lancaster are now lopped off except one frail, distant twig; for them Nemesis has done her work. So the drama ends with Edward of York once more upon the throne; incapacity of the monarch has again brought revolution; the Red Rose is plucked, and its petals scattered in the earth.

But, amid all these scenes of savagery, one man has shown himself to be the supreme savage — Richard, Duke of Gloster, brother of the King. His body is as misshapen as his soul; ominous breathings he has given out in the course of the play; demoniac rage impels him to the most cruel deeds. But ambition also has filled his thoughts; he wishes to be King — King he will be. Several of his nearest relatives stand between him and the throne; he will have to get them out of the way. Nemesis is again at work; she is here preparing a dire instrument for some terrible purpose of hers. The House of York, too, must be smitten to earth; Gloster is to be the scourge of his family, which now is destroyed from within. But this also will require for its treatment a new drama.

# RICHARD THE THIRD.

Not one member of the House of Lancaster remains; it has been torn up root and branch. It was begotten in revolution, in revolution it has perished. It had based its claim upon the competency of its rulers, and the nation had sanctioned this claim in the most emphatic manner; but it, too, has now furnished its incompetent monarch, to whom its own law must be applied with unswerving justice. But it would not submit to the principle which was the very origin of its existence — it resisted to the bitter end; nor does it cease the struggle till the last descendant of Bolingbroke is swept into the grave. The House of Lancaster, therefore, has decreed its own fate through its acts. Retribution is written in bloody letters over its corpse; let it now be buried out of sight of the world, which it will harass no more.

The House of York, the successful instrument of vengeance, is, however, left upon the face of the earth, and is sure to give trouble. It cannot stop in its bloody frenzy. But its enemies have perished; upon what object can it now fix its insatiate jaws? It will, indeed, find a most deserving object, namely, itself. Moreover, these furious sons of York, are they to be the rulers of England on the ground of competency — of fitness? Title they may have, but the nation declared in the great Lancastrian revolution something more than title to be necessary. The triumph of a vindictive party is not the triumph of the country; there is no rest yet possible. The true reconciliation can only be national; both sides must be united and harmonized in the ruler. Down with the bloody party; the House of York must be cleared away, like the savage forest, by the sharp, swift axe of justice before the soil of England will be blessed with the harvest of peace.

But what is the instrument for bringing retribution home to the House of York? We do not have to look far; it has within its own bosom the poisonous reptile which will sting it to death. In the woeful throes of civil war it has begotten a monster — a fire-breathing, blood-drinking monster — whose delight is to prey upon its own kindred. This is the function of Richard, Duke of Gloster, in the drama before us. He is to annihilate his own House by murdering all who have the misfortune to be connected with him in ties of relationship. The tender bond of the Family, which usually softens even the most obdurate heart, for him marks out the victim of destruction; he cannot rest as long as one of his blood be left to claim the throne of England. A doomed House is this House of York, whose executioner is Richard, one of its own children. Most bitter, yet true, is the reproach cast by Queen Margaret upon his mother:

> "From forth the kennel of thy womb hath crept
> A hell-hound that doth hunt us all to death —
> That dog that had his teeth before his eyes
> To worry lambs and lap their gentle blood."

Such a character is not a delightful object of contemplation, and, if the end of art be to give pleasure, then here it has lost its end. But the deep, reconciling principle must never be forgotten. Richard is a necessity of this world's justice—he is the instrument of retribution. The House of York has done that before God which makes it doomed—it simply must be extirpated. Richard, therefore, is tolerated because he is executing a just decree—the edict of impartial, incorruptible Nemesis. To consider him as a villain, pure and simple, destroying the innocent, is a view altogether one-sided; let him also be taken, on the other hand, as a hero who carries out in full measure a divine judgment. The primal law of man here below is responsibility for the deed; violation must bring punishment, and Richard is the man who wields the bloody rod; he thus is the vindicator—unconscious, it is true, but still the vindicator of that primal law. He is wicked, inexpressibly wicked—an incarnate fiend, red-hot from Hell, if you wish; but is he not the genuine product of this age—of these Wars of the Roses, whose diabolical atrocity culminates in him? Indeed, is he not the true—the truest—child of this House of York, both in birth and in character? He, the arch-fiend, is come to destroy Pandemonium; to burn it up in its own sulphur, with all the devils in it, himself included.

For Richard as a moral man there is clearly no defense, and none will be attempted here; but for Richard as the instrument of retribution—as the burning purifier of England—there is defense, and we may derive from his career even consolation. As the pitiless executor of a world-justice he must be considered in the present drama, if we are to have any relief at all from his portraiture; so he is certainly drawn by the Poet. In art, as well as in morals, there is no justification for him considered merely as an individual; but Richard as the destroying Nemesis of Hell-on-Earth is a necessity of History, and, hence, must belong to its artistic representation in the Historical Drama.

The tone of the play of *Richard the Third* is in the deepest harmony with the character of its one leading personage. Retribution is its beginning, middle, and end — the ominous sound uttered by all living shapes here, from the highest to the lowest. An over-mastering power hovers in the air above and swoops down upon the guilty world, requiting the wicked deed often with immediate destruction. Human actions must return, and return at once, to the doer, is the spirit of the whole work. It is, indeed, the drama of Retribution — Retribution to the Nation, to the Family, to the Individual. This trait is even too rigidly and too intensely drawn; mankind seems on the point of being crushed beneath the mace of retributive justice; mercy has quite fled from the world. Yet it is the true medicine for the diseased age; the conviction must sink deep into the minds of men that guilt is followed by retribution with the speed and power of the whirlwind.

There is another peculiarity of the present drama which ought to be mentioned — the frequent use of the curse. It is a terrific weapon, and is employed here with terrific violence. It seems to be something above the individual, dwelling in the Heavens — a mighty God, who, being invoked, rushes down from his Olympian height and dashes the frail human being to speedy death. The curse, however, is the mere utterance of retribution. In order to result in true fulfillment, it must be declared in view of the universal nature of the deed; its spokesman is a seer who looks far down into the consequences of an action, often unconsciously including himself in its operation.

Lady Anne, when she curses the future wife of Richard, utters the deepest truth of the situation; the wife of such a man must be accursed, because it lies in his character to make a woman wretched; still, Lady Anne marries him, and thus curses herself. A groundless imprecation is a monstrosity, to be excluded from every work of Art. The person who curses should only be a voice declaring judgment — the voice of Nemesis uttering the irrevocable penalty of the deed; petty personal spite is no ground for the curse.

The style of the drama will correspond to the matter. There is no rest to the impetuous torrent. dashing angrily down the sides of the mountain; grand, majestic movement of vast volume it has not. There is a terror in its expression — an unseen hand that almost smites to the earth. The language is mighty, furious, and feverish; it may be called frenzied at times. Titanic struggles and passions are hurled forth in words of Titanic strength and intensity. Human utterance has here reached its limit in some respects. It touches many chords, even the most diverse; at one moment the language of wrath and imprecation sends shudder after shudder through the soul, if not through the body; then follow the tenderest notes of sorrow, swelling into the loud wail of despair. Men gnash their teeth in agony, women weep for the slaughter of their innocent babes; but through all these cries is heard everywhere the demonic irony of Richard — a fiend scoffing over his victims. Many impurities of style may be pointed out — it is, indeed, the nature of the torrent to stir up the ooze and carry it along — but no grammatical cleansing process can possibly purify the torrent into the placid, crystalline brook.

Let us grasp the total action of play as it unfolds itself

before us. It moves from party triumphant and using success for partisan purposes to the complete national restoration which united both parties and was superior to both parties. The victory of York was the victory of one side — of a fragment of the nation ; the victory of Richmond was the victory of both sides — of the whole nation. The House of York, having overcome the Lancastrians, disintegrates within ; both parties, therefore, are quite annihilated. The surviving leaders, a man and a woman, join in marriage, and thus unite the White and the Red Rose. So the Tetralogy comes to an end in a new constructive epoch.

There are two distinct movements in the play, though they are of unequal length. Their fundamental principles are, respectively, the Guilt and Retribution of Richard ; or, what is the same thing from a different point of view, the Retribution of the House of York and the Retribution of Richard. The first movement portrays Richard destroying his own family ; he turns against his relatives — even against his own mother ; he tears asunder every domestic tie in order to reach the throne. Yet all these evils are the offspring of the guilty House — the consequences of its own deeds. Richard himself is its truest representative, though in punishing its crimes he is its greatest criminal. The second movement shows the Retribution brought home to Buckingham, Richard's worst satellite, and to Richard himself. The latter perishes on the battle-field, and his enemy mounts the throne.

Through all the folds and sinuosities of the action two threads can be seen moving, whose line of distinction is marked by sex. Among the men everywhere the central figure is Richard, who thus becomes the head of different groups, according to the different purposes which he is

seeking to accomplish. One relation of the family after
another is assailed by him, till every obstruction to his
permanent possession of the crown seems to be removed
— his brother Clarence, the Queen's kindred, Hastings,
his little nephews; such are the subordinate groupings.
The second thread is composed of the women of the
drama. It is difficult to separate this thread from the
rest of the play, but its employment is so peculiar and distinct that it must be looked at by itself. There are here
four Queens, two belonging to the defeated Lancastrians
and two belonging to the victorious Yorkists. Their chief
function, it must be confessed, is to curse their enemies;
then they have also to bewail their own unhappy lot.
Being royal women, they unite the political and domestic
relations; still, they represent here the Family in its manifold struggles and afflictions. All are wives and have lost
husbands; three are mothers and have lost children; one
has begotten the monster who is laying waste the country
and devouring his own kindred. With every new misfortune is heard the echo of female lamentation and imprecation; some one of them is wronged and bereaved in
these terrible times. The two Lancastrian women represent the lost House, but their loudest wail goes up for
their lost families. Queen Margaret is the embodiment of
the curse. Its substance is: As Lancaster has perished,
so York will perish. The judgment is fulfilled to the
letter; the aged Duchess of York, mother of monsters,
will be brought to curse her own brood. Most sad and
woeful is this chorus of high Queens, uttering the shrieks
of the Family as it is ground to death between the contending elements of the nation.

I. Following now our plan, let us grasp the character
of Richard in its very germ. He is resolved to wear the

crown of England. In his way to it stand two older
brothers and their children; they must be removed, one
and all — that is, he intends to destroy his kindred; his
means are dissimulation and murder. The great types of
deception he cites — Ulysses, Sinon, Proteus, Machiavel;
these he can equal — indeed, surpass — in treachery and
cruelty. The domestic emotion, strong even in the savage breast, he utterly abjures:

> " And this word, love, which gray beards call divine,
> Be resident in men like one another,
> And not in me; I am myself alone."

No feeling of affection, therefore, can swerve him from
his purpose; he is now to be let loose upon his family.

The first victim is his brother Clarence. He works
upon the weak, superstitious nature of King Edward, who
is failing in health; by means of " lies well steeled with
weighty arguments " Clarence is thrown into the Tower,
while the odium of his imprisonment is deftly turned aside
to the account of the Queen, Elizabeth — Richard pretending to sympathize deeply with Clarence. So he drives
the two brothers against each other, that they may perish,
while he is looking out for himself.

But this Clarence is by no means an innocent man,
though he dies of a charge of which he is not guilty.
His hands have been imbrued in blood during the civil
wars; now retribution has come, though from an unexpected quarter. As he lies in prison, conscience begins
to work upon him, and in a dream which he narrates there
is beheld the dark picture of his guilt. Perjury and
murder stain his soul, and, as he approaches the confines
of the future world, he hears the dire voices of accusation. He is a member of the guilty House — he is to be

cut down with his own vengeful instrument; his own deed
is to be served up to him. Listen to his confession: " I
have done those things, that now give evidence against my
soul, for Edward's sake;" and Edward has already signed
his death-warrant. The doomed family is executing judgment upon its own members — Clarence, the perjured
murderer, is himself treacherously murdered. Richard
has thus succeeded in his first attempt, and so let us pass
to his next plan against his House.

This is directed against the family of his reigning brother,
chiefly represented by the Queen, for this brother is
already dying of sickness, and need not be proceeded
against. She has two sons, still very young, by the present monarch, as well as sons by a former marriage; she
has also brothers. These relatives of hers are the natural
protectors and defenders of her small children; Richard
must first get them out of the way. He has already
excited much odium against them by representing them as
greedy adventurers and intriguers at court. The dying
Edward effects a hollow reconciliation between the two
hostile parties; but upon this scene of peace there falls
the sudden news of the death of Clarence.

Thereupon Edward is borne from the company in an
expiring condition. This is the second death — rapid is
the exit of these Yorkists. Edward falls by the torture
of disease, aided by the worse torture of conscience.
Before his departure he, too, opens his soul, and we behold
the agony there. A brother — to whom, more than to any
one else, he owed his throne — is murdered under his war-
rant. Retribution, again swooping down, infixes him;
forebodings for his family may well fill his last moments
with anguish, as he addresses those around him: " Oh,

God, I fear thy justice will take hold on me and you, and mine and yours, for this.'' God's justice is truly much to be feared in a Yorkian world.

Two brothers are, therefore, gone — cleared out of the way of Richard. Now succeeds the chorus of women and children — the wild, piercing lament of the disrupted Family. The mother, aged Duchess of York, is there with two orphaned grandchildren — son and daughter of Clarence; then comes the bereaved wife, Queen Elizabeth, mourning for her husband. The domestic relation is all torn and mangled; the mother, the wife, the child, sad trio of lamentation, utter their respective sorrows. But even through their present grief pierces the dim premonition of worse that is to come; both the Duchess and the Queen have felt, and recognize, the diabolical spirit which is casting the events for the annihilation of their House. A reflection of the same presentiment is given in the conversation of the two citizens; the gloomy foreboding of the future has descended into the minds of the people. ''O, full of danger is the Duke of Gloster,'' says one of these citizens; popular instinct points out the evil genius of the time with prophetic insight.

But Richard's work is far from being done. He thinks: Let me now knock down the supports of these orphaned heirs of Edward. Rivers, Grey, Vaughan — brother, son, friend of the Queen — are executed in prison. They, too, are caught in the net of the doomed House, for which they deserted their Lancastrian party; if not guilty participation, at least guilty indifference, is the charge against them. ''Now Margaret's curse is fallen upon our heads, for standing by when Richard stabbed her son,'' is the penitent cry of Grey. Yes, you did not interfere to save

an innocent boy from the butcher; on the contrary, you
went over to the party of the murderers, and shared in
their blood-dripping honors. Off with your heads; such
men as you must be got out of England before it is again
inhabitable by human beings. So shrieks Retribution,
smiting anew with vengeful ire.

The family of the Queen is thus destroyed or scattered
— Dorset, her other son, fleeing soon to France. Richard
now takes a step further. Hastings was an enemy of the
Queen's relatives; so far he could coöperate with the
designs of Richard. But he is a firm supporter of Edward's
young sons; at this point he stands in Richard's way to
the throne, and must be removed. Hastings is doubly
warned by his friend, Stanley, but he refuses to take the
advice. Suddenly Richard trumps up a false charge
against him, and demands his head before dinner. He,
too, falls under the curse of Margaret, having shared in
the bloody deeds of the Yorkists. He aided in destroying
the relatives of the Queen and exults in their death, holding himself to be "in better state than ere I was." He
should have been their ally; he is slaughtered for the
same offense as they — standing in Richard's way to the
throne. It is a harsh punishment for simple, blind Hastings, yet it gives back his own merely; when he exults in
the death of his enemies he is really exulting in his own
death. Let him be satisfied, says Nemesis, handing him
his deed. He sees, when it is too late, and repents:

> "I now repent I told the pursuivant,
> As too triumphing, how mine enemies
> To-day at Pomfret bloodily were butcher'd,
> And I myself secure in grace and favor.
> Oh! Margaret, Margaret, now thy heavy curse
> Is lighted on poor Hastings' head."

Now all the defenders are pretty much out of the way. But his assault upon his family is not yet ended; he orders his tools to "infer the bastardy of Edward's children"— nay, to declare that Edward himself was illegitimate. Richard thus impugns the honor of his own mother—the very origin of the Yorkian family is nullified as far as possible; even his own claim perishes with the legal right of his House. But, to make his title certain, the young boys of Edward are murdered by his orders. Thus all that stand between him and the throne are removed. Richard has attained the pinnacle in his destructive career toward his family. He has violated almost every domestic relation, one after another; he has passed the summit— now he begins to descend with violent speed.

But the butchery of these young children—what ground can Nemesis have for entangling them in her inevitable net? Innocent babes, smiling in infantile joy, prattling in unconscious prattle—why immolate them? the reader sternly demands. Red-mouthed Nemesis, in a frenzy, answers him: They, too, belong to this House of York, which must be got rid of—they are the young demonic brood, offspring of a fiend-begetting House; burn up the young devils in this general conflagration of Pandemonium. "God's justice" does, then, visit the sins of the parents upon the children. Both these families—York and Lancaster—have, with a blood-dripping scourge, smitten every family and every child in England; let now all their branches be cut off and consumed, down to the smallest tendril. Insatiate Nemesis, this may be a justice, and a justice indispensable to a Yorkian world, but it is not a high justice—not a justice through institutions.

At these last acts the chorus of female lamentation has

redoubled, and, indeed, the cause of grief is more than double what it was before. Yet these Queens have always a political element in their character which hardly consists with their domestic devotion. The loss of the throne affects Queen Elizabeth too deeply for a mother in great sorrow; "Ah, cut my lace asunder," she cries on hearing of Richard's usurpation. Still, the death of her two boys affects her maternal soul almost to distraction; but shortly afterwards her political ambition seems to get the upper hand, by Richard's proposition for her daughter. Strange woman, strange product of the age — the instinct of the mother and the ambition of the queen in eternal conflict, swaying from one side to the other in a tempest of passion. As wife and mother she has lost two husbands and two sets of children; still, she hopes to be — and, in fact, will be — Queen-mother. Her double nature rocks and tears her heart, but both principles remain in full force.

Then there is Queen Anne, wooed and won by Richard, the slayer of her husband, while she is weeping over the dead body of a father-in-law, slaughtered by the same hand. She is flattered by the wily suitor; nor can she resist his fair promises. She, too, is possessed with the demon of political ambition. To enter the domestic relation with a monster, it is a sacrifice of the woman in her to position. Domestic wretchedness has been hitherto her fate, but now death is the penalty of her choice. She takes to her bosom the destroyer of her family — hence of herself. A plaintive note she, too, utters in this female chorus, full of sad presentiment — then disappears:

> " For never yet one hour in his bed
> Did I enjoy the golden dew of sleep,
> But with his timorous dreams was still awaked."

But the Duchess, mother of monsters, has doubtless the saddest lot. All the misfortunes of the rest of the family are hers, with others peculiar to herself. Husband, children, grandchildren, she has lost; besides, she is mother of Richard, the death-breathing dragon who drinks the blood of his kindred. To give birth to the destroyer of her own offspring would seem to be the direst fate of motherhood. "Eighty odd years of sorrow have I seen;" both in the quality and quantity of the affliction her case is the extreme. What is her deed which has brought this mountain of horrors upon her? She has given to the world the House of York; the whole era of calamities goes back to her as its natural origin. Yet, personally, she commits no offense; she appears here as the best woman of them all — quite free from political ambition. Nor does Retribution punish her with death, but the crimes of her family rend her innocent bosom; when the offspring of her body are struck by the axe of justice, she, too, feels the blow. Thus every deed, every punishment of her guilty House, sweeps back to her, thrilling with pain her aged heart-strings. That is the tragic woman, if ever she was portrayed. But her last words are the most painful part of her painful life; after seeing her house perish, almost to the last member, she is compelled to lay her curse upon her only surviving son. Laden with that curse, Richard sinks rapidly to his fate.

This terrific calamity — whence does it come? It seems horrible, monstrous, unnatural. But the Poet is going to give its ground — it is retribution; this is uttered through the mouth of Margaret. Everything which has befallen the House of York is a picture of what it did to the House of Lancaster. Margaret was wife and mother; her husband and son were cruelly butchered by the York-

ists. The Yorkian Queens are now what she is — shorn
of family and of throne. Her curse has been fulfilled in
every particular, being based upon "God's justice;" she
gloats over the fall of her enemies, who are reduced to a
level with herself for the same crimes. Well may she
prophesy; in her own person already have prophecies been
fulfilled; she has but to read her own history and fate
to the proud victors. She has good reason to believe in
retribution, and she easily transfers to others what has
happened to herself.

So ends this wonderful chorus of Queens; it will be
heard no more in the second movement — the measure of
lamentation is full. A woeful undertone to the wicked
deeds and swift punishment of the men, it echoes along
the drama like fitful moans of the wind through forest;
it is the wail of women weeping for their disrupted domestic ties. The chorus has two parts, of different sound,
yet in deep harmony — both the Lancastrian and Yorkian
Queens, though enemies to each other, suffer the same
afflictions, and fundamentally sing the same song of sorrow. For Margaret's curse is merely her own grief, con-
cordant to the grief of Elizabeth. Man is punished for
his political deeds; woman, joined with him in the Family,
suffers along with him, even though she be innocent.

II. We are now ready for a rapid survey of the second
movement — the descent of Richard, which appears to
begin with his mother's curse. To ambition he has sacrificed his family, which now, in its supreme representative,
prays for his sacrifice. Richard changes; he begins to
woo the daughter of his brother, instead of slaying her —
it is a new policy for him. Queen Elizabeth seems to
yield to his suit, but afterwards we read that she has

promised her daughter to Richmond. It is an obscure
point in the Drama, but we may suppose that the Queen
deceives the butcher of her sons ; Richard fails in his new
plan — the star of his destiny is beginning to set. The
domestic tie, which he has so deeply injured, revenges
itself on him by a refusal.

Next, Richard destroys his most cunning and unprincipled tool, Buckingham, who hesitated at the murder of
the young Princes. Buckingham had managed successfully many important transactions, particularly the coronation ; it was folly in Richard to throw away such a use-
ful servant. But retribution thereby rays out the more
glaring light ; Buckingham is treated to that which he
has done to others — " underhand, corrupted, foul injustice, " inflicted upon him by the very man for whose benefit
his crimes were committed. He also sees the state of the
matter too late, and expresses the justice of his punishment :

> " Thus Margaret's curse falls heavy on my neck,
> Wrong hath but wrong, and blame the due of blame."

But Richmond has landed on the shores of England.
Let us give thanks, for he brings death to the monster,
death to this age, and an end to this Tetralogy. Messenger after messenger reports bad news — Richard loses his
poise amid danger ; he feels himself sinking. He marches
out to give battle ; the hostile camps lie facing each other,
when in the middle a strange vision passes before the
mind of both captains. The ghostly forms of those whom
Richard had murdered rise up before him and bid him
think on their wrongs, that he may be unnerved and lose
the battle. At the same time they give words of good-

will and encouragement to Richmond. The Poet has thus indicated that the hour of retribution is come; and the motives of the play, with its leading incidents, he summarizes in the vision.

Moreover, the scene will aid us in arriving at a judgment concerning Shakespeare's employment of ghosts and supernatural appearances. The conscious intention of the Poet is here so manifest that nobody can deny it, for the ghosts only reiterate what has been fully given in the play without this unreal form. Richard's overthrow and Richmond's victory has been amply motived; here it is cast into the unconscious presentiment of both leaders. In sleep the foreboding of the soul moulds itself into the distinct image, and there results the dream. The subjective nature of both men is thus shown — one buoyed up with a just cause, the other weighed down with his crimes. What Richard really is comes out in the vision; he might be able to suppress himself when awake.

Now he for the first time is frightened; the dream has fully revealed, not merely his character to himself — that he knew before — but the certainty of his punishment. It is the revelation of his own soul concerning his destiny, for Richard hitherto had no faith in retribution; his belief was in successful villainy. Hence his terror.

> "By the apostle Paul, shadows to-night
> Have struck more terror to the soul of Richard
> Than can the substance of ten thousand soldiers
> Armed in proof and led by shallow Richmond."

But he shuts his eyes, as it were, on the future; stamps out the rising remorse; "conscience is a word that cowards use." Utterly reckless, he gives the command to march on — "if not to Heaven, then hand in hand to Hell." So he rushes into the fight, seeking to drown conscience in death.

In Richmond we have the religious — and, in a higher sense, the national — hero, who unites the two parties into the nation. He stands above the dissension which produced the Wars of the Roses; his object is not partisan, but patriotic. With the battle of Bosworth Field a solution is given to the Yorkian Tetralogy — a solution which is essentially tragic, though it points beyond to a reconciliation. Both Houses have perished in all their immediate representatives; their names descend to remote members of each line, who proceed to disown the titles — York and Lancaster — and to found a new House of their own. A man and a woman — the heir of the Lancastrians and the heiress of the Yorkists — unite in marriage, and thus transform the political hate of the hostile Houses into the domestic love of the Family. But this Yorkian Tetralogy is truly one great historical tragedy; in fact, we may go back and include the whole eight plays, beginning with *Richard the Second.* It was, indeed, the tragic period of English History, in which, not an individual, but the entire nation, became tragic. But such is not the true destiny of England; there must. be a conclusion which is not tragic, as the nation is still surviving. The play of *Henry the Eighth*, therefore, is to follow; it will bring to a happy termination the English Historical series.

In this drama there is always felt to be something foreign to the genius of Shakespeare as revealed elsewhere in
his works. Much critical dissatisfaction has been expressed
concerning it, and some writers have even gone to the
extent of excluding the greater portion of it from the
genuine works of the Poet. To enter into the question of
authorship is not the purpose here; it is the domain of un-
limited, uncontrolled conjecture, upon which there are at
present many squatters, and which can accommodate many
more. Let the reader enter and make his choice for himself, since he has as good a right as anybody else. According to the external evidence, however, the claim of Shakespeare can hardly be gainsaid without danger of undermining all his other claims.

Still, the critical dissatisfaction just mentioned, as far
as it pertains to the quality of the work, has good grounds
— the drama of *Henry the Eighth* is certainly wanting in
unity of structure. It lies there in great masses, almost
disjointed; with a little change in the arrangement every
Act might be made into a play by itself, with its plot,
central figure, and catastrophe. Yet there are certain
characters and threads which run through the drama from
beginning to end, thus keeping up a connection of all the
parts; still, on the other hand, these connecting threads
constitute, not the main, but the subordinate, interest.
King Henry, for example, remains as a character of the

play from the first Act to the last; he is, however, hardly
more than a tool of mightier personalities in the first three
Acts.   There is the conflict between Wolsey and Buckingham first; second, between Wolsey and the Queen;
third, between Wolsey and the King.   Then Wolsey
drops out entirely.   Not enough concentration is brought
into the dramatic structure; too much of a tendency of
the parts to fall into independence is manifested.   This
is, indeed, owing mainly to its spectacular purpose, which
appeals to the eye rather than to the mind, and, hence, it
must look to immediate sensuous effects more than to the
long and careful preparation of dramatic motives.

The style, too, has in it many elements which are alien
to the best style of Shakespeare.   The versification has
been subjected to the so-called metrical tests; in accordance with these, the foreign portions have been designated.
But the difficulty reaches much deeper than the formal
meter; it extends to the coloring, to the figurative speech,
to the forms of expression — in fine, to the style generally.
Taking the drama as a whole, apart from single passages,
we miss the richness, the glow, the Shakespearian ecstasy;
when the language is elevated, it is emotional and subjective rather than sensuous and objective.   Single passages of great beauty may be found, undoubtedly; but
it is in the power of even fourth-rate poets to write beautiful lines now and then.   It is the sustained style which
marks the great work and great poet — not sudden spurts
amid dreary wastes of stupidity.

At this point we may be permitted to go out of the way
a little and make a further application of what has just
been said.   It is often declared by learned critics that
here and there, in some disputed play, they "see the hand

of Shakespeare;" that here is a scene which "Shakespeare alone could have written;" that lines occur in which "the hand of the Poet is plainly visible." Thereupon we have a dissection — certain scenes, passages, or even lines, being assigned to Shakespeare, the rest to somebody else. Now, the presupposition in such a case is radically false, namely, that every good line or beautiful image must be ascribed to Shakespeare. No fact in literary history is more common than that the mediocre poet may, in his very highest mood, rise to the level of the great Poet — but he cannot stay there. And, conversely, a play handed down as Shakespeare's, on the best evidence, should not be taken away from him on account of certain weak and unusual qualities. The Poet must be seen at his poorest, as well as at his best.

A word, too, should be said upon the characterization of the present drama. This is, for the most part, highly lauded, and deemed eminently worthy of the Poet. Yet, on the whole, it lacks completeness and clearness. For instance, Buckingham is one of the leading personages; still, as he stands portrayed, he is a contradiction. He is charged with treason — with even threatening the life of the King. The proof of this charge rests upon the testimony of his servants, but, then, opposed to it is his declaration of loyalty to the King. Was he innocent or guilty? It cannot be told from anything in the drama, yet this must be the central point of his character. There is left only the uncertain inference that Wolsey bribed his servants to commit perjury.

There is a similar doubt concerning Wolsey himself. His enemies charge him with every species of ambition and extortion; we are compelled to accept these accusations without seeing into his soul concerning their truth or falsity. The downfall of the Queen is laid at his door, yet the King explains the matter otherwise, and takes the burden of the separation entirely upon himself. Still, we must ascribe her untoward fate to Wolsey, though both he and Henry deny the charge. This capital fact of Wolsey's career is thus left in doubt; we can only surmise that he suborned the French Bishop who excited in Henry's mind the doubts concerning his marriage; in other words, Wolsey gave Henry the pretext for divorce. This is not good characterization, not Shakespeare's ordinary method, for here clearness and subtlety are both left out.

Objections also have been made to the outcome of the play, on account of its offense to ethical principles. Henry — at first a weak tool, then a sensual tyrant, always an unprincipled hypocrite — is rewarded in the end for his civil and domestic violations; while his wife, Catherine, though in the highest degree faithful to both Family and State, is punished — is cast off both as wife and Queen, and dies in her unhappy lot. The doubt, too, in the motiving of Buckingham and Wolsey leaves a very unsatisfactory feeling concerning the justice of their fate. Henry certainly deserves no such reward as the success of his unrighteous love and the birth of a Princess, whose glorification is one of the main objects of the play. In all these respects it is in marked contrast to the play which has just preceded — *Richard the Third* — wherein retribution follows so speedily and certainly the deed.

*Henry the Eighth* brings to a close the English Historical Drama, though its connection with that series cannot be termed intimate. The subordination of the turbulent nobility, which created so much trouble in the Wars of the

Roses, is manifested in the fate of Buckingham ; the crown has attained an unquestioned supremacy. The revival of letters and the importance of culture are often indicated ; learning has even come to the point of contesting the palm with rank. But the main point which is sought for by every reader as the very marrow of this period is the great religious revolution — the transition of England from Catholicism to Protestantism. Every other issue of that age sinks into insignificance in comparison ; there is no meaning in the reign of Henry the Eighth without the Reformation.

The present drama has, undoubtedly, the change of religion as its fundamental theme, for it could hardly have any other, but the event is portrayed with that dimness and ambiguity so characteristic of everything else in the work. The revolution of conscience is made to depend on a guilty passion of the King : the only morally heroic character is immolated to a movement whose essence was, if anything, the revolt of morality against corruption. Indeed, it must be confessed that in this moral and religious revolution, as here portrayed, morality and religion are quite left out. It is the *political* element which is brought into prominence, for the Reformation was also a political revolution.

Here is the key of the play — the standard by which it is to be judged — and every other test is inadequate. The political object of the See of Rome was the subordination of State to Church ; all nations of Christendom had ultimately to be subjected to the Pope — not alone in religious, but also often in civil, matters. The result was a perpetual strife between Church and State, even in ages of universal Catholic ascendency ; which strife finally culminated in a separation from the Church on the part of certain nations which were determined to be absolute, even in ecclesiastical matters. This gave rise to the Reformation, whose political principle was subordination of Church to State. To be sure, moral and religious freedom was coupled with political freedom, though the former is, not merely omitted, but repeatedly violated, in the present drama.

The action of *Henry the Eighth*, in general, moves from Catholic England to Protestant England; from Catherine of Aragon to Anne Boleyn as Queen; from Henry the instrument of Wolsey to Henry the uncontrolled arbitrary monarch; from the State ruled by a Cardinal of the Church to a State ruled by its own King. The revolution is purely political — at least, as here represented — though it is accomplished in the name and by means of the clerical profession. The civil subsumes the ecclesiastical organization. The revolt of conscience, the rise of the subjective judgment against formalism and dogma, are left out of sight, having not half the prominence as in *King John* — the very first play of the English Historical series.

It will, accordingly, be manifest that there is a culmination in the play which separates it into two movements, notwithstanding its otherwise disjointed character. This culmination is, in a general way, the fall of Wolsey and the marriage of Anne Boleyn; the one movement shows Henry, who is the central figure of the play as the instrument of Wolsey, till his enfranchisement; the second movement shows Henry freely acting in his religious, domestic, and political relations. The two movements may, hence, be named the Wolseiad and Henriad. Also, the threads should be taken as two — the King in his political relations, which manifest a variety of forms, and the King in his domestic relations towards the two Queens.

I. 1. The first thread of the first movement opens with the conflict between Wolsey and Buckingham; Henry stands in the background — the dupe and the instrument of the Cardinal's ambition. Buckingham is the central figure of a group of high-born relatives and friends; he represents the pride and privileges of the nobility against the new encroachments of " this butcher's cur " (Wolsey) and of the men of learning, for now " a beggar's book outworths a noble's blood." Buckingham is himself learned, eloquent, and popular; his birth places him next to Henry in the line of succession to the throne; he is, therefore, a very manifest object of the King's suspicion.

The point about which Buckingham and Wolsey came to an open breach was the alliance with France, which was favored by the latter, but opposed by the former. Particularly the recent meeting in the vale of Andren, which had impoverished so many nobles, was condemned by Buckingham, who saw in it an attempt to weaken his class. Other nobles, too, speak disapprovingly of it for having introduced the looseness and extravagance of French customs. Buckingham proceeds boldly, in spite of the warnings of his friends, and seems on the point of publicly accusing the Cardinal of treason, when suddenly he is arrested himself on the same charge. He sees his fate — " the net has fallen upon me;" he was open and reckless, while Wolsey proceeded with perfect secrecy till he was prepared with proof at every point. It is hard to tell the extent of Buckingham's guilt, in view of his denials; quite as difficult is it to discover the extent of

Wolsey's suborning of the witnesses.   It is a great blemish
in the characterization of these two leading men that the
guilt of each is thus left in doubt.   But Henry's suspicion
is aroused; Buckingham perishes, leaving a somewhat
uncertain impression of innocence; at least he is a most
imprudent talker, if his intentions be not bad.   But the
evidence against him is of doubtful truth, and, hence, no
inferences can be drawn from it respecting his character.

We must next try to find the supreme aim of Wolsey's
striving, and therefrom obtain a judgment of the man.
His great object in this life is the Papacy.   Hither every
look bends; every act, however contorted its course, ultimately leads to the Chair of Saint Peter.   He says in the
hour of humiliation that ambition ruined him; the highest
object of ambition in Christendom was the Papal Chair.
Thus he would be above all monarchs in name as well as
in reality — above Henry, who would have to submit to
him without disguise.   Such, then, was his ambition —
the love of supreme arbitrary domination, which the head-
ship of the Church alone could confer.

The acts of Wolsey must always be viewed with this
supreme end before the mind of the reader; it is a weakness of the play that Wolsey himself is not made to indicate his object more definitely, for we have to gather it
from the mouths of his most vindictive enemies.   His
alliance with France and his hostility to Spain have their
root in this same purpose.   He has failed in getting
the Archbishopric of Toledo, the stepping-stone to the
Papacy, through the opposition of the Emperor, Charles
the Fifth, relative of Queen Catherine; hence his solicitude to treat with France, the ancient foe of England.
Buckingham threw himself in the way of the French alli-

ance, and, therefore, he had to be crushed. Wolsey is utterly unscrupulous in his means of attaining his personal end; it is plain that he intends employing bribery at Rome. His immense accumulation of wealth at home is declared to be for the same purpose as his political combinations abroad.

Wolsey is, therefore, the very strongest representative of external domination over the State by the Church. He cares little or nothing for the spiritual purposes of the great religious organization; he wants it for its political supremacy. To be the head of Christendom is his ambition, to which he is just now immolating England. Is it not full time to sever such a relation? The State, to be adequate to its functions, must be supreme in its authority; the citizen also must find the highest pinnacle of political ambition inside, and not outside, of his country. Otherwise, the State is reduced to a means for the See of Rome; this is just what Wolsey is doing. Already he is Cardinal as well as Minister; the minister serves the cardinal. Disrupt the unholy tie: put the Church inside of the State, and not on the outside of it; nay, go further, put the Church inside of the Man — but this is getting beyond the present drama, indeed, we may say, beyond Protestantism in many of its phases.

After Buckingham, Wolsey's next conflict is with Queen Catherine. She has interfered strongly in favor of Buckingham; she has also caused through her influence certain onerous taxes to be repealed, the merit of which repeal Wolsey tries to turn to his own advantage when he cannot obtain the proceeds in money. But the chief ground of his hatred is that she is a Spaniard, and a relation of the Emperor; she thus stands in the way of Wolsey's highest ambition. The Cardinal had already infused

into the King's mind certain doubts about the rightfulness of his marriage with Catherine, and the doubts
were favored by the unhappy loss of all the male offspring of the royal pair. It is a subtle poison well calculated to work upon a character half hypocritical and half
superstitious, like that of Henry. Yet here the drama
again leaves us in a haze of uncertainty; the Queen
unquestionably looks upon Wolsey as the author of her
downfall, though he denies, and seems to disprove her
charges from the mouth of the King. Wolsey, therefore,
if Catherine's charge be true, must have instigated the
Bishop of Bayonne to question the legitimacy of the
marriage — so the reader with hesitation inclines to decide,
though such an inference lies wholly outside of the play.

The object of the Cardinal was to form a matrimonial
alliance with France, in order to further his own plan. He
uses the King as an instrument, yet Henry must not be
permitted to know his own situation, for his arbitrary
temper would render him exceedingly intractable. The
time has now arrived when Henry's capricious passion and
Wolsey's secret purpose will conflict. The King's love
for Anne Boleyn suddenly falls athwart the Cardinal's
scheme; the latter undertakes furtively to overreach the
King; he is found out — then comes his fall. The eyes
of the King are opened; henceforth he is resolved to reign
untrammeled by any restraint. This makes him an
immoral tyrant, but also it makes him the hero of English
Protestantism. He is as little governed by ethical ties as
by the authority of the Church.

Thus Wolsey with his great hopes is wrecked — wrecked
upon a caprice of the King. His end is hostile to England, at least external to England; though its chief minister, he has his eye upon another object than his country.

Thus the political relation of Rome to the State has become intolerable; it must be broken. Though we may think little of Henry's motives, the result is in the highest degree commendable, indeed necessary. The passion for Anne Boleyn was merely the occasion of what had soon to take place — the little spark that fired the powder magazine of ages. Without the powder, the spark would not have amounted to much. Let there be no more Cardinal Prime Ministers, with eye on Rome; Wolsey is to be the last representative of the class in England.

2. So much for the King in his political relations; we may now consider the second thread of his life — his domestic relations — though they cannot be wholly separated from the political thread. A grand entertainment is given by the Cardinal, at which Anne Boleyn is present; the Cardinal is thus the means of his own overthrow. King Henry also is present, full of gayety and fond of the ladies — not a domestic man. He beholds the fair Anne and exclaims: "By Heaven she is a dainty one" — and the fate of the Papacy in England is sealed. Wolsey — did he but know it as he sits there amid flattery — is falling into the lowest depths of humiliation and repentance, to death.

The change of Queens is now to take place — a change which runs parallel to the change of religion — and each Queen may to a certain extent be taken as the symbol of her faith. Anne is represented as an artless maid, full of sympathy with Catherine in her trial; she says that she would not be a queen, reading her destiny in Catherine's:

> —" 'Tis better to be lowly born,
> And range with humble livers in content,
> Than to be perk'd up in a glistering grief,
> And wear a golden sorrow."

The unexpected honors of the King overwhelmed her; she does not desert the Queen, yet she cannot resist the King — a simple maid, full of devotion and tenderness, yet without any strength of will or intellect.

Queen Catherine is the most beautiful character — the true heroine of the drama. In her double relation, as queen and as wife, she has been supremely true to both State and Family. She interfered for justice in the case of Buckingham; she came to the aid of the oppressed subjects in their grievances. Her devotion to her husband has been absolute — indeed, too great; she has suppressed all her likes and dislikes in his favor; it has been her great aim in life to dwell in complete unity with him. She combines two traits rarely found conjoined in woman — strength and sweetness; her force of character conflicts not in the least with her amiability. But in her person, though not through her fault, the two relations collide — political necessity demands a new queen for England. This horrible necessity tears asunder the conjugal bond — unqueened is unwifed. Again the Family is sacrificed to the State; domestic life is swept away by a national requirement.

Such is the historical justification of her fate, though there is no justification for the conduct of Wolsey and Henry. The decree of History is that England must change religions in order to attain to her true destiny. Though such a change involves the disruption of the domestic ties of sovereigns, it must, nevertheless, take place. Such is the conflict of the two irreconcilable principles; each has validity, but one must go down. Catherine is a Catholic, a Spanish Catholic, and relative of the Emperor, Charles the Fifth, the great supporter of the

Papacy; hence her political influence must be eliminated if England is to be free from external domination. But her political influence rests upon her being wife of the monarch — thus the domestic bond is involved. The reader may think that this result does not necessarily follow, but the poetic significance of Catherine is to be a representative of some principle; the divorce from her is the symbol of the divorce from the Church. It is true that the drama fails to bring into prominence this historical necessity, and exhibits only the wanton caprice of Henry; for this reason Catherine seems, not only an innocent, but an unnecessary, sacrifice. Thus, however, there is no real conflict in her destiny, and no tragic motive in her character.

II. The second movement shows Henry as absolute master, both in the political and domestic thread. Wolsey, Cardinal Prime Minister, ambitious of the Papacy, has come to an untimely end. The King's predilection now goes out towards Cranmer, a prelate who did not want the Papacy, but quite the opposite, namely, its annihilation. But Wolsey has left behind a faint reflection of himself in Gardiner, Bishop of Winchester, who is seeking to extirpate the "new opinions divers and dangerous," the main supporter of which he sees to be Cranmer. That there may be no doubt about the matter, the home of these new opinions is distinctly indicated to be Upper Germany. So the religious conflict comes out into bold prominence — the two prelates being the two champions of the respective sides.

Cranmer is on the point of being sent to the Tower by the Council, at the instigation of his enemy, when King Henry suddenly enters and takes the part of Cranmer.

This is the end of the politico-religious struggle—the King sides with the promoter of the new opinions. As before said, it is less a matter of Church than of State; with Henry it is not even a matter of State, but an arbitrary caprice of passion. Still, he receives the support of the nation; his successors to this day have upheld the same policy, or had to surrender the crown; the separation from the Papal family was, therefore, a national act. The ground thereof lies patent: England thus attains complete national autonomy—the supreme object of her striving since the beginning of her history; King Henry, therefore, was acting in harmony with the nation, which supported him; this is his historical justification. But as individual, judged by moral tests, he is a wretch, a bigot, yet a hypocrite—his deepest ruling principle being his passion. Defense there is for his deed—none at all for his motives. There ought, doubtless, to be punishment for his moral violation; his career, as shown in this drama, looks too much like a career of successful villainy. If Henry had consciously subordinated moral to political considerations, he might have attained the rank of a Hero, as is the case with a number of Shakespeare's characters. But the mainspring of his actions is capricious passion; the good results are an accident, and in no sense come from his intention.

2. The domestic thread, showing the Queens, remains to be considered. As Anne rises, Catherine descends; the brilliant coronation of the former and the mournful retirement of the latter stand side by side in the drama. Their connection with the general thought of the play is that each Queen is, to a certain extent, the representative of the colliding religions; the change of Queens is a reflection of

the change of faiths. Already Catherine has appealed to
the Pope — a jurisdiction beyond the State; this authority
is now to be broken by Henry — History's instrument. On
the other hand, Anne has been characterized by Wolsey
as "a spleeny Lutheran, and not wholesome to our cause."
Still, both are determined by the political movement of the
age, and are not by any means shown as religious zealots.

Catherine retires to Kimbolton, "sick to death;" there
she hears of the sad fate of her old enemy, the Cardinal,
who died "full of repentance, continual meditations, tears,
sorrows," whom she forgives and blesses. She herself
is approaching the last hour, though elevated into an ecstatic
mood. She beholds in a vision the crown of her future
bliss. But last of all she sends her dying message to the
man who had most deeply wronged her — "tell him in
death I blessed him, for so I will." Still, she yields not a
tittle of her rank and pride: "Although unqueened, yet
like a queen and daughter to a king inter me."

But the counterpart to this tragic side is the coronation
of the beautiful Anne Boleyn, amid brilliant ceremonies
and the hearty applause of the people. Another festival is
held at the christening of the new-born daughter, Elizabeth, terminated by the fervid prophecies of Cranmer.
For she will inherit the blessings of the present victory;
wisdom, virtue, and peace shall reign in her name. A
glance into the future reveals the prospect of untold happiness; still, in the somber background is beheld the
domestic tragedy, which deeply tinges the feelings. But
political enfranchisement has been reached; no foreign
domination of the Church will hereafter fetter the souls of
Englishmen; here we arrive at the true reconciling result
of this struggle.

Such is the happy termination of the play of *Henry the Eighth*, and therewith the happy termination of the whole English Historical series ; indeed, with a little stretch of our generalizing faculty, we may say — the happy termination of Shakespeare's World-Drama.   For this play, in spite of its faults, cannot be spared from Shakespeare's works ; it is an integral part of their complete development.   Perhaps its defects may be traced to the desire of the Poet to give something like completeness to these historical labors — for it is one of his latest plays.   Certainly the work is not well organized — not well thought out into clearness and harmonious proportion ; whether this resulted from haste, from mental changes, or from foreign interpolation, cannot be settled decisively.   Nor is the question of such transcendant importance ; the work remains just the same, whatever may be its origin ; the main duty is to comprehend it in its true inner thought and artistic worth.